Multilingualism and Pluricentricity

Language and Social Life

Editors
David Britain
Crispin Thurlow

Volume 20

Multilingualism and Pluricentricity

―

A Tale of Many Cities

Edited by
John Hajek, Catrin Norrby, Heinz L. Kretzenbacher and Doris Schüpbach

ISBN 978-1-5015-2741-8
e-ISBN (PDF) 978-1-5015-1197-4
e-ISBN (EPUB) 978-1-5015-1162-2
ISSN 2364-4303

Library of Congress Control Number: 2023941345

Bibliographic information published by the Deutsche Nationalbibliothek
The Deutsche Nationalbibliothek lists this publication in the Deutsche Nationalbibliografie;
detailed bibliographic data are available on the internet at http://dnb.dnb.de.

© 2025 Walter de Gruyter Inc., Boston/Berlin
This volume is text- and page-identical with the hardback published in 2024.
Cover image: Tim Perdue/Moment Open/Getty Images
Typesetting: Integra Software Services Pvt. Ltd.
Printing and binding: CPI books GmbH, Leck

www.degruyter.com

Contents

Catrin Norrby, John Hajek, Heinz L. Kretzenbacher and Doris Schüpbach
Introduction: Exploring multilingualism and pluricentricity in diverse urban settings —— 1

Part 1: **Multilingual policies in practice**

Doris Schüpbach and Claudine Brohy
1 **Bilingualism, multilingualism and diglossia: A tale of two Swiss cities** —— 27

Marie Nelson and Sofie Henricson
2 **The linguistic landscapes of Mariehamn and Kotka: A multilingual tale of local and national languages in Finland** —— 55

Zane Goebel
3 **Unity, diversity and the market: Television representations of multilingual diversity in Jakarta** —— 81

Francesco Goglia
4 **Multilingualism in Padua (Italy): The linguistic landscape of an emerging multiethnic neighbourhood** —— 99

Part 2: **Attitudes and identities**

John Hajek, Ambrin Hasnain and Carlie Hanson
5 **Exploring the Italianità of Melbourne's Little Italy: Lygon Street, Carlton** —— 123

Daniel Kaufman
6 **The Mixtec language in New York: Vitality, discrimination and identity** —— 147

Chloé Diskin-Holdaway
7 **Second language identities among recently-arrived migrants in Dublin, Ireland** —— 173

Claudia Maria Riehl and Sara Ingrosso
8 "The northernmost city of Italy": Italian immigrants in Munich —— 199

Part 3: Language across time and space

Peter Trudgill and Jane Warren
9 Norwich across time: A city of strangers —— 227

Bolormaa Shinjee and Sender Dovchin
10 The multilingual landscape of Ulaanbaatar, the capital city of Mongolia —— 249

Anu Bissoonauth and Jane Warren
11 Urban multilingualism in Mauritius: Exploring linguistic and ethnic diversity in Port-Louis —— 267

María Irene Moyna
12 Pluricentricity in Río de la Plata address: Montevideo is alike and a little different —— 291

Heinz L. Kretzenbacher, Doris Schüpbach, John Hajek and Catrin Norrby
Conclusion: Looking back and looking forward —— 321

Biographical notes —— 333

Index —— 337

Catrin Norrby, John Hajek, Heinz L. Kretzenbacher
and Doris Schüpbach
Introduction: Exploring multilingualism and pluricentricity in diverse urban settings

This volume explores linguistic diversity and complexity in a range of urban contexts, a number of which have been subject to relatively little or no sociolinguistic inquiry, especially in English. It seeks to diversify the sites under investigation in urban multilingualism studies, and advocates an exploration of multilingual practices that is not restricted to the large-scale contemporary Western metropolis. A novel mixture of cities from around the world is therefore studied, from megacities and lesser-known communities within well-researched cities to smaller cities on the national periphery, representing diverse types, sizes, contexts and languages.

We recognise that linguistic diversity and complexity exist beyond urban contexts and their presence in suburban and rural environments also deserve investigation. We are also aware that much current sociolinguistic scholarship may well be skewed towards cities and shaped by what Britain (2017, 2022) terms 'the urban gaze', where the notion of 'the city' is heavily influenced by preconceptions and ideological discourses of the urban (e.g. the city as diverse, innovative, multicultural etc.). Nevertheless, this volume focuses on urban contexts, viewed not as an explanatory concept but as sites where features under investigation may be more visible, more intensive or more frequent than outside cities and "therefore perhaps more noteworthy, more reportable" (Britain 2022: 70).

All chapters of this volume address multilingual and/or pluricentric aspects of linguistic diversity in urban areas, with the majority focusing on one urban centre. Six contributions investigate cities in Europe, while the remaining six focus on cities located on five other continents, namely Africa, Asia, North America, Oceania and South America. The sites include: Biel/Bienne and Fribourg/Freiburg (Switzerland), Dublin (Ireland), Jakarta (Indonesia), Kotka and Mariehamn (Finland), Melbourne (Australia), Montevideo (Uruguay), Munich (Germany), New York City (USA), Norwich (UK), Padua (Italy), Port Louis (Mauritius), and Ulaanbaatar (Mongolia). Five cities are national capitals, others are state or provincial capitals or re-

---

Note: We would like to acknowledge and thank Ambrin Hasnain for her invaluable assistance in preparing this chapter.

gional centres (for further details, see Appendix). They also reflect a variety of ways in which a city's linguistic profile can evolve, or not, over time.

The researchers who contributed to this volume also come from six continents. It was important to the volume editors to allow them to conduct and write up their research in ways that best reflect their own experiences and understanding of the world. As a result, their research, written in an accessible manner in order also to reach a broader audience, showcases diverse theoretical backgrounds and methodological approaches, ranging from investigations combining quantitative and qualitative methods and qualitative studies drawing on extensive ethnographic work or discourse analysis, to linguistic landscape studies and analyses of actual and reported language use. The chapters thus provide a broad overview of different current trends in sociolinguistic research on multilingual places and pluricentric languages.

1 Urban multilingualism

The study of urban multilingualism is central to much contemporary work in sociolinguistics, evident not least in the number of edited research volumes on the topic published in the last decade (Carson and King 2016; Smakman and Heinrich 2017; Mar-Molinero 2020a among others). However, a focus on language in the city and how different groups of people use and adapt their language repertoires in different situations has been central to much sociolinguistic research since the early days of the discipline. William Labov's seminal study of English in New York City, for instance, showed that community speech patterns correlated with social variables such as class (Labov 1966). This was the catalyst for a new type of research on urban speech communities, exemplified by Peter Trudgill's investigation of Norwich English (Trudgill 1974) and Barbara Horvath's study of the sociolects of English spoken in Sydney, which included ethnicity as a variable (Horvath 1985). Other research was also underway in Australia by Michael Clyne and colleagues who focused on the use and maintenance of languages other than English in multilingual communities (e.g. Clyne 1991; 2005; Kipp and Norrby 2006; Pauwels 1988; Romaine 1991).

The correlation of social characteristics and patterns of language use has greatly enhanced our understanding of how people communicate with one another. However, in today's mobile and globalising world, "studying sociolinguistics in the city necessitates a move away from the traditional approach of the 'sociolinguistics of distribution', where languages, speakers, social class, etc. are both well-defined and permanently fixed" (Smakman and Heinrich 2017: 9). More recent studies of urban multilingualism have been informed by the impact of today's increased scale of globalisation processes on cities and their inhabitants (Cadier and Mar-Molinero 2014; Wang et al. 2014; Carson and King 2016; Smakman and Heinrich 2017). The transnational movements of people and goods, intensified by large numbers of refugees fleeing their native countries as well as by global capitalism, and the resulting language contact both influence the language use of communities and individuals (Heller 2013). Urban settings have provided fertile contexts for studies of multilingualism as they are often subject to an increasing number of migrants arriving from different locations within a country as well as from other countries, and are typically the primary port of call for immigrants and refugees (Wang et al. 2014; Carson and King 2016). "The city as a site for experimentation and creativity in language practices" (Mar-Molinero 2020b: 12) gives rise to a dynamic linguistic environment, where people from diverse language backgrounds interact and communicate with one another in their everyday lives, thus using a variety of multilingual resources and producing new linguistic codes and repertoires (Otsuji and Pennycook 2010; Cadier and Mar-Molinero 2014).

In addition to complex linguistic practices in-place, the rise of the internet since the 1990s has further increased and diversified communication patterns, transnational interactions and information exchange (Blommaert 2013; Wang et al. 2014). Through increased access to various media, technology and information, as well as interactions through social media and connectivity via the internet and phones, migrants are more easily able to maintain transnational contact with their families and communities in their countries of origins and the wider diaspora. Transnational connectedness also extends to non-migrants, from residents of cosmopolitan cities to rural areas in most parts of the world (Blommaert and Rampton 2011; Dyers 2015). As a result of globalisation processes, migration streams and the internet, people today are able to access and create diverse, innovative language repertoires and communication practices on a daily basis – face-to-face as well as virtually.

'Superdiversity', a term coined by Steven Vertovec (2007), was proposed as an approach to the complexity of recent migration patterns resulting from globalisation processes, through a "multi-dimensional perspective on diversity" (p. 1026). It is also reportedly marked by more temporary migration patterns by smaller groups from more places, as opposed to more historical tendencies of larger groups from a limited number of places who settled permanently (Cadier and Mar-Molinero 2014; Li Wei 2018).

Superdiversity was quickly taken up by sociolinguists to describe and reassess linguistic diversity and patterns that are developing in such diverse spaces (Goebel 2018). It has been used as the contextual backdrop in many recent studies of multilingualism, especially in urban spaces and a range of books and edited volumes have been published on the subject in the past few years (Blommaert 2013; Duarte and Gogolin 2013; Goebel 2015; Arnaut et al. 2016a; 2016b; Creese and Blackledge 2018;

Mar-Molinero 2020a). However, the concept has also been strongly critiqued for a variety of reasons. Among them are: (a) its Euro-centricity (Flores and Lewis 2016; Goebel 2017; Pavlenko 2019) by largely applying it to Western settings or to other settings through a Euro-centric lens; (b) its rather ahistorical outlook by presenting it as a recent phenomenon (Britain 2016; Piller 2016), thus ignoring cases like Ancient Rome or Alexandria in Ancient Egypt; and (c) the perception of the underlying mobility as unprecendented in scale and scope (Britain 2016; Czaika and de Haas 2015).

The comparison of urban settings in this volume shows that superdiversity is not a required backdrop to urban sociolinguistic research in all settings nor is the phenomenon inherently monodirectional. With respect to the former point, researchers may not find it necessary or helpful to explore, even where diversity is marked. Only Diskin-Holdaway (Chapter 7) and Trudgill and Warren (Chapter 9) frame their contributions explicitly with respect to superdiversity. Kaufman in his chapter on New York (Chapter 6) on the other hand does not label it as such, although, arguably, the city can be described as stereotypically superdiverse. Moreover, it is not the case that all cities are necessarily becoming more diverse and multilingual over time. The arrival of migrants and refugees, for example, is often related to particular events or conflicts in countries of origin, as well as changes in the local conditions, which may make a location more or less attractive over time. Numbers can wax and wane, as can local multilingualism. A case in point would be Montevideo, the city dealt with in Moyna's contribution (Chapter 12). There was significant and linguistically rich migration, primarily from Europe to Montevideo in the 19th and early 20th centuries, with the last wave arriving in the post-WWII period (1945–1955). However, the deteriorating local conditions in the second half of the 20th century led to significant emigration from Uruguay starting in the 1960s, with spikes during the 1980s and the early 2000s. As a result, the population of Uruguay's national capital has grown relatively little in sixty years. The immigrant contingents of the 21st century tend to be Spanish-speaking Latin Americans (Venezuelan, Cuban, Dominican), whose impact is limited given their relatively small numbers. Today, Montevideo's linguistic profile is strikingly undiverse, compared to many other capital cities in the developed world. This pattern observed for Montevideo is consistent with a historical trend of long-term decline in immigration to Uruguay in general: in 1860, 35% of the nation's population was foreign-born, but since the late 1990s, it has never risen much above 3% (Aracena 2009).

Moreover, the inherent Euro-centric focus of superdiversity neglects the diversity and types of language contact in different parts of the world, particularly in the Global South (Flores and Lewis 2016). Many African, Asian and Pacific countries exhibit extreme linguistic diversity due to centuries of language contact through, for instance, nomadic lifestyles, trade relations, colonialism and the cohabitation of diverse ethnolinguistic groups, which enabled interconnections of various tribal and ethnic languages as well as languages introduced in colonial contexts (e.g. Makoni 2012; Pavlenko 2019). European languages were usually superimposed as official languages, adding to the linguistic diversity in a specific space, but often leading to more restrictive use of other languages due to asymmetric power relations. Port Louis, discussed in the chapter by Bissoonauth and Warren (Chapter 11), exemplifies a non-Western context in which today's linguistic diversity is a result of the city's colonial past. Initial colonisation by the French, the forced arrival of enslaved Africans, the occupation by the British, labour agreements with India and the migration of Chinese traders had created a complex linguistic situation by the time Mauritius gained independence in 1968. As is common with colonial languages, French and later English were superimposed as official languages, marginalising the use of Indian, African, Chinese and other language varieties spoken amongst the population, and leading to a progressive decrease in the number of speakers of these languages through language shift. Today, we have instead increasing convergence into a shared trilingual system that has taken centuries to develop in situ: Kreol, English and French, in contact with each other, are used in different domains, and associated with different social values, thus creating an interesting site for the study of multilingualism that is not primarily produced by modern-day immigration.

Despite the historically embedded linguistic diversity in non-Western settings, recent migration to Western societies from these areas has also resulted in much greater ethnic and linguistic heterogeneity in the latter, and is sometimes falsely contrasted with the host population's previous (perceived) monolingualism (Mar-Molinero 2020b; Pavlenko 2019). This discourse is further underpinned by the different impact migrant communities and their languages have on 'host' languages today. Trudgill and Warren's chapter on Norwich in this volume (Chapter 9) exemplifies this difference: migration by speakers of Old Danish in the ninth and tenth centuries, of Norman French, Flemish and Breton after the Norman conquest in 1066, and of Dutch in the 16th century, actively shaped the English language of Norwich, which can still be traced today through place names, grammatical features and vocabulary. Yet, recent migration has had little impact on the repertoire of the host population, and migrant languages now appear in the margins. To use the words of Pavlenko, "the only people who engage in the 'new' multilingual practices are immigrants themselves" (Pavlenko 2019: 157).

Current linguistic diversity is often viewed as a result of international migration, but as Goebel's case study of Jakarta in this volume (Chapter 3) demonstrates, this Asian megacity is characterised by 'superdiversity from within' (Goebel 2017), as opposed to transnational superdiversity. Indonesia's population speaks hundreds of ethnic and regional languages, such as Javanese, Sundanese, Balinese and many more, with the standardised *Bahasa Indonesia* (Indonesian) just one of many. Despite efforts to create a national identity through the circulation of Indonesian as the language of administration, education and the media, the devaluing of regional languages, and the construction of language hierarchies based on associated social values, a renewed emphasis was put on pride in ethnolinguistic diversity in the 1990s. The focus on 'diversity within diversity' can also be applied to studies of multilingualism in migrant contexts, as many migrant communities may use a range of languages and standardised and non-standardised language varieties in different spheres of their lives (Karatsareas 2020).

While big cities are the focus of most previous studies on urban multilingualism, it is crucial to note that cities are not necessarily linguistically diverse throughout their urban fabric. As Schneider (2020: 6) argues, how people interact with one another depends on their social networks, not on the city or physical place as such, and, while cities *as a whole* have the potential for extreme cultural and linguistic diversity, they are also marked by spatial, economic, and social compartmentalisation. By offering more spaces for specialised communities, large cities run the risk of promoting uniformity within social networks and consequently limited interaction between diverse members of their population. Furthermore, issues of class and unevenly distributed socio-economic conditions, coupled with racism and highly unequal access to the real estate market throughout a city may result in social segregation of its population across neighbourhoods. Attention to such differences and the diversity within a city is required to avoid too hasty generalisations, as argued by Schneider (2020). Multilingualism is not always inherently 'good' but layered and reconceptualised in different times and locations, even within a city (cf. Chik et al. 2019 on different dimensions of multilingualism in Sydney and Chik 2022 on the sixteen largest speech communities of Greater Los Angeles). In the present volume, authors show awareness of the varying distribution of linguistic diversity within the cities of their study. Thus, they focus on specific locations within the city in question (e.g. Melbourne, Kotka, Mariehamn, Norwich, Padua, Ulaanbaatar), demographic or ethnic groups (e.g. Dublin, Munich, New York, Port-Louis), and online or media representations (e.g. Biel/Bienne, Fribourg/Freiburg, Jakarta).

It is generally agreed that migration has increased diversity in Western Europe, but "migration does not necessarily increase ethnolinguistic diversity, as seen in Eastern European and Central Asian census data", as Pavlenko (2019: 153) notes (see also Wang et al. 2014; Schneider 2020). For example, small or geographically peripheral cities may not attract substantial numbers of international, culturally diverse migrant groups, but be limited to modest numbers of domestic migrants, whose settlement does not impact on the ethnic, cultural or linguistic diversity of a place. On the contrary, such locations might experience outward migration to larger urban centres. The Finnish city of Kotka, as discussed in the chapter by Nelson and Henricson (Chapter 2), represents a city that attracted immigrants from within Finland and from neighbouring Russia and Norway in the late 19th century, but has more recently experienced high unemployment rates and an outflux of its population to Helsinki. However, diversity is not directly related to size, as not all big cities are necessarily (super)diverse either. A case in point is Ulaanbaatar, the focal point of the chapter by Shinjee and Dovchin (Chapter 10). The city is home to 1.5 million residents and has been receiving in largely unabated fashion large numbers of domestic migrants since the end of Soviet style socialist rule in 1990, so much so that in 2017 and 2020 the municipal government placed bans on such arrivals. While there is some limited ethnic and linguistic diversity within the Mongolian population, there are still relatively few foreigners in Mongolia (only 0.7% in 2020). It is not surprising therefore, if on a global scale, Ulaanbaatar is not typically considered a particularly transnationally diverse location.

Some brief discussion of linguistic landscape studies is in order here, an approach which has caught on in urban linguistic research, including in many contributions to this volume. The concept 'linguistic landscape' was first introduced by Landry and Bourhis (1997) to refer to the visibility and prominence of languages on public and commercial signs in a particular territory. They argued that the language use on such signs displayed the relative power relationships between languages in multilingual communities and provided a means of measuring ethnolinguistic vitality. Since its first inception, linguistic landscape studies (LL for short) have gained increased traction in urban multilingualism (see e.g. the chapters in Shohamy et al. 2010) and several of the chapters in the present volume adopt an LL approach to take stock of the multilingualism present in the respective urban sites (see Section 3 below and also the concluding chapter).

Originally LL referred to the study of written inscriptions on signs in a particular geographical space, predominantly investigated through quantitative methods. Subsequently, the field has expanded its scope to also include all sorts of semiotic resources, such as images, photos, sounds and objects, captured by the label 'semiotic landscapes' (Jaworski and Thurlow 2010). Such a multimodal approach has also gone hand in hand with a shift towards qualitative, more discursive and ethnographic methods of investigation (for recent overviews, see Shohamy 2019; Yumul-Florendo and Muth 2022). Parallel to this development, human agency has become a focal point, where people are seen as active in the discursive and ideological construction of space, rather than passive consumers of signs (e.g. Barni and Bagna 2015; Jaworski and Thurlow 2010; Pennycook 2017). In other words, today LL research is a multifaceted field, characterised by a range of methodological approaches.

In the concluding chapter we discuss the individual chapters and their use of LL methodology in some detail as well as suggesting avenues for future development of this field.

2 Pluricentricity

Some of the chapters in this volume, e.g. Moyna's chapter on Montevideo, highlight a particular type of linguistic diversity – *pluricentricity* – which overlaps and intersects with multilingualism in different ways. It is thus an important element which is explored in more detail in some chapters. Typically, a pluricentric language has official status as the standard variety in more than one nation (Clyne 1992a)[1] or centre (Ammon 1995). This is the case of English and French, for example, which are spoken in a wide range of countries across different continents, and German and Dutch, both of which are predominantly spoken in neighbouring countries.

Key to the concept of pluricentricity are "power relationships between different varieties of pluricentric languages, in particular with regard to power asymmetries between national varieties, often expressed as dominant versus non-dominant varieties" (Norrby et al. 2020: 201). In the case of German, which has national official status in several European countries, standard German German can be regarded as the dominant variety, exerting influence over the other, non-dominant varieties of German such as standard Austrian German or standard Swiss German as regards language structure and attitudes, and taking the lead as the primary norm-setting centre (Clyne 1992b; Norrby et al. 2020: 203). Power relationships between dominant and non-dominant varieties are influenced by various factors. These include relative population size, economic and political power, historical role as a core or peripheral area, whether the variety is an official language or an 'unofficial' regional/minority language, and whether it is an indigenised or settler variety, that is, one that has been introduced via colonisation or immigration and has acquired native speakers in its new location (Norrby et al. 2020: 203; see also Clyne 1992c: 455; Muhr 2012: 26ff). All these factors also influence speakers' perceptions and attitudes to different varieties, and those in turn impact on their identification with a certain variety. Speakers of the dominant national variety, for instance, tend to view their variety as the standard, and other national varieties as sub-standard or old-fashioned. They also display limited understanding of the symbolic function of other national varieties for their speakers (Clyne 1992c: 459–460).

The power relationships between language varieties are often complex, and a pluricentric language can exhibit degrees of symmetry (Ammon 1989: 91). To take

---

[1] Clyne's concept of pluricentricity draws on Kloss (1978). Sociolinguist William Stewart first coined the notions *monocentric* and *polycentric* to describe different paths of language standardisation within a national context, the first where there is a set of universally accepted norms and the second where different sets of norms co-exist (Stewart 1968).

English as an example, there is not one sole dominant variety. National varieties can be put on a continuum with at one end the UK and the USA as the globally dominant varieties, settler varieties such as New Zealand English somewhere in the middle, and at the other end indigenised varieties such as Indian English. Power relationships can change over time, and a national standard variety can be both dominant and non-dominant. This is the case of standard Australian English, which is non-dominant in relation to, say, American English, but dominant in parts of the Pacific region. English also has a unique role as a global lingua franca, which adds to its pluricentric complexities – especially in multilingual settings (Kretzenbacher 2012, see also below). (For an overview of the field, see Norrby et al. 2020; see also the edited volumes Clyne 1992a; Muhr and Marley 2015; da Silva 2014.)

Pluricentricity is an evolving field of research, and recent discussions have focused on theoretical and methodological considerations. One area concerns certain limitations of the concept itself. A common understanding of pluricentricity is that the concept of nation equates to nation-state. Langer (2021) takes the example of national minority language North Frisian to show that this would not allow North Frisian the status of pluricentric language. It has also been argued that the term *pluriareality* which is not tied necessarily to a state (see e.g. Wolf 1994) is more appropriate than pluricentricity, particularly in relation to the German-speaking world, which can be viewed as a dialect continuum. According to this view, pluriareality better accounts for the fact that the boundaries of German varieties do not necessarily match national borders. It prioritises cultural/dialect rather than political/national borders and regional rather than national centres (Wide et al. 2021: 2). Auer (2021) for his part proposes a neutral term 'multi-standard language', which can deal with contexts in which a language has two or more standards and avoids the vagueness of terms such as 'centre' and 'periphery'. Oakes (2021) makes the case for an ethical dimension to pluricentricity, developing the idea of 'pluricentric linguistic justice', to support moral claims of non-dominant varieties in legitimising and promoting their variety. From an initial focus on describing language structure, the field has also expanded to include pragmatic and interactional differences between national varieties in naturally occurring conversations (e.g. Haugh 2017; Félix-Brasdefer and Placencia 2019; Lindström et al. 2019; Norrby 2021; Reber 2021).

As the above summary demonstrates, much work in pluricentricity has focused on standard national varieties used in different political entities. Importantly, the relationships between such national varieties have typically been described through a lens of power asymmetries, evident in abstract dichotomies such as dominance–non-dominance, and centre–periphery. In a discussion of urban multilingualism, it is important to consider such dichotomies further. On the one hand, large cities, in particular national capital cities, have often been treated as the obvious norm-setting centres of the respective standard national varieties, radiating outwards to the peripheries. As alluded to above, such a view does not fully account for the complex relationships that exist both between different national varieties and between sub-national varieties within a nation. For example, one national capital may act as the norm-setting centre in one nation-state, but be considered relatively peripheral in relation to a more dominant national variety and its norm-setting centre. The pluricentric engagement with the standard ideology of imagined monolingualism (cf. Clyne 2008), thus tends to downplay the linguistic diversity within nations and, accordingly, also the language practices of indigenous or minority groups. Previous work on multilingualism and the periphery (Pietikäinen and Kelly-Holmes 2013) suggests that the core–periphery dynamics need to be further unpacked in work on pluricentricity in order to shed light on how language ideologies, norms and practices are shaped and contested, not least in light of globalizing trends (and the global dominance of English). Several of the chapters in the current volume concern urban sites and communities which are peripheral in one or more ways, e.g., geographically remote from a perceived centre, linguistically distant from the mainstream majority, or have become peripheral due to historical or colonial developments.

There is an evident pluricentric thread running through this whole volume. Three chapters make explicit reference to a pluricentric context. In Chapter 2, Nelson and Henricson discuss the presence of Swedish in two urban sites, drawing on the fact that Swedish, spoken as a national language in Finland by a numerical minority of the population, is also the dominant national language of neighbouring Sweden. The city of Mariehamn represents an officially Swedish monolingual context in Finland, where Finnish is largely absent. This case highlights the very different conditions of the use of a pluricentric language in different national and regional contexts and shows that geography is important. Similarly, Moyna in Chapter 12 draws on pluricentric Spanish when she compares and contrasts the address pragmatics of the Uruguayan Spanish of Montevideo to the Argentine Spanish of Buenos Aires, which is the more dominant variety. Here multilectalism, which falls under the umbrella of multilingualism, comes to the fore. Montevideo and Buenos Aires are geographically close, separated by the Rio de la Plata estuary, with populations of approximately 1.4 million and 15.3 million respectively and which are also in frequent contact. In the context of sharing a language with a neighbouring country that is much more dominant, drawing on pluricentric theory, we would expect the dominant nation/city Buenos Aires to exert more influence on the less dominant variety. The real situation turns out to be more complex where Montevidean Spanish still retains some local address features that are not used in Buenos Aires, as illustrated by Moyna's results. Diskin-Holdaway in her chapter on perceptions of and identification with Dublin English by Chinese and Polish migrants to the city (Chapter 7), refers to the pluricentric nature of English where different national, as well as local, varieties are imbued with different indexical meanings of locality, power and prestige and explores how these differences play out in speaker attitudes in an increasingly diverse and multilingual city.

Other chapters deal with pluricentric languages in a range of contexts, for example, Kaufman's contribution on Mixtec speakers and their often fraught relationship with Spanish in Mexico as well as in New York (Chapter 6); or Schüpbach and Brohy's investigation of linguistic diversity and French/German bilingualism in the Swiss cities of Biel/Bienne and Fribourg/Freiburg (Chapter 1). In fact, most chapters include discussions of English, either as the dominant language (New York, Dublin, Melbourne, Norwich), as *de jure* official language of government and education (Port-Louis), as identity marker (Jakarta), regarding its role in the retail and hospitality sectors (Mariehamn, Ulaanbaatar) or as a lingua franca among migrants (Padua, Munich) as well as between members and institutions of the 'host' communities with migrants or visitors (Fribourg/Freiburg, Biel/Bienne, Kotka). This diversity of English-speaking contexts highlights not only the emergence of English as a lingua franca across the globe (Carson and King 2016) but also the pluricentricity of the language – with Irish, American, Australian, British, Mauritian, Nigerian and south-east Asian varieties of English referred to across the volume. We will return to the discussion of pluricentricity in the concluding chapter and how multilingualism and pluricentricity could be viewed as two sides of the same coin. We see great potential for future research in this field.

3 The volume

As has been noted, the volume takes an approach to linguistic diversity and multilingual practices that includes and moves beyond the huge contemporary Western city. As Wang et al. (2014: 26) point out with regards to globalisation studies, "less typical places [. . .] – peri-urban and rural areas, peripheral areas of countries, peripheral zones of the world, peripheral institutional zones where minorities are relegated – have been less quickly absorbed into current scholarship." Yet, smaller cities and regional centres provide interesting case studies to investigate if, and how, globalisation has impacted on more peripheral sites (Pietikäinen and Kelly-Holmes 2013), and the ways linguistic practices are at play there.[2] Including more

---

[2] See Heller (2013) for an exploration of how capitalism has contributed to the creation of the centre–periphery dichotomy and related language attitudes.

of these sites in current scholarship will create a more balanced representation of contemporary multilingualism, following a sociolinguistic tradition of studying urban contexts alongside remote or less urbanised communities, as in the pioneering work in sociolinguistics and linguistic anthropology by scholars like William Labov, John Gumperz, Dell Hymes and others (Wang et al. 2014). Showcasing non-central sites and societies helps also reduce the risk of a 'metropolitan bias' in the broader field, thus countering "the assumption that what occurs [in current centres] can and should be used as benchmark for studies elsewhere" (Wang et al. 2014: 28).

Some chapters take these issues into consideration by presenting studies of smaller and geographically more remote cities, some on national peripheries – considered small due to their population size, such as Mariehamn, a western outpost of Finland on the Åland Islands in the Baltic Sea, Kotka, located in Eastern Finland and close to the Russian border, and Fribourg/Freiburg in Switzerland, or in relation to other cities in their country, such as Norwich in the United Kingdom. These contrast with contributions on large cities such as Melbourne and Munich and the megacities Jakarta and New York, although the latter focuses on the linguistic experiences of the city's marginalised Mixtec community, which has not previously been subject to any scholarly attention. The inclusion of African, South American and Asian sites – including the Mauritian capital Port Louis, Uruguayan capital Montevideo, and the Mongolian capital Ulaanbaatar – also aims to add a global dimension. As far as we are aware, there have been no published studies on the complex language situation in Port-Louis. The study of multilingualism in Ulaanbaatar, a peripheral Asian city, also addresses a gap in current multilingual research, which tends to focus on multicultural, post-industrial, cosmopolitan Asian cities such as Singapore, Hong Kong and Dubai (e.g. Cavallaro and Bee Chin 2014; Jain 2021; Siemund and Leimgruber 2021; Tsiola 2023).

Other cities have received previous scholarly attention, but only to a limited extent, if at all, in English, and we present the linguistic situation in the respective cities to a larger audience for the first time. For example, Biel/Bienne and Fribourg/Freiburg are each well described in many respects in German and French but have previously not been well-documented in English. With regard to the Swedish-speaking population in Finland, there has been considerable research on language policy and language attitudes in different domains, with some available in English (e.g. Liebkind et al. 2007), but the sociolinguistic situations of the cities profiled here, Mariehamn and Kotka, have not previously been reported on in English.

The contributions illustrate a variety of theoretical and methodological approaches to multilingualism and linguistic diversity. These range from macro sociolinguistic analyses of multilingualism, language maintenance and language change, to qualitative analyses of actual and reported language use, including signs of language contact, where speakers draw on two or more languages, referred to in the volume by terms such as code-switching, language mixing or sign-switching. Linguistic ethnography (e.g. Tusting 2020) is a method which informs the analyses of several chapters where authors document linguistic diversity in the linguistic landscape, or perhaps more aptly referred to as semiotic landscapes (Jaworski and Thurlow 2010) to allow for the multimodal nature of any signage, through photographs of the built environment, observation, as well as interviews with members of the communities in question.

The twelve chapters have been organised across three parts. In part 1 – *Multilingual policies in practice* – authors examine multilingualism as it pertains to the relationship between language policies, official language(s) and actual language use. On a political level, language diversity evokes a variety of responses and language policies in different contexts, which are often informed by national and regional language ideologies (Tunger et al. 2010). However, these policies do not necessarily reflect the diverse language practices across the population, which may lead to the contesting of such policies (Skrandies 2016). As Skrandies (2016) notes, "multilingual policies and practices are simultaneously shaped from above, as politicians and policymakers try to manage and reconcile contradictory interests and ideologies, and from below, as communities struggle for the recognition of their needs and interests" (p. 115). The chapters in this section demonstrate four different approaches and responses to top-down discourses on multilingualism. The first two deal with tensions emergent from official bilingualism: the opening chapter explores different enactments of German/French bilingualism in two Swiss cities on the one hand, and the second examines two sites of local monolingualism (one Finnish, one Swedish) in the context of Finland's national bilingualism. The next two chapters in this section demonstrate expressions of language diversity and multilingualism in two contexts with language policies influenced in one way or another by what Clyne (2008) called a 'monolingual mindset': Inter-ethnic talk amongst Indonesians in Jakarta, and the linguistic landscape of a neighbourhood that is marked by international migrants in the Italian city of Padua.

Part 1 opens with *Doris Schüpbach* and *Claudine Brohy's* investigation of linguistic diversity in the Swiss cities Biel/Bienne and Fribourg/Freiburg. While Switzerland is characterised by territorial multilingualism, these cities are located on a language border and hold official or quasi-official bilingual French/German status. Other languages are also present, as well as diglossia in the German-speaking communities, with Swiss German dialects used in more informal settings and standard Swiss German in more formal ones. Following a historical overview of the language situation the chapter turns to a comparative analysis of contemporary language use, largely based on the two cities' official municipal websites. The results indicate that Biel/Bienne's symmetrical institutional bilingualism rather than its de facto multilingualism, is central to its officially promoted urban identity. In contrast, Fribourg/Freiburg has a language identity characterised by greater linguistic and cultural diversity than its French-German bilingualism, resulting in a dominance of French as well as more fluid discourses on bilingualism.

Chapter 2, by *Marie Nelson* and *Sofie Henricson*, compares the linguistic landscapes of the small Finnish cities Mariehamn and Kotka, located on opposite peripheries of Finland. As previously noted, Finland has two national languages, Finnish and Swedish. However, the Swedish-speaking population (a numerical minority of only 5%) is regionally unevenly distributed with varying official status. Mariehamn, on the Åland Islands is closer to Sweden than mainland Finland, and officially monolingual in Swedish. In contrast, Kotka is monolingually Finnish, with a very small Swedish-speaking community, constituting a so-called Swedish language island. The linguistic landscapes of each city echo both the respective region's officially monolingual status and the corresponding majority position of Swedish/Finnish, but also show traces of national bilingualism. The chapter thus contributes more generally to research on the use and visibility of Swedish in Finland.

In chapter 3 *Zane Goebel* explores media representations of inter-ethnic contact and multilingual diversity in Jakarta by analysing two popular soap operas, broadcast in 1998 and 2009. Based on excerpts from interactions between the characters, their multilingual repertoires are interpreted as habitual 'signswitching' between particular participant constellations. Such representations challenge state ideologies about purity and the need for Indonesian in inter-ethnic encounters, reconceptualising 'language' as open-ended and fluid, where fragments from many languages mesh into one. Further, participants constructed as belonging to particular territory-based ethno-linguistic groups are also represented as understanding and using languages not associated with those constructed ethnic identities. The chapter highlights the trend of inter-ethnic language commodification by showing that market forces behind the soap opera production exploit the linguistic and cultural diversity in order to attract a wider audience.

Chapter 4, by *Francesco Goglia*, explores how multilingualism is evidenced in the linguistic landscape of a fairly new and expanding multi-ethnic inner-city neighbourhood in the Italian city of Padua. In line with the monolingual approach to language policies in Italy (Machetti et al. 2018), local language policy in Padua requires the translation of all languages other than Italian. While Italian thus unsurprisingly represents the dominant language on public signs, Goglia demonstrates, amongst other things, that the inclusion of Italian on signs is adhered to more strictly in the major shopping street of the district than in secluded side-streets where more signs cater directly to immigrant groups. Other factors that influence the choice of languages include the use of English as a lingua franca between immigrant groups, and the retail orientations of some immigrant communities.

Part 2 – *Attitudes and identities* – probes into the attitudes displayed by community members towards the languages in question and examines how these attitudes as well as ideas of prestige and social values attached to languages and language varieties inform identity work at different levels. Identities are dynamic and continuously "negotiated in interaction with other individuals, collectivities and institutional structures" (Blackwood et al. 2016: xvii) – i.e., through language. Through increased mobility, transnational connectedness and language maintenance, languages have become important signifiers of identities amongst minority communities, as they are linked to cultural and social expressions. Yet, they are also intertwined with dimensions of power, as languages—and by extension their speakers – become more or less valued in relation to each other (Blackwood et al. 2016). Tensions between dominant languages in powerful positions and minority languages in less prestigious ones, including non-standardised varieties, create situations of contestation, which individuals and communities navigate through the use of various linguistic practices and repertoires, negotiating varying social identities in the process (Farr 2011; Karatsareas 2020). The chapters in part 2 demonstrate how such language attitudes influence the construction of individual and group perceptions and beliefs about languages and the self. All four chapters examine multilingualism from the perspective of immigrant communities and minority language speakers – an Italian enclave in Melbourne, the Mixtec community in New York, Polish and Chinese migrants in Dublin, and Italian immigrants in Munich.

Part 2 begins with a chapter by *John Hajek, Ambrin Hasnain* and *Carlie Hanson* which investigates the ways in which the *italianità* 'Italiannness' of Melbourne's Little Italy is expressed today through language and other means in the linguistic landscape of Lygon Street, Carlton – an area where Italian migrants were once heavily concentrated. They have largely gone but their presence is still strongly felt and visible, especially in relation to the largely symbolic use of language by food-oriented businesses that line the street. Following a pattern noted for ethnic or migrant enclaves elsewhere, this is a sign of the signalling and commodification of Lygon Street's Italian heritage that serves to attract visitors.

This is followed by *Daniel Kaufman's* exploration of the language use and attitudes in the community of Mixtec speakers in New York – a community which is largely invisible in the cityscape. A small group of estimated 25,000–30,000 speakers, the Mixtecs are dispersed throughout neighbourhoods within larger Spanish-speaking populations and typically live in a complex multilingual environment involving Mixtec, Chilango/Mexican Spanish, Caribbean Spanish/Spanglish, and English. Largely drawing from interviews with five members of the Mixtec community, Kaufman shows that a combination of historical trauma, ongoing discrimination and economic pressures conspire to suppress the use of Mixtec in public and prevent the passing on of Mixtec to the next generation. Kaufman also discusses the paradox between Mixtec speakers' apparent pride in their linguistic heritage and their patterns of language use which do not indicate significant language loyalty.

Taking a discourse analytical approach to interview data with a group of recently arrived Chinese and Polish migrants to Dublin, chapter 7, by *Chloé Diskin-Holdaway*, investigates attitudes to and perceptions of Irish English generally, and Dublin English in particular. Findings point to great heterogeneity in attitudes and diametrically opposite stances. For some participants, exposure to Dublin speech was a language shock, deviating from an imagined standard. For others, it was regarded as friendly and easy to learn. These widely different conceptualisations of Dublin English demonstrate that language attitudes and identities are subject to the participants' personal experience as well as their normative positionings of the repertoires they encounter. In light of this, the chapter also discusses the future position of globally non-dominant varieties of English and the ramifications for integration in increasingly diversified but socioeconomically segregated urban spaces.

Munich, and in particular its sizeable Italian community, is the focal point of chapter 8 by *Claudia Maria Riehl* and *Sara Ingrosso*. Munich, Germany's third largest city with a population of 1.5 million, is home to large numbers of immigrants from a variety of cultural and linguistic backgrounds. Historically, Italians and their language and culture have enjoyed a privileged position, setting them apart from other migrant groups. The chapter opens with a historical overview of Italian migration to Munich, followed by a detailed analysis of excerpts from language biographical interviews with Italian migrants in order to map the complexities and heterogeneity of this group through their individual trajectories of multilingualism, inclusion and exclusion in mainstream society, as well as comparing their experiences to other migrant groups in Munich.

The third part – *Language across time and space* – shines a spotlight on multilingualism resulting from historical and/or territorial language contact. The chapters in this section explore how multilingual practices have evolved in four urban multilingual settings which are not frequently associated with linguistic and cultural diversity. However, through historical and recent migration (Norwich, Port-Louis), territorial language contact (Montevideo) as well as recent shifts in political structures and policy (Ulaanbaatar) these cities demonstrate contrasting aspects of urban language practices.

This final part opens with *Peter Trudgill* and *Jane Warren*'s investigation of how and to what extent Norwich in past and current configurations has been a site of multilingualism and linguistic diversity. Traditionally, the capital of Norfolk has been stereotyped as a geographically remote and isolated part of the country, with a largely monocultural, white British population. However, closer analysis of the city's visual linguistic landscape reveals a much more complex and diversified image of cultural and linguistic practices than stereotypical images of the city lead us to believe. The authors compare the language situation in Norwich at three distinct periods in its history when the city experienced major linguistic change resulting from transnational population movements: the medieval period, the 16th century, and the present day. The chapter contrasts the different motivations behind the arrival of people and languages in the city during these periods, and the resulting linguistic layers evident in the city.

In chapter 10, *Bolormaa Shinjee* and *Sender Dovchin* explore multilingualism in the Mongolian capital Ulaanbaatar, as evident in the urban landscape. Ulaanbaatar, an Asian city with no significant immigration by other ethnic groups, has undergone tremendous change through rapid urbanisation in the period following the demise of the Soviet Union and communism, with a stark contrast between the modern urban Western lifestyle of Ulaanbaatar and the traditional nomadic lifestyle in rural areas. Increased foreign influence in recent years, combined with a laissez-faire language policy has resulted in some signs of greater linguistic diversity. The chapter analyses how the linguistic landscape of Ulaanbaatar is formed through diverse linguistic, cultural, and orthographic resources to achieve certain visual, communicative, and marketing purposes. Through the mixing and meshing of such resources, tokens of English, Russian and Korean are relocalised in creative ways in the urban context of Ulaanbaatar.

In chapter 11 *Anu Bissoonauth* and *Jane Warren* investigate multilingualism in Port-Louis, the capital of Mauritius, a city characterised by great linguistic and cultural complexity – a legacy of its colonial past. Based on historical documentation, demographic data, and semi-structured interviews with young Mauritians about language use and attitudes, the chapter reveals a complex multi-layered situation for language use where Kreol (French Creole) serves as lingua franca, but comes in contact with English and French as dominant languages, and with non-dominant Chinese and Indian ancestral languages. Further, the findings suggest the presence of two competing identities in the city: an ethno-linguistic identity based on one's cultural allegiances and a more fluid national identity grounded in Kreol as the shared resource.

In the final chapter, *María Irene Moyna* focusses on variation in the informal address system of Spanish in Montevideo, which is compared with Buenos Aires Spanish. Due to historical factors and the proximity of the two cities their local varieties of Spanish are mostly indistinguishable, with the exception of the informal address variation *vos/tú* in Montevideo. Variation by age group in Montevideo shows a consistent shift towards *vos*, evidencing Buenos Aires' influence as a dominant pluricentric variety of Spanish. However, not all *vos/tú* form variation in Montevideo is attributable to the influence of the larger sister city, as socioeconomic, educational, and interpersonal factors suggest that Montevideo speakers continue to avail themselves of *vos/tú* variation to express subtle social and pragmatic meanings that would be impossible to articulate if the latter address form disappeared, as it has in Buenos Aires.

Common to all chapters, explicitly or implicitly, is an acknowledgement of the importance of language contact. In sociolinguistics, urban areas have long been recognised as fertile ground for language shift as well as new ways of speaking. Without contact and interaction between individuals and groups, new localised varieties, or registers, would not surface. The volume ends with a concluding chapter that ties together methodologies and theoretical approaches presented – with a particular focus on the interplay between multilingualism and pluricentricity and the range of approaches to linguistic landscape research evident in the volume – and suggests possible avenues for future research particularly with respect to these contexts.

Appendix: Overview of cities and languages in the volume

City/Cities	Population	Status of city	Primary language(s) of city	Focus language(s) of chapter
Africa				
Port-Louis, Mauritius	148,147 (2017)	National capital	E, F, Kreol	Kreol, F, E
Asia				
Jakarta, Indonesia	10.56 million (2020)	National capital	Indo	Indo, ethnic languages (Betawi, Javanese, Chi-Indo), E
Ulaanbaatar, Mongolia	1.452 million (2017)	National capital	Mo	Mo, E, Ru, Kor

(continued)

City/Cities	Population	Status of city	Primary language(s) of city	Focus language(s) of chapter
Europe				
Biel/Bienne and Fribourg/Freiburg, Switzerland	B: 55,120 (2018) F: 38,829 (2017)	B: Capital of administrative district F: Capital of Canton (state)	B: G, F F: F, G	F, G, immigrant languages (I, E, etc.)
Dublin, Republic of Ireland	1.1 million (urban area, 2016)	National capital	E	Varieties of Irish E
Mariehamn and Kotka, Finland	M: 11,679 (2020) K: 52,126 (2020)	M: Capital of autonomous region of Åland K: Regional centre	M: Sw K: Fi	Languages other than the primary language of the cities
Munich, Germany	1.472 million (2019)	State capital	G	I, G
Norwich, UK	213,166 ('built-up area' 2011)	County town	E	E and contact languages
Padua, Italy	209,829 (2017)	Provincial capital	I	I, languages other than I (Chi, E etc.)
North America				
New York City, USA	8.419 million (2019)	Major global city	E	Mixtec, Sp
Oceania				
Melbourne, Australia	5.16 million (2020)	State capital	E	I, E
South America				
Montevideo, Uruguay	1.381 million (2017)	National capital	Sp	Varieties of Sp

Legend: G = German, F = French, I = Italian, E = English; Indo = Indonesian; Chi = Chinese; Sw = Swedish; Fi = Finnish; Ru = Russian; Sp = Spanish; Mo = Mongolian; Kor = Korean

References

Ammon, Ulrich. 1989. Towards a descriptive framework for the status/function/social position of a language within a country. In Ulrich Ammon (ed.), *Status and function of languages and language varieties*, 21–106. Berlin/New York: de Gruyter.

Ammon, Ulrich. 1995. *Die deutsche Sprache in Deutschland, Österreich und der Schweiz*. Berlin/New York: Mouton de Gruyter.

Aracena, Felipe. 2009. La contribución de los inmigrantes en Uruguay. *Papeles del CEIC* 47. 1–42.

Arnaut, Karel, Jan Blommaert, Ben Rampton & Massimiliano Spotti (eds.). 2016a. *Language and superdiversity*. New York/London: Routledge.

Arnaut, Karel, Martha Sif Karrebæk, Massimiliano Spotti & Jan Blommaert (eds.). 2016b. *Engaging superdiversity: recombining spaces, times and language practices*. Bristol: Multilingual Matters.

Auer, Peter. 2021. Reflections on linguistic pluricentricity. *Sociolinguistica* 35. 29–47.

Barni, Monica & Carla Bagna. 2015. The critical turn in LL: new methodologies and new items in LL. *Linguistic Landscape* 1(1–2). 6–18.

Blackwood, Robert, Elizabeth Lanza & Hirut Woldemariam. 2016. Preface. In Robert Blackwood, Elizabeth Lanza & Hirut Woldemariam (eds.), *Negotiating and contesting identities in linguistic landscapes*, xvi–xxiv. London: Bloomsbury.

Blommaert, Jan. 2013. *Ethnography, superdiversity and linguistic landscapes: chronicles of complexity*. Bristol: Multilingual Matters.

Blommaert, Jan & Ben Rampton. 2011. Language and superdiversity. *Diversities* 13(2). 1–21.

Britain, David. 2016. Sedentarism, nomadism and the sociolinguistics of dialect. In Nikolas Coupland (ed.), *Sociolinguistics: theoretical debates*, 217–241. Cambridge: Cambridge University Press.

Britain, David. 2017. Which way to look?: Perspectives on 'urban' and 'rural' in dialectology. In Chris Montgomery & Emma Moore (eds.), *Language and a sense of place: studies in language and region*, 171–188. Cambridge: Cambridge University Press.

Britain, David. 2022. 'Rural' and 'urban' in dialectology. In Beatrix Busse & Ingo H. Warnke (eds.), *Handbuch Sprache im urbanen Raum. Handbook of language in urban space*, 52–73. Berlin: de Gruyter.

Cadier, Linda & Clare Mar-Molinero. 2014. Negotiating networks of communication in a superdiverse environment: urban multilingualism in the City of Southampton. *Multilingua* 33(5–6). 505–24.

Carson, Lorna & Lid King. 2016. Introduction: multilingualism is lived here. In Lid King & Lorna Carson (eds.), *The multilingual city*, 1–16. Bristol: Multilingual Matters.

Cavallaro, Francesco & Ng Bee Chin. 2014. Language in Singapore: from multilingualism to English Plus. In John Hajek & Yvette Slaughter (eds.), *Challenging the monolingual mindset*, 33–48. Bristol: Multilingual Matters.

Chik, Alice, Phil Benson & Robyn Moloney (eds.). 2019. *Multilingual Sydney*. London/New York: Routledge.

Chik, Claire Hitchins (ed.). 2022. *Multilingual La La Land: language use in sixteen greater Los Angeles communities*. New York: Routledge.

Clyne, Michael. 1991. *Community languages: the Australian experience*. Cambridge: Cambridge University Press.

Clyne, Michael (ed.). 1992a. *Pluricentric languages: different norms in different countries*. Berlin/New York: Mouton de Gruyter.

Clyne, Michael. 1992b. Introduction. In Michael Clyne (ed.), *Pluricentric languages: different norms in different countries*, 1–9. Berlin/New York: Mouton de Gruyter.

Clyne, Michael. 1992c. Epilogue. In Michael Clyne (ed.), *Pluricentric languages: different norms in different countries*, 455–465. Berlin/New York: Mouton de Gruyter.

Clyne, Michael. 2005. *Australia's language potential*. Sydney: University of New South Wales Press.

Clyne, Michael. 2008. The monolingual mindset as an impediment to the development of plurilingual potential in Australia. *Sociolinguistic Studies* 2(3). 347–366.

Creese, Angela & Adrian Blackledge (eds.). 2018. *The Routledge handbook of language and superdiversity: an interdisciplinary perspective*. London/New York: Routledge.

Czaika, Mathias & Hein de Haas. 2015. The globalization of migration: has the world become more migratory? *International Migration Review* 48(2). 283–323.

da Silva, Augusto Soares (ed.). 2014. *Pluricentricity: language variation and sociocognitive dimensions*. Berlin: de Gruyter Mouton.

Duarte, Joana & Ingrid Gogolin (eds.). 2013. *Linguistic superdiversity in urban areas: research approaches*. Amsterdam/Philadelphia: John Benjamins.

Dyers, Charlyn. 2015. Multilingualism in Late-Modern Africa: identity, mobility and multivocality. *International Journal of Bilingualism* 19(2). 226–35.

Farr, Marcia. 2011. Urban plurilingualism: language practices, policies, and ideologies in Chicago. *Journal of Pragmatics* 43(5). 1161–1172.

Félix-Brasdefer, César J. & Maria Elena Placencia. 2019. *Pragmatic variation in service encounter interactions across the Spanish-speaking world*. London: Routledge.

Flores, Nelson & Mark Lewis. 2016. From truncated to sociopolitical emergence: a critique of superdiversity in sociolinguistics. *International Journal of the Sociology of Language* 241. 97–124.

Goebel, Zane. 2015. *Language and superdiversity: Indonesians knowledging at home and abroad*. New York: Oxford University Press.

Goebel, Zane. 2017. Superdiversity from within: the case of ethnicity in Indonesia. In Karel Arnaut, Martha Sif Karrebæk, Massimiliano Spotti & Jan Blommaert (eds.), *Engaging superdiversity: recombining spaces, times and language practices*, 251–276. Bristol: Multilingual Matters.

Goebel, Zane. 2018. Superdiversity. In Jan-Ola Östman & Jef Verschueren (eds.), *Handbook of pragmatics*, 221–238. Amsterdam: John Benjamins.

Haugh, Michael. 2017. Mockery and (non-)seriousness in initial interactions amongst American and Australian speakers of English. In Donald Carbaugh (ed.), *The handbook of communication in cross-cultural perspective*, 104–117. New York: Routledge.

Heller, Monica. 2013. Repositioning the multilingual periphery. In Sari Pietikäinen & Helen Kelly-Holmes (eds.), *Multilingualism and the periphery*, 17–34. Oxford: Oxford University Press.

Horvath, Barbara. 1985. *Variation in Australian English: the sociolects of Sydney*. Cambridge: Cambridge University Press.

Jain, Ritu (ed.). 2021. *Multilingual Singapore: language policies and linguistic realities*. Abingdon/New York: Routledge.

Jaworski, Adam & Crispin Thurlow (eds.). 2010. *Semiotic landscapes: language, image, space*. London: Continuum.

Karatsareas, Petros. 2020. Uncovering variation within urban multilingualism. In Clare Mar-Molinero (ed.), *Researching language in superdiverse urban contexts*, 106–130. Bristol: Multilingual Matters.

Kipp, Sandra & Catrin Norrby (eds.). 2006. Community languages in practice in Australia. *International Journal of the Sociology of Language* 180.

Kloss, Heinz. 1978. *Die Entwicklung neuer germanischer Kultursprachen seit 1850*. 2nd ed. Düsseldorf: Schwann.

Kretzenbacher, Heinz L. 2012. The emancipation of Strine: Australian English as an established post-colonial national standard of English. In Rudolf Muhr (ed.), *Non-dominant varieties of pluricentric languages*, 129–142. Frankfurt am Main/Vienna: Peter Lang.

Labov, William. 1966. *The social stratification of English in New York City*. Washington: Center for Applied Linguistics.

Landry, Rodrigue & Richard Y. Bourhis. 1997. Linguistic landscape and ethnolinguistic vitality: an empirical study. *Journal of Language and Social Psychology* 16(1). 23–49.

Langer, Nils. 2021. Pluricentricity and minority languages: the difficult case of North Frisian. *Sociolinguistica* 35. 73–90.

Liebkind, Karmela, Tom Moring & Marika Tandefelt (eds.). 2007. The Swedish-speaking Finns. *International Journal of the Sociology of Language* 187/188.

Li Wei. 2018. Linguistic (super)diversity, post-multilingualism and translanguaging moments. In Angela Creese & Adrian Blackledge (eds.), *The Routledge handbook of language and superdiversity*, 16–29. Abingdon/New York: Routledge.

Lindström, Jan, Catrin Norrby, Camilla Wide & Jenny Nilsson. 2019. Task-completing assessments in service encounters. *Research on Language and Social Interaction* 52(2). 85–103.

Machetti, Sabrina, Monica Barni & Carla Bagna. 2018. Language policies for migrants in Italy: the tension between democracy, decision-making, and linguistic diversity. In Michele Gazzola, Torsten Templin, & Bengt-Arne Wickström (eds.), *Language policy and linguistic justice*. 477–498. Cham: Springer.

Makoni, Sinfree. 2012. A critique of language, languaging and supervernacular. *Muitas Vozes* 1(2). 189–199.

Mar-Molinero, Clare (ed.). 2020a. *Researching language in superdiverse urban contexts: exploring methodological and theoretical concepts*. Bristol: Multilingual Matters.

Mar-Molinero, Clare. 2020b. Researching multilingual urban contexts. In Clare Mar-Molinero (ed.), *Researching language in superdiverse urban contexts: exploring methodological and theoretical concepts*, 8–27. Bristol: Multilingual Matters.

Muhr, Rudolf. 2012. Linguistic dominance and non-dominance in pluricentric languages: a typology. In Rudolf Muhr (ed.), *Non-dominant varieties of pluricentric languages: getting the picture*, 23–48. Frankfurt am Main/Vienna: Peter Lang.

Muhr, Rudolf & Dawn Marley (eds.). 2015. *Pluricentric languages: new perspectives in theory and description*. Frankfurt am Main/Berlin: Peter Lang.

Norrby, Catrin. 2021. Interaction and variation in pluricentric languages: communicative patterns in Sweden Swedish and Finland Swedish. *Sociolinguistica* 35. 267–276.

Norrby, Catrin, Jan Lindström, Jenny Nilsson & Camilla Wide. 2020. Pluricentric languages. In Jan-Ola Östman & Jef Verschueren (eds.), *Handbook of pragmatics* 23, 203–222. Amsterdam: John Benjamins.

Oakes, Leigh. 2021. Pluricentric linguistic justice: a new ethics based approach to pluricentricity in French and other languages. *Sociolinguistica* 35. 49–71.

Otsuji, Emi & Alastair Pennycook. 2010. Metrolingualism: fixity, fluidity and language in flux. *International Journal of Multilingualism* 7(3). 240–254.

Pavlenko, Aneta. 2019. Superdiversity and why it isn't: reflections on terminological innovation and academic branding. In Barbara Schmenk, Stephan Breidbach & Lutz Küster (eds.), *Sloganization in language education discourse*, 142–168. Bristol: Multilingual Matters.

Pauwels, Anne (ed.). 1988. The future of ethnic languages in Australia. *International Journal of the Sociology of Language* 72.

Pennycook, Alistair. 2017. Translanguaging and semiotic assemblages. *International Journal of Multilingualism* 14(3). 269–282.
Pietikäinen, Sari & Helen Kelly-Holmes. 2013. Multilingualism and the periphery. In Sari Pietikäinen & Helen Kelly-Holmes (eds.), *Multilingualism and the periphery*, 1–16. Oxford: Oxford University Press.
Piller, Ingrid. 2016. *Linguistic diversity and social justice: an introduction to applied sociolinguistics*. Oxford: Oxford University Press.
Reber, Elisabeth. 2021. On the variation of fragmental constructions in British English and American English post-match interviews. *Sociolinguistica* 35. 217–241.
Romaine, Suzanne. 1991. *Languages in Australia*. Cambridge: Cambridge University Press.
Schneider, Britta. 2020. The urban myth: a critical interrogation of the sociolinguistic imagining of cities as spaces of diversity. *Working Papers in Urban Language & Literacies* 267. 1–27.
Shohamy, Elana. 2019. Linguistic landscape after a decade: an overview of themes, debates and future directions. In Martin Pütz & Nele Mundt (eds.), *Expanding the linguistic landscape: linguistic diversity, multimodality and the use of space as a semiotic resource*, 62–86. Bristol: Multilingual Matters.
Shohamy, Elana, Eliezer Ben-Rafael & Monica Barni (eds.). 2010. *Linguistic landscape in the city*. Bristol: Multilingual Matters.
Siemund, Peter & Jacob R. E. Leimgruber (eds.). 2021. *Multilingual global cities: Singapore, Hong Kong, Dubai*. Abingdon/New York: Routledge.
Skrandies, Peter. 2016. Language policies and the politics of urban multilingualism. In Lid King & Lorna Carson (eds.), *The multilingual city*, 115–148. Bristol: Multilingual Matters.
Smakman, Dick & Patrick Heinrich. 2017. Introduction: why cities matter for a globalising sociolinguistics. In Dick Smakman & Patrick Heinrich (eds.), *Urban sociolinguistics: the city as a linguistic process and experience*, 1–11. New York: Routledge.
Stewart, William. 1968. A sociolinguistic typology for describing national multilingualism. In Joshua A. Fishman (ed.), *Readings in the sociology of language*, 530–545. The Hague/Paris: Mouton.
Trudgill, Peter. 1974. *The social differentiation of English in Norwich*. Cambridge: Cambridge University Press.
Tsiola, Anna 2023. Social actors in the Singaporean LL: sign uptake, market ideology, and language hierarchies. *Linguistic Landscape* 9(1). 59–85.
Tunger, Verena, Clare Mar-Molinero, Darren Paffey, Dick Vigers & Cecylia Barłóg. 2010. Language policies and "new" migration in officially bilingual areas. *Current Issues in Language Planning* 11(2). 190–205.
Tusting, Karin (ed.). 2020. *The Routledge handbook of linguistic ethnography*. London: Routledge.
Vertovec, Steven. 2007. Super-diversity and its implications. *Ethnic and Racial Studies* 30(6). 1024–1054.
Wang, Xuan, Massimiliano Spotti, Kasper Juffermans, Leonie Cornips, Sjaak Kroon & Jan Blommaert. 2014. Globalization in the margins: toward a re-evaluation of language and mobility. *Applied Linguistics Review* 5(1). 23–44.
Wide, Camilla, Catrin Norrby & Leigh Oakes. 2021. Introduction: new perspectives on pluricentricity. *Sociolinguistica* 35. 1–7.
Wolf, Norbert. 1994. Österreichisches zum österreichischen Deutsch. *Neuphilologische Mitteilungen* 113(4). 497–509.
Yumul-Florendo, Maria Rosario & Sebastian Muth. 2022. The pragmatics of linguistic landscapes. In Andreas H. Jucker & Heiko Hausendorf (eds.), *Pragmatics of space*, 523–548. Berlin/Boston: de Gruyter Mouton.

Part 1: **Multilingual policies in practice**

Doris Schüpbach and Claudine Brohy
1 Bilingualism, multilingualism and diglossia: A tale of two Swiss cities

> Today Biel is the most bilingual city of Switzerland, (. . .) Fribourg itself is a bilingual city (. . .) which forms an interesting contrast with Biel. (Weinreich [1953] 2011: 127, 129)

1 Introduction

Switzerland is a multilingual country with four national and official languages (German, French, Italian and Romansh) and many immigrant languages. However, due to the principle of territoriality which ascribes the national languages to certain territories, institutional bi- and multilingualism is restricted to relatively few areas, notably those along the "language borders" (see Zimmerli 1891–1899; Rash 2002; Schedel and Meyer Pitton 2018). Even though some of these run along geographic boundaries, in some instances municipalities are actually located *on* a language border and are considered bilingual.

In this chapter, we consider the two prime examples of French-German bilingual cities in Switzerland: Fribourg/Freiburg – with a French-speaking majority – and Biel/Bienne – with a German-speaking majority.[1] Due to immigration, both cities also have sizeable alloglot minorities – i.e. residents who have a language other than the local languages French and German as their first language – and both cities are thus in reality multilingual rather than bilingual. In addition to bi- and multilingualism, as generally in German-speaking Switzerland, there is also a diglossic situation among the German-speaking communities of the two cities: the Swiss German dialects are the varieties spoken in all but the most formal situations and more recently also used in informal written exchanges, whereas the Swiss variety of Standard German is generally used in written discourse and orally in certain formal contexts (see Ferguson 1959; Rash 1998, 2003; Stępkowska 2012).

We discuss and illustrate issues associated with bilingualism, multilingualism and diglossia in the context of the two cities. We first summarise relevant previous research and present our framework and the research questions. We then

---
[1] The dual naming used here reflects the names of the cities in both languages: Fribourg (French), Freiburg (German); Biel (German), Bienne (French), with the respective majority language mentioned first.

provide an overview of the historic and demolinguistic development of the two cities and summarise their language policies and legislation. We investigate the official discourse in Biel/Bienne and Fribourg/Freiburg on bilingualism, multilingualism and linguistic diversity, using the municipalities' official websites as principal data sources. We explore the interplay of official bilingualism and actual multilingualism, the role allocated to the immigrant languages and the influence of Swiss-German diglossia. By comparing the situation in the two cities, we identify and discuss major differences as well as commonalities which are linked to historical, demographic, social, as well as political and individual factors.

2 Previous research

There is a considerable amount of folk linguistic material,[2] illustrating the general public's interest in the language situation in these two locations and highlighting that this kind of language situation is perceived as atypical in Switzerland given the prevailing principle of territoriality (see Brohy 2009; Elmiger 2015: 35–36; Kużelewska 2016). Some unpublished research at lower academic levels (by high school, undergraduate and master students) is also available. These contributions are mostly concerned with French/German bilingualism in one of the two locations. Similarly, most existing academic research on Biel/Bienne and Fribourg/Freiburg focuses on bilingualism and considers other languages only to a limited extent or not at all. Only few contributions examine both localities and/or take a comparative perspective. And even though Weinreich ([1953] 2011, quoted above) alludes to significant differences between the two cities, they were not the focus of his study.

First and foremost among the comparative studies is Kolde's (1981) seminal and wide-ranging work on language contact in bilingual cities, in which he investigated language competence, language use and attitudes towards the other language among young people in Biel/Bienne and Fribourg/Freiburg. He found that in both cities, the French speakers made less use of the other language, and displayed a lower competence and a more negative attitude towards it than their German speaking counterparts. However, the difference between the two groups

---

2 These include letters to editors, opinion pieces, radio programs, a recent comparative volume written by a local journalist (Schneuwly 2019) and an exhibition in Biel/Bienne's local museum „Le bilinguisme n'existe pas: Biu/Bienne, città of njëqind Sprachen" (Neues Museum Biel/Nouveau Musée Bienne, 22/6/2019 – 22/3/2020, http://www.nmbiel.ch/index.php?id=4&lang=de&eid=66).

was less pronounced in Biel/Bienne than in Fribourg/Freiburg. More specific and narrower in focus are for example Brohy's (2005) comparison of perceptions of bilingualism, Conrad (2005) on bilingual communication, Brohy and Schüpbach (2016) on language policies in the two cities, and studies on their linguistic landscape (e.g. Brohy 2011).

Several larger studies cover the language situation in Biel/Bienne. The most comprehensive one – *bil bienne, bilinguisme à Bienne, Kommunikation in Biel* 'bil bienne, bilingualism in Bienne, communication in Biel' – was conducted in the early 2000s (Conrad and Elmiger 2010; Elmiger and Conrad 2005a; Conrad et al. 2002; see also Elmiger 2015: 38–42 and Schüpbach 2008: 159–161 for short summaries in English) and investigated the language choices monolingual and bilingual residents of Biel/Bienne make in their everyday lives. Their choices of a (common) language of interaction seem to depend on a range of factors, among them the language repertoires available to the interlocutors, their relationship and status, the context as well as issues of identity (Elmiger 2015: 40–41). While there are no strict rules for any given situation, interactions between speakers from different language groups very often follow what is termed the Biel/Bienne model (a term coined by Kolde 1981, cf. Conrad and Elmiger 2010: 36–37), where the person who initiates the interaction also determines its language. The study also briefly compares practices in Biel/Bienne and Fribourg/Freiburg (Conrad and Elmiger 2010: 45–52) and notes that in Fribourg/Freiburg the majority language French dominates and is considered the default language choice. At a more general level, the authors propose a linguistic *social contract* to describe the city's bilingualism. In this contract "each linguistic group accepts and tolerates, individually as well as collectively, the other language group and claims the same for itself" (Elmiger 2015: 42). More recently, an ethnographic study examined language practices at local call centres and the ways Biel/Bienne's bi- and multilingualism was used to attract these companies (Flubacher and Duchêne 2012; Duchêne and Flubacher 2015). It shows that the official bilingualism and inherent multilingualism form an integral part of Biel/Bienne's promotional discourse and are discursively constructed by the authorities as an economic resource and as an asset. The language skills of individual workers, on the other hand, are taken for granted and thus not separately remunerated. A recurring project, the *Bilingualism Barometer*, is a survey conducted roughly every ten years. It aims to gauge attitudes towards bilingualism and the two major speech communities in Biel/Bienne (Fuchs and Werlen 1999; Brohy 2008, 2009, 2012; Forum für die Zweisprachigkeit 2016). Its results generally confirm that bilingualism in Biel/Bienne is widely accepted and forms an integral part of the local identity. However, they also highlight that the linguistic minority is less satisfied with the current implementation of bilingualism and sees more scope for improvement of its status.

Less published research is available about Fribourg/Freiburg and much of it is quite specific in nature. Lüdi (1985), for example, analyses the multilingual council minutes of the 15th century; Brohy (1992) details the urban linguistic context of bilingual couples and families; Haas (2008) discusses aristocrats' language use in the 18th century; Altermatt (2005) reviews the city's institutional bilingualism, mostly focusing on its political and historical development. More recent research deals with linguistic landscape, signage and naming (Brohy 2017b; Anderegg 2018).

3 Framework, methodology and sources of data

Our conceptual framework derives from contact linguistics and the ecology of language (see for example Haugen 1972; Weinreich [1953] 2011) which study the history and practice of groups using different languages in shared territories and the interplay between languages and the environment. In a comparative perspective, we analyse bilingualism as a social practice, the official discourse of bi- and multilingualism and the traces of bilingualism and multilingualism (or their absence). Our main focus is on the diverging perception and hence implementation of bilingualism in these two German-French bilingual cities in Switzerland. More specifically, we explore the following questions:

(1) In which ways do the two cities differ in their discourses on language(s), bilingualism and multilingualism?
(2) To what extent do history and demography help explain current official attitudes and discourses on language, bilingualism and multilingualism?
(3) Do the local policies and discourses on bilingualism support or constrain a broader multilingualism and if so, in what way?
(4) What role does language (and bilingualism and multilingualism in particular) play in the cities' self-perception and identity?

In addition to summarising the history, demography and language legislation of the two cities, we analyse their public discourse with regard to bilingualism, multilingualism and other languages. We focus on the contexts in which these terms are mentioned, how they are conceptualised and the role they are assigned in the construction of the cities' official identity.

Our data consist of official documents published by the municipal authorities of the two cities with a focus on their official websites; where appropriate, other published materials, media reports and personal observations are also included. Websites are prime examples of official discourse and therefore rich data sources, particularly in this context: they show how the city presents itself to locals and outsiders alike; they discursively construct the city's identity and are embedded in the discourse of promotion (Flubacher and Duchêne 2012) and branding. As they also provide information and services, they are social representations *about* languages as well as representations *in* and *through* languages and discourse (Moore and Py 2011).

While we also rely on statistical data, their comparability across time and locations is an issue: firstly, the Federal Statistical Office and the local authorities in Biel/Bienne and Fribourg/Freiburg respectively focus on different types of data. Secondly, the mode of data collection at the national level has changed recently: until 2000, a full census was conducted every ten years. Since 2010 data are primarily sourced from public registers, supplemented by samples from so-called "structural surveys". As a consequence, figures are less reliable for smaller cohorts and results less fine-grained. In addition, some answer options have been modified; until 2000, respondents could only indicate a single "mother tongue" and separately one "principal language", while in the current structural surveys up to three principal languages are allowed. This makes direct comparisons over time very difficult and we use these figures cautiously, primarily to help identify trends.

4 Biel/Bienne and Fribourg/Freiburg

4.1 The context

Switzerland is a federal state consisting of 26 cantons which – among many other issues – decide on their official language(s), manage their cultural policy, and are in charge of education. Three of the cantons are officially bilingual, in that they have two official languages: the canton of Bern/Berne has a German-speaking majority and a French-speaking minority; in the cantons of Fribourg/Freiburg and Valais/Wallis French is the majority language, German the minority language; and one canton – Graubünden/Grischun/Grigioni – is officially trilingual (German, Romansh, Italian) with a German-speaking majority.

Biel/Bienne is located in the canton of Bern/Berne, Fribourg/Freiburg is the capital of the canton of the same name. While both cities are tiny by world standards (see Table 1), they are considered cities in the Swiss context: Biel/Bienne is the 10th largest by population, Fribourg/Freiburg the 14th and as the capital the most significant centre within the canton.

The two cities are only about 50 km apart and both are situated on the German-French language border. As a consequence, the imagined border *line* morphs into a *space*, and the personal principle – the right of each individual to use the language of their choice – prevails over the territorial principle applied elsewhere in Switzerland, where cantons (and in some instances districts and towns) have the right to determine their official language(s) while taking into account the traditional territorial distribution of languages (Brohy 2009: 307; 2011: 107; Elmiger 2015: 36).

Table 1: Demographic indicators (Source: Federal Statistical Office).[3]

	Biel/Bienne	Fribourg/Freiburg	Switzerland
Population 2018	55,159	38,365	8,544,527
Foreign nationals 2018	34.2%	37.1%	25.1%
Employed 2017			
Total	40,349	33,730	5,180,170
Industry	9,452 (23.4%)	2,314 (6.9%)	1,078,704 (20.8%)
Services	30,847 (76.4%)	31,908 (93.1%)	3,938,561 (76%)
Principal languages 2015–2017			
German	55.0%	19.8%	62.8%
French	39.4%	70.6%	22.8%
Italian	9.0%	4.6%	8.2%
Romansh	-	-	0.5%
English	4.7%	5.2%	5.2%
Other languages	25.2%	30.2%	18.5%

Table 1 presents some basic demographic indicators for the two cities as well as for Switzerland as a whole. Notable is the high proportion of residents without Swiss nationality in both locations (and in Switzerland). This is in large part due to the complex naturalisation process which requires a very long period of residence before an application for naturalisation can be lodged.

The employment figures hint at the character of the two cities: in Fribourg/Freiburg the service sector is dominant, which includes the cantonal administration and a large education sector with, among others, bilingual institutions at secondary and tertiary levels. Biel/Bienne still has a relatively strong manufacturing sector with watchmaking and precision engineering the most important industries,

---

[3] https://www.bfs.admin.ch/bfs/de/home/statistiken/regionalstatistik/regionale-portraets-kennzahlen/gemeinden/gemeindeportraets.html and https://www.bfs.admin.ch/bfs/de/home/statistiken/bevoelkerung/sprachen-religionen/sprachen.html (accessed 24 January 2021) and Patricia Zocco, personal communication 30 August 2019.

but also a growing service sector with tertiary education and communication its major proponents.

In terms of languages, the totals add up to more than 100 per cent as up to three languages can be nominated. French and German are the strongest languages in both locations with Italian the most important alloglot language in Biel/Bienne and the fourth in Fribourg/Freiburg (behind Portuguese and English). Noteworthy in this context is the ambivalent status of Italian as a national language of Switzerland with official status at the national level, and as an important language of immigrants in the two cities discussed here. It is also important to point out the different status of the respective majority languages in the two cities: Biel/Bienne's majority language, German, is also the majority language in Switzerland overall, and the French speakers of Biel/Bienne are thus a minority group locally and nationally. We term this *parallel minority status* as opposed to an *embedded minority status* in Fribourg/Freiburg, where German is the minority language at a local and cantonal level but the majority language nationally – consequently, French is the local majority but a minority language nationally.

4.2 History

Biel/Bienne was founded in 1220 AD as a German-speaking settlement with a French-speaking hinterland to the North, situated on the border of what was to become, in 1353, the canton of Bern. Politically, Biel/Bienne was associated with the Bishopric of Basel, a traditionally bilingual entity. It remained relatively insignificant, overshadowed in importance and size by neighbouring towns which dominated the all-important trade routes. In 1815, Biel/Bienne and most of its hinterland were allocated to the canton of Bern in compensation for the loss of other territories. Biel/Bienne remained predominantly German-speaking until the mid-19th century when the local authorities introduced generous tax breaks to attract watchmakers from the French-speaking Jura region. Between 1844 and 1859 around 1700 watchmakers and their families moved to the town, which led to a rapid change in its linguistic composition. Biel/Bienne quite rapidly developed from a small town adjacent to the language border to a medium-size city on the border, and from a German-dominated town to a bilingual centre – an image successfully promoted by the local authorities from the first half of the 20th century onwards. In 1952, Biel/Bienne's bilingualism was officially recognised by the canton of Bern in its new constitution.

Fribourg/Freiburg was founded in 1157 AD by Duke Berthold IV of Zähringen – himself the son of a Burgundian mother and a Swabian father. From the beginning the population was linguistically mixed, initially with a German-speaking majority. The status of the two languages, however, has changed multiple times, in line with the distribution of power in emerging Switzerland and beyond. As a case in point, when in 1481 Fribourg/Freiburg and its rural hinterland became a member of the then exclusively German-speaking "Swiss" Confederation, it was the first canton with a part-French-speaking population and consequently its language policy was strongly weighted in favour of German. On the other hand, the strong position of France in Europe in the 17th and 18th centuries worked in favour of French, the most prestigious language in Europe at the time. French was instituted as official language after the Napoleonic invasion in 1798, but after 1814 (the so-called Restoration) the pendulum swung back in favour of German. In 1830, French again became the official language, while the 1857 constitution implicitly declared French and German official languages, with French providing the legally binding texts. French – the language of prestige, government and the upper classes – was favoured again in the domains of education, politics, culture, and economy. This led to inequalities and discrimination against the German-speakers. Only from the 1950s onwards was the situation slowly rectified, driven in particular by a lobby organisation, the *Deutschfreiburgische Arbeitsgemeinschaft* 'Association of German-speakers of Freiburg', established in 1959.[4]

4.3 Language demography

How did this history translate into language demography? Figure 1 is based on census data and shows the development of the language groups from 1888 to 2000 in Biel/Bienne and Fribourg/Freiburg. In both cities, the proportion of speakers of French as their main language is relatively stable over time, while German is seen to decline. Italian had by the 1960s a greater presence in industrial Biel/Bienne due to a higher number of immigrant workers from Italy; it has, however, declined in numbers in both localities since the 1970s – a result of re-migration of Italian workers and of language shift in the second generation. The number and

---

[4] In 2017, the Association merged with another group to form *KUND Kultur Natur Deutschfreiburg* 'Culture [and] Nature [in] German-speaking Freiburg'.

proportion of alloglot speakers have risen steadily in Biel/Bienne since 1970, and in Fribourg/Freiburg since the 1950s.

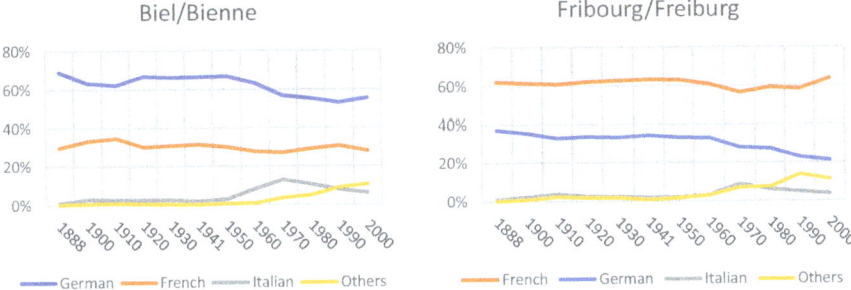

Figure 1: Language demographic development in Biel/Bienne and Fribourg/Freiburg, 1888–2000 (Source: Federal Statistical Office).[5]

For both cities, data are also available for the preferred language of correspondence (French or German) the inhabitants have lodged with the local authorities. The longitudinal data for Biel/Bienne (see Figure 2) illustrate the historic development outlined earlier and show that the gap between the two languages has been closing over time.

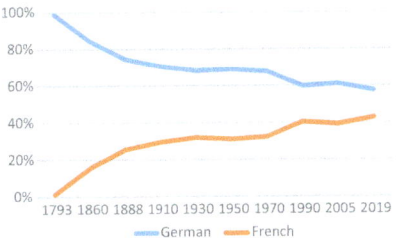

Figure 2: Biel/Bienne – Preferred language of correspondence 1793–2019 (Sources: Racine 2003: 12; Stadt Biel).[6]

For Fribourg/Freiburg, consistent numbers of preferred language of municipal correspondence (here termed language of contact) have only been available since 2012

---
5 https://www.pxweb.bfs.admin.ch/pxweb/de/ and https://www.bfs.admin.ch/bfs/de/home/dienstleistungen/historische-daten.html (accessed 2 September 2019).
6 Biel/Bienne: Statistisches Fact Sheet. Données statistiques, https://www.biel-bienne.ch/public/upload/assets/912/pra_sm_fact_sheet_jun20_d_f.pdf (accessed 24 January 2021).

(see Table 2), with the proportion of French steadily rising and the gap between the languages thus increasing. As in Biel/Bienne, the immigrant population predominantly adopt French as their preferred language of administration (particularly those from a Romance language background). This development strengthens the French-speaking linguistic minority in Biel/Bienne and the French-speaking linguistic majority in Fribourg/Freiburg.

Table 2: Fribourg/Freiburg – Preferred language of municipal correspondence 2012–2019 (Source: Ville de Fribourg).[7]

	2012	2013	2014	2015	2016	2017	2018	2019
French	82.3%	82.5%	83.2%	83.5%	83.6%	83.7%	84.1%	84.3%
German	17.7%	17.5%	16.8%	16.5%	16.4%	16.3%	15.9%	15.7%

At the individual level, reliable and comparable data on languages other than French and German are quite difficult to find. Aggregated data for 2015–2017 indicate that 38.9 per cent of the population in Biel/Bienne and 40 per cent in Fribourg/Freiburg indicate a language other than French or German as their (co-)principal language (see Table 1). Table 3 lists the break-down by language. As already mentioned, these add up to more than 100 per cent, as up to three languages could be nominated.

Table 3: Principal languages spoken by residents over 15 years of age 2015–2017 (Federal Statistical Office).[8]

Biel/Bienne		Fribourg/Freiburg	
German	55.0%	French	70.6%
French	39.4%	German	19.8%
Italian	9.0%	Portuguese	11.7%
English	4.7%	English	5.2%
Albanian	4.6%	Italian	4.6%
Portuguese	3.8%	Spanish	3.8%
Spanish	3.4%	Albanian	3.5%
Serbo-Croatian	2.2%	Turkish	2.0%
Turkish	1.9%	Arabic	1.3%
Arabic	1.5%	Serbo-Croatian	1.0%
Other languages	7.8%	Other languages	6.9%

---

7 Nicolas Wolleb, personal communication 12 January 2019 and Rapports de gestion, https://www.ville-fribourg.ch/conseil-communal (accessed 24 January 2021).
8 Patricia Zocco, personal communication 30 August 2019.

In Biel/Bienne, Italian is still the most important alloglot language. In Fribourg/Freiburg the Portuguese speakers are the largest group after the local languages, followed by English and Italian. Due to the relatively crude sampling for this survey, these percentages cannot be taken at face value but indicate the strength of the various language groups.

It is important to note that neither Biel/Bienne nor Fribourg/Freiburg show distinct or consistent spatial clustering or segregation, neither of the two local language groups, nor of immigrant groups (Stadt Biel, Henri Graber, personal communication 9 January 2012; Etat de Fribourg, Service de la statistique, personal communication 5 November 2016).

4.4 Language legislation and policies

In terms of language legislation, the situation in Biel/Bienne is quite straightforward and we can speak of an official, explicit, legislated bilingualism. The first article of the city's statute[9] forms the basis for full institutional bilingualism:

> *Die Stadt Biel ist eine eigenständige zweisprachige Gemeinde innerhalb des Kantons Bern;*[10]
> The city of Biel/Bienne is an independent bilingual municipality within the canton of Bern;

The institutional bilingualism of Biel/Bienne is further spelled out in article 3 of its statute:

> [1] *Deutsch und Französisch sind gleichberechtigte Amtssprachen im Verkehr mit städtischen Behörden und mit der Stadtverwaltung.*
> [2] *Städtische Erlasse und amtliche Mitteilungen an die Bevölkerung sind in deutscher und französischer Sprache abzufassen.*[11]
> [1] German and French are equal official languages in dealings with local authorities and the local administration.
> [2] Municipal regulations and official communications with the public are to be made available in German and in French.

---

[9] Stadtordnung/Règlement de la Ville 1996, www.biel-bienne.ch/lawdata/SGR/pdf/100/101.1.pdf (accessed 11 April 2019).

[10] We quote the relevant legislation of Biel/Bienne in German (although it is available in both languages), and in French for Fribourg/Freiburg (where most is only available in French). The translations into English are ours unless otherwise attributed.

A complete overhaul of the statute of Biel/Bienne is underway; judging by the draft before local parliament, no major changes with regard to languages are suggested.

[11] www.biel-bienne.ch/lawdata/SGR/pdf/100/101.1.pdf (accessed 11 April 2019).

As a consequence, all official documents are available in both official languages and both versions are legally binding. Matters relating to language are mentioned in 25 (of about 160) municipal regulations.

Fribourg/Freiburg, on the other hand, has never declared itself *officially* bilingual. The corresponding article 1 of the local statute states:

> *La Ville de Fribourg est une commune du Canton de Fribourg.*[12]
> The city of Fribourg is a municipality of the canton of Fribourg.

Language is not mentioned. Implicitly, however, the current constitution of the canton acknowledges the city's bilingualism by stating that:

> *Sa capitale est la ville de Fribourg, Freiburg en allemand.*[13]
> Its capital is the city of Fribourg, Freiburg in German.

In Fribourg/Freiburg language use is mentioned only in a handful of official regulations. For instance, the section comparable to Biel/Bienne's article 3 cited above makes no mention of language,[14] but bilingualism is mentioned for example in the legislation ruling the municipal parliament:[15]

> *¹ Les membres s'expriment en français ou en allemand.*
> *² Sur demande du Bureau, les documents importants sont fournis aux membres en français et en allemand. Dans tous les cas, les messages comportent un résumé dans l'autre langue.*
> ¹ Members express themselves in French or German.
> ² If requested by the Bureau, important documents are made available to the members in French and German. In all cases, the communications include an abstract in the other language.

Overall, thus, Biel/Bienne addresses language use directly and makes its institutional bilingualism explicit in legislation, while Fribourg/Freiburg, by not explicitly mentioning it, relegates bilingualism to a quasi-official status.

---

12 Règlement fixant l'organisation générale de la ville de Fribourg 2000, www.ville-fribourg.ch/sites/default/files/2018-06/011_organisation_gen_de_la_vf_et_statut_membres_ducc_2017.pdf (accessed 11 April 2019).
13 Constitution du canton de Fribourg 2004, art. 2/2, https://bdlf.fr.ch/app/fr/texts_of_law/10.1 (accessed 11 April 2019).
14 Règlement fixant l'organisation générale de la ville de Fribourg . . . 2000, art. 16/2, www.ville-fribourg.ch/sites/default/files/2018-06/011_organisation_gen_de_la_vf_et_statut_membres_ducc_2017.pdf (accessed 11 April 2019).
15 Règlement du Conseil général de la Ville de Fribourg du 18 septembre 2018, art. 44, www.ville-fribourg.ch/actualites/reglement-du-conseil-general-du-18-septembre-2018 (accessed 19 April 2019).

5 The discourses on languages on the municipal websites

As noted earlier, websites constitute social representations about languages as well as representations in and through languages. Hence, we examine two aspects: (1) language use on the official websites as an example of official language practices of the respective cities and (2) the discourses about languages, bilingualism and multilingualism present on the websites.[16]

5.1 Bilingualism

In Biel/Bienne the full content of the website is available in parallel versions in German and French. The website of Fribourg/Freiburg makes the full content available in French along with a slightly shorter parallel version in German (approximately 85 per cent of the French website). Some documents – although listed on the German website – are only available in a French version; among them are press releases or some communications of the local council.[17]

Biel/Bienne's website has the URL www.biel-bienne.ch, with /de or /fr added to distinguish between the two language versions; www.biel.ch and www.bienne.ch also link to the respective German or French sites. Fribourg/Freiburg's URL, on the other hand, is www.ville-fribourg.ch for the French version and www.ville-fribourg.ch/de for the German one (www.stadt-freiburg.ch also links to the German site), making the French website the principal version and highlighting the primacy of French.

5.1.1 Bilingualism and self-perception

Bilingualism is mentioned as part of the welcome message on Biel/Bienne's home page (see Figure 3) and serves as the predominant label of self-perception or identity:

---

[16] The initial analysis was conducted on the websites as of August 2016 (and confirmed in early 2019). In the meantime, substantial design changes to both websites have occurred; their underlying structure and content, however, have remained largely unchanged.

[17] For example www.ville-fribourg.ch/de/actualites/le-site-internet-de-la-ville-fait-peau-neuve or www.ville-fribourg.ch/de/actualites/credit-detude-de-1689735-francs-pour-la-requalification-de-la-place-de-la-gare-et-de-ses (accessed 16 April 2019).

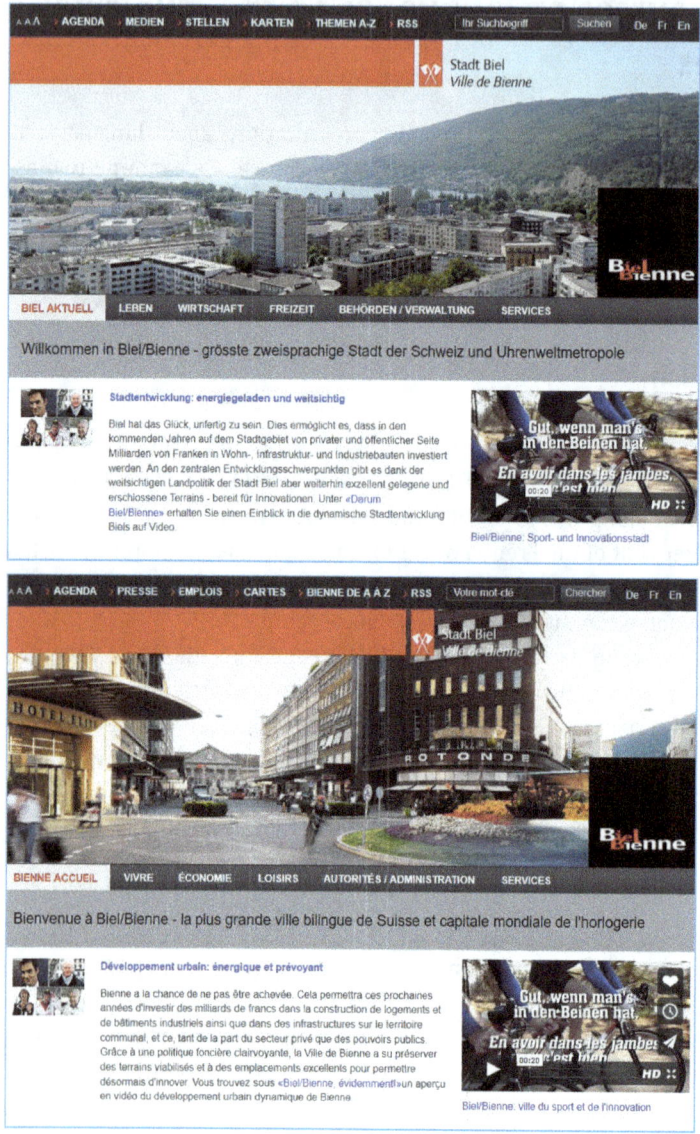

Figure 3: Screen shots of the Biel/Bienne homepages in German and French, © Stadt Biel/Ville de Bienne.[18]

---

18 www.biel-bienne.ch/de/pub/biel_aktuell.cfm and www.biel-bienne.ch/fr/pub/bienne_accueil.cfm (accessed 8 November 2016).

1 Bilingualism, multilingualism and diglossia: A tale of two Swiss cities — 41

Figure 4: Screen shots of the Fribourg/Freiburg homepages in French and German, © Ville de Fribourg/Stadt Freiburg.[19]

---

19 www.ville-fribourg.ch/ and www.ville-fribourg.ch/de (accessed 8 November 2016).

> *Willkommen in Biel/Bienne – grösste zweisprachige Stadt der Schweiz und Uhrenweltmetropole* (G)
> *Bienvenue à Biel/Bienne – la plus grande ville bilingue de Suisse et capitale mondiale de l'horlogerie* (F)
> Welcome to Biel/Bienne – the biggest bilingual city in Switzerland and the world capital for watchmaking

This predominance extends across the entire website and the official documents available through it. While other labels refer to innovation or to particular industries (watchmaking, communication, precision engineering) and more recently to sport, bilingualism is the main selling point, for example for attracting new residents:

> *Wo sonst lernt Ihr Kind bereits im Sandkasten Französisch?*
> Where else does your child already learn French in the sandpit?
> *Ici votre enfant apprend l'allemand dès le bac à sable*
> Here, your child learns German starting at the sandpit
> *Wohnen in Biel bedeutet hohe Lebensqualität à la bilingue*
> Living in Biel means high quality of life bilingual style[20]

The *Portrait of Biel/Bienne*,[21] a promotional brochure available on the website in German and French versions, mentions bilingualism on eight of its twelve pages. Other descriptive phrases used in this brochure (and elsewhere) include: *weltoffen, tolerant, lebendig, . . . die wichtigste Brücke zwischen Deutschschweiz und Romandie, . . . eine charmante Mischung verschiedener Kulturen und Mentalitäten,* 'open to the world, tolerant, vibrant, . . . the most important bridge between German and French-speaking Switzerland, . . . a charming mix of diverse cultures and mentalities'.

Fribourg/Freiburg's self-perception labels, on the other hand, do not mention bilingualism. If languages are mentioned at all, it is not a binary distinction but rather multiples. The initial messages on its home pages state:

> *Fribourg, naturellement (F)*
> *Freiburg, natürlich (G)*
> Fribourg/Freiburg – naturally/of course

and its online portrait[22] (see also Figure 4) is entitled:

> *Une cité naturellement ouverte sur le monde*
> A city naturally open to the world

---

20 www.biel-bienne.ch/de/pub/biel_aktuell.cfm and www.biel-bienne.ch/de/pub/leben.cfm (accessed 19 April 2019).
21 see www.biel-bienne.ch/files/pdf11/pra_zid_1_BielBienne_Portraet_D.pdf (accessed 19 April 2019).
22 www.ville-fribourg.ch/presentation-fribourg (accessed 19 April 2019).

Eine weltoffene Stadt

A city open to the world

Overall the majority of Fribourg/Freiburg's identity labels is focused on its culture and history (in addition to research and innovation in connection with its status as a university town) and the metaphors of crossroads and bridge at linguistic and cultural boundaries figure prominently. For example:

> (. . .) au point de rencontre des Suisses romande et alémanique
> Placée à un carrefour des chemins linguistiques et culturels au cœur de l'Helvétie, la ville de Fribourg (. . .) joue un rôle de "pont" à nul autre pareil. (. . .) Notre cité est de surcroît un lieu de mixité aux origines linguistiques plurielles[23]
> (. . .) at the meeting point of French- and German-speaking Switzerland
> Situated at a cross-roads of linguistic and cultural paths in the heart of Switzerland, Fribourg (. . .) plays an exemplary bridging role. (. . .) What is more, our city is a melting pot of multiple language backgrounds

While these labels are also present in Biel/Bienne, they are much more prominent in Fribourg/Freiburg. Its function as a bridge between regions and communities is underlined on the website by appropriate images of Fribourg/Freiburg's numerous bridges and becomes thus the defining label of self-identification.

Figures 3 and 4 also illustrate the self-identification of the two cities through their logos. Biel/Bienne's logo is bilingual, with the two names closely interwoven, while Fribourg/Freiburg has a monolingual French logo. A new, more modern one – also monolingual – was rejected by the city parliament in 2013, and the issue has been postponed due to a since abandoned plan to merge Fribourg/Freiburg and eight surrounding municipalities.

5.1.2 Discourses on bilingualism

Consistent with its self-perception projected on its official website, Biel/Bienne – unlike Fribourg/Freiburg – has a separate page on bilingualism.[24] The fact that this page is associated with the mayor's office and until recently listed under "Economy/City marketing" highlights that bilingualism in Biel/Bienne is part of the brand and seen as a competitive advantage in the context of local economic development.

The page's subheadings – *Biel, die grösste zweisprachige Stadt der Schweiz* 'Biel the largest bilingual city in Switzerland' in German, *Bienne, la ville qui vit au*

---

23 www.ville-fribourg.ch/presentation-fribourg (accessed 19 April 2019).
24 www.biel-bienne.ch/de/pub/verwaltung/stadtpraesident_praesidialdi/wirtschaft_statistik/zweisprachigkeit.cfm (accessed 19 April 2019).

rythme du bilinguisme 'Bienne the city that lives to the rhythm of bilingualism' in French – reiterates the city's defining self-identification. Furthermore, the page lists basic facts and statistics of language use in Biel/Bienne and highlights official involvement in promoting bilingualism, particularly through the *Forum für die Zweisprachigkeit/Forum du bilinguisme* 'Forum for bilingualism', an organisation jointly funded by the city and the cantonal and federal governments to promote bilingualism and to monitor and support inter-community relations.

While not present on the website, bilingualism (and its status) is a recurring topic in political debates in Fribourg/Freiburg's parliament. Most recently two submissions targeted the official recognition of bilingualism. This led to the commissioning of a report on introducing German as co-official language (Coray and Berthele 2018). Arguing against a prescriptive top-down approach, it recommended gradually strengthening German as a working language in the municipal administration, without currently recognising it as a co-official language nor making Fribourg/Freiburg's de facto bilingualism official. Taking into account long-standing fears among the French-speaking population of increasing "Germanisation" and the costs associated with official bilingualism, the local authorities accepted these recommendations and vowed to continue practical measures to strengthen German within the current frame, which they term "pragmatic bilingualism".

5.2 Other languages and multilingualism

Both cities have higher than average proportions of speakers of other languages (see Table 1), and both localities claim that they host people of well over 100 different nationalities. Again, drawing on the official websites and official documents available through them, we consider how languages other than the local ones (German and French) are presented, whether they are present at all, and what views of multilingualism are communicated.

5.2.1 Other languages

Other languages are present on the websites to varying degrees. In Biel/Bienne there is limited content in English, promoting the city as a business location and a tourist destination. No mention of any other languages is made on the home page and no information in other languages is available on the website. The assumption seems to be that alloglot local residents will use the French or German versions and that alloglot outsiders will be mostly interested in doing business or visiting – in English as a lingua franca.

The Fribourg/Freiburg website provides limited content in languages other than French and German. The analysed version has – in addition to the language "buttons" (DE for German and FR for French) – one for "Other languages", revealing a drop-down menu listing the available languages – in English! –, namely English, Spanish, Italian, Portuguese, Arabic, Tigrinya, Turkish, Serbian and Albanian. The information provided in these languages is aimed at immigrants who have recently moved to the city. The pages contain information about and links to: (1) a service tasked with facilitating contacts between immigrant families and the schools of their children; (2) waste disposal (including a brochure on how to correctly dispose of waste); and (3) an invitation to the annual welcome event for new residents. For English, Spanish, Italian and Portuguese the page also features a welcome message by the mayor and a downloadable brochure summarizing relevant information for new residents, information which is also available in German and French on the website.

The choice of languages for the brochure was explained in a press release in 2017[25] as representing the four most commonly spoken first languages by new residents, namely Portuguese, German, Spanish and Italian. This explanation shows the primacy of French – which as the source or "master" language is not mentioned –, the lower status of German which is listed among the other languages, and the role of English which often serves as a lingua franca.

5.2.2 Multilingualism

To explore the views of multilingualism communicated on the cities' websites, we searched for the term itself and for similar and related expressions, and we examined the contexts in which these terms appear.

Biel/Bienne
Multilingualism appears in two areas on the Biel/Bienne website: (1) as a selling point for new businesses ("A region of many languages – a great advantage when recruiting staff and when marketing"[26] (cf. Flubacher and Duchêne 2012 for an analysis of this aspect); and (2) on a page about non-compulsory extra-curricular courses in students' heritage languages and cultures. In this context, multilingualism and the students' heritage languages, even though presented as an asset, take second place behind one of the local languages. The German version of the site, for example, states:

---

25 www.ville-fribourg.ch/actualites/information-aux-nouveaux-habitants-enrichie (accessed 19 April 2019).
26 www.biel-bienne.ch/en/pub/economy/location_for_business.cfm (accessed 28 February 2019).

> *Die Förderung der deutschen Sprache sowie die Entwicklung von mehrsprachigen und interkulturellen Kompetenzen stellen grundlegende Bildungsaufgaben der Volksschule dar.*
> The promotion of the German language and the development of multilingual and intercultural competencies are among the basic tasks of compulsory education.[27]

There is a clear expectation or even an obligation to learn German or, by implication, French. Biel/Bienne's official integration policy[28] conceptualises integration as expected in three connected domains: socially, economically, linguistically. Knowledge of at least one local language is thus seen as a cornerstone of integration. The policy does, however, not only require the immigrants to learn a local language but also the employees of the local administration to develop better intercultural competences, thus postulating some reciprocity.

The view that the entire population needs to be involved in the process is also apparent in the city's statement on immigrants.[29] This statement describes diversity – which presumably includes linguistic diversity – as an asset and aims for mutual understanding and respect of local and immigrant groups, framing integration as a two-way process involving locals as well as new residents. However, it then puts the onus back on immigrants, as they are expected to understand the language, the rules and functioning of the local society. It is noteworthy that the term "language" is used in the singular, and no mention is made of the bilingual situation of the city.

The terminology used in these webpages and documents is worth highlighting: the terms *Fremdsprachige* 'alloglots', *Ausländer/Ausländerinnen* 'foreigners' and *Migranten/Migrantinnen* 'immigrants' are used more or less interchangeably. However, most Germans, Austrians and French, for example, may be foreigners (i.e. non-citizens of Switzerland) and immigrants but they are unlikely to be alloglots; people from the Italian-speaking areas of Switzerland are alloglots in the local context and domestic migrants but not foreigners. This suggests that the city's integration policy applies to people who are alloglot, non-Swiss *and* immigrant.

Overall, Biel/Bienne's official discourse on multilingualism and speaking languages other than the official ones is clearly and closely associated with immigration from outside Switzerland.

---

27 www.biel-bienne.ch/de/pub/leben/kinder_jugendliche/5-12_schule_-_aber_nicht_nur/fremdspra chigkeit/kursangebot_fremdsprachige.cfm (accessed 21 April 2019).
28 *Integrationskonzept*, www.biel-bienne.ch/files/pdf6/dss_if_integrationskonzept_juni_2015_d2. pdf (accessed 3 November 2016).
29 www.biel-bienne.ch/de/pub/leben/soziales/migranten_migrantinnen.cfm (accessed 18 April 2019).

Fribourg/Freiburg

Like bilingualism, multilingualism as such is not a topic on the Fribourg/Freiburg website. Information for new residents on the Fribourg/Freiburg website is part of the section *S'installer à Fribourg* 'Settling in Fribourg' which is aimed at all new residents – Swiss or non-Swiss, from outside the country or from within. Unlike Biel/Bienne, it does not single out immigrants, alloglots or foreigners.

Cohésion sociale 'social cohesion', Fribourg/Freiburg's equivalent of Biel/Bienne's statement on integration, takes a positive view of diversity. It also makes a clear link between integration and social cohesion, and states that integration measures are aimed at the entire population. It thus covers similar ground as in Biel/Bienne, but extends beyond immigrants to neighbourhood initiatives, local clubs etc., and aims to encourage active community participation of the entire population.[30]

The only mention of language(s) is found in a subsection of *S'installer à Fribourg* on language and integration courses:

> *Vous ne maîtrisez pas le français et/ou l'allemand et souhaitez améliorer vos connaissances? Nous avons sélectionné pour vous des cours qui se déroulent en ville de Fribourg.*
> *Si vous souhaitez élargir le périmètre de vos recherches, vous pouvez consulter la brochure des Cours de langues pour migrants dans le canton de Fribourg (. . .)*[31]
> 'Do you not have a good command of French and/or German and would like to improve your level?
> We have made a selection of some of the language courses taking place in the City of Fribourg.
> If you wish to widen your search, you can consult the Language courses for migrants' brochure (. . .)'

Again, this is inclusive as it is aimed at anyone wishing to learn or improve their knowledge of French or German, and not limited to immigrants or alloglots. In addition, it is not framed in terms of expectations but highlights the agency of the new residents.

5.3 Diglossia

The diglossic situation among the German-speaking communities and the Swiss-German dialects are hardly mentioned in official discourse on the websites (and beyond).

---

30 www.ville-fribourg.ch/cohesion-sociale (accessed 18 April 2019).
31 www.ville-fribourg.ch/sinstaller-a-fribourg, translation taken from the English language brochure www.ville-fribourg.ch/sites/default/files/inline-files/1_nouveaux_citoyens_ANGLAIS_08.06.2018.pdf (accessed 25 April 2019).

There are only two instances where Swiss-German dialect is referred to in the entire Biel/Bienne website: dialect as a language option in the municipal parliament, and dialect courses for staff of the local administration – presumably for those who did not grow up in Biel/Bienne and whose first language is a language other than German. This can be interpreted as an implicit admission that the diglossic situation may disadvantage resident non-native speakers of German – French speakers and alloglots alike.

The dialect and the diglossic situation do not figure in Biel/Bienne's integration policy either.[32] Its expectation of linguistic integration does not differentiate between the two varieties of German: in practice, Swiss German dialect is more useful for social integration, but economic integration requires knowledge of the standard variety as well. There is no acknowledgement (in the integration policy) that this can be a considerable obstacle for learners of German. The finding by the *bil.bienne – bilingualism in Biel/Bienne* study of 2005 seems to remain valid: the diglossic situation is considered a marginal aspect in the discourse of bilingualism in Biel/Bienne and this diglossia is not perceived as an additional bilingualism by its speakers (Elmiger and Conrad 2005b). This stands somewhat in contrast with the folk-linguistic discourse in Switzerland, where the Swiss German dialect is often named as the "mother tongue" and Standard German as the "first foreign language".

Neither Swiss German dialect nor diglossia is mentioned in the Fribourg/Freiburg website. This is in line with the current language practice: French is the default language and if German is used in interaction with French speakers or alloglots, or by French speakers, it is predominantly the standard variety. If dialect is used, it is mainly with fellow dialect speakers. This contrasts with Biel/Bienne where dialect use is much more present given the majority status of German. It also reflects the local acquisition patterns of the other language: the French speakers growing up in Biel/Bienne often acquire dialect informally (in addition to Standard German at school) and have at least receptive competence (Brohy 2011: 118), whereas the majority of French speakers in Fribourg/Freiburg learn German predominantly at school – i.e. Standard German. As a consequence, they often feel that they have to learn two languages to be able to communicate proficiently in German.

Overall, different reasons are at play for neglecting diglossia in public discourse in the two cities: it is of marginal importance in Fribourg/Freiburg, as dialect is not an obvious part of the local audioscape; in Biel/Bienne, on the other

---

[32] As Flubacher (2013: 171) posits, it seems to be the case throughout German-speaking Switzerland that "the ideological representation of diglossia as matter-of-fact leads to its erasure in public debates and legal texts concerned with the acquisition of the 'local language' by migrants".

hand, it is viewed as a "natural" or integral part of the local bilingualism without being recognised as such.

6 Conclusion

The two cities investigated have a range of commonalities. They have the same set of languages and varieties to deal with – French, German and Swiss German (in a stable diglossic situation), and immigrant languages.[33] Both have a higher language diversity than the Swiss average and a higher proportion of individual bi- and multilingualism. However, as implied in our first research question and shown in the analysis of the municipalities' websites, their discourses on bilingualism and multilingualism present themselves quite differently.

In Biel/Bienne, the two local languages German and French are officially on equal terms, that is, Biel/Bienne officially commits to a symmetrical, straightforward institutional bilingualism, and has had a coherent positive discourse on bilingualism for close to 100 years. In this sense, the city has a settled, but also a quite fixed linguistic identity. In Fribourg/Freiburg, on the other hand, French is the dominant, privileged language and while bilingualism is present and acknowledged to some extent ("pragmatic bilingualism"), it is not official and the discourse is more varied and fluid (Brohy 2011: 110).

As foreshadowed in our second research question, we anticipated that history and demography would help explain these diverging discourses and attitudes. In particular, differences in size and status of the minority language are important factors in this context. In Fribourg/Freiburg the smaller proportion of German speakers results in less weight to the minority language. However, the status of German as the majority language at a national level and the embedded minority status of French – majority on the local level but minority on a national level – have made the local French-speaking majority more defensive and more fearful of losing their status, whether this loss is actually realistic or not. Thus, the notion of "Germanisation" has been part of the folklinguistic discourse on bilingualism in Fribourg/Freiburg, despite the share of German-speakers steadily decreasing. Strengthening bilingualism has traditionally been perceived as strengthening German and the German-speaking minority and, consequently, as weakening the po-

---

33 In Fribourg/Freiburg, we also find Bolz, a "mixed language" or hybrid urban code. It comes in two varieties, one with German, the other with French as its matrix language. These days it is spoken by a few hundred people and is part of the traditional urban identity of the Basse-ville, part of Fribourg/Freiburg's old town (see Brohy 2017a).

sition of the French majority (Conrad and Elmiger 2010: 45). While this somewhat anxious attitude is still present to some extent, it is now changing quite rapidly, possibly due to an increased appreciation of multilingualism, particularly among younger people (see Brömmelsiek 2014: 122–127).

History is an important factor as well: while Fribourg/Freiburg – bilingual from its foundation in the 12th century – could be expected to be more at ease with its bilingualism than Biel/Bienne, it is actually the reverse. The more recent but linear and constant development towards symmetrical bilingualism in Biel/Bienne and its official promotion helped establish it as a firm part of its identity. In Fribourg/Freiburg, the history of a changing power balance between the two major language groups has promoted uncertainty and a fear that the current balance could change again.

Our third research question addresses potential tensions between policies and discourses on bilingualism and those on multilingualism. Immigration has a different impact on the linguistic equilibrium in the two cities. While in Biel/Bienne it strengthens the local minority, in Fribourg/Freiburg it reinforces the majority language. In terms of bilingualism and multilingualism, competing discourses are indeed at work in both locations. In Biel/Bienne the official institutional bilingualism takes precedence over the actual multilingualism and linguistic diversity. It even seems to constrain support for a broader multilingualism, as argued by Ricento (2013), who posits that linguistic dualism can inform and influence public attitudes and even more so official local language policies, and has the potential to marginalise other languages, and therefore multilingualism as well. In Fribourg/Freiburg the opposite is the case. Linguistic and cultural diversity are foregrounded and French-German bilingualism in the two local languages is subsumed under this multilingualism.

Not surprisingly, the focus of Fribourg/Freiburg's official identity and self-perception is therefore on its location at cross-roads and on a bridging function, rather than on bilingualism as it is in Biel/Bienne. Regarding our fourth research question about the role of languages in the cities' self-perception, we can thus conclude that language, in particular bilingualism, is at the core of Biel/Bienne's official urban identity and self-perception. Simultaneously, Biel/Bienne, has – as already mentioned – a settled, but also a quite fixed linguistic identity, while Fribourg/Freiburg's identity is more diverse and bypasses language issues.

The now abandoned merger of Fribourg/Freiburg with surrounding, predominantly French-speaking municipalities would have further affected the linguistic equilibrium of the region. Similarly, talk of intensified collaboration or even potential mergers of municipalities is tentatively (re-)emerging in the Biel/Bienne area. While such developments are on halt in Fribourg/Freiburg and only "thought bubbles" in Biel/Bienne, they will most likely give rise to further discussion of the linguistic status and language policies, and this discourse surrounding languages, bilingualism and multilingualism will be interesting to observe.

References

Altermatt, Bernhard. 2005. Die institutionelle Zweisprachigkeit der Stadt Fribourg-Freiburg: Geschichte, Zustand und Entwicklungstendenzen. *Bulletin VALS-ASLA* 82. 63–82.

Anderegg, Jean-Pierre. 2018. Namen im Kontakt: Freiburgische Strassen-, Orts- und Familiennamen. *Freiburger Volkskalender* 2018. 109–115.

Brömmelsiek, Björn. 2014. Wenn individuelle Zweisprachigkeit kollektive Sprachkonflikte löst: Sprachgrenze und Identitätsdiskurse in Fribourg/Freiburg (CH): die Sicht junger bilingualer Erwachsener. PhD thesis, Montréal University.

Brohy, Claudine. 1992. *Das Sprachverhalten zweisprachiger Paare und Familien in Freiburg*. Freiburg: Universitätsverlag.

Brohy, Claudine. 2005. Perceptions du bilinguisme officiel et interactions bilingues à Biel/Bienne et Fribourg/Freiburg. *TRANEL* 43. 111–127.

Brohy, Claudine. 2008. Anticyclone sur Biel/Bienne – mit einigen Wolkenfeldern. *Babylonia* 4. 62–63.

Brohy, Claudine. 2009. Entre protection des minorités et promotion du plurilinguisme en Suisse: mesures et dispositifs. In Paulo Feytor Pinto, Claudine Brohy & Joseph-G. Turi (eds.), *Direito, lingua e cidadania global – Droit, langue et citoyenneté mondiale – Law, language and global citizenship*, 307–326. Lisbon: APP.

Brohy, Claudine. 2011. Les langues s'affichent: signalétique, publicité et paysage linguistique dans deux villes bilingues suisses, Biel/Bienne et Fribourg/Freiburg. *Cahiers de l'ILOB* 2. 105–124.

Brohy, Claudine. 2012. Bilingualism and the city: measuring linguistic conviviality in two bilingual cities in Switzerland. In Claudine Brohy, Theodorus du Plessis, Joseph-G. Turi & José Woehrling (eds.), *Law, language and the multilingual state. Proceedings of the 12th International Conference of the International Academy of Linguistic Law*, 103–123. Bloemfontein: Sun Media.

Brohy, Claudine. 2017a. Frontière des langues et urbanolecte hybride: le cas du bolze à Fribourg (Suisse). In Mzago Dokhtourichvili, Julie Boissonneault & Ali Reguigui (eds.), *Les langues et leurs territoires: entre conflit et cohabitation*, 77–102. Sudbury: Université Laurentienne.

Brohy, Claudine. 2017b. Spuren der Mehrsprachigkeit im öffentlichen Raum. *Sprachspiegel* 4. 98–117.

Brohy, Claudine & Doris Schüpbach. 2016. Protection des minorités ou promotion du plurilinguisme? Droits linguistiques, politique et pratiques dans deux villes bilingues suisses. *Droit et Cultures* 72. 181–224.

Conrad, Sarah-Jane. 2005. Zweisprachige Kommunikation: Biel/Bienne und Freiburg im Vergleich. *Bulletin VALS-ASLA* 82. 43–62.

Conrad, Sarah-Jane, Alexis Matthey & Marinette Matthey. 2002. Bilinguisme institutionnel et contrat social: le cas de Biel-Bienne (Suisse). *Marges Linguistiques* 3. 159–178.

Conrad, Sarah-Jane & Daniel Elmiger (eds.). 2010. *Leben und Reden in Biel/Bienne: Kommunikation in einer zweisprachigen Stadt. Vivre et communiquer dans une ville bilingue: une expérience biennoise*. Tübingen: Narr.

Coray, Renata & Raphael Berthele. 2018. *Deutsch als Amtssprache der Stadt Freiburg i.Ü.? Bestandesaufnahme und Analysen aus historischer, juristischer und soziolinguistischer Perspektive: Bericht zuhanden des Gemeinderates von Freiburg*. Freiburg: Institut für Mehrsprachigkeit.

Duchêne, Alexandre & Mi-Cha Flubacher. 2015. Quand légitimité rime avec productivité: la parole-d'œuvre plurilingue dans l'industrie de la communication. *Anthropologie et Societés* 39(3). 173–196.

Elmiger, Daniel. 2015. Equal status, but unequal perceptions: language conflict in the bilingual city of Biel/Bienne. *International Journal of the Sociology of Language* 235. 33–52.

Elmiger, Daniel & Sarah Conrad (eds.). 2005a. Le projet bil.bienne – bilinguisme à Bienne * Kommunikation in Biel. *TRANEL* 43.

Elmiger, Daniel & Sarah Conrad. 2005b. Un bilinguisme peut en cacher un autre: bilinguisme et diglossie à Biel/Bienne. *Bulletin VALS-ASLA* 82. 31–42.

Ferguson, Charles A. 1959. Diglossia. *Word* 15. 325–340.

Flubacher, Mi-Cha. 2013. Language(s) as the key to integration? The ideological role of diglossia in the German-speaking region of Switzerland. In Erzsébet Barát, Patrick Studer & Jiří Nekvapil (eds.), *Ideological conceptualizations of language: discourses of linguistic diversity*, 171–192. Frankfurt am Main: Peter Lang.

Flubacher, Mi-Cha & Alexandre Duchêne. 2012. Eine Stadt der Kommunikation: urbane Mehrsprachigkeit als Wirtschaftsstrategie? *Bulletin VALS-ASLA* 95. 123–145.

Forum für die Zweisprachigkeit. 2016. *Schlussbericht 'Barometer für die Zweisprachigkeit der Stadt Biel-Bienne 2016': Zweisprachigkeit ist Ihre Wahl!* Biel: Forum für die Zweisprachigkeit.

Fuchs, Gabriele & Iwar Werlen. 1999. *Zweisprachigkeit in Biel/Bienne: Untersuchungen im Rahmen des Bieler-Bilingualimus-Barometers 1986–1998*. Bern: Universitäres Forschungszentrum für Mehrsprachigkeit.

Haas, Walter. 2008. Deutsch im Freiburg des Ancien Régime. *Freiburger Geschichtsblätter* 85. 109–132.

Haugen, Einar. 1972. *The ecology of language*. Stanford: Stanford University Press.

Kolde, Gottfried. 1981. *Sprachkontakte in gemischtsprachigen Städten: vergleichende Untersuchungen über Voraussetzungen und Formen sprachlicher Interaktion verschiedensprachiger Jugendlicher in den Schweizer Städten Biel/Bienne und Fribourg/Freiburg i. Ü*. Wiesbaden: Steiner.

Kużelewska, Elzbieta. 2016. Language policy in Switzerland. *Studies in Logic, Grammar and Rhetoric* 45(1). 125–140.

Lüdi, Georges. 1985. Mehrsprachige Rede in Freiburger Ratsmanualen des 15. Jahrhunderts. *Vox Romanica* 44. 163–188.

Moore, Danièle & Bernard Py. 2011. Introduction: discourse on languages and social representations. In Geneviève Zarate, Danielle Lévy & Claire Kramsch (eds.), *Handbook of multilingualism and multiculturalism*, 263–270. Paris: Éditions des archives contemporaines.

Racine, A. Jean. 2003. *Über die Bedeutung der Zweisprachigkeit im Amtsbezirk Biel*. Biel: Forum für die Zweisprachigkeit.

Rash, Felicity. 1998. *The German language in Switzerland: multilingualism, diglossia and variation*. Bern: Peter Lang.

Rash, Felicity. 2002. The German-Romance language border in Switzerland. *Journal of Multilingual and Multicultural Development* 23(1–2). 112–136.

Rash, Felicity. 2003. Language and communication in German-speaking Switzerland. In Joy Charnley & Malcolm Pender (eds.), *Living with languages: the contemporary Swiss model*. 107–127. Oxford/New York: Peter Lang.

Ricento, Thomas. 2013. The consequences of official bilingualism on the status and perception of non-official languages in Canada. *Journal of Multilingual and Multicultural Development* 34(5). 475–489.

Schedel, Larissa Semiramis & Liliane Meyer Pitton (eds.). 2018. Linguistic borders (in Switzerland): new approaches, critical perspectives. *Bulletin VALS-ASLA* 108.

Schneuwly, Rainer. 2019. *Bilingue – wie Freiburg und Biel mit der Zweisprachigkeit umgehen*. Baden: Hier und Jetzt.

Schüpbach, Doris. 2008. Franco-German language contact in Switzerland: the case of Biel-Bienne. In Jane Warren & Heather Benbow (eds.), *Multilingual Europe: reflections on language and identity*, 149–166. Newcastle upon Tyne: Cambridge Scholars Publishing.

Stępkowska, Agnieszka. 2012. Diglossia: a critical overview of the Swiss example. *Studia Linguistica Universitatis Iagellonicae Cracoviensis* 129. 199–209.

Weinreich, Uriel. [1953] 2011. *Languages in contact: French, German and Romansh in twentieth-century Switzerland*. Amsterdam: John Benjamins.

Zimmerli, Jakob. 1891–1899. *Die deutsch-französische Sprachgrenze in der Schweiz*. Vol. 1–3. Geneva/Basel: H. Georg.

Marie Nelson and Sofie Henricson

2 The linguistic landscapes of Mariehamn and Kotka: A multilingual tale of local and national languages in Finland

1 Introduction

This chapter explores multilingualism in the linguistic landscapes of Mariehamn and Kotka, two cities in Finland. Mariehamn is situated in the Åland archipelago in the Baltic Sea between Sweden and Finland, and Kotka is a coastal city in southeastern Finland. The two cities are located on the same latitude, about 370 kilometres apart. As Figure 1 shows, Mariehamn is in the west, closer to Sweden than to mainland Finland, and Kotka is in the east, near the Russian border. Finland is officially bilingual with Finnish and Swedish as its two national languages (see statistics in Figure 1).

The linguistic history and demography of the two urban areas reflect their geographical placement, and in many aspects Mariehamn and Kotka show opposite patterns for Swedish and Finnish. In the current study, we investigate whether these differences are mirrored in their respective local linguistic landscapes.

Linguistic landscape (LL) is a relatively young and rapidly growing research area, with many edited volumes (e.g. Shohamy and Gorter 2009; Gorter et al. 2012; Pütz and Mundt 2018), special issues, and the scientific journal *Linguistic Landscape*, established in 2015. The term was coined through Landry and Bourhis' (1997) investigation of the link between linguistic landscapes and ethnolinguistic vitality. Today, LL research can broadly be described as the study of languages in place. The field encompasses various theoretical and methodological approaches, data collection procedures, and analytical foci (Gorter 2018: 41–42).

Multilingualism and the copresence of several languages, particularly in urban areas, are recurrent topics of LL research. Some studies, such as Cenoz and Gorter (2006) and Barni and Bagna (2010), compare the visibility of distinct minority languages and ethnolinguistic groups in different cities. There is often a focus on learning more about the visibility and power relations between languages, the

---

Note: We are grateful for the constructive comments offered by anonymous reviewers as well as the editors of the volume. We also wish to thank Klara Skogmyr Marian for valuable language proof reading and Cornel Marian for crucial help with the Russian data. Naturally, all remaining errors are our own. The authors have contributed equally to the chapter.

Figure 1: Statistics and map of Finland, with Mariehamn and Kotka. Modified map with CC by-licence from National land survey of Finland © 2020.

dynamics of ongoing changes in language demography, and the linguistic vitality of minority groups. English is a language that has been reported to be "omnipresent in virtually all of the linguistic landscapes, irrespective of whether or not it is actually spoken by any sizeable share of the population" (Backhaus 2007: 56–57). Previous research on the presence of English in Finland, Sweden and Norway suggests that this also holds for linguistic landscapes in Scandinavia (Syrjälä 2012; Norrby 2014; Herberts 2017).

The current study contributes to the research field of minority languages in urban linguistic landscapes by investigating the public visibility of minority languages in two linguistically and geographically distinct cities of Finland. The analysis of linguistic landscapes in Mariehamn and Kotka sheds light on the diversity of the Swedish-speaking regions of Finland, and highlights two extremes of Swedish as one of two national languages.

The aim is to investigate and compare linguistic landscapes at two distinct geographical locations in Finland in relation to language demography and policy. Our approach has many parallels with Cenoz and Gorter's (2006) study on minority languages in two cities in Friesland and the Basque Country, where the main differences concern the visibility of the cities' minority languages (Frisian/Basque), a result that is related to differences in language policy. Inspired by this study, we have narrowed down our focus to the visibility of languages other than the local majority languages, Swedish (83%) in Mariehamn and Finnish (90%) in Kotka. Our data consist of photographed linguistic signs collected in the two cities. We address the following research questions:

(1) Inventory: What languages other than the local majority languages (Swedish/ Finnish) are publicly visible in the city centres of Mariehamn and Kotka?
(2) Function: In what contexts and for what purposes are the languages used, and by whom?
(3) Contextualisation: Is there a relationship between linguistic signs, language demography and linguistic power relations?

The frequency and functions of minority languages in Mariehamn and Kotka are discussed in relation to language demography, language policy and present-day societal processes, such as tourism and migration. As a starting point, and following Ben-Rafael et al. (2006: 7), Barni and Bagna (2010: 4, 15), and Blackwood (2015: 39), for example, we interpret LL items in minority languages as visible symbols of these languages in the public space, without reading the linguistic landscape as a direct representation of the vitality of languages or ethnolinguistic groups.

We start with an overview of Swedish in Finland and the two research sites, Mariehamn and Kotka (section 2), followed by a description of our data and method (section 3). We then present the analysis of linguistic landscapes in Mariehamn and Kotka (section 4), and our conclusions (section 5).

2 Swedish in Finland

Finland has two national languages, Finnish and Swedish. Finnish is spoken as first language by the vast majority of the population (87%), whereas Swedish is spoken by a small minority (5.2%) (OSF 2020). All Finnish citizens register one language as their official first language. As a result, all multilingual individuals must choose one of their available languages. A person can change his/her official first language at any point in time, independent of actual language skills or origins. This policy enables rapid changes to be captured in the language statistics in the case of larger societal shifts in language attitudes (Liebkind et al. 1995: 57).

Given the small Swedish-speaking minority, the Swedish language has exceptionally strong constitutional rights.[1] On a national level, Finnish and Swedish have

---
[1] See Liebkind et al. (2007) for a comprehensive overview of Swedish in Finland.

equal status, and language legislation guarantees equal linguistic rights for speakers of either national language. On a regional level, linguistic rights and opportunities vary from one region to another. Language legislation (Ministry of Justice, Finland, 2003) builds upon a combined personal and territorial principle. The personal principle gives each citizen the right to use the national language of his/her choice in court and with other state authorities. The territorial principle, on the other hand, states that linguistic rights when communicating with municipal authorities depend on the linguistic status of each municipality. The general rule is that municipalities are bilingual when a minority group of at least 8%, or 3,000 individuals, are registered as speakers of the other national language, otherwise they are considered monolingual in Finnish or Swedish. In addition, monolingual municipalities can opt for bilingual status, a choice that implies obligations but also offers economic advantages.

There are historic reasons for this language policy. Until the early 19th century, Sweden and Finland were part of the same political entity. Within its borders, Swedish, Finnish and Sami had been spoken for centuries, although Swedish was the dominant language in society. In 1808–1809, Sweden and Russia fought the so-called Finnish war. As a consequence, the Swedish-Finnish political entity was split into two, leading to the creation of the nations we today call Sweden and Finland. In Sweden, Swedish remained the main language. Swedish also remained important in Finland, despite Finland becoming an autonomous part of the Russian Empire. Russian was used in certain official domains but played a rather marginal role in Finnish society, whereas Finnish entered new and more official domains. When Finland obtained independence in 1917, Finnish and Swedish became its two constitutionally defined national languages.[2]

Until the middle of the 19th century, Swedish remained the dominant language in Finnish society, even though the majority of the population has always been Finnish-speaking. At the end of the 19th century, the Swedish-speaking group constituted about 13–14% of the total population (Finnäs 2012); this has subsequently decreased to 5.2% in 2019 (OSF 2020). Traditionally, speakers of Finnish as a first language inhabited the inland areas, whereas their Swedish-speaking counterparts lived on the coast. This geographical division remained relatively distinct until the early 20th century, but it has since lost its clear-cut contours. In 2017, about half of all Swedish-speaking Finns lived in municipalities with a Finnish-speaking majority (AFLRA 2017). There is notable variation between regions, and Swedish-speaking

---

[2] Swedish thereby became a pluricentric language, with official status in two countries, i.e. Sweden and Finland. For a thorough analysis of the historical processes behind the language policy in Finland, see Engman (2016).

Finns live in diverse linguistic surroundings, from municipalities with more than 90% of Swedish-speaking inhabitants, such as Larsmo in Ostrobothnia, to municipalities with fewer than 5% of Swedish-speaking inhabitants, such as Vantaa in southern Finland (AFLRA 2017).

In some officially monolingual Finnish municipalities, there are small Swedish-speaking groups that maintain a Swedish-speaking society despite decreasing demographic numbers. Colloquially, these are called Swedish language islands in Finland, and Kotka is among the largest and most long-standing (Henricson 2013). In Kotka, Finnish is the only official language, spoken by 90% of the population, while the Swedish-speaking population amounts to 1%. Kotka also has a Russian-speaking minority, constituting 5% of the population (OSF 2020).

The only Finnish region with officially monolingual Swedish municipalities is Åland, an island group with about 30,000 inhabitants (OSF 2020). There are many small villages on the islands, but Mariehamn is the only populated area referred to as a city. Since 1921, Åland has been an autonomous, demilitarised and monolingually Swedish region of Finland, with nationally ensured protection of the Swedish language, culture and local customs on the islands (Loughlin and Daftary 1999; Engman 2016; Nelson 2016). In Mariehamn, Swedish is the only official language, spoken by 83% of the inhabitants. The Finnish-speaking population amounts to only 5%, while other languages are spoken by 12% (ÅSUB 2020).

Against this background, we consider the cities of Mariehamn in Åland and Kotka in southeastern Finland as two extremes of the Swedish-speaking continuum in Finland. Studying their linguistic landscapes, and how they reflect language demography and policy, contributes to our knowledge about the link between linguistic visibility and linguistic power relations. In the following sections (2.1–2.2), we introduce the two cities and briefly summarise their language demography.

2.1 Mariehamn

The archipelago of Åland includes more that 26,000 islands and skerries, of which about 60 are inhabited and constitute 16 Swedish-speaking municipalities (ÅSUB 2020). The city of Mariehamn was founded in 1861, and has grown steadily over the years. At the end of 2019 Mariehamn had 11,679 inhabitants, constituting about 39% of the total population of the islands (ÅSUB 2020).

Mariehamn's location, on a narrow peninsula of an island, makes the city ideal for both shipping and tourism. The port of Mariehamn is of strategic and economic importance, particularly since Åland is exempt from Value Added Tax.[3] As a result of this tax exemption, ferries between Finland and Sweden make a brief stop in Åland to enable tax-free shopping onboard. During 2019, over two million travellers arrived in Åland, 1,661,000 from Sweden and 367,000 from mainland Finland (ÅSUB 2020).

The highly autonomous status of Åland is exceptional within Finland. Since 1954, Åland has had its own flag, and today has its own stamps, licence plates, and internet domain (.ax). Moreover, Mariehamn is often referred to as "the capital of Åland", further supporting Åland's status as an autonomous entity distinct from Finland.

In accordance with the *Act on the Autonomy of Åland* (Ministry of Justice Finland, 1991) and in contrast to mainland Finland, Åland and Mariehamn are officially monolingual Swedish. The Act further states that Swedish is the language of education in Åland, and hence Finnish is not a mandatory subject in school. In mainland Finland, both national languages are compulsory elements of education (Ministry of Justice Finland, 1998). English, however, is a mandatory subject in both Åland and mainland Finland. Åland has been criticised for being negative towards the Finnish language, for example when it comes to Finnish-speaking pupils' limited opportunities to study Finnish in school (Allardt Ljunggren 2008: 9). This suggests a rather complex relationship between Åland and the Finnish language.

The Swedish language has a strong position in Mariehamn, not only regarding language policies and laws, but also in terms of attitudes and number of speakers.[4] The number of Swedish-speaking citizens has increased steadily since 2000, but as a proportion of the whole population, it has consistently decreased (from 92% in 2000 to 83% in 2019). This is not due to a growing Finnish-speaking population in Mariehamn,[5] but rather a result of globalisation and migration, leading to an increasing number of other languages present.[6] The current proportion of Swedish speakers in Åland as a whole is 87% (ÅSUB 2020), a figure that is slightly higher than Parkvall's (2009: 105) estimation that about 85% of the popula-

---

[3] https://ec.europa.eu/taxation_customs/business/vat/eu-vat-rules-topic/territorial-status-eu-countries-certain-territories_en (accessed 22 March 2019).
[4] For a discussion on language attitudes and identity in Åland, see Nelson (2016).
[5] The Finnish-speaking population in Mariehamn has decreased from 6.1% in 2000 to 4.9% in 2019 (OSF 2020).
[6] The statistics (ÅSUB 2020: 49) show that the largest minority languages in Åland, after Finnish with 1,405 speakers, are: Romanian (449 speakers), Latvian (402), Estonian (201), Thai (154), Russian (149), English (143), Arabic (123) and German (107). In total, 35 languages with more than 10 speakers are listed in the statistics.

tion of Sweden has Swedish as their mother tongue. As a result, Åland is notionally a more Swedish-speaking area than Sweden itself (Nelson 2016).

2.2 Kotka

The city of Kotka was founded in the late 19th century, at a time when the local forestry industry attracted migrants, not only from different parts of Finnish-speaking Finland but also from the Swedish-speaking surroundings, and from Russia and Norway (Halila 1978: 21). Besides being an important industrial centre, Kotka has one of Finland's main export ports, offering shipping services to continental Europe and Russia.[7] Passenger cruisers also benefit from Kotka's strategic position between Helsinki and St. Petersburg. At the time of data collection, Russian tourists constituted more than 80% of all foreign tourists in Kotka, and the vast majority of the city's tourism revenue came from Russian tourists.[8]

Since the city's foundation, its population has increased from about 1,000 to the current 52,126 inhabitants, due mainly to municipal amalgamations and immigration. Swedish and Norwegian immigration was particularly evident in the newly founded city, and Russian immigration has increased rapidly in the 21st century. Throughout, Finnish-speaking immigrants have by far outnumbered Swedish-speaking and Russian-speaking immigrants. In 2019, Finnish was the main language for 90% of the population in Kotka (OSF 2020).[9] In the last few decades, Kotka has struggled with high unemployment rates and a decreasing population.

Until the early 20th century, the Swedish-speaking minority constituted a highly influential group in local society, as Swedish and Norwegian businessmen occupied the most central positions within city administration, industry, and trade (Anttila 1957: 221–242). As in Finland generally, the number and in particular the proportion of Swedish-speakers in Kotka has declined. In the late 19th century, the Swedish minority represented almost 17% of the entire population (Halila 1978: 21), whereas in 2019, it amounted to a mere 0.9% (OSF 2020). Due to the small proportion and number of speakers, the Swedish language has no local legal status in Kotka. Nevertheless, the Swedish minority maintains its own socie-

---

7 Port of HaminaKotka 2020, https://www.haminakotka.com (accessed 27 February 2020).
8 https://docplayer.fi/18489355-Ulkomaiset-matkailijat-suomessa-ja-kymenlaaksossa.html, slide 16 (accessed 14 March 2019). It should be noted that this describes circumstances before the Russian invasion of Ukraine in February 2022.
9 The ten largest minority languages are: Russian (2,499 speakers), Swedish (491), Estonian (349), Arabic (249), Kurdish (137), English (135), Persian/Farsi (114), Albanian (92), Turkish (92), Somali (89). In total, 36 languages with more than 10 speakers are listed in the statistics (OSF 2020).

tal infrastructure, such as Swedish education from kindergarten to secondary school, and has done so for more than a century. However, in the 20th century, Swedish in Kotka lost domains such as politics and media to Finnish (Henricson 2013).

Russian immigration to Kotka began in the early days of the city, and for a while, the Russian-speaking minority represented as much as 8% of the population (Halila 1978: 21). However, Russian immigrants did not settle permanently, and during the era of the Soviet Union, the Russian-speaking minority in Kotka remained small. Since the 1990s, Russian immigration to Finland has greatly increased, and Russian is now the most spoken foreign language in the country (OSF 2020). In Kotka, Russian immigration has been growing since the early 21st century and by 2019, the Russian-speaking minority amounted to about 2,500 individuals, i.e. 4.8% of the local population.

With 4.8% of Russian speakers and 0.9% of Swedish speakers, Kotka shows a contrasting pattern to Finland overall, with 5.2% of Swedish speakers and 1.5% of Russian speakers (OSF 2020). Swedish has the status of national language, but locally, neither of the two minority languages has any official status.

3 Data and method

The empirical data for the study were collected in parallel during one and the same day, January 27 2019. We each visited one city centre (Nelson in Mariehamn and Henricson in Kotka) and took photographs of all visible signs in public spaces that included a language other than the majority language (Swedish in Mariehamn and Finnish in Kotka), be it on its own or in addition to the majority language. As a rule, photographs were only taken outdoors.

Both city centres are situated within a limited geographical area on an island. During data collection, we covered large parts of each urban centre, such as main streets, public transportation centres, central squares, parks, as well as facades of churches, city halls, and libraries. Although we have not exhaustively explored the linguistic landscapes of Mariehamn and Kotka (cf. Blackwood 2015: 41), the targeted survey areas were largely covered, providing enough data to give a representative view of the linguistic landscapes in the two city centres. We did not limit data collection to specific domains or modalities, and our data comprise not only public signs, commercial signs, street signs and tourist indications, but also other items such as recycling instructions on wastebaskets, and graffiti.

Both datasets were coded and then analysed using quantitative and qualitative methodologies (as discussed in Blackwood 2015). In the quantitative analysis, we follow Backhaus' (2007) unit of analysis, and count every text "within a spatially definable frame" (p. 66) as one unit. As an example, texts that were photographed on different sides of a single object are counted as separate units within a multilingual frame.

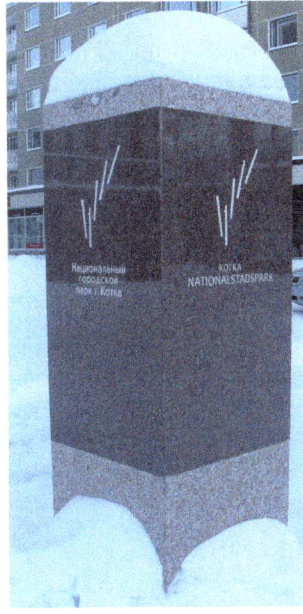

Figure 2: Monolingual signs in a multilingual object in Kotka (Photo: Sofie Henricson).

Figure 2 illustrates our method of coding. The granite monument has text on four sides, with *Kotka national urban park* written on one side each in Finnish, in Swedish, in English, and in Russian.[10] As we exclude monolingual signs in the local majority language, this monument was counted as three monolingual signs (Swedish, Russian, English), which are part of a multilingual frame consisting of four languages (Swedish, Russian, English, Finnish). A small number of signs could not be attributed to a certain language; these signs have been categorised as "universal". As an example, two stickers from Mariehamn contain the text *Helsinki*, which is used for the Finnish capital in many languages, but not in Swedish ('Helsingfors').

The two datasets consist of 631 linguistic signs, with 22 different languages represented. Items are coded as either monolingual or multilingual signs. The multilingual signs are coded according to language combinations. For the qualita-

---

10 The Russian and Swedish sides are included in Figure 2.

tive analysis, we further analyse the signs as regards domain of use, and whether community members or institutions produced the signs, i.e. if they constitute official, "top-down" signs, or non-official, "bottom-up" signs (see Backhaus 2007: 57). The detailed analysis of the LL items is inspired by the coding schemes presented in Ben-Rafael et al. (2006: 14–15) and Backhaus (2007: 65). This includes dividing the top-down and bottom-up categories into different sub-groups, such as governmental signs, commercial signs, and graffiti. As top-down signs we include official signs produced by national or local authorities and institutions, and as bottom-up signs we include texts by individuals or businesses (cf. Ben-Rafael et al. 2006).

4 Linguistic landscapes of Mariehamn and Kotka

For each city, we discuss the functions of the signs as well as the relationship between the city's linguistic landscape and local factors relating to language demography, language policy and present-day societal processes, e.g. tourism. The section begins with a comparison of the visible languages in each location, followed by separate city analyses.

4.1 Inventory of languages: Mariehamn and Kotka

The Mariehamn dataset consists of 202 linguistic signs, of which 132 are monolingual (65%) and 70 are multilingual (35%). The Kotka dataset, in contrast, consists of 429 items, of which only 166 are monolingual (39%) and 263 multilingual (61%). In Table 1, we give an overview of languages on the monolingual signs (excluding majority language Swedish in Mariehamn and Finnish in Kotka (=n/a), as mentioned above), divided into top-down (official) and bottom-up (non-official) items.

In both datasets, English is by far the most frequent language on monolingual signs, amounting to between 67% (Mariehamn) and 87% (Kotka) of all such signs. In addition, the two national languages Finnish and Swedish are visible in the city where they do not have local status as an official language. Both city centres also display monolingual Russian signs. In both cities, and particularly in Mariehamn, we also find monolingual signs representing other languages.

Table 1: Monolingual signs in Mariehamn and Kotka.

	English	Finnish	Russian	Swedish	Other	Total
Mariehamn	88	16	5	n/a	23*	132
Top-down	18	3	1	n/a	11	33
Bottom-up	70	13	4	n/a	12	99
Kotka	142	n/a	12	7	5**	166
Top-down	8	n/a	2	4	0	14
Bottom-up	134	n/a	10	3	5	152
Total	223	16	17	7	28	298

*13 different languages.
**4 different languages.

Table 2 illustrates the main combinations of languages included on multilingual signs. The dominance of the local majority language – Swedish in Mariehamn and Finnish in Kotka – is a common, and expected, feature of the multilingual signs in both cities. In addition, English is also highly visible in both locations. Another shared feature is the presence of the national language that does not have official local status, i.e. Finnish in Mariehamn and Swedish in Kotka.

Table 2: Multilingual signs in the two cities (S=Swedish, F=Finnish, E=English, R=Russian), in any order.

Mariehamn		Kotka	
SFE	27	FE	134
SE	25	FS	38
FS	8	FSE	35
FE	1	FER	25
FSER	1	FSER	5
Other	8	RE	3
		FR	2
		SE	1
		Other	20
Total	**70**	**Total**	**263**

A characteristic of the multilingual signs in Kotka is the presence of Russian, a language that appears in different combinations with the two national languages and omnipresent English. In total, a greater number of languages (20) are represented in Mariehamn than in Kotka (14).

4.2 The linguistic landscape of Mariehamn

In a city of under 12,000 people, of whom 83% are first language Swedish-speaking, a total of 19 visible languages besides Swedish may be considered astonishingly high. However, 12 of the languages are represented by a single sign, six of which are posters in the city library windows. The posters introduce different Swedish-speaking authors, with translated quotations from their writing in Arabic, Estonian, Persian, Somali, Turkish and Vietnamese.[11] A further three languages are on consulate signs (Dutch, Korean and Norwegian), two on restaurant signs (Hindi and Italian), and one on a sticker (Polish). Thus, the majority (9 of 12) of single language appearances have top-down origins. Overall, there are more bottom-up signs (139 items or 69%) than top-down signs (63 items or 31%) in the city's linguistic landscape. Among the bottom-up items, eight are written by hand – in the snow, on a piece of paper, or on wood. There are also three signs containing a single word (*Camping*) that has the same form in different languages, and these are therefore coded as universal signs.

As Table 1 shows, most monolingual signs in Mariehamn (88) are written in English. A majority of these signs (70) are bottom-up items, 60 of which are produced and used within the commercial domain. At the time of data collection, English was prominent due to "Sale" signs in some shop windows, and signs for the upcoming Valentine's Day, an imported English-language tradition.[12] The windows of a bookstore were decorated with cards containing Valentine's Day greetings in English, such as *LOVE is magic* and *I Love You Forever*. These findings correlate with Norrby's (2014) observations in a shopping mall in Stockholm, where "Sale" and related advertisements in English were highly prominent.

Although Finnish is a majority and national language in Finland and English is not, monolingual English signs are almost six times more common than monolingual Finnish signs in our data from Mariehamn (see Table 1). As mentioned in

---

[11] The number of speakers of these languages in Åland in 2018: Arabic 123, Estonian 201, Persian 52, Somali (not listed = less than 10), Turkish 16, and Vietnamese 19 (ÅSUB 2020: 49).
[12] Valentine's Day, in Swedish *Alla hjärtans dag* (lit. 'Day of all hearts'), is a rather new tradition in the Nordic countries, initiated by shopkeepers from English-speaking parts of the world (see e.g. https://www.nordiskamuseet.se/aretsdagar/alla-hjartans-dag).

section 2.1, Finnish has never had a strong position in Åland, and this finding is therefore not completely unexpected. The result also shows the strong position of English, similar to the situation in many other parts of the world (see e.g. Gorter 2006: 4).

With the exception of a poster about an author presentation in the library window (top-down), the only monolingual signs in Russian are four pieces of graffiti in the snow (bottom-up). These ephemeral items are written in letters from the Russian alphabet, three on benches outside the church in Mariehamn, and the fourth on the ground next to one of the benches. Two are insults, and the other two have connections to the Russian language and country (see Figure 3). An English monolingual sign is also written in the snow, and expresses a ghostly greeting: *Boo*.

Figure 3: Monolingual (Russian) bottom-up sign: Россий, possessive form of Russia, written in the snow (Photo: Marie Nelson).

German, Spanish and Thai are visible in three monolingual signs each and French in two. Most of these are bottom-up items that occur in businesses related to eating and drinking.

Turning now to the multilingual signs, the most common combination and order of languages is Swedish-English (17 of 70 items), followed by Swedish-Finnish-English (16 of 70). Finnish appears on a total of 41 multilingual signs, English on 60 signs, and Swedish on all multilingual signs but three (67). Of these latter signs, two are bottom-up items from private businesses and one is a film poster in English and Finnish (see discussion below). As Table 2 shows, Swedish,

English and Finnish are the most common languages in multilingual signs in Mariehamn (a total of 27 signs in five different orders of the languages). Most of these trilingual signs are top-down and they are typically found in the harbour area or outside tourist or cultural services. With one exception, Finnish is never dominant in font size or shape in multilingual signs, whereas both Swedish and English are. The exception is a sign outside the city library that announces *Satuhetki* 'Storytelling' in a logo-like illustration and in large and colored letters. The rest of the information is however written in Swedish only, under the Swedish title *Sagostunder på finska våren 2019* 'Storytelling in Finnish during spring 2019' (see Figure 4). The fact that Swedish and English are visually dominant in multilingual signs, together with the numerous appearances of Swedish (67) and English (60), indicates the superior status of Swedish and English vis-à-vis other languages on multilingual signs.

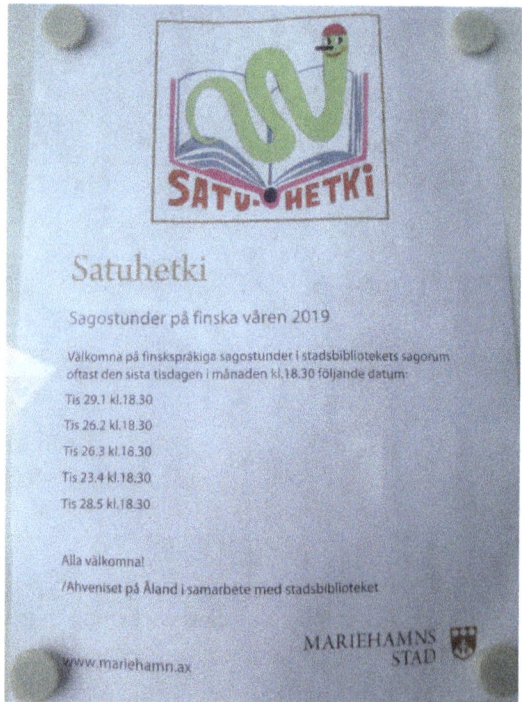

Figure 4: Bilingual (Finnish-Swedish) sign 'Storytelling' at library information board in Mariehamn (Photo: Marie Nelson).

Among "other" languages in multilingual signs, we find single appearances of different combinations of languages, e.g. Swedish-Korean on a consulate sign and Finnish-English on a film poster. An employee at the local theatre pointed out that film posters in Finland are only printed in Finnish and English. This is the case in our data: we have documented seven film posters – three in English, three in Finnish and one in Finnish and English.

Table 2 also shows that Russian is not a common language on multilingual signs. We only find Russian on one multilingual item, illustrated in Figure 5, a sign on a door to a bank informing, in four languages (Finnish-Swedish-English-Russian), that a *Digital recording system* is in use. The order and number of languages and the domain name, .fi, give reason to believe that this sign is made for the Finnish mainland market.

Figure 5: Quadrilingual (Finnish-Swedish-English-Russian) bottom-up sign outside a bank (Photo: Marie Nelson).

The analysis of signs written in languages other than Swedish shows that Mariehamn constitutes a dynamic linguistic landscape, with a certain dominance of English. Finnish, the majority language in mainland Finland, is also visible in Mariehamn but it is used predominantly in combination with other languages and typically in a non-dominant position.

Russian was the third most visible language on monolingual signs on the day of data collection although more than half are of an ephemeral nature. This reminds us about the potentially rapid shifts in linguistic landscapes, especially in a city where weather and tourism affect what is visible across the seasons.

As for additional languages, they appear either as a result of Mariehamn's position as an administrative centre (foreign consulates) or in the cultural domain where an exhibition in the library made several languages with only a few local speakers visible.

In sum, Swedish occupies a strong position in Mariehamn, as does English, which is by far the second most visible language. Finnish is mainly used on signs with instructions or that focus on cultural events and tourism – and on occasional stickers posted on lampposts and walls. The Finnish language is sometimes a forced import from the mainland. Linguistic diversity plays a crucial role in informative signs in Mariehamn, but is also used to attract guests to restaurants, museums and the library. Nevertheless, the language that sells – is English.

4.3 The linguistic landscape of Kotka

Kotka is nearly five times larger than Mariehamn at roughly 52,000 inhabitants, but the city centre has fewer visible languages. There are 14 languages in the Kotka dataset, of which ten appear in a total of only 19 signs (Chinese, Dutch, Estonian, French, German, Italian, Latin, Norwegian/Danish, Polish, Spanish).[13] In addition, six signs include items coded as universal. Four of the ten less visible languages occur in a small set of signs (Chinese in seven signs, German and Italian in five signs each, French in four signs). The Chinese signs are all related to a Chinese restaurant, while Italian, German and French are visible in more heterogeneous contexts, e.g. in business names and in multilingual marine signs at the port areas. At the bus station in Kotka, a touristic sign with a map of the city centre welcomes visitors in seven languages; Finnish, German, Swedish, Russian, English, French and Estonian. Six of the ten less visible languages occur only once (Dutch, Estonian, Latin, Norwegian/Danish, Polish, Spanish). The languages with

---

[13] The number of speakers of these languages in Kotka in 2019: Chinese 60, Dutch 20, Estonian 349, French 48, German 47, Italian 19, Latin –, Norwegian/Danish less than 10, Polish 29, Spanish 62 (OSF 2020).

single or few occurrences typically appear in multilingual signs, of which most also include Finnish and/or English (17 of 19).

The remaining signs contain one or several of the following languages, in descending order: English, Finnish, Swedish, and Russian. As a rule, only some of these four languages are combined in the same sign, and the cases where all four languages are included mainly concern tourist information. In this section, we discuss linguistic signs containing one or more of these four languages, as they clearly dominate the linguistic landscape of the city. Due to limited space, we focus especially on Swedish and Russian, as these two minority languages have a historical and current presence in Kotka and thus are of specific importance in the city in focus.

Under 4% (10 of 263) of all multilingual signs in Kotka do not include Finnish, which clearly reflects the fact that Finnish is the local majority language and the only official language of the city, as well as the national language of majority status.[14] In most multilingual signs (86%, 225 of 263), Finnish is the first language cited and in more than half (51%, 135 of 263), the Finnish text dominates, for example through font size or amount of content. Most monolingual signs written in a language that is not the local majority language are bottom-up signs, produced by community members (see Table 1).

English is clearly the most frequently occurring language apart from Finnish, as evidenced in Tables 1 and 2, and is particularly dominant on bottom-up signs, especially in the business domain. English also appears relatively often on public signs addressed at tourists, such as road and site signs, and visitor information at larger museums. In addition, English is the main language of graffiti and stickers (14 of 16 items).

Swedish occurs in a total of 88 signs, of which 81 are multilingual – 51 top-down and 30 bottom-up. This distribution can, at least in part, be explained by the status of Swedish. On the one hand it is a national language, and on the other a local minority language without any official status, but with a historically strong position in society and a continued presence with its own local institutions, mainly in the domain of education. This interpretation is supported by an analysis of the 38 bilingual Finnish-Swedish signs, of which 22 are top-down. The bilingual top-down signs include public signs about topics such as parking and postal services, and information from national and local organisations and authorities.

---

14 As we have not collected Finnish monolingual signs, Finnish only appears in multilingual signs.

The bilingual warning sign in Figure 6, for example, can be found in similar versions at railway stations across the country,[15] and both reflects and exemplifies how the national position of Swedish as an official language adds to the visibility of Swedish on a local level also in officially monolingual Finnish cities such as Kotka. The usual order of top-down bilingual signs in the main official languages is Finnish-Swedish. A reverse order (Swedish-Finnish) is however found on the information sign at the entrance to Kotka's Swedish kindergarten, illustrating the presence of local Swedish institutions, and reflecting the fact that Swedish is often only one of the languages spoken in the childrens' families. All the 16 bilingual bottom-up signs are related to business, and 14 of these are produced by companies operating on a national level, not by local shops.

Figure 6: Bilingual (Finnish-Swedish) warning sign 'Danger of death' at the harbour railway station (Photo: Sofie Henricson).

The 35 trilingual signs with Finnish, Swedish, and English follow a similar distribution with 21 top-down and 14 bottom-up signs, ten of which are produced by businesses or organisations operating at a national level. The remaining four bottom-up signs are produced by local shops, and show the continued presence of Swedish-speakers in Kotka. Figure 7 is an example of a trilingual information sign by a local authority, with equal amounts of information given in all three languages (although with a spelling error in Swedish, *säkerhetskontrol* instead of *säkerhetskontroll*). The collection also includes signs where only part of the information is provided in languages other than the local majority language, Finnish.

---

15 There are also monolingual versions of the same message at railway stations in Finland.

Figure 7: Trilingual (Finnish-Swedish-English) information about forbidden items at the entrance to the sports arena in Kotka (Photo: Sofie Henricson).

Of seven monolingual Swedish signs, four are top-down. Two contain the name of the Swedish kindergarten,[16] and two are part of a multilingual frame (Finnish-Swedish and Finnish-Swedish-Russian-English). Local businesses have authored two of three bottom-up signs, whereas the third is a piece of graffiti, *FÖR JA E FI FI FI FI FINLANDSSVENSK* 'cause I am Fi Fi Fi Fi Finland Swedish', carved on a rain gutter near the central park.

Russian, the largest minority language in Kotka, is also very visible in the linguistic landscape of the city centre. Russian is mostly included in multilingual signs (37 compared to 12 monolingual). While the multilingual signs are directed to both visitors and inhabitants, most of them have tourists as the main target group. This is not surprising, as at the time of data collection Russian visitors constituted the major tourist group in Kotka.

A combination of Finnish, English and Russian is most common on multilingual signs including Russian (25 of 37), and with very few exceptions, the languages are written in that order, with Finnish as the dominant language. This is illustrated by Figure 8, which shows a sign at Kotka's aquarium, the Maretarium. The Finnish text states that the attraction is closed, provides information about

---

[16] The Swedish kindergarten is maintained by a private organisation (Kotka Svenska Samskolas Garantiförening r.f.), and is partially funded by the municipality of Kotka.

the reasons for the closure and the expected timetable for reopening, and also gives tips about updates on Facebook. The English text includes the same information without the link to Facebook, whereas the Russian text simply informs visitors that the Maretarium is closed.

Figure 8: Trilingual (Finnish-English-Russian) information at the Maretarium (Photo: Sofie Henricson).

Among the multilingual signs there are 16 top-down items containing information about the city and its sites, museums, and public transportation. Most of these are information boards, with detailed facts about the city sites, history, and characteristics. The main target group appears to be visitors rather than inhabitants. The nine bottom-up Finnish-English-Russian signs concern local businesses. The shopping centre, for example, provides customer information in the three languages.

The three bilingual Russian-English signs are related to local businesses, including two bilingual diplomas in the display window of a beauty parlour. These diplomas have Russian as the dominant language and indicate that the local business has Russian-speaking employees or owners, which also functions as an invitation to Russian-speaking customers. Two further Russian texts are included in bilingual Russian-Finnish items, one of which is a memorial sign of Lenin's visit to Kotka in 1907.

The monolingual Russian signs are usually bottom-up (10 of 12). Six of these consist of religious brochures, placed on a stand in front of the central shopping centre. In addition, two Finnish brochures are displayed on the same stand. For these Russian items, the frame is thus bilingual, and Russian is the most dominant language. Only three monolingual Russian items appear without parallel texts in other languages, and these have Russian tourists and visitors as the target group. Two items inform shop customers of the possibility of tax-free shopping and product delivery to Russia, and the third is a public sign in front of Kotka church, requesting silence during services.

Swedish and Russian, and possibly other languages, are combined on seven signs related to tourism, museum information, and wastebaskets. The presence of the two local minority languages in recycling information can be related to the linguistic groups represented in the local population. When Swedish and Russian recycling information is written on wastebaskets, they share the space with Finnish and English, as in Figure 9. Figure 9 also illustrates that Finnish is the dominant language on these signs just as it is in the local society overall: it is written first, has a larger font, and often contains some additional information.

Figure 9: Quadrilingual (Finnish-Swedish-English-Russian) information on wastebasket (detailed information on prohibited glass types written below in Finnish only) (Photo: Sofie Henricson).

To sum up, the linguistic signs including Swedish or Russian share certain features, but also differ in many aspects. Both languages often occur in combination with Finnish and English (see Table 2), and bottom-up signs are not as common as they are for English. Most signs including Swedish are top-down (51 of 81), whereas for Russian the ratio is more balanced (25 top-down of 49). Reflecting its status as a national language and the bilingual policy of Finland, Swedish is visible in a larger number of signs, with a predominance of top-down signs. These include texts from national authorities and organisations, and relate to topics such as education as well as national transportation, domains in which the Russian language is not as visible. The Russian top-down signs are mainly written for tourists, whereas only a few tourist signs include Swedish. Both Swedish and Russian often occur in commercial contexts, but Russian is only present in signs by local businesses, whereas most of the commercial signs including Swedish are related to companies operating at a national level. Both Swedish and Russian are therefore visible minority languages in the city centre of Kotka, but their visibility is related to fairly distinct societal domains.

5 Conclusion

This chapter has told a tale of multilingualism and linguistic visibility in two Finnish cities. The analysis is based on parallel case studies of the linguistic landscapes of Mariehamn and Kotka, two urban centres located at end points on a scale between a monolingual Swedish societal frame and a monolingual Finnish societal frame. The data were collected on one specific day and hence the results reflect the linguistic landscapes as evidenced at the time of the snapshot, including temporary signs such as writings in the snow or current holiday greetings. The analysis consists of an inventory of languages and their frequency, how they relate to one another in public displays, and their functions as regards contexts, authors and target readers. We have further studied possible links between linguistic signs, language demography and linguistic power relations.

In Mariehamn, the number of languages present is striking, especially the number of visible languages with less than one hundred speakers in Åland. This use of a wide range of languages suggests an openness in the city to adopting a multicultural and global approach. It also reflects Mariehamn's status as a popular tourist destination. The superior position of English is clearly visible, particularly in commercial bottom-up items. The relationship between the non-national language English and the national language Finnish is also noteworthy. Finnish is the main language of ten times as many individuals in Åland (1,397 speakers) as

English (134 speakers). Despite this, 67% of the (non-Swedish) monolingual signs are written in English but only 12% in Finnish. A clear majority of monolingual items in English and Finnish are bottom-up signs, whereas multilingual signs containing Swedish, Finnish and English are typically top-down. These trilingual signs, found particularly in the harbour and at tourist attractions, illustrate the presence and importance of transportation and tourism in Mariehamn. Russian was the third most visible language in Mariehamn on the day of the data collection, but without the four ephemeral pieces of graffiti in the snow, Russian would have been placed sixth, after German, Spanish and Thai. The majority language in Mariehamn, Swedish, is present on all but three of the multilingual signs collected. This shows a clear pattern: if a sign in Mariehamn is written in more than one language, Swedish is one of them – and often combined with only English. In Mariehamn Swedish is visibly the language of majority and of power, often accompanied by English.

The distinctive feature of Kotka is the visibility of the two largest local languages besides Finnish, i.e. Swedish and Russian, and the qualitative analysis has primarily focused on signs that include these two languages. The majority language Finnish is present on almost all multilingual signs. In addition, the linguistic landscape in Kotka contains many signs with the universally present English language, and a smaller number of instances of ten other languages. Swedish is mostly included in top-down signs, and often appears through its status as a national language. Swedish is also visible as a local minority language with institutional organisations of its own. Russian is a local minority language with an increasing number of speakers, but also the main language of tourists from abroad. This is reflected in the linguistic signs including Russian, which are relatively evenly split between top-down and bottom-up, and relate to tourism and local businesses. Some signs also acknowledge the presence of Russian inhabitants, such as the signs indicating Russian-speaking shop employees or owners.

A comparison of the lingustic landscapes of Mariehamn and Kotka reveals many similarities, such as the relationship between top-down and bottom-up signs, and the presence of the local majority language on multilingual signs. In both cities the local majority language usually dominates in multilingual signs, for example through font size, positioning and amount of information, and in both cities the majority language is included in 96% of the multilingual signs. Hence, a clear dominance in visibility is given to Swedish in Mariehamn and to Finnish in Kotka. This result has strong parallels to the findings in Cenoz and Gorter (2006), which show a clear dominance of the majority language in the urban centres they explored, i.e. Dutch in Ljouwert and Spanish in Donostia, as regards both the quantity of occurrences and the prominence in multilingual signs.

Another common feature is the salience of English, especially as regards commercial signs. Today English is a global language with a strong position and a great influence on speakers, languages, and societies, and the growing presence of English is a well documented fact within research on linguistic landscapes (Gorter 2006: 1; Backhaus 2007: 56–57; Norrby 2014: 17). This is also supported by our study. In our data, the strong position of the English language and Anglo-American culture is illustrated for example by the Valentine's Day decorations in Mariehamn. None of the signs documented carry a Valentine's Day greeting in Swedish: they are all written in English.

However, a comparison also reveals differences in the visibility of languages in the two cities, which can be related to their divergent linguistic contexts. Inspired by Barni and Bagna (2010), we chose to let the characteristics of each city guide the data collection and analysis, which in our case led to the exclusion of the majority language as primary focus in order to concentrate on the analysis of other languages. This process allowed us to highlight the linguistic profile of the two cities. The minority linguistic landscape in Mariehamn strongly favours English while the largest minority language Finnish has low visibility, a tendency that can be related to language policy, the monolingual regional constitution, the history of the autonomous islands, the closeness to Sweden and the large number of Swedish and international tourists. In contrast, the minority linguistic landscape in Kotka strongly favours local minority languages Swedish and Russian and reflects their main domains of use in the local context, but also mirrors national Finnish-Swedish bilingualism.

Although linguistic landscapes cannot be interpreted as direct representations of ethnolinguistic vitality (as noted e.g. by Ben-Rafael et al. 2006 and convincingly demonstrated in Barni and Bagna 2010), new insights in urban multilingualism can be gained from reading them in relation to language policy, language demography and societal processes, such as tourism. The linguistic landscapes of Mariehamn and Kotka clearly echo both the officially monolingual status and the majority position of Swedish/Finnish, but also show some traces of national bilingualism in the officially monolingual local contexts, such as evident e.g. in bilingual signs used across the country. In Kotka, the distribution and type of signs display a clear connection to the two largest languages besides the majority language, i.e. Swedish and Russian. These two languages are found on signs that reflect their main domains in the city. Examples of this are the Russian signs related to tourism and those that make visible the growing local Russian-speaking minority. Mariehamn, on the other hand, displays a broad palette of minority languages, irrespective of actual speakers present, showing the value attributed to these languages in the cultural sphere. The linguistic landscapes of the two cities, situated at the extremes of Finland's bilingual Finnish/Swedish continuum, thus reflect linguistic demographics and rights, domains of use and historical background of different languages, and present-day lives in a society where speakers of different languages meet.

References

AFLRA (Association of Finnish local and regional authorities). 2017. *Svensk- och tvåspråkiga kommuner: Bakgrundsinformation 2008–2017* [Swedish and bilingual municipalities: background information 2008–2017]. https://www.kommunforbundet.fi/sites/default/files/media/file/2017-02-svensk-och-tvasprakiga-kommuner_0.pdf (accessed 1 February 2019).
Allardt Ljunggren, Barbro 2008. *Åland som språksamhälle: språk och språkliga attityder på Åland ur ett ungdomsperspektiv* [The Åland islands as a language environment: languages and language attitudes from an adolescent perspective]. Stockholm: Stockholm University.
Anttila, Leo. 1957. Kotka som industristad [Kotka as an industrial city]. In Leo Anttila, Aimo Halila, Väinö Meltti, Gabriel Nikander, Ragnar Rosén & Carl-Michael Runeberg (eds.), *Kotka stads historia I* [The history of Kotka I], 193–415. Helsinki: Frenckellska Tryckeri.
ÅSUB (Statistics and Research Åland). 2020. *Statistical yearbook of Åland*. Mariehamn: ÅSUB.
Backhaus, Peter. 2007. *Linguistic landscapes: a comparative study of urban multilingualism in Tokyo*. Clevedon: Multilingual Matters.
Barni, Monica & Carla Bagna. 2010. Linguistic landscape and language vitality. In Elana Shohamy, Eliezer Ben-Rafael & Monica Barni (eds.), *Linguistic landscape in the city*, 3–17. Bristol: Multilingual Matters.
Ben-Rafael, Eliezer, Elana Shohamy, Muhammad Hasan Amara & Nira Trumper-Hecht. 2006. Linguistic landscape as symbolic construction of the public space: the case of Israel. In Durk Gorter (ed.), *Linguistic landscape: a new approach to multilingualism*, 7–30. Clevedon: Multilingual Matters.
Blackwood, Robert. 2015. LL explorations and methodological challenges: analysing France's regional languages. *Linguistic Landscape* 1(1–2). 38–53.
Cenoz, Jasone & Durk Gorter. 2006. Linguistic landscape and minority languages. *International Journal of Multilingualism* 3(1). 67–80.
Engman, Max. 2016. *Språkfrågan: Finlandssvenskhetens uppkomst 1812–1922* [The language issue: the rise of Finland-Swedishness 1812–1922]. Helsinki: The Society of Swedish Literature in Finland.
Finnäs, Fjalar. 2012. *Finlandssvenskarna 2012: en statistisk rapport* [The Swedish-speaking Finns 2012: a statistical report]. Helsinki: The Swedish Assembly of Finland.
Gorter, Durk. 2006. Introduction: the study of the linguistic landscape as a new approach to multilingualism. In Durk Gorter (ed.), *Linguistic landscape: a new approach to multilingualism*, 1–6. Clevedon: Multilingual Matters.
Gorter, Durk. 2018. Methods and techniques for linguistic landscape research: about definitions, core issues and technological innovations. In Martin Pütz & Neele Mundt (eds.), *Expanding the linguistic landscape: multilingualism, language policy and the use of space as a semiotic resource*, 38–57. Bristol: Multilingual Matters.
Gorter, Durk, Heiko F. Marten & Luk Van Mensel (eds.). 2012. *Minority languages in the linguistic landscape*. New York: Palgrave Macmillan.

Halila, Aimo. 1978. Kotkan vaiheita: satama- ja teollisuuskaupunki 100-vuotias. [Stages of Kotka: the 100-year-old city of harbour and industry]. In Jorma Savikko (ed.), *Satavuotias Kotka: juhlakirja vuonna 1978.* [Kotka 100 years: Festschrift in 1978], 1–34. Kotka: City of Kotka.

Henricson, Sofie. 2013. *Svenska i finsk miljö: interaktion, grammatik och flerspråkighet i samtal på svenska språköar i Finland* [Swedish in Finnish surroundings: interaction, grammar and language contact in conversations within Swedish speech islands in Finland]. PhD thesis, University of Helsinki.

Herberts, Kjell. 2017. Flerspråkighet eller English only? Om språklandskapen i Vasa och Umeå [Multilingualism or English only? On linguistic landscapes in Vasa and Umeå]. *Sprog i Norden* 2017. 39–54.

Landry, Rodrigue & Richard Y. Bourhis. 1997. Linguistic landscape and ethnolinguistic vitality: an empirical study. *Journal of Language and Social Psychology* 16(1). 23–49.

Liebkind, Karmela, Roger Broo & Fjalar Finnäs. 1995. The Swedish-speaking minority in Finland: a case study. In Juha Pentikäinen & Maria Hiltunen (eds.), *Cultural minorities in Finland: an overview towards cultural policy.* 2nd ed., 48–83. Helsinki: Finnish National Commission for Unesco.

Liebkind, Karmela, Tom Moring & Marika Tandefelt (eds.). 2007. The Swedish-speaking Finns. *International Journal of the Sociology of Language* 187/188.

Loughlin, John & Farimah Daftary. 1999. Insular regions and European integration: Corsica and the Åland Islands compared. *ECMI Report* 5.

Ministry of Justice, Finland. 1991. *Act on the autonomy of Åland.* 1144/1991.

Ministry of Justice, Finland. 1998. *Basic education act.* 628/1998.

Ministry of Justice, Finland. 2003. *Language act.* 423/2003.

Nelson, Marie. 2016. Swedish on the Åland Islands: a non-dominant yet dominating variety. In Rudolf Muhr, Kelen Ernesta Fonyuy, Zeinab Ibrahim & Corey Miller (eds.), *Pluricentric languages and non-dominant varieties worldwide: pluricentric languages across continents – features and usage,* 415–429. Frankfurt am Main: Peter Lang.

Norrby, Catrin. 2014. English in Scandinavia – monster or mate? Sweden as a case study. In John Hajek & Yvette Slaughter (eds.), *Challenging the monolingual mindset,* 17–32. Bristol: Multilingual Matters.

OSF (Official Statistics of Finland). 2020. *Population structure.* Helsinki: Statistics Finland. http://www.stat.fi/til/vaerak/tau_en.html (accessed 7 November 2020).

Parkvall, Mikael. 2009. *Sveriges språk – vem talar vad och var?* [Languages in Sweden – who speaks what and where?]. Stockholm: Stockholm University.

Port of HaminaKotka. 2020. Official website https://www.haminakotka.com (accessed 27 February 2020).

Pütz, Martin & Neele Mundt (eds.). 2018. *Expanding the linguistic landscape: linguistic diversity, multimodality and the use of space as a semiotic resource.* Bristol: Multilingual Matters.

Shohamy, Elana & Durk Gorter (eds.). 2009. *Linguistic landscape: expanding the scenery.* New York: Routledge.

Syrjälä, Väinö. 2012. *Två lingvistiska landskap i Norden: om språk i Helsingfors Metro och Oslos T-bane* [Two linguistic landscapes in Scandinavia: about languages in the Metro of Helsinki and Oslo]. Helsinki: University of Helsinki.

Zane Goebel
3 Unity, diversity and the market: Television representations of multilingual diversity in Jakarta

1 Introduction

The question this chapter seeks to address is how Indonesian television has represented multilingualism in Jakarta, Indonesia's capital and largest city. I focus on representations of language practices in Jakarta, to highlight a trend in Indonesian television where fragments of linguistic signs associated with some of Indonesia's hundreds of ethnic languages are mixed with the national language, *Bahasa Indonesia* 'Indonesian'. In building on my earlier work (Goebel 2008; 2015), I focus on representation of inter-ethnic contact in Jakarta to note that these representations have helped produce an alternate language ideology to that regimented by the Indonesian state. The state narrative sees the unification of its hundreds of ethnolinguistic groups (i.e., unity in diversity) as being facilitated though Indonesian (Dardjowidjojo 1998) and sees Indonesian as a pure unmixed medium to be used in such interactions, in government settings and as the language of the national mass media. Even so, where television is concerned, representations of city life in Jakarta have increasingly modelled language practices as occurring in a mix of colloquial Indonesian and ethnic languages, such as Javanese and Betawi. To account for this trend, I draw upon a stream of linguistic anthropology that has paid increasing attention to relationships between languages, markets, and political regimes (Agha 2007; Blommaert 2010; Heller and Duchêne 2012). This work has helped us understand that the underlying driver of sociolinguistic change is a process that assigns some sort of value to a particular set of signs (linguistic and otherwise). In the case

---

Note: Much of what I present in this contribution uses data analysis presented in other papers, although my focus here develops my argument around valuation processes and how it relates to ideologies of what constitutes language in the Indonesian context. More specifically, excerpt 1 uses some data previously presented in my article "Enregistering, authorizing and denaturalizing identity in Indonesia" published in 2008 in the Journal of Linguistic Anthropology (18:54–55). The data and parts of the analysis have been reprinted with permission of the American Anthropological Association. Excerpts 2 and 4 were originally published in 2015 in my book entitled "Language and superdiversity: Indonesians knowledging at home and abroad" (pp. 98–99 and 162–163). They have been reproduced by permission of Oxford University Press https://global.oup.com/academic/product/language-and-superdiversity-9780199795420?cc=au&lang=en&. For permission to reuse this material, please visit http://global.oup.com/academic/rights.

of television markets, some languages are more valuable than others for attracting audiences, and thus potential consumers of the goods and services advertised as part of the television programming.

After synthesizing scholarship on language and value in section 2, I then take a historical view of the different value projects that have impacted the representation of language practices in Indonesian television since the early 1990s (section 3). This section provides the necessary background to understand television representations of social life in Jakarta, which become the main focus of section 4. In particular, section 4 examines the language practices found in two soap operas (*sinetron*) extracted from a database of around 400 hours of broadcast recordings collected between 1995 and 2009 (Goebel 2015). I have chosen these soaps (broadcast in 1998 and 2009) because they represent inter-ethnic contact. While the representation practices I identify in section 4 resemble the use of tokens from multiple languages, often referred to with terms, such as polylanguaging, translanguaging, and metrolingualism (Garcia and Li Wei 2014; Jørgensen et al. 2011; Pennycook and Otsuji 2015), I do not use these terms. This is so for two reasons. First, while a number of these concepts offer new conceptualisations of context, their limitations typically lie in an inability to account for the language labels used in such studies and a lack of focus on the multimodal nature of communication. Second, these labels often conflate the product of interaction and the practice of mixing.

Building on Goebel (2010; 2014; 2015; 2019; 2020) and Goebel et al. (2020), I use the term "contact register" to refer to the emergent and often ephemeral product of social practice, while I use the term "signswitching" to refer to the actual practice of alternating between signs (linguistic and otherwise) stereotypically associated with named languages. The concept of signswitching refers to the local recognition of moving between signs stereotypically associated with named languages to achieve an interactional outcome, as well as the multimodal nature of other switching practices that we find in everyday talk, such as changes in tempo, pitch, use of proximity, gesture, facial expressions, and so forth. To keep my contribution short, I will not focus on the multimodal nature of the interactional data that I examine. Importantly for this paper, the idea of signswitching invites us to account for how we come to label interactional practices as occurring in one language/code or another. For example, are such labels based on nation-state generated ideologies, folk notions about language, scholarly labels, or interactionally in situ generated ones? Thus, while signswitching acknowledges well-recognised problems with older views about the relationship between linguistic form, community, and territory (Blommaert 2010; Heller 2007) – that is, where language was conceptualised as having clear boundaries, and mixed language practices and codeswitching meant the movement between two separate unitary languages – it also points to the limitations of current alternates that continue to use language labels without accounting for them. In concluding, I point out how these types of representations produce images of and imaginaries about unity in diversity in Jakarta.

2 Language and social value

> [U]tterances are not only (save in exceptional circumstances) signs to be understood and deciphered; they are also signs of wealth, intended to be evaluated and appreciated, and signs of authority, intended to be believed and obeyed. (Bourdieu 1991: 66)

Much linguistic anthropological thought about language has been inspired by Bourdieu's (1991) ideas about the social value of language and about language in social life and/or by Foucault's (1978) ideas about how certain practices are monitored or policed in a way that engenders perceptions of the naturalness and social value of certain communicative practices (Agha 2007; Woolard 1998). Other scholars have explored how certain languages and language practices become valued in a world where almost everything is monetised and enumerated (Blommaert 2010; Heller and Duchêne 2016; Kelly-Holmes 2016; Pietikäinen et al. 2016).

There are three parts to this latter group's argument. First, language is seen as an index of pride that is linked to ideas of identity. Second, language is also increasingly commodified; that is, it is seen as a means of making profit and gaining market share, often via claims of authenticity. Drawing upon Wallerstein's (2004) insights about processes of globalisation, this literature argues that market saturation and the continued search for profits in new niche markets is one driver of processes of language commodification. Third, these processes of revaluing and commodifying languages have recursively imitated value formulas that consist of pride in a particular language as a symbol of a nation, territory, and a group inhabiting this territory. For example, minority languages have been marketed as signs of territory, group, and of the authenticity of goods and services in Canada (Heller et al. 2015).

While nationally authorised and codified versions of a language are still imagined as important in some of these markets – as found in the tourist bureaus in the mining frontiers of Canada (Heller et al. 2015) – what is just as common is the use of just enough fragments of a minority language to give the appearance of authenticity (Pietikäinen et al. 2016). This strategy of mixing fragments of nationally authorised languages and minority or ethnic languages (and other signs of ethnic-ness) as a way of gaining some sort of market advantage can be seen across the world (Pietikäinen and Kelly-Holmes 2013). For example, Pietikäinen and colleagues (2016) analyse the case of Welsh sea salt sold in a container that has the following text as part of its label: "Natural Halen Môn Anglesey Sea Salt". In this case, "Halen Môn" is classified as Welsh, and mixed with the rest, which is in English. The use of the Welsh and the place name "Anglesey" are argued to enhance the authenticity and desirability of the product because they point to, or index, the origin of the place and the speaking population stereotypically associated with that place. In doing so, these marketing activities that represent language as mixed create tensions with older ideas about language as a unitary construct anchored to place and group.

While much of this work highlights the need to understand the processes behind these changes and the consequence that they have for those who benefit from or are marginalised by these processes (Heller and Duchêne 2016: 148), typically it is the latter that is the focus of most analysis. Explanations of processes are often relegated to a loose correlation between economic activity and language practices. In related, but more theoretical work, Agha (2007) has clarified these processes of valuation. There are five elements to this process, one of which is a product of these same processes from another time and space or "scale" (Blommaert 2010). These are: semiotic register, metasemiotic commentary, imitation, authorisation, and mass circulation.

Here I will start with defining semiotic register, but as the following discussion will show – and in what might initially appear to be a cyclical argument – there needs to be a pre-existing semiotic register to engender evaluation processes. Drawing on Agha (2007) we can define a semiotic register as follows:

> A semiotic register is a group of signs or semiotic features that have become associated with each other over time through their recirculation via commentaries about these signs' social value. The term semiotic register covers what is commonly referred to as "language" and "dialect", but also includes the indexical relationships that linguistic signs have with speakers, social practices, and ideas about morality and epistemology.

Semiotic register formation is dependent on tokens of an emergent register being commented upon. Following Agha (2007), we can refer to these commentaries as "metasemiotic commentaries". Metasemiotic commentaries evaluate a particular language practice and those engaged in the language practice. Such commentaries thus also contribute to a re-use or "imitation" of tokens of this emergent register as well as to its categorisation (e.g. as a named language, poor language, slang, etc.).

Imitation of tokens of an emergent register is the third ingredient in processes of semiotic register formation. Imitation is similar to replication, but it acknowledges two points (Bauman and Briggs 1990; Lempert 2014). First, as semiotic features move across contexts their meanings change. Second, and related to the first point, most forms of replication are not repetition as precise copy, but rather have something old (making the configuration somewhat recognizable), and something new (which can attract attention to the configuration). For example, the adaption of a novel to television or film replicates much of the story, while adding multimodal features to the representations of language and social relations found in novels along with a change in mediation technology.

Another element needed in processes of semiotic register formation is authorisation of the use of tokens of an emergent register. This is achieved by use of these tokens by someone who is socially valued (e.g. a teacher, politician, celebrity, sports star) or through authorisation of their mass mediation. The last element needed in this process is a means of mass circulation within one-to-many participation frameworks, such as television and radio or mass schooling, where the programming content or teacher is the "one" and the audience or students are the "many".

The inter-relationships between these five elements – which together we can refer to as "infrastructures for social value" – can be summed up as follows: chains of authorised metasemiotic commentaries drive semiotic register formation and thus changes in the social value of language practices in multiple social domains. Typically, change can occur simultaneously in multiple social domains (e.g. television representations, language policy for schools, local emergent norms for interacting in urban contact zones). The existence of these overlapping chains enables some of the features of emergent semiotic registers to be more widely recognised – that is, "enregistered" (Agha 2007; Silverstein 2003), while also enabling comparisons of their value vis-à-vis other semiotic registers. Blommaert (2010) sees the creation of multiple semiotic registers as also enabling the formation of language hierarchies. For example, one where national languages are at the top, ethnic and minority languages below national ones, and youth language and associated slang are even further below. Such hierarchies are not fixed, however, as the work above points out, but are impacted upon by changes in how capital is mobilised, by efforts to manage linguistic diversity more generally (Errington 2001; Gal 2012), and by and through regime change, as we will see in the following section.

It is also important to point out that processes of enregisterment engender what Blommaert (2010) refers to as "localisation". Localisation refers to the process whereby semiotic forms (e.g. linguistic tokens stereotypically associated with a particular territory and group) become recognised as being of local providence. For example, the imitation of tokens stereotypically associated with English can become habitual to the extent that they attract no commentary from others who hear or view such tokens. In short, such tokens become locally perceived as of "local providence".

3 Researching the valuation of sociolinguistic diversity: From nation to city

In Indonesia, infrastructures for social value as they relate to language have had a long history. As highlighted above, understanding this history will help in our analysis of valuation processes as they relate to representations of language practices in Jakarta which we will turn to in section 4. More specifically the methodologies used to historicise these valuation processes relate to examining the when and where of value statements and how they relate to subsequent ones (i.e. imitations of commentaries about social value). These methodologies are complemented with other historical work that embed these commentaries in the socio-economic and political circumstances of the day. The analysis of actual transcripts of talk that we do in section 4 will draw upon these accounts of valuation processes and the important contextual elements accompanying such accounts. The television broadcasts from which this data is extracted were gathered as part of two larger projects in 1996–1998 (Goebel 2010) and 2009 (Goebel 2015). The former gathered this material as a supplementary form of data and was not a product of systematic recording, while the latter involved systematic recording of eleven television channels over the course of a month in 2009, resulting in some 400 hours of recordings.

Existing semiotic register formations in Indonesia have their basis in a long history of Dutch thought and Dutch colonial administrative practices (Errington 2001; Moriyama 2005; Sneddon 2003). The massive diversity encountered by Dutch missionaries, governors, administrators, educators, and settlers was typically simplified through administrative and educational practices (Errington 2001; Moriyama 2005). This process was imitated by subsequent political regimes, including during the Japanese occupation in World War II (Goebel 2015). We know little about processes of semiotic register formation in the period between when Indonesian Independence was declared and when an anti-communist regime was established in 1966.

What we do know is that Indonesia's attempts to create and maintain a unified state essentially devalued regional languages (*Bahasa daerah*). This was so because of their association with ethnicity, territory, religion, political parties, and regional independence movements (Feith 1962; Legge 1961; Liddle 1972). Large-scale investment in nation building started to occur in Indonesia in the late 1960s (Dick 2002). Nation building and building a sense of pride in Indonesia were achieved through investment in schooling (Bjork 2005), communication (Kitley 2000), transportation infrastructures (Dick 2002), and language planning activities (Dardjowidjojo 1998). These activities and the people they involved contributed to the imitation and regimentation of earlier ideas that languages were unitary and pure, and that using 'proper Indonesian' (*Bahasa Indonesian yang baik dan benar*) – especially with those who did not speak your regional language – was part of what it meant to be a citizen.

Importantly for this paper, during the early 1990s the ideology of language as pure, unitary, and anchored to a territory and particular group started to contrast with representations of such interactions in the domain of television. Market forces in the area of television production and consumption helped usher in a period where the representation of ethnic-ness became highly profitable because of its ability to attract wider and niche audiences (Goebel 2008; Kitley 2000; Loven 2008). Most of these television representations used just enough emblems of ethnicity and tokens stereotypical of a particular ethnic language to engender a sense of ethnic-ness. The upshot of these practices was that televised representations of everyday co-ethnic conversations were characterised by the formation of contact registers and the practice of signswitching.

This commodification of ethnolinguistic identity in the domain of television co-occurred with the primarily positive revaluation of ethnolinguistic identity in multiple other domains (Goebel 2015: 42–51). To sum up the period between 1966 through to 1998 (often referred to as the New Order period), we can say that there was a large-scale massification in the mechanisms that facilitated the circulation and valuation of ideas linking language, region, and ethnic social types. These processes produced a semiotic register that included the tight association of linguistic forms with particular regions and groups to the extent that when Indonesians talked of themselves as speaking a regional language, such as Javanese, Sundanese, Balinese, this also frequently pointed to the same ethnic identity (Boellstorff 2002). At the same time, and in line with ideals laid out in the Indonesian constitution and operationalized through language policy, speaking Indonesian had become ideologically associated with doing unity in diversity among an ethnolinguistically diverse citizenship.

Even so, by the 1990s, these infrastructures for social value had also created a hierarchy of languages within Indonesia. This hierarchy can be summarised as one where English (only recognised and spoken by elites) sat at the very top of this hierarchy, followed by standard pure Indonesian (typically of the written academic type or the type spoken on national television and radio). Beneath this was a handful of standardised pure prestigious versions of ethnic languages with large numbers of speakers, such as Javanese, Balinese, and Sundanese. In the case of Javanese, the label "Javanese" often referred to more prestigious *kromo* varieties of Javanese, even though these were actually increasingly uncommon in many communicative contexts (Errington 1998; Goebel 2007). These prestigious versions of ethnic languages sat above much less valued everyday colloquial forms of language. These typically ephemeral mediums included ethnic languages, Indonesian, and varieties of Malay, both of which varied significantly from region to region, and even from neighbourhood to neighbourhood (Goebel 2010). Everyday communicative contexts were typically characterised by the use of tokens of Malay, Indonesian, and ethnic languages in co-ethnic interaction (Errington 1998; Kuipers 1998) and inter-ethnic interaction (Goebel 2002; Jacob and Grimes 2006). At the base of this language hierarchy, there were the endangered and dying ethnic languages from the island peripheries (Kuipers 1998). As with spoken forms of ethnic languages from Java and Bali, these were valued neither by the nation-state nor by their own speakers because of the social value of Indonesian, especially the perception that it was a means of social and economic mobility.

Since 1998, there has been significant social, economic, political, and cultural change in Indonesia (Aspinall and Fealy 2003; Davidson and Henley 2007; Holtzappel and Ramstedt 2009). These changes contributed to a positive valuation of ethnicity and ethnic languages (Davidson and Henley 2007; Goebel 2018b). As sociolinguistic research on contemporary language practices in Indonesia emerges, we know that formerly powerless institutions now have the resources and the political and constitutional support to further promote ethnic languages (for a recent summary see Goebel 2018a). This positive revaluation of ethnic languages can be seen in increased discourses about entitlement and authenticity, increases in the use of ethnic languages for political purposes, teen literature, the internet, consumer goods, everyday conversations among university students, within the Indonesian bureaucracy, and on Indonesian television (e.g. Goebel 2007; 2014; 2015; and the papers in Goebel et al. 2020). In the case of televised representations of interaction, an analysis of 400 hours of recordings of Indonesian television from August 2009 shows that practices of representing tokens of ethnic languages could be found in almost all television genres, including children's shows, quiz shows, celebrity gossip shows, soaps, and local language news services (Goebel 2015). Below I narrow my focus by examining whether and to what extent these Indonesia-wide television trends existed at the city scale. I will especially focus on television representations of inter-ethnic contact in Jakarta, drawing upon representations of inter-ethnic contact in soap operas (*sinetron*) broadcast in 1998 and 2009.

4 Representing the doing of diversity

Excerpts 1 and 2 are taken from a long running popular television series *Si Doel Anak Sekolahan* 'Doel an educated lad'. I recorded this particular episode, (*Meniti Batas Mimpi* 'Walking along the edge of a dream') in mid-1998. *Si Doel* is set in the poor outskirts of Jakarta and is a story about the lives of a family who are portrayed as belonging to an ethnic group referred to as Betawi. This group has been stereotyped as a group who have historically struggled economically, been quite pious in their Islamic practices, been anti-education, and quick tempered. It is a story that has undergone many iterations (Loven 2008), all authorised by some infrastructure for social value. For example, the original novel upon which this soap is based, *Si Doel Anak Betawi* (Aman [1932] 1971), was authorised by the then Dutch colonial regime via their publishing arm, *Balai Pustaka*. While the soap opera itself is authorised by a different regime, as with the novel and earlier film versions, the very fact that these stories became mediated at all attests to their social value. At this point it is also important to note that both the novel and the soap contained or engendered discourses that not only addressed the social value of these representations, but also the social value of the languages used in these representations.

For example, within the preface to the novel and then the accompanying story, the medium of interactions among the main characters were labelled as occurring in a language of a particular ethnic group, the Betawi (Goebel 2015: 28–29). In the case of the televised soap, commentaries by the producer and then by those who liked or disliked the language used help imitate these same ideas that labelled the linguistic forms used in co-ethnic interaction as a named language, Betawi (Goebel 2008; Loven 2008). This discursive work essentially contributed to an emerging semiotic register associated with Betawi-ness, which was spoken by the main characters who were part of an extended Betawi family, all living in the same house (Lela the mother of Doel and Atun, and older sister to Mandra). Over the course of multiple seasons, other personas from different ethnic backgrounds were also constructed. Of note here is Karyo, who is constructed as a migrant from Central Java who speaks a language different to that of Betawi, in this case tokens of a variety of Javanese (in early episodes this difference was highlighted through the use of Indonesian subtitles when he was using Javanese). At this point, we can briefly return to my discussion in section 3 about the need to note how and by whom linguistic forms are labelled. In this case, it is producers of the film, actors involved, those who comment on usage, a number of Indonesian research assistants, and myself; all of whom have imitated earlier versions of language labels constructed by state infrastructures of social value.

Excerpt 1 is preceded by a shot of Karyo raising a birdcage up a pole located beside a house in a large yard. He then moves to a nearby *warung* (a small canteen type construction selling food and home necessities), where he starts his conversation with Lela in a mixture of linguistic forms stereotypically associated with Indonesian and Betawi. To keep my analysis manageable, I have focused just on linguistic forms in my analysis.

Excerpt 1: Television representations of doing unity in diversity (Source: Karno 1998)

Karyo
1   **MAKNYAK, BANG** mandra sudah jalan   MUM, BROTHER Mandra has already gone *heh*?
    toh
Lela
2   *udah*   *Yeah*.
Karyo
3   **kok tumben loh** pagi pagi   *Gee that's unusual* [for him to get up] so early.
Lela
4   **IYÉ** mau ke rumahnya munaroh   YEAH, [he] wants to go to Munaroh's house.
Karyo
5   ke rumah munaroh   To Munaroh's house?
Lela
6   iya   Yeah.
Karyo
7   **ngelamar** ya   [He] wants to **propose** [marriage] yeah?
Lela
8   **Nggak**, cuma mau **nanyain**, kapan   **No**, [he] only wants to **ask** when [is the best time to
9   lamarannya bisa DITERIMÉ, *gitu*   propose so that] it is ACCEPTED [by his girlfriend's parents].
Karyo
10 Oh, jadi belum ya **mak** ya   Oh, so not yet heh **Mum** yeah?
Lela
11 ya BELON *dong*   Yes, *no of course* NOT YET.
Karyo
12 atun ada MAK   Is Atun around MUM?
Lela
13 ada NOH lagi sarapan   Yeah, THERE having breakfast.

Key: plain font = Indonesian; **BOLD SMALL CAPS** = Betawi; ***bold italics*** = forms which cannot be classified as Betawi or Indonesian.

This excerpt is interesting because it represents an encounter conducted in a mixed medium among those who have been identified in the story as coming from different ethnolinguistic backgrounds. In this inter-ethnic encounter, we have Karyo using and understanding tokens of Betawi on lines 1, 4, 9–13. This contrasts with the state narrative that ideologises Indonesian as the language of such encounters. It is important to note here that such usage is situational and in other parts of the soap Karyo uses and is spoken to in Indonesian in interactions with those he does not have close social relations. He only uses Betawi tokens when interacting with familiars.

For example, Atun is Karyo's romantic partner and in his interactions with her, he is also represented as using tokens of Betawi, Javanese, and Indonesian. By looking at wider interactional patterns we find that such mixed usage is, in fact, habitual among different sets of characters (as we will see in excerpt 2). Importantly, while these representations contrast with the state language ideology, they represent an example where doing unity in diversity is modelled as conducted in a contact register. In doing so, such models of inter-ethnic encounters are valued, albeit via a different infrastructure for social value. In this case, it is a market-generated infrastructure rather than a state-generated one.

Excerpt 2 is taken from the same episode as excerpt 1. This time we have Karyo (who as noted earlier is represented as a migrant from Central Java), and Mandra, who is represented as a local Betawi who has little education, is illiterate, and unable to control his emotions. In the lead up to this scene, both have had a bad day; Mandra's marriage proposal was rejected, and Karyo could not get a loan to pursue a business venture because his identity card still showed that he did not live in Jakarta. Up to this point, Karyo does all of the talking. Mandra just nods his head, while looking down at the ground. This bit of talk occurs after Mandra gives his identity card to Karyo, which, as Karyo points out, has expired. This time, talk is littered with tokens of Betawi and with tokens stereotypically associated with Javanese.

Excerpt 2: Representations of inter-ethnic talk (Source: Karno 1998)

Karyo
1	Loh, iss. Ini masa berlakunya, sudah abis	What! Hey! This card is expired, you
2	gini loh. **Sampeyan** ni **piyé toh**, Ini loh	know. **What is up with you**! Here have
3	**mbok** diliat tu, masa berlaku, lima februari,	a look! **didn't** [you] see this! Valid until
4	sembilan tujuh.	the 5th of February 97.
5	Berarti telat setaun,	That means it has [already been expired]
6	**sampeyan kudu** ngurus ke	for one year! **you must** go to the local
7	kelurahan lagi.	government office again.
8	Ini sudah ndak laku.	[This one] is already expired!

Mandra
7	Sini. Emangnya GUWA	Give it here! It doesn't matter, I'M not a
8	pendatang kayak ELU. GUWA betawi asli.	newcomer like YOU! I'M a genuine
9	Biar gak punya ktp,	Betawi! Even if [I] don't have an identity card it is
10	juga gak apa apa, ngak bakal ditangkap.	okay. I'll never be arrested.
11	Emangnya kayak ELU, ditangkep LU, kalo	Not like YOU. YOU'LL be arrested if you don't have
12	ngak punya ktp Jakarta, tolol.	a Jakartan identity card, idiot!

Key: plain font = Indonesian; BOLD SMALL CAPS = Betawi; **bold** = tokens stereotypically associated with Javanese

In the above excerpt, we see a representation of an inter-ethnic encounter where both participants are portrayed as understanding languages that are stereotypically not their own: Mandra is represented as understanding bits of Javanese on lines 2, 3, and 6, while in the extended dialogue, not reproduced here, Karyo is also represented as understanding bits of Betawi of the type found on lines 7–8, and 12 (and in excerpt 1). In other places in this episode, and indeed in this series, Karyo is also represented as interacting with familiars using tokens of Javanese, e.g. in his interactions with his romantic partner, Atun. Again, these representations of inter-ethnic encounter contrast with the national ideology that Indonesian would be used in such encounters. Such usage co-occurs with the projection of ethnolinguistic boundaries between those who are Betawi and those who are not (lines 7–12). Just as importantly, this imitation of Javanese tokens also contributes to a localisation of these forms in the story world as well as for consumers of such soaps.

Put in terms of signswitching, what we have is a representation of signswitching as habitual between particular participant constellations. Such representations challenge state ideologies about purity and the need for Indonesian in inter-ethnic encounter. These representations also denaturalise links between ethnic languages and territory because here we have participants who are constructed as belonging to particular territory-based ethno-linguistic groups, yet they are also represented as understanding and using languages not associated with these constructed ethnic identities. As noted earlier, the type of language commodification examined in the above soap opera continued in 2009. Below are two examples of this continued commodification of ethnic languages in inter-ethnic encounter in Jakarta. They are extracted from the soap entitled *Bukan Romeo Juliet* 'This is not Romeo and Juliet'.

It is framed (via trailers and the constructed story) as a comedy about inter-ethnic relations, especially interactions among migrants locally known as Indonesians of Chinese ancestry and Indonesians of Arab ancestry. In doing so, *Bukan Romeo Juliet* explicitly engages with what has historically been a very problematic relationship between Indonesians of Chinese ancestry and other Indonesians (Purdey 2006). Of import to my larger argument is that, like most of the television footage, talk between participants is never represented as talk in pure Indonesian or pure ethnic languages, but typically a contact register.

The story is set in one low-income Jakarta neighbourhood and revolves around two sets of romantic relationships. The first is between Zaenab, a young Betawi Muslim woman, Alung, a non-Muslim man of Chinese ancestry, and Melani, a young Indonesian woman of Chinese ancestry, who is also economically better off than both Zaenab and Alung. The second emerging romantic relationship is between Sutini, a Javanese migrant, and two potential partners, Liong who is Alung's uncle and Wan who is Zaenab's father.

As with my representation of language practices in the last two excerpts, when considering the next two excerpts it is useful to remind the reader that while I use labels to refer to languages (e.g., Javanese, Chinese-Indonesian, and Indonesian), what I refer to is just small lexical tokens that are stereotypically associated with named languages. I identified and labelled these as such, via reference to a number of Indonesian consultants, my own experiences with these languages, a number of dictionaries, and what we know about the infrastructures of social value described in section 3. The interaction in excerpt 3 is preceded by Sutini and Liong dancing to music. They are then joined by Wan, who like Liong, fancies himself as a potential romantic partner for Sutini. Wan and Liong then bump into each other on purpose while dancing until Sutini storms off.

Excerpt 3: Representations of inter-ethnic talk among old generation migrants

Sutini
1   Kalau gini caranya **tak** matiin aja, hum,   If this is how it is, [then] **I'll** just turn off
2   nggak asyik   [the music]. It's not enjoyable!
Babah Liong
3   Nih gara gara **lu olang**   This is **your** fault.
Wan Abud
4   gara **ENTÉ**   **YOUR** fault.
Babah Liong
5   **Oweh** lagi senang senang **lu olang** masuk   I was having fun [and] **you** joined in.

Key: plain font = Indonesian; **CAPS** = tokens that are stereotypically associated with those of Arab decent; **bold** = tokens stereotypically associated with Javanese; **bold underline** = forms that can be classified as Chinese-Indonesian

In excerpt 3, we can observe a mix of Indonesian and non-Indonesian forms. In the case of non-Indonesian, typically these are tokens for self and other reference, including *tak* 'I', *oweh* 'I', *lu olang* 'you', *enté* 'you'. This mixing is common and represented as habitual and not noticed or commented upon by any of the other characters throughout the episode. In short, a contact register is represented as "the medium of interaction" (i.e. it is the medium of interaction rather than two separate mediums used together). As with excerpts 1 and 2, this medium contrasts with nation-state regimented language ideologies where inter-ethnic exchanges are ideologised as being in pure Indonesian. It is also the case, again as with excerpts 1 and 2, that both participants are represented as both a member of a particular territory-bound ethnolinguistic group, and someone who is able to comprehend tokens of language not their own.

This 2009 representation of inter-ethnic talk in a Jakartan neighbourhood not only imitates models of language in social life from other television soaps (e.g. *Si Doel* described earlier), but it also continues to offer a meta-semiotic commentary about the value of such representations. The very fact of it not being censored and thus being authorised and circulated in a one-to-many participation framework attests its social value. In sum, we have an infrastructure for social value – in this case one associated with a market where tokens of language continue to be commodified – that contributes to the enregisterment and localisation of a contact register that is associated with contact among those of differing backgrounds.

Excerpt 4 is an interaction between Melani, represented as an Indonesian of Chinese ancestry who was born and raised in Indonesia, and Sutini, who is represented as a Javanese migrant. As with previous excerpts, different fonts are used to represent different named languages.

Excerpt 4: Representations of inter-ethnic talk and localisation

Melani
1   **MORNING** *mbak* sutini   **MORNING** *Sister* Sutini.
Sutini
2   eee **GOOD MORNING**, um *mbak* melani   Oh, **GOOD MORNING**, um [you are]
3   kan   *Sister* Melani right?
Melani
4   Betul   Yes.
Sutini
5   lah, mesti ke sini cari *mas* alung   So, [you] must have come here looking for *Brother* Alung.
Melani
6   iya dong, habis *aku* kangen sih *mbak*   Of course. I miss [him] so much, you know, *Sister*.
Sutini
7   loh *mbak*, **YOU** kan udah tahu, kalau   What Sister? **YOU** already know right, that
8   **misalé** *mas* alung dah ada   **FOR example** Brother Alung already has a
9   **GIRLFRIEND**nya, nanti **misalé** rebut lagi   **GIRLFRIEND**. Later if **for example**, [you both]
10 kaya waktu itu **piyé**   fight again like before, **then what**?
Melani
11 (Her facial expressions show she is upset with what Sutini has said.)
Sutini
12 aduh *mbak*, maksud **I AM** nggak gitu loh,   Gee Sister, **I** didn't mean it like that.
13 aaa ndak usah   Um [you] don't need
Melani
14 udah udah, ndak apa apa *mbak*, ndak apa   [It's] ok. [It's] ok, [it's] alright *Sister*, [it's]
15 apa   alright

Key: plain font = Indonesian; **bold** = tokens stereotypically associated with Javanese; *italics* = fragments that are of ethnic origin, in this case Javanese; **BOLD CAPS** = English

Note that like excerpt 3, this encounter is represented as an inter-ethnic one, although unlike excerpts 1 to 3 it is an encounter among relative strangers. This is evidenced via the need for Sutini to check whether she has Melani's name correct (lines 2–4). Despite this unfamiliarity, we see the representation of another encounter characterised by a contact register and signswitching. For example, we can observe a particular type of representation of morphological localisation where an Indonesian form that indicates possession (*nya*) is affixed to an English form, "girlfriend" (line 9) in an utterance that also has other English tokens "you", localised Javanese kin terms of address (*mbak* and *mas* on lines 7–8, Indonesian lines 7–10), and Javanese tokens (*misalé* and *piyé* on lines 9–10). In sum, and as with the previous three excerpts, we can say that the commodification of language practices here contributes to the emergence of a market-generated counter-narrative to two interrelated state narratives; the first that inter-ethnic encounter is to be conducted in pure Indonesian, and the second that unity in diversity can be achieved solely with recourse to Indonesian.

5 Conclusion

In this chapter, I have examined television representations of language practices in inter-ethnic encounters in one of Indonesia's mega-cities, Jakarta. In doing so, I have drawn upon sociolinguistic scholarship on semiotic register formation and its relationship to social value and the market to add to a burgeoning field that seeks to understand processes that discursively value and label languages in multilingual settings (Blommaert 2010; Heller et al. 2015; Heller and Duchêne 2012; Pietikäinen et al. 2016). In contrast to much of this scholarship, which uses long-term ethnographic research to focus on the consequences of these valuation processes (i.e. who benefits and who is marginalised), this contribution has the more modest aim of examining the processes that enable particular ideas about what constitutes language to become widely circulating.

For this purpose, I have drawn on scholarship on processes of semiotic register formation (Agha 2007) in one social domain, that of Indonesian television. Part of this approach requires us to take a historical view, embedding television in wider social, political and economic events in a way that highlights how we can think of all of this in terms of infrastructures for social value. This historicising move enabled me to show how the market, as just one driver of sociolinguistic change in the domain of television, related to these events and how languages were conceptualised by state and non-state actors. For example, we started with looking at how the state valued and conceptualised language as unitary and unmixed before the 1990s, noting that pure forms of Indonesian were idealised as the medium of inter-ethnic encounter and the medium for doing unity in diversity. We then examined how television programming provided an alternative to this state narrative by representing language practices in inter-ethnic encounter in the urban neighbourhoods of Jakarta as mixed.

In the cases presented here, the product of interaction (a contact register) and the practice of signswitching were represented as habitual and mundane in social life found in Jakartan neighbourhoods. In authorising such representations, this programming also contributed to a localisation of linguistic tokens typically associated with other territories and groups of speakers. In concluding, it should also be noted that the data presented here is now over ten years old and it would be worthwhile to see what is happening in contemporary Indonesia. For example, the rise in nationalism that is currently underway (Aspinall 2016) may counter the market forces and the effects described above, and perhaps even contribute to a move back toward a valuing and regimentation of pure and unmixed Indonesian in such encounters.

References

Agha, Asif. 2007. *Language and social relations*. Cambridge: Cambridge University Press.
Aman. 1971[1932]. *Si Doel anak Betawi*. 8th ed. Jakarta: Balai Pustaka.
Aspinall, Edward. 2016. The new nationalism in Indonesia. *Asia & Pacific Policy Studies* 3(1). 72–82.
Aspinall, Edward & Greg Fealy (eds.). 2003. *Local power and politics in Indonesia: decentralisation and democratisation*. Singapore: Institute of Southeast Asian Studies.
Bauman, Richard & Charles Briggs. 1990. Poetics and performance as critical perspectives on language and social life. *Annual Review of Anthropology* 19. 59–88.
Bjork, Christopher. 2005. *Indonesian education: teachers, schools, and central bureaucracy*. New York: Routledge.
Blommaert, Jan. 2010. *The sociolinguistics of globalization*. Cambridge: Cambridge University Press.
Boellstorff, Tom. 2002. Ethnolocality. *The Asia Pacific Journal of Anthropology* 3(1). 24–48.
Bourdieu, Pierre. 1991. *Language and symbolic power*. Cambridge: Polity Press.
Dardjowidjojo, Soenjono. 1998. Strategies for a successful national language policy: the Indonesian case. *International Journal of the Sociology of Language* 130. 35–47.
Davidson, Jamie & David Henley (eds.). 2007. *The revival of tradition in Indonesian politics: the deployment of adat from colonialism to indigenism*. London: Routledge.
Dick, Howard (ed.). 2002. *The emergence of a national economy: an economic history of Indonesia, 1800–2000*. Crows Nest: Allen & Unwin.
Errington, Joseph. 1998. *Shifting languages: interaction and identity in Javanese Indonesia*. Cambridge: Cambridge University Press.
Errington, Joseph. 2001. Colonial linguistics. *Annual Review of Anthropology* 30. 19–39.
Feith, Herbert. 1962. *The decline of constitutional democracy in Indonesia*. New York: Cornell University Press.
Foucault, Michel. 1978. *The history of sexuality. Volume 1: an introduction*. New York: Pantheon Books.

Gal, Susan. 2012. Sociolinguistic regimes and the management of "diversity". In Monica Heller & Alexandre Duchêne (eds.), *Language in late capitalism: pride and profit*, 22–42. Hoboken: Routledge.

Garcia, Ofelia & Li Wei. 2014. *Translanguaging: language, bilingualism and education*. Basingstoke: Palgrave Macmillan.

Goebel, Zane. 2002. Code choice in inter-ethnic interactions in two urban neighbourhoods of Indonesia. *International Journal of the Sociology of Language* 158. 69–87.

Goebel, Zane. 2007. Enregisterment and appropriation in Javanese-Indonesian bilingual talk. *Language in Society* 36(4). 511–531.

Goebel, Zane. 2008. Enregistering, authorizing and denaturalizing identity in Indonesia. *Journal of Linguistic Anthropology* 18(1). 46–61.

Goebel, Zane. 2010. *Language, migration and identity: neighborhood talk in Indonesia*. Cambridge: Cambridge University Press.

Goebel, Zane. 2014. Doing leadership through signswitching in the Indonesian bureaucracy. *Journal of Linguistic Anthropology* 24(2). 193–215.

Goebel, Zane. 2015. *Language and superdiversity: Indonesians knowledging at home and abroad*. New York: Oxford University Press.

Goebel, Zane. 2018a. Language diversity and language change in Indonesia. In Robert W. Hefner (ed.), *Routledge handbook of contemporary Indonesia*, 378–389. New York: Routledge.

Goebel, Zane. 2018b. Reconfiguring the nation: re-territorialisation and the changing social value of ethnic languages in Indonesia. In Sjaak Kroon & Jos Swanenberg (eds.), *Language and culture on the margins: global/local interactions*, 27–52. New York: Routledge.

Goebel, Zane. 2019. Contact discourse. *Language in Society* 48(3). 331–351.

Goebel, Zane. 2020. *Global leadership talk: good governance in Javanese Indonesia*. New York: Oxford University Press.

Goebel, Zane, Deborah Cole & Howard Manns (eds.). 2020. *Contact talk: the discursive organization of contact and boundaries*. New York: Routledge.

Heller, Monica. 2007. Bilingualism as ideology and practice. In Monica Heller (ed.), *Bilingualism: a social approach*, 1–22. Basingstoke: Palgrave Macmillan.

Heller, Monica & Alexandre Duchêne (eds.). 2012. *Language in late capitalism: pride and profit*. Hoboken: Routledge.

Heller, Monica & Alexandre Duchêne. 2016. Treating language as an economic resource: discourse, data and debate. In Nikolas Coupland (ed.), *Sociolinguistics: theoretical debates*, 139–156. Cambridge: Cambridge University Press.

Heller, Monica, Lindsay Bell, Michelle Daveluy, Mireille McLaughlin & Hubert Noel. 2015. *Sustaining the nation: the making and moving of language and nation*. New York: Oxford University Press.

Holtzappel, Coen & Martin Ramstedt (eds.). 2009. *Decentralization and regional autonomy in Indonesia: implementation and challenges*. Singapore: Institute of Southeast Asian Studies/Leiden: International Institute for Asian Studies.

Jacob, June & Barbara Grimes. 2006. Developing a role for Kupang Malay: the contemporary politics of an Eastern Indonesian creole. Paper presented at 10th International Conference on Austronesian Linguistics, 19–20 January, Puerto Princesa City, Palawan, Philippines.

Jørgensen, Jens Normann, Martha Sif Karrebæk, Lian Malai Madsen & Janus Spindler Møller. 2011. Polylanguaging in superdiversity. *Diversities* 13(2). 22–37.

Karno, R. 1998. *Si Doel anak sekolah*. Jakarta: Karnog Film.

Kelly-Holmes, Helen. 2016. Theorising the market in sociolinguistics. In Nikolas Coupland (ed.), *Sociolinguistics: theoretical debates*, 157–172. Cambridge: Cambridge University Press.

Kitley, Philip. 2000. *Television, nation, and culture in Indonesia*. Athens: Ohio University Press.
Kuipers, Joel. 1998. *Language, identity and marginality in Indonesia: the changing nature of ritual speech on the island of Sumba*. Cambridge: Cambridge University Press.
Legge, John. 1961. *Central authority and regional autonomy in Indonesia: a study in local administration, 1950–1960*. Ithaca: Cornell Uiversity Press.
Lempert, Michael. 2014. Imitation. *Annual Review of Anthropology* 43. 379–395.
Liddle, R. William. 1972. Ethnicity and political organization: three East Sumatran cases. In Claire Holt (ed.), *Culture and politics in Indonesia*, 126–178. Ithaca: Cornell University Press.
Loven, Klarijn. 2008. *Watching Si Doel: television, language, and cultural identity in contemporary Indonesia*. Leiden: KITLV Press.
Moriyama, Mikihiro. 2005. *Sundanese print culture and modernity in nineteenth-century West Java*. Singapore: National University of Singapore Press.
Pennycook, Alastair & Emi Otsuji. 2015. *Metrolingualism: language in the city*. New York: Routledge.
Pietikäinen, Sari & Helen Kelly-Holmes (eds.). 2013. *Multilingualism and the periphery*. New York: Oxford University Press.
Pietikäinen, Sari, Helen Kelly-Holmes, Alexandra Jaffe & Nikolas Coupland. 2016. *Sociolinguistics from the periphery: small languages in new circumstances*. New York: Cambridge University Press.
Purdey, Jemma. 2006. *Anti-Chinese violence in Indonesia, 1996–1999*. Singapore: National University of Singapore Press.
Silverstein, Michael. 2003. Indexical order and the dialectics of sociolinguistic life. *Language and Communication* 23. 193–229.
Sneddon, James. 2003. *The Indonesian language: its history and role in modern society*. Sydney: University of New South Wales Press.
Wallerstein, Immanuel. 2004. *World-systems analysis: an introduction*. Durham: Duke University Press.
Woolard, Kathryn A. 1998. Introduction: language ideology as a field of inquiry. In Bambi B. Schieffelin, Kathryn A. Woolard & Paul V. Kroskrity (eds.), *Language ideologies: practice and theory*, 3–47. New York: Oxford University Press.

Francesco Goglia
4 Multilingualism in Padua (Italy): The linguistic landscape of an emerging multiethnic neighbourhood

1 Introduction

In the last 20 years, the number of immigrants in Italy has rapidly increased. In 2003, immigrants numbered around one and a half million; by January 2015, their numbers had risen to more than five million (Caritas and Fondazione Migrantes 2015). This sudden increase has led to the emergence of significant linguistic and cultural diversity in specific parts of urban centres, where immigration has had a greater impact than elsewhere. The Veneto region, because of its job opportunities, is among the Italian regions with the largest number of immigrants.[1] In the city of Padua immigrants represent about 15% of the total population of 210,440 (Nalon and Foresta 2018). It is thus an ideal location in which to investigate the emergence of multilingualism involving immigrant languages and, in particular, its impact on the linguistic landscape (LL) of the city. In this chapter, I will focus on the LL of Padua's railway station neighbourhood, where a large number of immigrants have settled and opened shops and businesses in the past 20 years.

Padua has a large and well-known university and is a major financial and economic centre in the Veneto region. The railway station is an important junction in the Italian rail network along main routes, such as the Venice-Rome and the Venice-Milan lines. The traditional sociolinguistic situation of the city is one of de facto bilingualism with Italian as the only official (national) language and the local Veneto dialect[2] widely used in everyday communication. Since 2014, the Padua city council, in line with other city councils in Italy, has required that advertising messages and shop signs in foreign languages show the Italian translation and that the translation be easily recognisable to Italian-speaking customers (Comune di Padova 2014: Article 26). This by-law was promulgated by anti-immigration political parties, which are very strong in the Veneto region and in the city of Padua. The largest

---

[1] The term 'immigrant' (and thus the numbers listed in this chapter) may also include the second-generation, as children of immigrants, even if born in Italy, can only apply for Italian citizenship when they are 18.
[2] The Italian dialects, like Italian (Tuscan), are also derived from Vulgar Latin, but today they are not official or fully standardised. Depending on the region, some dialects are still widely used in everyday communication.

immigrant communities in Padua are shown in descending order in Table 1. Some of these communities, for example the Nigerian, Chinese and Moroccan, began to arrive in the early 1990s, others in the 2000s.

Table 1: The largest immigrant communities in Padua by country of origin (Nalon and Foresta 2018).

	Country	No.		Country	No.
1	Romania	9,333	8	Bangladesh	1,338
2	Moldova	4,010	9	Sri Lanka	897
3	China	2,872	10	Ukraine	802
4	Nigeria	2,622	11	Tunisia	486
5	Philippines	1,876	12	Pakistan	484
6	Morocco	1,815	13	India	448
7	Albania	1,418	14	Cameroon	441

Immigrants live in all six city districts (*quartieri*) into which the city is subdivided. The demographic situation of immigrant communities in Padua does not provide a clear picture of the languages they speak. Neither the Italian national census nor Padua city council statistics has data on the languages of immigrants. Focusing on the first eight nationalities in Table 1, we can assume that the most commonly spoken languages are Romanian, Moldovan, Chinese, Nigerian English/ Nigerian Pidgin English, Tagalog, Moroccan Arabic (and Berber), Albanian, and Bengali. The case of Nigerians, for example, is particularly complex as they are not a homogenous group. Individuals of this immigrant group may belong to different ethnic, religious and linguistic subgroups. In Padua, Nigerians are mainly Yoruba, Edo and Igbo who also speak English and Pidgin English as lingua francas for interethnic communication among Nigerians and other English-speaking African immigrants (Goglia 2011; 2015).

2 Railway station neighbourhood: Background

The multiethnic neighbourhood that I have chosen to focus on incorporates parts of two city districts: part of the residential *quartiere Nord,* and the neighbouring *quartiere Centro* where the main shopping area and the old city are located. Although very central, this area around the station has been neglected and abandoned by local inhabitants and shopkeepers over recent decades – a phenomenon also common to other Italian cities. From the 1990s onwards, immigrant entrepreneurs have bought properties in the area at affordable prices and started opening businesses (grocery stores, hairdressers, etc.) for a largely immigrant clientele, first north of the station and later also south of it. The inhabitants of Padua and local media label this area as the *quartiere etnico*, 'the ethnic quarter'. The businesses owned and/or managed by immigrants, and the open spaces near them (pavements, small squares and parks) also function as meeting places for certain immigrant groups, particularly first-generation male migrants. A subway below the railway station links the two parts of the multiethnic neighbourhood. While the station itself is at its centre, with its mainstream shops and services it is an altogether different world compared to the rest of the neighbourhood. Commuters and tourists mainly head for the city centre via *Corso del Popolo*, a long avenue that links the station to the historical city centre (see also Figure 1). Given the proximity to the railway station and the adjacent public transport (buses, the tram and the coach station), the surveyed area is also frequented by immigrants who come from other parts of Padua or from outside Padua to do their shopping or to meet friends from the same countries of origin.

Table 2 provides an overview of the nationalities of the immigrant population in the two city districts where the multiethnic neighbourhood lies. We can see that over 40% of Romanians, Nigerians, Chinese, and Filipinos in the city of Padua live in these two districts.

Table 2: The distribution of immigrant nationalities in Padua as a proportion of overall individual community size in the Centro and Nord city districts (Nalon and Foresta 2018).

	Centro	Nord
Romania	6%	34%
Moldova	6%	28%
China	17%	40%
Nigeria	3%	38%
Philippines	16%	25%
Morocco	6%	24%
Albania	10%	20%
Bangladesh	7%	67%
Ukraine	15%	20%
Other	16%	28%
Total in Padua	10%	32%

3 The study of the linguistic landscape (LL)

Landry and Bourhis initially defined linguistic landscape research as the study of "the visibility and salience of languages on public and commercial signs in a given territory or region" (1997: 23). The LL of a given area comprises both "private" – commercial signs on storefronts, advertising billboards – and "government" signs – public signs used by municipal and government bodies (Landry and Bourhis 1997). The former are also referred to as bottom-up and the latter as top-down signs by Ben-Rafael et al. (2006: 10). Landry and Bourhis (1997: 28) maintain that private signs are more revealing of the linguistic diversity of a particular area but also of the power relations and the ethnolinguistic vitality of the linguistic communities in the given territory. Later studies, particularly studies of multiethnic neighbourhoods, have demonstrated that the relationship between the visibility of a language in public space and its ethnolinguistic vitality is not straightforward but rather complex and dynamic, depending on a variety of social and linguistic factors (Ben-Rafael et al. 2006; Barni and Bagna 2015). Social factors may include the power relations between dominant and subordinate groups, the drive of a particular community to present itself in the LL with its identity markers (including languages), and the choices of the individuals who produce the signs in order to include/exclude a particular audience (Ben Rafael et al. 2006). Linguistic factors may include the hierarchy of languages and issues of prestige in the linguistic repertoires of immigrant communities, the presence of products and cultural items for which there is no translation, and the use of lingua francas. Cenoz and Gorter (2006: 67–68) see LL as linked to the specific sociolinguistic context because LL may both reflect the use of languages in the social world and influence the speakers' perception of the languages used in the signs and linguistic practices. Recent trends in LL research have extended the analysis of the LL to non-linguistic signs such as visual images, colours, icons and the built environment, as these signifiers contribute to the construction of the public space (Jaworski and Thurlow 2010: 2). Additionally, the role of those involved in the production or consumption of signs has been investigated via ethnographic approaches, including interviews with the authors of the signs and observation (Barni and Bagna 2015: 7). I will draw on these recent research approaches for the analysis of multilingualism in the LL of the emerging multiethnic neighbourhood around the Padua railway station. The specific research questions of this study are the following:
(1) What languages are visible in the LL of the neighbourhood?
(2) What factors influence the visibility of immigrant languages?
(3) What functions do particular languages have on the signs?

Before explaining the methodology and presenting the data in section 5, I will briefly review the existing literature on the LL of multiethnic neighbourhoods in Italy that has informed this study.

4 Linguistic landscape studies of Italian multiethnic neighbourhoods

The literature on the LL of multiethnic neighbourhoods of Italian cities includes studies that have investigated different linguistic and extra-linguistic factors influencing the presence of immigrant languages in the LL.

The first major study on immigrant languages and their presence in the Italian LL was conducted by Barni and Bagna (2006; 2010) on the visibility and vitality of immigrant languages in the *Esquilino* neighbourhood near Rome's central railway station. This research not only gathered a large amount of quantitative data due to the innovative use of georeferencing software, but also allowed for the comparison of data over time. The study of *Esquilino* revealed the presence of 24 languages, but the highest occurrences of signs were in Chinese, Italian as a local lingua franca and English as the lingua franca for many south-Asian immigrants present in the area, where they dominate small trade. It also showed that languages of large immigrant communities in *Esquilino*, such as Filipinos, Romanians and Poles, were not visible in the LL. The authors maintain that the absence of these languages was because members of these communities are mainly working as housekeepers and caretakers rather than entrepreneurs. In 2010, the same researchers conducted a follow-up study of the *Esquilino* neighbourhood. The results, reported in Barni and Vedovelli (2012), showed a decrease in the visibility of immigrant languages and an increase in bilingual signs, with Italian and immigrant languages present on shop signs in the neighbourhood due to the implementation of a local by-law requiring the use of Italian on all multilingual signs.

Minuz and Forconi (2018) focused on the LL of *Bolognina*, a multiethnic neighbourhood in Bologna. The aim of this study was twofold. Firstly, it mapped the LL of the neighbourhood and found Chinese to be the most visible immigrant language, in line with Barni and Vedovelli (2012). Furthermore, the study found that bilingual signs displaying immigrant languages and Italian are more frequent due to the local council language policy requiring foreign language signs to provide an Italian translation. Secondly, using focus groups and interviews, the study investigated how residents, members of associations and other stakeholders perceived the neighbourhood, as well as their attitudes towards immigrant languages in the LL. Whilst the neighbourhood was perceived by some as a Chinatown because of Chinese signs and shops, for other participants in the study the LL was not the main component in their perception of multiculturalism; instead, it was mostly linked to the presence of immigrants, immigrant-owned shops, colours, smells and clothing (Minuz and Forconi 2018: 269).

In a study on two multiethnic neighbourhoods in Milan (*Baggio* and *Giambellino*), Uberti-Bona (2016) offered an analysis of shop signs, including Spanish and Arabic, two of the most widely represented immigrant languages in the neighbourhoods, in combination with Italian. This study found that signs are either in Italian only or in Arabic/Spanish only. Contrary to the cases discussed in Barni and Vedovelli (2012) and Minuz and Forconi (2018), Italian translation of the signs in immigrant languages was nearly always absent despite Milan city council's by-law mandating the provision of an Italian translation.

All recent studies have shown the high visibility of signs in Chinese in multiethnic neighbourhoods in Italy. Desoutter and Gottardo (2016) focused on the Chinatown in Milan. They adopted an ethnographic approach, interviewing the authors of the signs, and offered, for the first time, an analysis of the signs in Chinese produced by Italian people and businesses, in addition to those produced by members of the Chinese community. They found that Italian shopkeepers use Chinese signs for two main reasons: to attract Chinese customers and to symbolically reinforce the identity of the local Chinatown.

5 Methodology

The selection of the area for data collection must be driven by the purpose of the study (Huebner 2009). As the area around the railway station has seen an increase in the presence of immigrants' shops over the last few decades, it is therefore an ideal setting in which to investigate the visibility of immigrant languages in the LL. North of the station the first immigrants' shops started appearing at the end of the 1990s, while they later expanded south of the station into the side streets off *Corso del Popolo*, which as previously noted is the main avenue that links the railway station to the city centre (see Figure 1).

Following Backhaus' definition, in this study, a sign is "text within a spatially identifiable frame" (2007: 66). The analysis that follows is both quantitative and qualitative. I will first present the quantitative results (the number of visible languages, and their frequency in monolingual and multilingual signs) before providing a qualitative analysis of a selection of signs in an attempt to identify the linguistic and extra-linguistic factors that are linked to a particular use of the language(s) on a sign. In this study, the unit of analysis for the quantitative overview is the individual sign, including store name, advertising posters and any information notices. However, for the qualitative analysis, I took a more holistic approach with the whole shop front as the main analytical object. This distinction allowed me to account for individual factors influencing the use of languages in each sign without ignoring any connections between several signs in the same shop front. In July 2018, I photographed 297 signs in all immigrants' shops in the selected area.

I will also draw on local demographic information and my own knowledge of the area where, through the years, I have conducted fieldwork in immigrant shops for other projects.

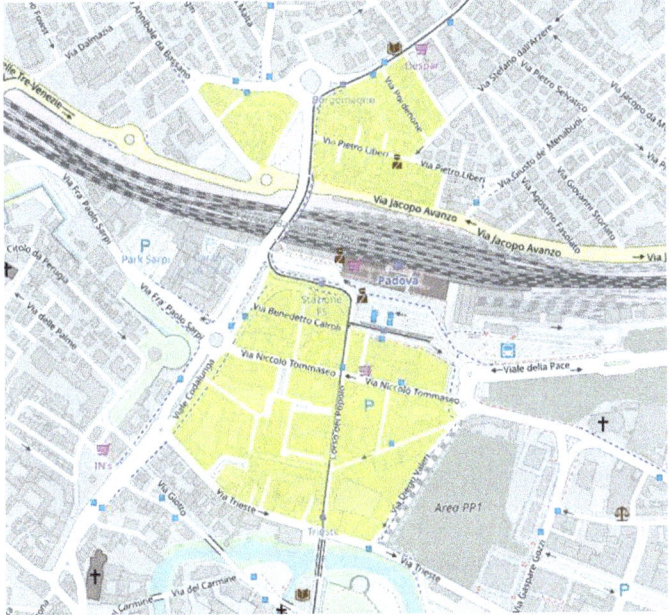

Figure 1: Map of the railway station area of Padua, surveyed area in green (map data Google © 2019).

6 Findings

The corpus is mainly composed of private signs of a wide variety of types: name-bearing signboards above a store entrance, advertising posters on the shop front, handwritten messages, menus, and lists of services provided. Some government signs were also collected: public administration signs reading "no smoking" and "no alcohol consumption", which some shopkeepers choose to display.

A comprehensive list of the languages displayed in the corpus of photographs includes 16 languages: Albanian, Arabic, Bengali, Chinese, Serbian/Croatian, English, French, German, Hindi, Italian, Romanian, Russian, Spanish, Tagalog, Tamil and Urdu. All these languages were publicly visible from the sidewalk. The number of occurrences and the patterns of representation of the languages in multilingual signs also varies. For example, Chinese is highly visible in the linguistic landscape, appearing in a wide range of signs (shop names, posters, hand-written notices), both monolingual and multilingual, while Urdu appears only once in a monolingual handwritten notice. Most signs were monolingual (208, 70%), while the rest were multilingual with two languages (80), three languages (3), four languages (5) or five languages (1). Table 3 summarises the use of languages in the monolingual and multilingual signs, in descending order of appearance in multilingual signs.

Table 3: Languages used on monolingual, bilingual and multilingual signs.

Monolingual (208)	Bilingual (80)	Multilingual (9)
Italian (112)	Chinese-Italian (32)	*Trilingual (3)*
Chinese (42)	Italian-Chinese (10)	Italian-English-Chinese (2)
English (30)	Italian-English (7)	Chinese-Italian-English (1)
Romanian (8)	English-Bengali (6)	
Arabic (6)	Italian-Arabic (5)	*Quadrilingual (5)*
Bengali (3)	Bengali-English (4)	English-Italian-French-Chinese (2)
Albanian (1)	Chinese-English (4)	Italian-English-German-French (2)
Serbian/Croatian (1)	Arabic-English (3)	Arabic-Italian-French-English (1)
French (1)	English-Italian (3)	
Hindi (1)	Arabic-Italian (1)	*Pentalingual (1)*
Russian (1)	Bengali-Italian (1)	Chinese-English-Italian-French-Spanish (1)
Tamil (1)	English-Hindi (1)	
Urdu (1)	Romanian-Italian (1)	
	Tagalog-English (1)	

In the next sections, I will discuss the use of languages on the signs of my corpus. First, I will discuss the dominance of Italian, then the use of Chinese and English, and finally summarise occurrences in other languages.

6.1 Signs in Italian

Italian on monolingual signs is the most frequently visible language (112) on shop fronts. This is not surprising given that Italian is both the only official language and the lingua franca used by immigrants in cross-group communications. Customers who do not belong to the immigrant group of a particular shop are addressed in Italian if they do not share any other language(s) (my longstanding observation based on previous fieldwork in the neighbourhood; cf. also Blommaert (2013) and Blommaert and Maly (2016) for the use of Dutch in ethnic neighbourhoods in Antwerp and Ghent and Lipovsky (2019) for the use of French in the Parisian neighbourhood of Belleville). Italian is also used in code-switching in communication between customers of the same immigrant groups (my own observation in Nigerian and Bangladeshi shops in the surveyed area).

Italian is also very present on bilingual signs (61), both as a more visible language (26) and as a secondary language (43). The local language policy, which requires the use of Italian together with any foreign languages, helps to explain this finding. A similar dominance of Italian in multilingual signs, together with a smaller number of monolingual signs in immigrant languages, was observed in other studies as a result of local council requirements in favour of a mandatory Italian translation (Barni and Vedovelli 2012; Minuz and Forconi 2018).

Another factor that may have inflated the number of Italian signs is the availability of standard signs in Italian (as well as hand-made replicas of them), such as those forbidding smoking, alcohol consumption or the entry of dogs, or open/closed signs. These signs are not compulsory, but they are ready-made, and shopkeepers may choose to display them.

A small number of signs in Italian are written by shopkeepers. Figure 2, for example, shows a notice in Italian produced by a Bangladeshi owner of a grocery shop: *perfavore non lasciate botteglie in perchiggio* [sic] (standard Italian: *per favore non lasciate bottiglie nel parcheggio*) 'please do not leave bottles in the car park' with errors that reveal that a non-native speaker wrote it.

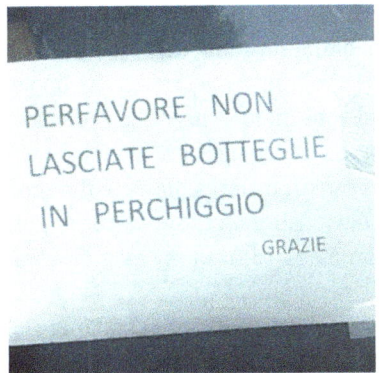

Figure 2: Notice in Italian L2 (Photo: Francesco Goglia).

6.2 Signs in Chinese

Chinese is the second most frequently visible language, appearing on 45 monolingual signs and 46 bilingual signs (32 times as the first/dominant language).[3] This finding is in line with other Italian studies (cf., Barni and Bagna 2006; 2010; Barni and Vedovelli 2012; Minuz and Forconi 2018). In the last decade, an increasing number of Chinese businesses have opened in the area around Padua's railway station, particularly grocery shops, hair salons and beauty shops, photography and electronics shops. The Chinese community is growing and settling permanently in the area. Chinese immigrants are the most numerous foreign entrepreneurs in Padua, mainly in retail and manufacturing (Nalon and Foresta 2018), and are the largest immigrant community in the two administrative suburbs in which the surveyed area lies (see Table 2). In the surveyed area, Chinese has an informational rather than symbolic function for the Chinese community, as is the case in more well-established Chinatowns where Chinese signs contribute to selling the neighbourhood as a tourist destination (Lou 2010; Amos 2016). A shop front in a side street off *Corso del Popolo* can serve as an example. The name of the shop, written only in Chinese, 鹏达肉食品店, 'Peng Da meat food store' in the traditionally auspicious red colour, appears prominently in the shop window. There is no Italian counterpart for the name of the shop, so non-readers of Chinese do not know what to expect and are not the intended clientele. Moveover, the sign is not in line with the local by-law on the use of foreign languages on messages and shop signs (see introduction). All other signs in the front window are only in Italian: the standard opening hours and the open/closed signs and two signs on alcohol consumption: *vietato consumare alcool davanti al negozio* 'it is forbidden to drink alcohol in front of the shop' and *non vendiamo e non serviamo alcolici ai minori di 18 anni* 'we do not sell and serve alcoholic drinks to anyone under the age of 18'. The latter two signs are photocopies of standard signs, which reveal communication with non-Chinese speakers. These signs are found on many other shop fronts; they reflect the implementation of a locally mandated ban on alcohol consumption near shop premises and in particular on the selling of alcohol to minors. These signs are intended both as a warning to the immigrant men who congregate in the area opposite the shop and may potentially consume alcohol, and as a demonstration to Padua authorities of compliance with the local by-law (information obtained from my own observation and questions directed to shopkeepers).

---

[3] I am grateful to my colleague Dr Yue Zhuang for her help in translating and interpreting the meanings of the Chinese signs in my corpus.

The shops along *Corso del Popolo*, the main walking and public transport route from the railway station to the historic city centre, display more bilingual signs, clearly targeting a wider clientele, as is the case for the electronics shop in Figure 3. The name of the shop is provided in both Chinese and Italian; the Chinese 梦想科技, 'dream technology', appears on top between two icons, a PC and an electron orbit, also indexing the type of shop, while the Italian translation of the shop name, *La Tecnologia dei Sogni*, appears in the centre in a larger print size. Below the name of the shop, a list of the services offered appears in Italian in capital letters but in smaller font: *vendita cellulari, accessori & computer; riparazione cellulari e PC;* 'mobile phones, accessories & computers sold here; mobile phone and PC repair'.

Figure 3: Chinese electronic shop (Photo: Francesco Goglia).

In some shops, mainly restaurants, Chinese identity may also be indexed via the shop name and images on the shop front, as is the case for the restaurant in Figure 4. Its name, 外婆家, 'grandmother's home', in the traditional Chinese red colour, appears first in a circle in traditional calligraphy style, then in Chinese writing followed by the Italian *Ristorante Waipojia* 'Waipojia restaurant' i.e. the transliteration of the Chinese name. The ideogram for 'maternal grandmother' reveals a particular Chinese regional identity, as it is used only in southeastern China (Yue Zhuang, personal communication). Drawings on the top left and top right show lotuses painted using traditional Chinese techniques and traditional southeastern Chinese vernacular architecture. The restaurant name and the drawings aim to evoke the idea of southern Chinese homemade food, targeting the Chinese community in Padua, mainly from the southeast. Two laminated coloured posters with images of dishes served in the restaurant appear in the shop window. The image in the left window advertises Chinese breakfast with a text in Chinese and in Italian: *colazione aperto 8.00*, 'breakfast open 8 am'.

Figure 4: Chinese restaurant (Photo: Francesco Goglia).

The image in the poster is unlikely to target Italian customers, who are used to a quick on-the-go breakfast with cappuccino and a croissant. Similar posters are displayed in the Chinatown in Milan, which has many second-generation Italian-Chinese residents, and where Chinese breakfast may be more popular. The poster thus appears to be imported from a more established bilingual and bicultural Chinatown.

Some Chinese shops also target other immigrant groups as potential customers, as is the case for the following example. The name of the shop in Chinese, 中非食品店, 'Chinese and African food store', appears both in the middle of the shop window in red and on the side in the traditional vertical writing. Below the Chinese, in red capital letters, is the translation in English – *Cina & Africa Market* – with Italian spelling used for China. In this example, the shop owner chooses to use English to attract English-speaking African immigrants, in particular Nigerian customers, who are numerous in the area. This use of English exemplifies the good-reasons principle, the rational consideration of alternative languages by LL stakeholders to attract potential clients (Ben-Rafael et al. 2006; Cenoz and Gorter 2009).

Desoutter and Gottardo (2016) found several instances of commercial signs in Chinese produced by Italian companies and businesses in the Chinatown in Milan, which has a more established economy targeting the Chinese-speaking residents of the area. In the Padua corpus, however, there was only one commercial sign from an Italian company that included Chinese, namely an advertisement in Italian, English and Chinese by the telecommunications company *Wind*.

6.3 Signs in English

The third most visible language in the corpus is English, present in 30 monolingual and 29 bilingual signs. We need to distinguish between signs with English as an international lingua franca already widely present in commercial signs (for example, advertising by Italian companies) and signs with English as an immigrant lingua franca, produced by English-speaking immigrants such as Nigerians to communicate with members of their community or other English-speaking African immigrants.

Typical examples of the use of international English are internet points and money transfer agencies. On their shopfronts, both Italian and English are used to advertise services (international money transfer, internet access, printing facilities, and flight booking), aimed at all immigrants (see Blommaert (2013) and Maly (2016) for a discussion of similar shop fronts in Antwerp and Ostend).

Signs with English as an immigrant lingua franca are produced by immigrants from English-speaking countries such as Nigeria. There are several Nigerian shops in the surveyed area and they were among the first to appear in the neighbourhood, particularly north of the station. I am very familiar with these grocery shops as I conducted previous research in these sites and I still regularly visit them. They are all run by Igbo shop owners but target all Nigerians and other African customers as well. They are more than just grocery shops, and function as meeting points for the Nigerian community, where Nigerians can chat over a beer or seek advice on work and Italian legal documents. Although Igbo and other Nigerian languages are widely used by Nigerian immigrants in Italy, I did not find any signs in these languages in the surveyed area. The sole presence of English in the LL of these shop fronts reflects its use as the lingua franca and main written language by Nigerians and other African English-speaking immigrants (Goglia 2015; 2018).

Figure 5 shows a notice in English only, written by the shopkeeper of a Nigerian shop north of the railway station: "Due to August holidays, this shop will remain closed from 9.00 am to 2.00 pm from Monday 21st till further notice".

Figure 5: Notice in English on the shop front of a Nigerian shop (Photo: Francesco Goglia).

Figure 6 shows the entrance of another Nigerian shop with signs in Italian and English. The name of the shop, *Adonai*, 'my Lord', a Hebrew-origin English word widely used by Nigerians, appears at the top of the shop front in large-sized capital letters. Below and in smaller writing, the subtext specifies the type of shop: *African store, boutique, alimentari & non-alimentari*, 'African store, boutique, food and non-food goods'. The majority of words and the syntax are English, with two insertions of the Italian word *alimentari*, 'food'; in the second instance, this word is used with the English prefix *non-*. The shop name and the subtext *African store* index the Nigerian community and are used without translation into Italian. There are other signs in the shop window: a standard notice in Italian stating that no alcohol will be sold to anyone below the age of 18 and a notice produced by the shopkeeper in both Italian and English about the consumption of food and drink on the shop premises (see above for other examples of such signs). Two posters are in English: one advertises services for immigrants (translations, photocopies, etc.), the other a Pentecostal religious event taking place in Padua. Both posters target the Nigerian and other African customers of the shop. To the left of the door, there are two more posters. One advertises a concert by Nigerian singer Rude Boy in Padua, reflecting the presence of the large and deep-rooted Nigerian community in the city which is able to organise and provide an audience for such an event in a local stadium. The second poster announces the 15th anniversary celebration of a Nigerian couple. As noted previously, Nigerian languages such as Igbo, Yoruba and Edo are completely absent from the LL of the neighbourhood, and the Nigerian identity in the immigrant context is indexed via English as a pan-Nigerian language (Goglia 2015).

Figure 6: Nigerian shop front window (Photo: Francesco Goglia).

All posters on the shop front door and the side column of the Nigerian shop discussed above advertise either cultural or community events related to the life of Nigerian immigrants in Padua.

6.4 Other immigrant languages

This section discusses Arabic, Romanian and Bengali, the three languages with some visibility in Padua's LL, and considers the absence of languages one would expect to be present based on population numbers (see Table 1).

Arabic follows Italian, Chinese and English as the most visible language in both monolingual (6) and multilingual signs (10) in combination with Italian (see Table 3). Arabic is displayed mainly on the shop fronts of Moroccan and Bangladeshi grocery shops and is used in the name of the shop and on the bilingual *halal* sign noting the selling of food prepared according to the tenets of the Quran. On bilingual signs, the most frequent pattern shows the Italian translation displayed side by side with the text in Arabic. The front window of a Moroccan butcher's shop uses both Arabic and English; the Arabic sign 'Halal butchery' is written on a picture showing different kinds of meat in the top left-hand corner of the shop front, and next to it, the name of the shop, *Padova market*, is partly in English with English syntax and occupies a larger area. The text is in black on a white background with red and green at the sides and on the bottom, mimicking the Italian flag. The name of the shop does not provide the exact translation of the Arabic but instead complements it. Overall, the Arabic sign attracts a Muslim clientele, while the name of the city together with the colours of the flag indicate "Italianness", thereby welcoming Italian customers as well. The word 'market' is widely used in shop names in Italy and particularly in immigrant shops.

The visibility of Arabic is not high despite Moroccans forming the sixth largest immigrant community in the city and given that another relatively large immigrant group, Tunisians, also speaks Arabic. In her study on Belleville in Paris, Lipovsky (2019) found that Arabic was never used there in monolingual signs on any shop fronts but was always used in combination with French and English. The presence of monolingual signs in Arabic in Padua is due to the more recent immigration of Moroccans and Tunisians, who are not always fluent in French. It is worth noting here that I did not find any instances of French text on Maghrebi or North African shop fronts, so French does not seem to act as a lingua franca within the community, which is mainly composed of Arabic and Berber speakers.

Romanian appears on only eight monolingual signs. The small number is quite striking given that Romanians and Moldovans, who share the same language, are the two largest immigrant communities in Padua. Barni and Bagna

(2010) found a similar result in their LL study on neighbourhoods in and around Rome and Florence, where Romanians also represented one of the largest immigrant communities at the time of their research (see also Minuz and Forconi 2018). The authors explained the low number of signs in Romanian with the non-retail orientation of the group, but they also found that the lack of visibility of Romanian in the LL did not mean lack of use and maintenance of the language among Romanian families. In Padua, Romanians and Moldovans were among the first foreign entrepreneurs, but they are involved more in the manufacturing and construction sectors and less in retail (Redivo 2018: 186). Romanian appears on windows of grocery shops and travel agencies. Figure 7 shows the front windows of a Romanian grocer. The name of the shop *Magazin Alimentar*, 'food store' is in Romanian only, in breach of the Padua council by-law. As these shops often sell Eastern European products, they target, as the sign on the right window reads, *moldovenesc, rusesc, ucrainesc*, 'Moldovans, Russians, and Ukrainians'. Smaller signs on the window are standard government signs in Italian (no smoking, no alcohol sold to anyone under 18 years of age, no dogs allowed), but two are in Romanian: one is a travel advert for a van service from Italy to Moldova, the other is a bilingual notice in Romanian (top) and Italian (bottom) asking customers not to drink alcoholic beverages on the premises. The shopkeeper's choice to display a translation in Romanian seeks to maximise the exposure of Romanian-speaking customers to the local ban on alcohol consumption.

Figure 7: Romanian shop front (Photo: Francesco Goglia).

Bengali is used in three monolingual signs, in ten bilingual signs with English and only once with Italian (see Table 3). More than two-thirds of Padua Bangladeshis reside in the *quartiere Nord* (see Table 2), the northern area of the surveyed area. Figure 8 shows the front of a Bengali grocery shop north of the railway station. There are three signs in Bengali on the shop window: the first is a poster advertising the Bengali brand *Tatka* selling frozen fish, the second a hand-written notice produced by the shopkeeper listing the vegetables sold in the shop and their prices, and the third a poster advertising a trip to Geneva from Padua for the Bangladeshi community. Although they are of different kinds and material, the three signs index the presence of the Bangladeshi community.

Figure 8: Bangladeshi shop front (Photo: Francesco Goglia).

English was also found on this shop window. At the top is an advertisement for a Bangladeshi product, *frooto* drink, that states *iftar time, frooto time*. *Iftar* is the evening meal with which Muslims end their daily Ramadan fast at sunset. The advert at the bottom in the same window is for a frozen foods company. These posters, imported from Bangladesh, replicate the LL of grocery shops in Bangladesh with their bilingual use of English and Bengali.

The lack of visibility in the public space of signs in Albanian (only one), Tagalog (only one), Tamil (only one) and Ukrainian (none) is striking, as these communities are highly represented in the surveyed neighbourhood. In Padua, Filipinos, Sri Lankans and Ukrainians are mainly employed in the domestic sector and as caregivers (with a very high proportion of women) and tend not to be entrepreneurs and shopkeepers (Redivo 2018: 180; cf. Barni and Bagna 2006). Meanwhile, Albanians (like the Romanians mentioned earlier) were among the first foreign entrepreneurs in Padua, although not in retail and services. In much the way that the Romanian shop front in Figure 7 also targeted Moldovans, Russians and Ukrainians, some Chinese shops also sell Filipino products. The only sign in Tagalog in the corpus was found on the front door of a Chinese grocery shop, confirming that Chinese urban spaces often serve "as multi-ethnic, multilingual hubs for Chinese immigrants and for other Asian immigrants as well" (De Klerk and Wiley 2010: 309).

7 Conclusion

This chapter focused on the LL of Padua's multiethnic neighbourhood located around the railway station to the north of the city centre. Quantitative data were used to obtain an overall picture of the visible languages in the surveyed area; I then focused on a qualitative discussion of some shop-front signs to understand the function of particular immigrant languages and which linguistic and extra-linguistic factors may have contributed to such uses. To do so, I have made use of Padua city council statistics on immigrant communities in the city, for example, information on a particular community in relation to the surveyed area and main occupations. The results of this study have provided an initial picture of the visibility of immigrant languages in a relatively new and expanding multiethnic neighbourhood.

Findings show the prominence of Italian in both monolingual and multilingual signs. This reflects the fact that Italian is a lingua franca used by immigrants, both in communication with Italians and with immigrants from different countries. Indeed, the use of Italian in some notices (such as the message in Figure 2) revealed the appropriation of the language by immigrants to communicate with customers or passers-by. The high number of signs in Italian is also linked to the status of Italian as the sole official language, imposed at the local level via the by-law on advertising (cf. Barni and Vedovelli 2012; Minuz and Forconi 2018). Despite this legal requirement, immigrant languages are still visible both in monolingual signs and in bilingual signs with a language other than Italian. The quantitative results have shown that, apart from Italian, the most visible languages in the surveyed area are Chinese, English, Romanian, Arabic and Bengali. Chinese is the second most visible language in the neighbourhood, where a new Chinatown is emerging. Shops along the more affluent *Corso del Popolo* that offer services to a wider clientele, including Italians, show more adherence to the local language policy, with all signs, including the name of the shop, provided in both the immigrant language and Italian. In more secluded side streets, shops are more in-group focused and in breach of the requirement to translate all messages into Italian. In these shops, signs in immigrant languages are mainly informational as the shops function as hubs for first-generation immigrants who not only buy products but also exchange information. The results have revealed that (Igbo-run) Nigerian shops make exclusive use of English as a pan-Nigerian language. This explains why, although widely used in oral communication, Nigerian languages such as Igbo and Yoruba are completely absent in the LL of Padua. English may also be used for inter-group communication; for example, Nigerian shops also reach other English-speaking African communities in Padua such as Ghanaians and Cameroonians. Signs in English as an international lingua franca are a minority compared to signs in English as an immigrant lingua franca, and only appear on shop fronts of internet points and money transfer agencies, which target all immigrants. These results are different from previous research in Strasbourg and Paris, which showed that the use of English mainly indicates a global culture and is used to communicate with tourists (Bogatto and Hélot 2010; Lipovsky 2019). A possible explanation for this could be the presence of a large, well-established Nigerian community and the non-tourist focus of the area. Little attention has been given so far to the role of English as an immigrant language in the LL of multiethnic neighbourhoods in Italy (cf. Barni and Bagna 2006).

Arabic, Romanian and Bengali signs can be found respectively in Moroccan, Romanian and Bangladeshi grocery shops on both monolingual and bilingual signs. Other immigrant languages are either not visible or only used in few instances, even if they are spoken by sizable communities in the neighbourhood. This absence may be because some immigrant groups are involved in domestic work rather than retail, as is the case of Filipino and Ukrainian immigrants (Barni and Bagna 2006), or they may do their shopping in other immigrant groups' shops. Some shop signs suggest the presence of other immigrant groups as customers.

This initial discussion on the LL of an emergent multiethnic neighbourhood in Padua has revealed the main factors that are contributing to the LL of the area: the local language policy, the use of lingua francas, the strategic choice of language(s) by shopkeepers to address a particular clientele, and the retail behaviours of certain immigrant groups. Further research, including ethnographic observation and interviews or focus groups with shop owners and other residents of the area, would be necessary to gain a deeper understanding of the LL of the city.

References

Amos, William. 2016. Chinatown by numbers: defining an ethnic space by empirical linguistic landscape. *Linguistic Landscape* 2(2). 127–156.

Backhaus, Peter. 2007. *Linguistic landscapes: a comparative study of urban multilingualism in Tokyo.* Clevedon: Multilingual Matters.

Barni, Monica & Carla Bagna. 2006. Per una mappatura dei repertori linguistici urbani: nuovi strumenti e metodologie. In Nicola De Blasi & Carla Marcato (eds.), *La città e le sue lingue: repertori linguistici urbani*, 1–43. Naples: Liguori Editore.

Barni, Monica & Carla Bagna. 2010. Linguistic landscape and language vitality. In Elana Shohamy, Eliezer Ben-Rafael & Monica Barni (eds.), *Linguistic landscape in the city*, 3–18. Bristol: Multilingual Matters.

Barni, Monica & Carla Bagna. 2015. The critical turn in LL: new methodologies and new items in LL. *Linguistic Landscape* 1(1/2). 6–18.

Barni, Monica & Massimo Vedovelli. 2012. Linguistic landscape and language policies. In Christine Hélot, Monica Barni, Rudi Janssens & Carla Bagna (eds.), *Linguistic landscape, multilingualism and social change*, 27–38. Bern: Peter Lang.

Ben-Rafael, Eliezer, Elana Shohamy, Muhammad Hasan Amara & Nira Trumper-Hecht. 2006. Linguistic landscape as symbolic construction of the public space: the case of Israel. *International Journal of Multilingualism* 3(1). 7–28.

Blommaert, Jan. 2013. *Ethnography, superdiversity and linguistic landscapes: chronicles of complexity.* Bristol: Multilingual Matters.

Blommaert, Jan & Ico Maly. 2016. Ethnographic linguistic landscape analysis and social change: a case study. In Karel Arnaut, Jan Blommaert, Ben Rampton & Massimiliano Spotti (eds.), *Language and superdiversity*, 197–217. New York/London: Routledge.

Bogatto, François & Christine Hélot. 2010. Linguistic landscape and language diversity in Strasbourg: the 'Quartier Gare'. In Elana Shohamy, Eliezer Ben-Rafael & Monica Barni (eds.), *Linguistic landscape in the city*, 275–291. Bristol: Multilingual Matters.

Caritas & Fondazione Migrantes. 2015. XXV *Rapporto immigrazione 2015*. https://www.migrantes.it/wp-content/uploads/sites/50/2019/05/Sintesi.pdf (accessed 30 January 2020).

Cenoz, Jasone & Durk Gorter. 2006. Linguistic landscape and minority languages. *International Journal of Multilingualism* 3(1). 67–80.

Cenoz, Jasone & Durk Gorter. 2009. Language economy and linguistic landscape. In Elana Shohamy & Durk Gorter (eds.), *Linguistic landscape: expanding the scenery*, 55–69. London: Routledge.

Comune di Padova. 2014. Deliberazione del consiglio comunale: tributi comunali; regolamenti comunali sulla pubblicità. Padua: Comune di Padova, Segretaria generale. http://www.padova net.it/sites/default/files/attachment/C_1_Allegati_19316_Allegato.pdf (accessed 20 February 2019)

De Klerk, Gerda & Terrence Wiley. 2010. Linguistic landscape as multi-layered representation: suburban Asian communities in the Valley of the Sun. In Elana Shohamy, Eliezer Ben-Rafael & Monica Barni (eds.), *Linguistic landscape in the city*, 307–325. Bristol: Multilingual Matters.

Desoutter, Cécile & Maria Gottardo. 2016. Il paesaggio linguistico della Chinatown di Milano e Parigi: non solo i cinesi scrivono in cinese. *Mondi Migranti* 2016(2). 203–222.

Goglia, Francesco. 2011. Code-switching among Igbo-Nigerian immigrants in Padua (Italy). In Eric A. Anchimbe & Stephen A. Mforteh (eds.), *Postcolonial linguistic voices: identity choices and representations*, 323–342. Berlin: Mouton de Gruyter.

Goglia, Francesco. 2015. Multilingual immigrants and language maintenance: the case of the Igbo-Nigerian community in Padua. In Sara Gesuato & Mariagrazia Busa (eds.) *Festschrift for Prof. Alberto Mioni*, 701–710. Padua: CLEUP.

Goglia, Francesco. 2018. Code-switching and immigrant communities: the case of Italy. In Wendy Ayres-Bennett & Janice Carruthers (eds.) *Manual of Romance sociolinguistics*, 694–714. Berlin: Mouton de Gruyter.

Huebner, Thom. 2009. A framework for the linguistic analysis of linguistic landscapes. In Elana Shohamy & Durk Gorter (eds.), *Linguistic landscape: expanding the scenery*, 88–104. London: Routledge.

Jaworski, Adam & Crispin Thurlow. 2010. Introducing semiotic landscapes. In Adam Jaworski & Crispin Thurlow (eds.). *Semiotic landscapes: language, image, space*, 1–40. London: Continuum.

Landry, Rodrigue & Richard Y. Bourhis. 1997. Linguistic landscape and ethnolinguistic vitality: an empirical study. *Journal of Language and Social Psychology* 16(1). 23–49.

Lipovsky, Caroline. 2019. Belleville's linguistic heterogeneity viewed from its landscape. *International Journal of Multilingualism* 16(3). 244–269.

Lou, Jia Jackie. 2010. Chinese on the side: the marginalization of Chinese in the linguistic and social landscapes of Chinatown in Washington, DC. In Elana Shohamy, Eliezer Ben-Rafael & Monica Barni (eds.), *Linguistic landscape in the city*, 96–114. Bristol: Multilingual Matters.

Maly, Ico. 2016. Detecting social changes in times of superdiversity: an ethnographic linguistic landscape analysis of Ostend in Belgium. *Journal of Ethnic and Migration Studies* 42(5). 703–723.

Minuz, Fernanda & Giulio Forconi. 2018. La percezione del panorama linguistico in un'area della città di Bologna. *Lingue e Linguaggi* 25. 253–275.

Nalon, Silvio & Andrea Foresta. 2018. *Residenti a Padova con cittadinanza straniera: anno 2018*. Padova: Comune di Padova, Settore Programmazione Controllo e Statistica. http://www.padovanet.it/sites/default/files/attachment/Stranieri%202018.pdf (accessed 5 November 2019)

Redivo, Gianpaolo. 2018. *Gli imprenditori stranieri in provincia di Padova*. Padova: Camera di Commercio Padova. https://www.pd.camcom.it/gestisci-impresa/studi-informazione-economica/dati-e-analisi-economiche-1/archivio-pubblicazioni-fino-al-2018/dinamica-demografia-imprese (accessed 20 February 2019)

Uberti-Bona, Marcella. 2016. Esempi di eteroglossia nel paesaggio linguistico Milanese. *Lingue Culture Mediazioni* 3(1). 151–166.

Part 2: **Attitudes and identities**

John Hajek, Ambrin Hasnain and Carlie Hanson
5 Exploring the Italianità of Melbourne's Little Italy: Lygon Street, Carlton

1 Introduction

The migration of Italian people to Australia dates to the early days of its colonial settlement but rose dramatically in the 1950s and 1960s. As a result, Italians were for decades the largest non-English-speaking migrant group to settle in Australia, with the greatest concentration resident in the city of Melbourne. Carlton, a suburb just north of Melbourne's city centre, has been a major destination for immigrants since the late nineteenth century, and by the mid-twentieth century, its central artery, Lygon Street, had become Australia's best-known 'Little Italy', the core of an ethnic enclave where Italians and their businesses were concentrated.

Today, Lygon Street is a busy retail and restaurant strip drawing pedestrians with many different food-related businesses, as well as a popular cinema, book shop, boutiques and other businesses. Restaurants spill out on the broad sidewalks to offer al fresco dining, giving the street at least in part a European promenade feel. In addition, important cultural institutions such as the *Museo Italiano*, CO.AS.IT (*Comitato Assistenza agli Italiani*),[1] as well as the *La Mama* Theatre and a public library are located just off Lygon Street on Faraday Street. The area has also long been promoted by local and state governments as Australia's premier Italian destination where visitors and tourists are invited to enjoy Italian cuisine, style and *la dolce vita*.[2]

In this case study we aim to explore how *italianità* 'Italianness' is constructed on Lygon Street through a multimodal approach to the neighbourhood's linguistic landscape (LL), focussing on an analysis of the interplay between linguistic signs and images, as well as objects and other indicators of Italianness. In doing so, we aim to understand the lasting impact of past Italian settlement in Carlton but also to explore how the Italian language in particular is used, alongside English, and modified to meet the requirements of its potential audience. Our research is guided by the following questions:
(1) To what extent is Italianness present in the LL of Lygon Street, and how does it manifest itself?

---

[1] The Italian Assistance Committee is a community based social welfare organization.
[2] https://www.visitvictoria.com/regions/melbourne/destinations/carlton (accessed 19 November 2022).

(2) In what way does the expression of Italianness, whether through language or other means, point to a shift in the nature and status of Lygon Street as a Little Italy?
(3) What are the features of Italian in a language contact situation that is dominated by English?

In line with research on Little Italies elsewhere (Becker 2015; Gabaccia 2006), answering these research questions also allows us to understand the function today of the use of Italian and how this interacts with any interpretation of Lygon Street as some kind of an Italian space.

2 The context: Italians in Carlton

The number of Italians resident in Australia accelerated after World War II, particularly after the signing in 1951 of a formal migration agreement between Italy and Australia. As a result, some 305,000 Italians arrived in Australia between 1951 and 1973, comprising the largest non-English speaking immigrant group in this period (Cresciani 2003). By 1961 alone, 227,689 Italian-born persons were resident in Australia, 40% of whom had settled in the state of Victoria with almost all of these located in the country's major industrial centre, Melbourne, looking for work in factories. In many cases however, they set up small businesses, catering to their own community as well as to the general population (Dal Borgo 2006).

Eventually, due to improving economic conditions in Italy by the 1970s, the number of Italians arriving in Australia declined dramatically, leading to long-term effects on the size of the resident Italian community in Victoria. In 1971, Italian-born residents in Victoria numbered 121,758 (O'Neill 1972), dropping to only 70,527 in 2016 (ABS 2016). Reported use of Italian in the home shows a similar pattern of decline, falling from 173,995 individuals in 1991 to 112,272 in 2016 (ABS 2016; Castles 1993). These trends are a result of the ageing demography of the Italian-born immigrant community, as well as the tendency of grandchildren and great-grandchildren of the post-WWII migrant generation to speak only English at home (Bradshaw 2013).

Carlton, an inner-city suburb in Melbourne, mirrors the broader immigration history of Italians to Australia. Drawn by the suburb's cheap rent and its proximity to inner-suburban factories, the first wave of Italians moved to Carlton in the second half of the nineteenth century (Dal Borgo 2006). Between the two World Wars, a second wave of Italians settled in Carlton, drawn by, and in turn expanding, the already existing Italian community in this neighbourhood (Jones

1964), a process which was repeated again on a much larger scale after World War II (CO.AS.IT n.d.; Cresciani 2003; Dal Borgo 2006; Jones 1964). Census data for the City of Melbourne, the local government area which includes Carlton, show a steep increase in the number of Italian-born residents between 1921 and 1961, rising from 237 in 1921, to 1,612 in 1947, and 9,958 in 1961 (Archer 1963; Jones 1962). While Carlton was not counted separately in the census before 2001, there are estimates of the Italian population in this neighbourhood:

> In June 1960 Italians in the Carlton area were estimated to number between 4,900 and 5,500 persons, 19 to 21 per cent of the total population, and this includes only the first generation of Italian immigrants, those born in Italy. The inclusion of their Australian-born children raises the estimate to between 6,350 and 7,000 persons, 25 to 27 per cent of the total population. (Jones 1964: 92)

By the end of the 1960s, with one quarter of Carlton's residents now of Italian origin, the neighbourhood became known as Melbourne's Little Italy, a label which persists to this day (Dal Borgo 2006). Lygon Street became the place where Italian residents opened restaurants, food stores and other shopfront businesses, providing a wide range of goods and services to the Italian community in the area. By 1960, the number of Italian-owned shops had risen to forty-seven, compared to only fourteen in 1947 (Jones 1964). However, this burgeoning of the local Italian community was not to last long at all: attracted by more affordable property prices and rents as well as by a desire for more space and more modern housing due to growing families, Italians quickly began to move away from Carlton to newer suburbs further afield. This departure of Italians, clearly evident by the 1970s, was accompanied by the arrival into the suburb of gentrifying waves of artists and professional workers, as well as students and teachers from the nearby universities. As a result, by the 1990s few Italians continued to reside in the suburb, even though many Italian-owned businesses remained. Change through gentrification and subsequent waves of migration from around the world has been ongoing and today, Carlton houses a very diverse mix of immigrants and refugees from lower socio-economic backgrounds, more affluent residents from mostly Anglo-Australian backgrounds as well as students from Australia and increasingly from overseas (Dal Borgo 2006).

Recent census figures confirm the very limited presence of Italian-born and Italian-speaking residents in Carlton. Over the past two decades, Carlton has seen a large influx of migrants from Asian countries such as China, India, Indonesia, Malaysia and Singapore, making Italy the twelfth most common country of birth (Table 1). This demographic shift is also reflected in census data on languages spoken at home (Table 2). Apart from English, Mandarin, Cantonese and Indonesian are the most widely spoken languages at home in Carlton, with only 331 residents reporting the use of Italian in 2016, putting it in seventh place.

Table 1: Carlton's three most common countries of birth, and Italy (no 12) (ABS 2002; 2017).

	Number of Residents	
Country of Birth	2001	2016
1. Australia	4,259	5,212
2. China (excl. SARS & Taiwan)	197	4,284
3. Malaysia	741	1,218
12. Italy	160	255

Table 2: Carlton's three most common languages spoken at home, and Italian (no 7) (ABS 2002; 2017).

	Number of Residents	
Language spoken at home	2001	2016
1. English only	4,653	6,440
2. Mandarin	801	4,860
3. Cantonese	704	806
7. Italian	267	331

Interestingly, the long-term demographic decline of the local Italian community has been slightly reversed in more recent times. While the number of Italian speakers dropped from 267 in 2001 to 238 in 2011, it rose to 331 in 2016. Similarly, the number of Italian-born residents in Carlton dropped from 160 in 2001 to 140 in 2011, before rising again to 255 in 2016 (ABS 2002; 2012; 2017). These increases reflect the arrival of young Italians, mostly on temporary working holiday visas, who have come to Melbourne looking for work due to difficult economic conditions in Italy since the global financial crisis of 2007–2008 (Armillei and Mascitelli 2016). Many of these temporary visa holders have found employment in Italian food-related businesses, especially restaurants, on Lygon Street, helping to enhance the *italianità* and noticeably boosting the audible use of Italian in Carlton.

3 Linguistic landscape as a methodological approach

We examine the Italian character of Lygon Street through a multimodal analysis of its LL (Pütz and Mundt 2018; Shohamy 2018). LL research is a burgeoning area of sociolinguistics that explores the visual display and representation of language, while more recently also considering other communicative devices. In their seminal paper, Landry and Bourhis (1997) explain that "Linguistic Landscape refers to the visibility and salience of languages on public and commercial signs in a given territory or region" (p. 23). Their work laid the groundwork for LL research as a diagnostic tool for researchers to grasp whether an area is mono- or multilingual, which languages are being used and which languages dominate the visual landscape, often through the quantitative analysis of languages on public signs. As LL research has evolved, this initial method has been criticised for its static approach towards linguistic diversity, as the quantitative analysis of shop signs does not accurately reflect its complexities and patterns (Shohamy 2018).

Incorporating an ethnographic approach, LL research became increasingly interested in examining the symbolic function served by specific linguistic and communicative choices in the public. Rubino (2019), who explores the LL of two traditionally Italian suburbs in Sydney, argues that "linguistic choices can be symbolic practices that contribute to the construction of a social space as the expression of ever evolving ethnic identity. LL indexes linguistic communities as well as diachronic changes" (p. 184). This understanding of LL is underpinned by the idea that a geographical, physical space becomes a place with a sociocultural identity through the social, cultural and political practices performed by its inhabitants, as well as through their interactions with and within the space and the institutions that govern it (Allon, 2002; Ben-Rafael et al. 2010; Britain, 2011). As language is an essential part of individual as well as collective identity (Gaiser and Matras 2016), people create a sense of familiarity and belonging to a place through the ability to understand and communicate in the language(s) used in that place. In this sense, LL research is a useful tool to analyse power relations and dynamics between the dominant culture and other cultures through the occurrences and authorship of LL items (Landry and Bourhis 1997; Ben-Rafael et al. 2006; 2010; Blommaert 2013; Woldemariam and Lanza 2015; Gaiser and Matras 2016; Rubino 2019). Communicative choices made by public and private authors can inscribe a place with a certain cultural identity and give people of the corresponding language communities a sense of value and status. At the same time, this may lead to feelings of exclusion amongst people that belong to different language, ethnic and cultural communities.

Since its initial phase, the boundaries and constituents of LLs have been subject to continuous debate, and have been expanded to allow an interdisciplinary and multimodal approach (Shohamy 2018). A shift to the concept of 'semiotic landscape' considers places "not as mere geographically defined areas but as symbolic representations of social, cultural and political values" (Pütz and Mundt 2018: 4). This approach is interested in the interplay of, and meaning-making through, non-linguistic elements in a landscape, such as images, food, sounds, architecture, smells, people and other non-textual communication tools (Jaworski and Thurlow 2010; Shohamy 2018). It thus works to "describe communication practices in terms of the textual, aural, linguistic, spatial and visual resources – or modes – used to compose meaningful messages" (Pütz and Mundt 2018: 5), opening up an opportunity to analyse the complexities of ethnic representation in an area. Shohamy (2018) gives an insightful overview of the development of LL approaches and themes and defines LL as "any display in public spaces which communicates varied types of messages" (p. 27).

Ethnic enclaves, such as Little Italies, are highly pertinent neighbourhoods for multimodal LL analyses. Created through the influx of a group of people who share a cultural identity into the same neighbourhood, an ethnic enclave is characterised by containing both ethnic residents as well as ethnic businesses (Terzano 2014). Understood as "a voluntarily segregated space" in which "a minority group and its group members share a language, culture, ethnicity, or nationality [. . .] as means to strengthen economic, sociocultural, and political development within the community" (Kim 2018: 276–277), ethnic enclaves offer recent migrants socioeconomic opportunities and a sense of security and reassurance. These are achieved through employment, a support network by people who share experiences of migration as well as a mutual language, the provision of goods and services found at home, and the ability to maintain strong cultural ties to the homeland despite dislocation (Gabaccia 2006; Kim 2018; Krase 2004; Terzano 2014).

The dissolution of ethnic enclaves often occurs in response to demographic shifts. While the relocation of a resident ethnic community can be entirely self-motivated, for example to move closer to family and jobs or to find better housing, it can also be linked to changes brought about through new residents (Kosta 2019; Terzano 2014). The influx of people from 'other' communities may lead to a re-diversification of the neighbourhood in residents and businesses. For example, the area might assume a more culturally diverse identity, or develop into a different ethnic enclave altogether (Krase 2012; Terzano 2014). Moreover, gentrification processes can also be set in motion by the arrival of a more affluent population, changing the traditional socio-economic profile of the neighbourhood (Murdie and Teixeira 2011), something which has also occurred in Carlton.

Yet notwithstanding any demographic shifts, the ethnic identity of a neighbourhood can outlast the specific community linked to it. Terzano (2014) suggests that if an area "becomes diversified in residents but not businesses", (p. 343) its ethnic identity may be used as branding for the neighbourhood. For example, in his account of Little Italy in the Bronx, Kosta (2019) observes, "while a pattern of white flight and incoming minorities resulted in residential de-Italianization, the commercial strip of the area had experienced intensification of its Italian identity over the same decades" (p. 1101). This commodification of ethnic identity, which is often accompanied by the labels 'Little' and 'town', such as Little Italy and Chinatown, is often supported by local councils or municipalities to maintain a coherent neighbourhood image that attracts tourists (Terzano 2014). Kim (2018) labels an ethnic enclave that has become commodified for tourists a 'transclave', which she defines to be "a commercialized ethnic space that exists exclusively for consumption, leisure, and entertainment" (p. 277). Often packaged for tourists and non-residents of the neighbourhood, the commodification of ethnic enclaves also raises the issue of authenticity (Hackworth and Rekers 2005).

Hence, analysis of a neighbourhood's LL can give insight into the status and identity of an ethnic enclave. Shop and restaurant signs typically play a crucial role in the construction of the identity of a business – and its neighbourhood by extension. Through the "choice of materials, symbolic signs, images and languages" (Izadi and Parvaresh 2016: 183) on its sign, a shop indexes its intended customers. For example, languages other than the dominant language on signs or culturally specific imagery may be used to communicate messages and offers for a specific community, promising familiar and authentic products and services. Conversely, shop signs which convey all information in the dominant language but include an ethnic name or other non-communicative messages may be using this language symbolically, i.e., to index their ethnic identity rather than to communicate. Lastly, two or multiple languages may be used together on signs to communicate same or different messages with different customer groups. This often indicates that the shop is still serving its ethnic customers while also acknowledging the need to communicate with other customers (Izadi and Parvaresh 2016).

4 Data collection

The corpus for this case study was extracted from data captured through the mobile app LinguaSnapp Melbourne.[3] LinguaSnapp is a smartphone app developed originally at the University of Manchester to carry out LL research (see Gaiser and Matras 2021). The app allows users to document multilingual signs, flyers, and posters by taking and uploading a picture and entering certain information, including information about language(s) and translation(s), the context of the sign and a basic analysis of the sign's purpose, audience, etc. With GPS turned on, the phone geo-tags the photo and uploads it, after some back-end processing, to its geographical location on a map of the city. This map is publicly accessible and displays all the photos that have been successfully uploaded. Pictures on the map can be filtered by different languages, alphabets, outlets, and other relevant information for the purposes of analysis.

For this study, we were interested in signs that feature the Italian language along Lygon Street in Carlton. To filter our results, we first searched for 'Italian' on the LinguaSnapp map and exported all results (n = 174). We then selected those (n = 75) fitting the latitude and longitude of Little Italy on Lygon Street in Carlton (see below) and classified these LL items into categories such as 'restaurant and café', 'food product', 'entertainment venue/ cultural institution', 'street sign', 'personal message', 'newspaper clippings' and 'others'. After removing duplicates and signs that were falsely identified as Italian (we will elaborate on some below), sixty-three pictures remained, which we colour-coded according to whether the items feature 'Italian', 'Italian and English', or 'Italian, English and other languages'. This gave us a good basis from which to perform a qualitative analysis of the captured images which we report on below.

5 Results

While Lygon Street extends north past Carlton, running through Carlton North, Brunswick East and Brunswick, the area traditionally known as Little Italy is located in Carlton with its centre on a stretch of Lygon Street bordered by Elgin Street to the north and Victoria Parade to the south. Data gathered with LinguaSnapp shows a high concentration of Italian LL items along this specific stretch of roadway (Figure 1), as well as on neighbouring side streets (Faraday Street, Grattan Street, Argyle Place and Pelham Street). Despite the small numbers of Italian-

---

[3] https://www.linguasnappmel.manchester.ac.uk/.

born and -speaking residents, Italian language signs continue to be more prominent than signs in languages of larger resident ethnic communities. Whereas Mandarin, Cantonese, Arabic, Indonesian and Vietnamese all have more speakers than Italian in this particular suburb, signs in these languages are still less common—but increasing in number over time, particularly in streets near Lygon Street (Figure 2).

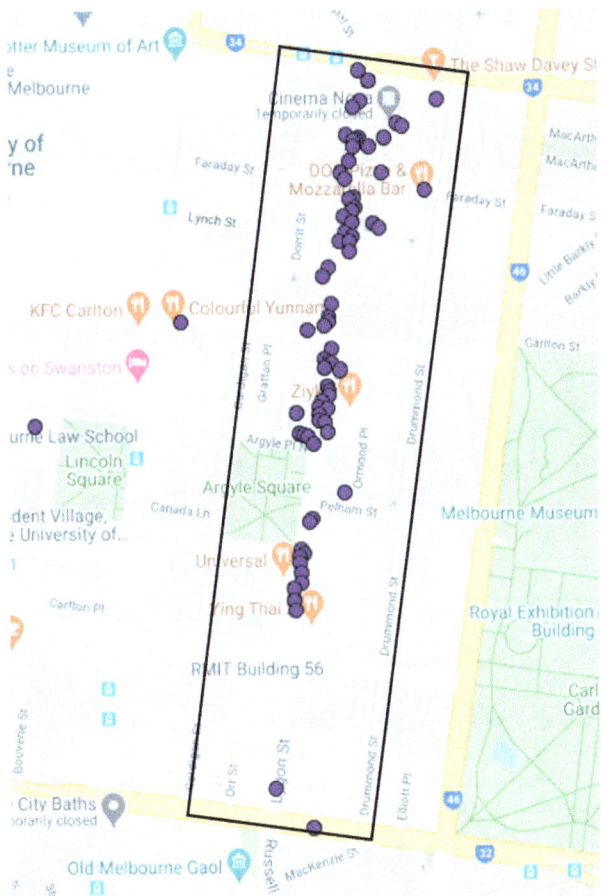

Figure 1: Screenshot of the LinguaSnapp map showing the location of all signs in Carlton and the Lygon Street District (within the black rectangle) that were identified as containing Italian (Source: LinguaSnapp Melbourne).

LinguaSnapp users uploaded and geotagged sixty-three pictures on Lygon Street on which they identified Italian words (Figure 1). Thirty-eight pictures (60%) show a restaurant or café name or menu (of 34 different businesses), ten pictures (16%)

Figure 2: Screenshot of the LinguaSnapp map showing the location of signs in the four most commonly spoken languages other than English in Carlton and the Lygon Street District. 'Chinese' includes traditional and simplified characters and thus writing produced by Mandarin and Cantonese speakers (Source: LinguaSnapp Melbourne).

show Italian food products, sold in groceries or cafés, and five pictures (8%) show inscriptions, newspaper clippings and personal messages. Four pictures (7%) show place names and street signs, two of which are signs for the same place in different locations, two pictures (3%) are of entertainment venues and cultural institutions, and two pictures (3%) show merchandise and clothing stores. Two pictures (3%) were categorised as 'other': (a) a bicycle with the Melbourne brand 'allegro', and (b) a multilingual product tag for a cheese grater.

In our corpus of Italian LL items on Lygon Street, only three pictures (5%) appear to be signs from official authorities, while the remaining 95% are created by the private sector and individuals. Only one place carries an Italian name, namely the *Piazza Italia*, which sits within Argyle Square, a small public park. The *Piazza* functions as an outdoor square that hosts community events and festivals, such as the annual Italian *Festa*. Opened in 2006, the *Piazza Italia* was developed by the City of Melbourne in collaboration with Melbourne's Italian sister city Milan in an effort to display the continuing relationship between Lygon Street and the city's Italian community. Using stone imported from Italy, and traditional Italian masonry techniques, the hand-paved plaza with its large sundial and surrounding benches was envisioned to replicate the look and feel of an Italian *piazza* (Helzer, 2008). While ethnic neighbourhoods may naturally develop a resemblance to the look, flair and atmosphere of the street life 'back home' (Gabaccia 2006), in this instance it was created through a local council initiative.

Furthermore, three official street signs were identified as Italian, which point to the community cultural institutions *Museo Italiano* and *La Mama* Theatre (Figure 3). However, the sign for *La Mama* Theatre, while commonly understood by passers-by to involve Italian, is done so in error. The theatre is in fact modelled and named after a theatre venue in New York City, the 'La MaMa Experimental Theatre Club', which was named after its founder Ellen Stewart, who was commonly known as 'Mama' (Coveney 2011). Thus, the name is only assumed to be Italian due to the theatre's location in Melbourne's Italian precinct, and to a misunderstanding that *la mama* is Italian, rather than the correct *la mamma*. While we did not include this sign in our count, this example demonstrates the way that non-Italian words can still

Figure 3: Blue street signs to the *Museo Italiano* and to *La Mama* Theatre (Photos: LinguaSnapp Melbourne).

contribute to the Italianness of an area, as long as they are understood to be Italian by tourists or other visitors to the area.

Regarding the language composition of the Italian LL items found on Lygon Street, thirty-two (52%) are bilingual (Italian and English), twenty-three (37%) appear with Italian text only, and seven (11%) show text in Italian and other languages, such as Chinese, German and French. Examination of the bilingual signs shows that most essential information, such as opening hours, contact information, menus or type of business, is given in English or inclusive Italian.[4] There are eleven restaurant and shop signs displayed on the outside of businesses which use Italian only, seven of which only display their Italian business name. The additional four include inclusive use of Italian such as *gelateria*, *dal 1870* 'since 1870', *cucina italiana* 'Italian cuisine' and a website address. However, all of these shops and restaurants use English elsewhere in their establishments, for example on their menus and product labels. All bilingual outdoor shop signs provide either overlapping or complementary information in English, i.e., they either provide only some of the information given in Italian in English or vice versa, or they provide different pieces of information in English and Italian (Reh 2004). For example, *Casa Del Gelato* provides information in Italian and English that it sells *Gelati* and 'Ice Cream', but it tells customers only in Italian that it is a *Gelateria Italiana*, and only in English that its ice cream is 'home-made' (Figure 4). Other complementary information commonly given in English and Italian respectively include words that have entered the English vocabulary (often inclusive Italian referring to Italian products on offer), e.g. *Pizza*, *Pasta*, or that refer to liquor licencing, e.g. 'B.Y.O.'[5] or 'Fully Licensed'.

It is also important to observe the size and arrangement of bilingual information on signs (Reh 2004). For example, *Il Cantuccio* 'The Corner' or 'Nook' has printed the restaurant name in large letters, while clarifying in smaller but uppercase letters that it offers *cucina italiana* and in even smaller and lowercase letters that it is 'Fully Lic/BYO Wine' (Figure 5). By putting its Italian name in a dominant position, the restaurant aims to emphasise its Italianness.

As these two examples suggest, an overwhelming majority of signs, posters and other instances of written Italian found in the LL of Lygon Street are situated in a food context. Of sixty-three pictures, fifty-three images (84%) capture Italian inside or outside of a restaurant, café or grocer, while only ten pictures (16%) depict items that are not related to food. Within food-related LL items, there are

---

[4] Inclusive Italian refers to Italian words that are either widely known, such as *pasta* or *gelato*, or easily understood from the context, while exclusive Italian refers to words and phrases that are more likely to be understood only by proficient Italian speakers.
[5] Bring Your Own (Alcohol).

Figure 4: Shopfront of an ice cream shop in Lygon Street (Photo: LinguaSnapp Melbourne).

Figure 5: Sign at *Il Cantuccio* restaurant (Photo: LinguaSnapp Melbourne).

thirty images of restaurant and café names (57%), followed by ten images of food products (19%) and four images of menus that are visible from the outside (8%). Other items include newspaper clippings, decorations, and personal messages.

Italian is most commonly used in the names of restaurants and cafés, with varying naming practices. Many of the business names are derived from Italian first or family names. For example, *Donnini's* is owned and operated by members of the well-known Donnini family, who have owned a number of restaurants in Melbourne since the 1950s. Other restaurant and café names may use non-food related Italian words, such as *Café Italia* 'Italy Café', *Piccolo Mondo* 'Small World' and *Café Cavallino* 'Pony Café', or reference typical Italian products, such as *gelato* or *pasta*, to create an

Italian flair.[6] Ice cream shops found along Lygon Street include *Il Dolce Freddo* 'The Cold Dessert' and *Casa Del Gelato* 'House of Ice Cream' (Figure 4), while others advertise *gelato* and display *gelateria* signs. Besides the pasta restaurant *Pasta Rustica Ristorante*, there are two restaurants whose names are derived from the iconic Italian pasta, *spaghetti*: *La Spaghetteria Ristorante* and *La Spaghettata*.

Other naming practices use Italian creatively, such as through unusual spellings, or specific grammatical structures as well as fake or pseudo-Italianisms. For instance, while *ti amo* 'I love you' appears as *Tiamo* as the name of a well-known restaurant (and popularly also referred to as *Tiamo's*), it remains easily identifiable as the Italian declaration of love. In addition, Italian may be influenced by English grammatical structures creating a hybridization of Italian and English. Family names which clearly evoke Italian origins may appear with the English genitive, e.g., *Donnini's*. Less obviously, *Pasta Rustica Ristorante* and *La Spaghetteria Ristorante*, unlike examples such as *Café Cavallino*, follow an English word order in which the name precedes rather than follows the word for restaurant. This reflects the need for English syntactic structure to facilitate comprehension by English speakers. Furthermore, the restaurant name *Seasons Provedore* was also identified as Italian – understandably so as the name is accompanied by 'Authentic Italian Cuisine' and an image of the Italian flag – even though *provedore* (a supplier of goods, often food-related) is a pseudo-Italianism of likely Portuguese origin. The name of the ice cream franchise chain *Gelatissimo*, which is not Italian-owned or founded, is another example of a pseudo-Italianism, as this word-suffix combination as a noun (rather than an adjective) is not typically Italian but clearly designed in this case to evoke a sense of Italianness.

The restaurant *Stuzzichino* shows a more dynamic mix of English and Italian, using inclusive as well as exclusive Italian. While its sign uses well-known Italian words and expressions to tell its passers-by it is a *ristorante e bar* and a *pizzeria artigianale*, it also uses exclusive Italian on its sign, as the words *spuntini* 'snacks' and the café name *Stuzzichino* 'Appetizer' or 'Snack' are not widely known. In addition, the caption *È tempo di caffè* calqued on the English 'it's coffee time' (rather than the more natural *è l'ora del caffè*), runs around the menu board. The restaurant *Delizio* 'Delight' also employs a mix of inclusive and exclusive Italian on their signs. One sign champions the restaurant name in large print, which is complemented by an English list of the food on offer: 'woodfired pizza, pasta, steak, seafood—Fully Licensed—BYO wine only'. A second sign reads *autentica cucina italiana* 'authentic Italian cuisine', which is easily understood by non-Italian

---

6 Somewhat ironically the French form *café* prevails over Italian *caffè* in Australia – even for Italian-style cafés where Italian food and coffee are served.

speakers, but to understand the phrase *se la provi t'innamori* 'if you try it, you'll fall in love' written underneath, one needs a deeper knowledge of Italian. Another interesting text on the sign is the inclusion of *pizzaiola Chiara*, referring to the pizza chef Chiara in Italian.

Imagery that provokes Italianness is also commonly found on business signs. The Italian flag and its colours (green, red, and white) is featured on twelve signs, either as a decoration or in the form of text colours. Other imagery found on signs evokes associations with Italian food, one image depicts a woman eating a plate of spaghetti and meatballs and another shows a Roman angel holding a pizza. In addition, the restaurant *Villa Romana* displays its *italianità* with an old Fiat 500 outside their business, which is also decorated with the Italian flag.

The second most common category of Italian use (n = 10) relates to food products found inside of shops. Serving a range of customers, including Italian- and non-Italian speakers, delicatessens use Italian names for local and imported products and ice cream shops label their flavours in Italian. Just three of the ten pictures of food products are in Italian only. The other seven items are mostly bilingual (Italian and English), including two trilingual signs (with French and German as the third languages), and for the most part show Italian product names with English descriptions and details.

Examples captured through LinguaSnapp include packets of *Pasta di Grano Duro da agricoltura biologica* 'Durum wheat pasta from organic farming', and boxes of *Torrone*, a nougat confection, labelled in Italian with fragmented English translations. The alcohol shop *Bottega Tasca* (lit. 'Pocket Shop' with correct Italian word order) advertises the wine varieties *Valpolicella* and *Pinot Grigio* by the Italian wine label *Paolovino* on a poster outside of their shop. In addition, one grocer displays a whole range of imported *Lurisia* soft drinks in their shop window with use only of Italian evident in the product labelling visible to potential customers. *Brunetti*, a famous Italian café and eatery, is an excellent example of the use of *italianità* to attract customers, by emphasizing Italian-style interior design, as well as by hiring young Italian workers and displaying Italian labels. For example, pastries and ice cream flavours are labelled in Italian, but feature English descriptions and ingredient lists to help customers not familiar with Italian.

The name of the well-known Italian food business, *D.O.C.*, which incorporates a delicatessen, an espresso bar and a pizza restaurant, is an abbreviation known to all Italians: *Denominazione di Origine Controllata* (literally 'Controlled Designation of Origin'). This term is used to indicate high quality wine and traditionally also some food products from a specific region. *D.O.C.* also provides an example of a shop that employs large numbers of young Italian staff to cater to Italian-speaking customers, promoting a resurgence of spoken Italian. While all *D.O.C.* staff speak

Italian, their deli signage is also largely, albeit not exclusively, in Italian. For example, the board detailing their deli specials is written in a mix of Italian names of food products and English, e.g. *Vitello Tonnato* [veal in tuna sauce], combine it with a glass of *Malandrino* [Italian red wine variety], and they advertise *Salumi* and *Formaggi del mese* 'cured meats and cheeses of the month' (Figure 6). Furthermore, *D.O.C.* presents product information boards in Italian. The board giving information about a French cheese is labelled in Italian, including the categories *prodotto* 'product', *origine* 'origin', *latte* 'milk', *descrizione* 'description' and *prezzo etto* 'price per hectogram' (Figure 7). While the product information is specified in English, other signs continue to target Italians and Italian speakers exclusively. For example, the deli displays a blackboard that reads *Al deli le lavagne in vetrina sono migliori se vuote!* 'At the deli, the boards in the windows are best if empty!'. In addition, they have an old-fashioned newspaper stand that reads *giornali* 'newspapers' and *riviste* 'magazines'.

Figure 6: Boards at *D.O.C.* using a mix of Italian names of food products and English (Photo: LinguaSnapp Melbourne).

In addition to eateries and food products, there are a few other instances of food-related uses of Italian recorded. A newspaper clipping in the window of *Il Dolce Freddo* is from the local Italian newspaper *Il Globo* and reports on the proprietor's ice cream making practice. The article is written entirely in Italian with no translation provided.

Figure 7: Product board for a French cheese at *D.O.C.* using Italian labels and English descriptions (Photo: LinguaSnapp Melbourne).

Beyond food-related businesses, the use of assumed Italian names is rare. Italian fashion and design shops with goods imported from Italy were once prominent along Lygon Street but have now almost entirely disappeared, with only two of any kind remaining. *Bonaparte* is a men's fashion boutique that offers "quality clothing from Germany, Italy and Spain".[7] Apart from its name, the store has no other signage that can be linked to Italian. The shop *Forza Italia* (lit. 'Come on Italy!') sells merchandising linked to famous Italian brands, sport teams and cities, such as Ferrari jackets. Finally, there is the cultural institution *Museo Italiano Melbourne* 'Italian Museum Melbourne' which sits within CO.AS.IT and displays records, images and objects from the Italian Historical Society. Next to the Italian name of the museum written in large letters on the side of the CO.AS.IT building, a mural depicts a woman looking into the distance together with a ship, the silhouette of a man with a suitcase and seagulls. It is intended to evoke the immigration history of the Italian community to Melbourne (Figure 8).

---

7 https://bonapartemensboutique.com.au/ (accessed 19 November 2022).

Figure 8: Large-scale mural for the *Museo Italiano Melbourne* on the side of the CO.AS.IT building (Photo: LinguaSnapp Melbourne).

6 Italian overtones on Lygon Street: Little Italy as a linguistic transclave

Our study of Lygon Street through the LL lens gives insight into the narrowing scope to which *italianità* is present in Melbourne's Little Italy. During the residential heyday of Italians in Carlton, the use of Italian served a practical function. It reflected actual language use in the area, encouraged language maintenance and use, and created a sense of community and home. Given the large-scale departure of Italians from Carlton in the late 1960s and 1970s, Italianness on Lygon Street has become indexed primarily through the public visibility of Italian language, culture and style. Corresponding with Rubino's (2019) findings in Italian neighbourhoods in Sydney, the multimodal use of Italian language and cultural aspects in eateries, shops and delis on Lygon Street aims to index the authenticity of products and services, aiming to create an Italian aesthetic to attract non-Italian customers and tourists who are seeking an Italian experience. In addition to linguistic items, other modes of Italianness include Italian cuisine, food products and merchandise, names, architecture (including building materials and techniques), decorations, the size and arrangement of texts on signs, imagery, as well as staff working in cafés. While most of these are exhibited by businesses, the *Piazza Italia* seems to be the only major attempt by the local and state governments to explicitly display the continuing relationship between Lygon Street and Melbourne's Italian community. Most of the signs in our sample are bilingual which supports the impression that Italian mostly serves a symbolic function on Lygon Street. Businesses use Italian to index their Italianness, and English to communicate with their mostly English-speaking customer base.

The Lygon Street neighbourhood mirrors the development of an ethnic enclave into a 'transclave' (Kim 2018; Krase 2004), as the ethnic and cultural identity of Italians has come to be increasingly packaged for symbolic consumption by non-Italians. The Lygon Street neighbourhood displays a simultaneous de-Italianisation of residents on the one hand, counterbalanced on the other by the presumed Italian identity and nature of many local businesses (Kosta 2019), a heavy investment of local and state governments in its branding and promotion as Little Italy, as well as in redesigning the streetscape to make it more attractive to tourists (Terzano 2014), all of which facilitates a commodification of Italian identity and culture (Hackworth and Rekers 2005; Kim 2018). The marked overrepresentation of Italian in the context of restaurants and food on Lygon Street, for instance, corresponds with other research that has found a strong connection between the conspicuous presence of restaurants and eateries and the commodification of ethnic enclaves. For example, Amos (2016) has shown the strong association of restaurants with Chinese culture in Liverpool, while Hackworth and Rekers' (2005) findings show that in North America 'Little Italies' in particular demonstrate a strong focus on Italian restaurants and food as representation of Italian culture.

The size and arrangement of bilingual information on signs also reflects the attempt to uphold Italian identity. By presenting an Italian restaurant name or food label in a dominant position (see *Il Cantuccio,* Figure 5), businesses ensure that the Italian name or word attracts immediate attention, conveying their Italianness to potential customers. The creative use and hybridisation of Italian in names, such as *Donnini's, Tiamo* and *Gelatissimo* is a commonplace phenomenon. Interpreting these (pseudo-)Italianisms around the world, Bagna and Machetti (2012) claim that "Italian is no longer just the language of the Italians, but is recreated to form new words, often with a contribution from local languages, and always with the aim of evoking traits of Italianness" (p. 220).

Being situated in an English-dominated language context, the use of Italian on Lygon Street features recurring linguistic patterns, such as the use of Italian names alongside grammatical hybridisation. The connotative meaning of the Italian language, i.e. its cultural and emotional associations, is "linked to the perception of aspects of Italianness such as quality of life, well-being, dynamism and creativity" (Bagna and Machetti 2012: 219). The use of Italian family names can be reinforced by the inclusion of newspaper articles in Italian (see *Il Dolce Freddo*), by exclusive Italian (see *Stuzzichino*) or by adding dates in Italian to signs, as exemplified by the ice cream shop *Lavezzi*, with its shopfront use of *dal 1870*. As in the example of *Stuzzichino*, the use of lesser-known Italian words does not alienate or exclude non-Italian speakers, as none of these words and phrases need to be understood by customers to know the purpose of the business. They simply need to be recognised as Italian. As such, they aim to further strengthen the Italian character of the restaurant. Similarly, the *Delizio* sign gives the impression that it uses Italian communicatively. Disguised as an exclusive use of Italian, *se la provi t'innamori* 'if you try it, you'll fall in love' seems more symbolic in function. Even though the Italian phrase is too complex to be easily understood by a non-Italian speaker, its message appears to be directed at non-Italians. The inclusion of this phrase and the Italian names of the chefs also serve to amplify the level of Italian authenticity represented by *Delizio*. While Italian business names may evoke Italianness, they do not guarantee Italian ownership or even origins. Some eateries have continued to carry the names of former Italian owners to build from an already established reputation. Others have taken on Italian names to benefit from the association with Little Italy to attract customers (Becker 2015). Hence, it is not easily discernible from names alone if eateries with Italian names are indeed under Italian ownership.

The only two clothing and merchandise stores with any expression of Italianness on Lygon Street also tap to different degrees into the Italian identity of the neighbourhood to attract customers. By offering Italian menswear (as well as German and Spanish), *Bonaparte* refers back to the time when Lygon Street was the centre of Italian fashion and design in Melbourne. *Forza Italia* on the other hand offers tourists the opportunity to buy Italian merchandise far away from Italy and uses the association of Lygon Street with the Italian community to its advantage. As Italian fashion, shoe and design stores along the strip have gradually disappeared, a narrowing focus of Italianness on food-related activity and products has helped to transform the characterisation of Lygon Street into a largely commodified ethnic transclave.

Yet despite all this, for Italo-Australians, the use of Italian on Lygon Street still links the area to their heritage and home country. Experiencing one's ethnic identity on visible and sometimes audible display helps to create a space to experience, if not speak, one's heritage language particularly in those businesses where Italian is used regularly by Italian-speaking staff. This can play an important role in both identity and language maintenance (Rubino 2019). The connection between the

Italo-Australian community and the sense of place and Italianness evoked by Lygon Street manifests itself most strongly during sporting events in which Italy participates. For example, when Italy won the Euro Cup in 2021, thousands of Italian-Australian soccer fans congregated on Lygon Street to watch the match and to celebrate the victory (Johnson 2021).

7 Conclusion

In this case study, we explored how *italianità* 'Italianness' is constructed and expressed on Lygon Street in Melbourne. Through our multimodal approach to the neighbourhood's LL, we found that the Italian language as well as objects and imagery appear frequently and are used to construct *italianità* in an ethnic space that has however also become largely commodified, most conspicuously through the presence of Italian in the food sector. This particular use of the language not only marks space but serves also to evoke the positive values and attitudes more generally associated with Italian cuisine and food practices (Hajek and Giannelli 2002). The symbolic use of the Italian language and culture in business signs and shops on Lygon Street indexes Italianness to tourists and English-speaking Australians, including those of Italo-Australian descent, as opposed to the practical function it used to serve for the Italian migrant community for a large part of the twentieth century. This status shift also demonstrates that Lygon Street's Little Italy has transformed from an ethnic enclave where Italians once lived in large numbers to a transclave that attracts visitors. Being positioned in an English-dominant context, Italian has also become subject to linguistic hybridization to meet the requirements of its non-Italian-speaking audience, such as its insertion into English grammatical structures and word orders.

Finally, we must also recognise that Linguistic Landscapes are dynamic and stratified. Today, despite the evidence of *italianità* we have presented, the neighbourhood around Lygon Street is also strongly multilingual and multicultural, and subject to ongoing transformation. Alongside the frequent symbolic use of Italian, we also find signs which use Thai, Arabic, Vietnamese, Chinese, French, Spanish, Japanese and Turkish. Even Italian restaurants have to adjust by not only catering for English but also for Chinese speakers now, for example by advertising their menus with Chinese signs (Figure 9). Such a step is a telling linguistic response to the burgeoning number of local residents who are of Chinese-speaking background (Tables 1 and 2) as well as Chinese-speaking visitors from elsewhere in Melbourne and from overseas – a sign in turn of the wider demographic transformation of Australian society under way at present.

Figure 9: The Copperwood menu displays 'This restaurant has a Chinese menu' in Chinese characters (Photo: LinguaSnapp Melbourne).

References

ABS (Australian Bureau of Statistics). 2002. *2001 Census Community Profile Series: Carlton*. Canberra: Commonwealth of Australia.

ABS (Australian Bureau of Statistics). 2012. *2011 Census of Population and Housing: Basic Community Profile: Carlton*. Canberra: Commonwealth of Australia.

ABS (Australian Bureau of Statistics). 2016. *2016 Census Community Profiles: Victoria*. https://www.abs.gov.au/census/find-census-data/community-profiles/2016/2

ABS (Australian Bureau of Statistics). 2017. *2016 Census of Population and Housing: General Community Profile: Carlton*. Canberra: Commonwealth of Australia.

Allon, Fiona. 2002. Translated spaces/translated identities: the production of place, culture and memory in an Australian suburb. *Journal of Australian Studies* 26(72). 99–110.

Amos, H. William. 2016. Chinatown by numbers: defining an ethnic space by empirical linguistic landscape. *Linguistic Landscape* 2(2). 127–156.

Archer, K.M. 1963. *Census of the Commonwealth of Australia, 30th June, 1961: Volume II, Victoria*. Canberra: Commonwealth Bureau of Census and Statistics. https://www.ausstats.abs.gov.au/ausstats/free.nsf/0/38AF442D361E193BCA25787900175504/$File/1961%20Census%20-%20Volume%20II%20-%20Part%20I%20VICTORIA%20Analysis%20of%20Population%20in%20LGA.pdf

Armillei, Riccardo & Bruno Mascitelli. 2016. *From 2004 to 2016: a new Italian 'exodus' to Australia?* Melbourne: COMITES Comitato degli Italiani all' estero Victoria and Tasmania.

Bagna, Carla & Sabrina Machetti. 2012. LL and (Italian) menus and brand names: a survey around the world. In Christine Hélot, Monica Barni, Rudi Janssens & Carla Bagna (eds.), *Linguistic landscapes, multilingualism and social change*, 217–230. Frankfurt am Main: Peter Lang.

Becker, Elisabeth. 2015. Little of Italy? Assumed ethnicity in a New York City neighbourhood. *Ethnic and Racial Studies* 38(1). 109–124.

Ben-Rafael, Eliezer, Elana Shohamy & Monica Barni. 2010. Introduction: an approach to an 'ordered disorder'. In Elana Shohamy, Eliezer Ben-Rafael, & Monica Barni (eds.), *Linguistic landscape in the city*, xi–xxviii. Bristol: Multilingual Matters.

Ben-Rafael, Eliezer, Elana Shohamy, Muhammad Hasan Amara & Nira Trumper-Hecht. 2006. Linguistic landscape as symbolic construction of the public space: the case of Israel. *International Journal of Multilingualism* 3(1). 7–30.

Blommaert, Jan. 2013. *Ethnography, superdiversity and linguistic landscapes: chronicles of complexity*. Bristol: Multilingual Matters.

Bradshaw, Julie. 2013. The ecology of minority languages in Melbourne. *International Journal of Multilingualism* 10(4). 469–481.

Britain, David John. 2011. Conceptualizations of geographic space in linguistics. In Alfred Lameli, Roland Kehrein & Stefan Rabanus (eds.), *Language and space: an international handbook of linguistic variation. Vol. 2: language mapping*, 69–97. Berlin: de Gruyter Mouton.

Castles, Ian. 1993. *Census characteristics of Victoria: 1991 Census of Population and Housing*. Canberra: ABS, Commonwealth of Australia. https://www.ausstats.abs.gov.au/ausstats/free.nsf/0/3585CA25F44B73B6CA2574BE00835F50/$File/27102_1991_90_Census_Characteristics_of_Victoria.pdf

CO.AS.IT (Comitato Assistenza Italiani/Italian Assistance Association). n.d. *Fact Sheet: Italians in Carlton*. Carlton: Italian Historical Society.

Coveney, Michael. 26 January 2011. Ellen Stewart obituary: Energetic founder of the pioneering experimental theatre club La MaMa. *The Guardian*. https://www.theguardian.com/stage/2011/jan/26/ellen-stewart-obituary

Cresciani, Gianfranco. 2003. *The Italians in Australia*. Cambridge: Cambridge University Press.

Dal Borgo, Alice Giulia. 2006. Signs of Italian culture in the urban landscape of Carlton. *Italian Historical Society Journal* 14(1). 2–9.

Gabaccia, Donna Rae. 2006. Global geography of 'Little Italy': Italian neighbourhoods in comparative perspective. *Modern Italy* 11(1). 9–24.

Gaiser, Leonie & Yaron Matras. 2016. *The spatial construction of civic identities: a study of Manchester's linguistic landscapes*. Manchester: University of Manchester.

Gaiser, Leonie & Yaron Matras. 2021. Using smartphones to document linguistic landscapes: the LinguaSnapp mobile app. *Linguistics Vanguard* 7(s1). 20190012.

Hackworth, Jason & Josephine Rekers. 2005. Ethnic packaging and gentrification: the case of four neighborhoods in Toronto. *Urban Affairs Review* 41(2). 211–236.

Hajek, John & Luciano Giannelli. 2002. L'impatto della cucina mediterranea nel Pacifico. In Domenico Silvestri, Antoniette Marra & Immacolata Pinto (eds.), *Saperi e sapori mediterranei: la cultura dell'alimentazione e i suoi riflessi linguistici*, 1205–1229. Napoli: Università degli Studi di Napoli 'L'Orientale'.

Helzer, Jennifer. 2008. Veggie patches & piazzas: Italia in the Australian landscape. *FOCUS on Geography* 51(2). 9–17.

Izadi, Dariush & Vahid Parvaresh. 2016. The framing of the linguistic landscapes of Persian shop signs in Sydney. *Linguistic Landscape* 2(2). 182–205.

Jaworski, Adam & Crispin Thurlow. 2010. Introducing semiotic landscapes. In Adam Jaworski & Crispin Thurlow (eds.), *Semiotic landscapes: image, text, space*, 1–40. London: Continuum.

Johnson, Katie. 29 July 2021. Lygon St comes alive after Italy's win before plunging into lockdown. *Inner City News*. https://www.innercitynews.com.au/lygon-st-comes-alive-after-italys-win-before-plunging-into-lockdown

Jones, Frank Lancaster. 1962. The Italian population of Carlton: a demographic and sociological survey. PhD thesis, Australian National University.

Jones, Frank Lancaster. 1964. Italians in the Carlton area: the growth of an ethnic concentration. *The Australian Journal of Politics and History* 10(1). 83–95.

Kim, Jinwon. 2018. Manhattan's Koreatown as a transclave: the emergence of a new ethnic enclave in a global city. *City & Community* 17(1). 276–295.

Kosta, Ervin. 2019. Commercial gentrification indexes: using business directories to map urban change at the street level. *City & Community* 18(4). 1101–1122.

Krase, Jerome. 2004. Italian American urban landscapes: images of social and cultural capital. *Italian Americana* 22(1). 17–44.

Krase, Jerome. 2012. *Seeing cities change: local culture and class*. New York: Routledge.

Landry, Rodrigue & Richard Bourhis. 1997. Linguistic landscape and ethnolinguistic vitality. *Journal of Language and Social Psychology* 16(1). 23–49.

Murdie, Robert & Carlos Teixeira. 2011. The impact of gentrification on ethnic neighbourhoods in Toronto: a case study of Little Portugal. *Urban Studies* 48(1). 61–83.

O'Neill, J.P. 1972. *Census of Population and Housing, 30 June 1971: Bulletin 1: summary of population. Part 2: Victoria*. Canberra: Commonwealth Bureau of Census and Statistics.

Pütz, Martin & Neele Mundt. 2018. Multilingualism, multimodality and methodology: linguistic landscape research in the context of assemblages, ideologies and (in)visibility: an introduction. In Martin Pütz & Neele Mundt (eds.), *Expanding the linguistic landscape*, 1–22. Bristol: Multilingual Matters.

Reh, Mechthild. 2004. Multilingual writing: a reader-oriented typology, with examples from Lira Municipality (Uganda). *International Journal of the Sociology of Language* 170. 1–41.

Rubino, Antonia. 2019. Multilingualism in the Sydney landscape. In Alice Chik, Phil Benson & Robyn Moloney (eds.), *Multilingual Sydney*, 180–192. London/New York: Routledge.

Shohamy, Elana. 2018. Linguistic landscape after a decade: an overview of themes, debates and future directions. In Martin Pütz & Neele Mundt (eds.), *Expanding the linguistic landscape*, 25–37. Bristol: Multilingual Matters.

Terzano, Kathryn. 2014. Commodification of transitioning ethnic enclaves. *Behavioral Sciences* 4(4). 341–351.

Woldemariam, Hirut & Elizabeth Lanza. 2015. Imagined community: the linguistic landscape in a diaspora. *Linguistic Landscape* 1(1–2). 172–190.

Daniel Kaufman
6 The Mixtec language in New York: Vitality, discrimination and identity

1 Introduction

The Endangered Language Alliance's language map of New York City (Perlin and Kaufman 2019; Kaufman and Perlin 2018) reports over 640 languages in the greater metropolitan area, likely representing the highest linguistic diversity of any city in the world. The foreign-born population of New York has doubled from the 1970s to the present day, where it stands at over a third of the general population, but our knowledge of the various linguistic communities within this third is highly uneven and lags far behind the facts on the ground. Much has been written on New York's Spanish, Russian, Mandarin Chinese and Yiddish speaking communities (e.g. Garcia and Fishman 2002) but smaller language communities are only described in passing and these descriptions are largely anecdotal in nature.

Despite a population of well over half a million people, New York's Mexican-born community has traditionally been thought of as a monolithic Spanish-speaking bloc when it is in fact one of the most multi-ethnic and multilingual populations in the city. This diversity has only recently come to light for a larger segment of the public due to the catastrophic impacts of the Trump administration's anti-immigrant policies and the Coronavirus pandemic of 2020. City agencies scrambling to communicate with previously neglected populations have for the first time created messaging in Indigenous languages of Latin America but the inadequate resources to meet growing needs for interpretation in languages such as Nahuatl, Mixtec, Zapotec, Mam and K'iche' have rightly been considered a crisis of its own (Nolan 2020; Torrens 2011).

In the present chapter, I focus on the linguistic predicament of Mixtec New Yorkers with a view towards understanding language use and attitudes in the community. The primary research question, which is approached here for the first time, is whether Mixtec will survive as a spoken language among the younger, New York born members of the community. While we cannot prognosticate how the landscape

---

Note: This research would not have been possible without the generous assistance and facilitation of Thelma Carrillo (NYCDOHMH), Krystal Reyes (NYCDOHMH), Jackeline Alvarez (Hunter College), Ross Perlin (ELA), Irwin Sanchez (ELA), Maximiliano Bazan (ELA), Wendy Mirón (LSA Health Center), Inginia Garcia (LSA Health Center) and all of our interviewees. I also sincerely thank the editors of this volume and the anonymous reviewers for many helpful comments that led to improvements.

may change over the decades to come, we can make fairly clear projections about what would happen were the current sociolinguistic and economic conditions to continue as they are.

The primary data which this chapter is based on come from several related sources. Most of the interviews cited here were undertaken as part of "A Qualitative Study of Well-Being and Cultural Continuity through Language Among Indigenous Latin American Immigrants in New York City" (DOHMH IRB#17-132), a collaborative effort led by the Endangered Language Alliance (ELA) and sponsored by the New York City Department of Health and Mental Hygiene. The project collected 30 hour-long interviews across members of six ethnic groups in New York (Nahuatl [Mexico], Mixtec [Mexico], K'iche' [Guatemala], Mam [Guatemala], Garifuna [Honduras, Guatemala and Belize], and Kichwa [Ecuador]) and sought to better understand the contexts in which Indigenous languages are used in New York City, language transmission, issues of access and discrimination, as well as prevalent health issues in the six communities.[1] I rely most heavily on interviews with five Mixtec speakers, whom I refer to with pseudonyms to maintain their anonymity. Our Mixtec co-researcher in the project, Maximiliano Bazan, who carried out most of the interviews, is cited by name.[2] From the same project, I also cite group discussions I led together with collaborators around questions of language. These were held at the LSA Health Center in East Harlem with Mixtec-speaking mothers living in the same neighbourhood.[3] In two cases – (1) and (15–16) below – I make use of previous interviews and discussions I have undertaken with Mixtec speakers as part of ELA, the original sources for which can be found in the notes.

The chapter is organised as follows. First I present the requisite socio-historical background on the Mixtec people both in Mexico and New York and give a brief historical and typological overview of the Mixtec language, including the state of

---

[1] Our approach sought to empower community members as co-researchers by training one person from each group to carry out the interviews in their native language, make time-aligned translations of the recordings, and assist in the interpretation of the transcripts themselves. This is rather unique in the literature on Indigenous migrants in the US, as all studies heretofore have been based on interviews in Spanish, carried out with or without the help of insider co-researchers. This excludes a crucial population of Indigenous migrants we have striven to include here, those who fall within a range of being fully monolingual to not expressing themselves fully in Spanish.
[2] I also make use of ancillary group discussions conducted as part of the larger project as well as interviews conducted prior to this project. Quotes not attributed to any of the pseudonymised interviewees below come from this material.
[3] I use the first person plural throughout to refer to findings from the collective interview project which serves as the primary source material for the current analysis.

the language in New York City. In section 2, I discuss the division of Mixtec speakers' language use by domain, which I argue is crucial to understanding the language's vitality in the diaspora. In section 3, I briefly examine experiences of linguistic discrimination and the potential effects of this discrimination and its perception on language use. In section 4, I look at insider perceptions of the value of the Mixtec language and the factors that will determine its future in diaspora. I conclude with a note on the remaining gaps in our knowledge and directions for further study.

1.1 The Mixtecs in Mexico and New York

The majority of Mexican-born New Yorkers have migrated over the last 35 years, entering predominantly Spanish-speaking neighbourhoods long associated with Puerto Rican and Dominican communities, such as East Harlem, Corona and the South Bronx. Mexican migration to New York increased considerably in the 1980s and 1990s due in large part to the amnesty granted to previously undocumented migrants and the subsequent family reunifications, as part of the Immigration Reform and Control Act of 1986 (IRCA), which conferred legal status on those undocumented immigrants who arrived before 1982. Up until that point, the Mexican state of Puebla was the most significant source of Mexican immigration to New York and the immigrants were largely from the rural mestizo (mixed European/Indigenous ancestry) population. The pre-IRCA migrants from Puebla to New York have been described most prominently in Smith's (2005) ethnography, which examines various aspects of a transnational immigrant community from a single town as they negotiate the social, economic and cultural pressures of leading parallel lives across an American inner city and a rural Mexican *rancheria*. The tightly organised, transnational communities described by Smith may be typical of the mestizo Mexican migrants who benefitted from IRCA. However, in more recent years the state of Guerrero has become the dominant sending region for migrants to the Northeast US (Massey et al. 2010) and the more recent arrivals from Guerrero are of a significantly different profile. A larger proportion are of Indigenous ancestry, belonging to the Mixtec, Nahuatl, Amuzgo and Tlapanec ethnolinguistic groups, among others. The Mixtec speakers, our focus here, comprise the fourth largest Indigenous group in Mexico but are historically among the least integrated into the Mexican state, both socially and economically.

As with many Indigenous groups of Mexico, the Mixtecs are most widely known by the Nahuatl name given to them by the Aztecs. Their popular contemporary endonym, *Ñuu Savi*, descends from earlier Mixtec *Ñudzahui* 'people of the rain/clouds'. The language is referred to commonly as *Tu'un Savi, Sa'a Savi* or a variant thereof, meaning 'language of the rain/clouds'.

Mixtec civilisation is evidenced by a rich archeological record and a large number of Spanish and Mixtec language manuscripts produced during the early Spanish colonial period (see Terreciano 2001 for a comprehensive overview) as well as a vibrant oral culture.

The small-scale agriculture practiced by Mixtecs for millennia provided a viable subsistence until the introduction of livestock by the Spanish (Pérez-Rodríguez 2016; Amith 2005), which altered the landscape considerably and had far reaching consequences on the economy and livelihood of the Indigenous population. More recently, a major turning point emerged in the 1990s, when conditions suddenly worsened as the value of produce depreciated with new US subsidised competition introduced by the North American Free Trade Agreement (NAFTA) (Stephen 2007: 122–131; Gálvez 2018). The negative economic consequences of NAFTA on small-scale farmers were severe enough to single-handedly force thousands to find alternative means of survival. When Indigenous migrants from Guerrero speak of migration, they therefore describe it as a necessity more often than an opportunity. The ensuing Mixtec diaspora now comprises communities throughout the western states of California, Oregon and Washington. However, the northward migration is very much based on village and regional networks. Consequently, we find that the majority of Mixtecs on the west coast originate from communities in Oaxaca but the vast majority of communities in New York and the east coast originate from the neighbouring state of Guerrero with few migrants from Oaxaca.

There is a dramatic disparity in the percentage of speakers of Indigenous languages among the Mexican born population in New York and Mexico itself. Official statistics report that 6.2% of Mexicans over the age of five speak an Indigenous language,[4] while a survey of 1,500 people conducted by the Mexican consulate in New York found that 17.26% spoke an Indigenous language, almost three times the rate of that reported for Mexico itself. Assuming that the estimate of half a million Mexicans in New York City is correct, this puts speakers of Indigenous languages at roughly 86,300 individuals. Two factors lie behind this disparity. Firstly, emigration push factors appear to disproportionately affect Indigenous people regardless of country or region.[5] Secondly, over the last three decades the source of migration to

---

4 Census data 2020, https://www.inegi.org.mx/temas/lengua/#Informacion_general (accessed 14 November 2022).
5 Cohen (2004: 70, 92–3), for instance, notes that speakers of Indigenous languages in areas of Oaxaca appeared more likely to emigrate to the US than to migrate internally and surmises that anti-Indigenous discrimination within Mexico may account for this. Urbanisation (i.e. internal migration) has also been shown to affect Native Americans of the United States and Canada dis-

New York has shifted from towns and cities dominated by mestizos to some of the most linguistically diverse regions of Mexico, where over 20% of the population speaks an Indigenous language.

The more recent Mixtec migrants to New York have far fewer hometown organisations than earlier Mexican immigrants. Their social networks are the extended family unit and, due to their work schedules and family obligations, they typically have little opportunity to congregate with others from their hometown. Furthermore, they are dispersed throughout far-flung neighbourhoods within larger Spanish-speaking populations, such as Corona, East Harlem, Sunset Park, the South Bronx, and the Richmond Hill area of Staten Island. As commented upon elsewhere (e.g. Hernández Corchado 2014: 245), it seems impossible to estimate the number of Mixtecs in New York City with any accuracy, but a figure of 25,000–30,000 has been posited by Martino-Velez (2010), which appears reasonable based on the number of migrants from Guerrero.

1.2 The Mixtec language

1.2.1 Historical and typological overview

Mixtec is best considered a subgroup within the larger Otomanguean family, rather than a single language. Estimates of the number of Mixtec languages based on linguistic criteria vary between 20 to 50. Almost every individual town has an identifiable variety of the language and these varieties can differ considerably within relatively short distances. Varieties of Mixtec are thought to be spoken by over half a million people across Mexico.[6] There is no good estimate for how many Mixtec speakers live in the United States.

All Mixtec varieties are tone languages, most of which have intricate systems of realizing combinations of tones and highly irregular inflectional paradigms in which tense, aspect, mood and person agreement are also indicated at least in

---

proportionately, as well as Indigenous populations from Asia. A recent survey done within the Nepali immigrant community in New York showed that 58% of the respondents belonged to Indigenous "Adivasi" ethnicities, contrasting sharply with their minority status in Nepal itself, where they are only 36% of the general population (Hangen and Ranjit 2010:10). Nonetheless, in the Mexican case, at least, anti-Indigenous discrimination continues largely unabated in the US (Stephen 2007, Holmes 2013).

6 2020 census data show 526,593 speakers of Mixtec languages in Mexico over the age of three, https://www.inegi.org.mx/app/tabulados/interactivos/?pxq=LenguaIndigena_Lengua_05_b53071ff-aae2-48d6-84d1-13a3eb054601&idrt=132&opc=t (accessed 14 November 2020).

part by tone changes. Syntactically, Mixtec is a head-initial language with a basic clausal word order of Verb-Subject-Object. There are roughly two dozen modern descriptive grammars and grammar sketches of Mixtec varieties, most of which were authored by members of the Summer Institute of Linguistics from the 1980s onwards.[7] There also exist hundreds of articles and unpublished theses on various aspects of Mixtec phonetics, phonology and grammar. Pioneering work by Longacre (1957), Josserand (1983) and Dürr (1987) have improved our understanding of the historical development and diversification of the Mixtecan languages, although much work still remains to be done to understand the subgroup's internal diversity and its relation to other Otomanguean subgroups (Campbell 1997, Campbell 2017).

Mixtec already had a two thousand-year-old written tradition when the Spanish arrived in the mid-16th century, but within a relatively short time, Indigenous manuscripts and knowledge of writing were almost completely destroyed. Remnants of Mixtec pictographic writing are still actively being deciphered (see Jansen and Pérez Jiménez 2011 for a recent overview), but detailed knowledge of its use was erased. Mixtec is now written in the Latin alphabet and is promoted by the Mixtec Language Academy, *Ve'e Tu'un Savi* 'House of the Mixtec Language', a non-governmental organisation, through orthography design and literacy workshops, as well as by governmental organisations such as INALI (Instituto Nacional de Lenguas Indígenas). *Ve'e Tu'un Savi* is mainly concerned with *normalización*, the creation of a written standard that can be applied widely within the Mixtec speaking area. The internal diversity of Mixtec has become politicised as the work of INALI in identifying and cataloguing Mixtec "languages" counters the understanding of community organisations such as *Ve'e Tu'un Savi*, who prefer to speak of varieties of a single language. The Mixtec language activists and intellectuals associated with *Ve'e Tu'un Savi* understandably fear that the presentation of Mixtec as a multitude of independent languages only serves to further fragment the community and will ultimately frustrate the creation of a common standard. This is the converse of an earlier but still ongoing struggle to recognise Indigenous languages of Mexico as *lenguas/lenguajes* 'languages' as opposed to *dialectos* 'dialects', as per the common Spanish practice. The Spanish usage carries over to the present day, in which *hablar dialecto* 'to speak dialect' is still the common parlance for speaking an Indigenous language in Mexico.

---

7 Macaulay's (2016) grammar of Chalcatongo Mixtec is probably the most complete description of any variety while Zylstra's (2012) grammar sketch of Alacatlatzala Mixtec is the best description for varieties of the Guerrero region discussed here.

Currently, there is little multilingualism across speakers of Indigenous languages in Guerrero. Even though there are several areas, especially Metlatonoc and Tlapa, where speakers of various Indigenous languages have lived side by side for generations, we have not encountered anyone in New York who can understand multiple Indigenous languages. This was not always the case, but it does appear to hold widely today at a time when Spanish is the uncontested lingua franca.[8] Nonetheless, Mixtec New Yorkers typically live in a complex multilingual environment involving Mixtec, Chilango/Mexican Spanish, Caribbean Spanish/Spanglish, and English.

1.2.2 The language in New York

With regard to New York's linguistic landscape, Mixtec, and Otomanguean languages more generally, are entirely invisible. They have no written representation, neither in signage nor in informal writing. This might be expected given that the vast majority of the language community has no experience reading and writing in their mother tongues; however, even the symbolic use of language, as seen for instance in the widespread use of Nahuatl names of restaurants and other establishments, is completely absent for Mixtec. The Mixtecs, like many other Indigenous peoples of Mexico, had to contend with multiple erasures, first that suffered under the Aztec conquest, then the one imposed by the Spanish colonisers, and now that of the Anglophone world in which many are forced to earn their living.

Another factor in the invisibility of Mixtec is that only the youngest migrants may have had exposure to their mother tongue as a medium of instruction; bilingual education in Guerrero is a relatively new phenomenon and is not distributed evenly throughout the region. More surprising than the absence of written Mixtec in New York is the relative absence of spoken Mixtec on the streets and workplaces, given the large number of speakers. As discussed below, Mixtec speakers typically prefer to use Spanish in the workplace, if possible.

In New York's school system there is no official recognition of any Indigenous Latin American languages being spoken by the student population. All too often, children whose families speak Indigenous languages at home are incorrectly assumed to be Spanish speakers and placed in a Spanish language track, often with negative consequences (Velasco 2010; 2014; Pérez et al. 2016: 259). Velasco and Ka-

---

[8] Sicoli (2011:171) makes an interesting observation that the tendency for speakers of different Otomanguean languages to use Spanish between themselves has led the borderlands between language groups to become areas of increased shift to Spanish.

buto (2019: 142) note that, "[w]hen registering their children for school, Mixteco families rarely share that they are Mixteco speakers when reporting home languages on formal school documents or in conversations during parent-teacher conferences." Indigenous languages have been so denigrated over the last several centuries in Mexico that, for many speakers, they are no longer considered to belong to the same ontological category as Spanish and English. They are unwritten *dialectos* with neither status nor grammar.[9] Furthermore, for those who came in the 1980s and early 1990s, there is a strict separation between the Spanish domain of education and the Mixtec domain of the home. Transgression of this barrier in school often resulted in physical punishment.

It is only within the last three years that city agencies have begun responding to the need for translation and outreach to Mixtec speakers with occasional promotions and informational material in Mixtec, among a handful of other Indigenous languages from the region.[10]

2 Language domains

The work of Joshua Fishman (1965; 1972 and following) bestowed a key role on the notion of social domains in understanding language maintenance and revitalisation, specifically, the question of "Who speaks what language to whom and when?". As shown in a large body of subsequent work, language shift proceeds by domain, as does effective revitalisation. Overall, all Mixtec interviewees were aware of changes in language use after arriving in New York City, which uniformly consisted of an increase in Spanish use, and few reported any significant use of English (although many made efforts to acquire English through free classes). However, to assess the present state of Mixtec in New York and the prospects of its survival it is essential to understand language choice in context and which (if any) social spaces remain for the language in the diaspora. A summary assessment of language use is offered in the following for the domains of work (2.1), school (2.2), religion (2.3), healthcare (2.4), the home (2.5), and written communica-

---

9 Attitudes toward Indigenous languages are improving in Mexico amid increased efforts at rehabilitating their prestige. Most important among these efforts are the amendments to the Mexican Constitution implemented in 1992 that seek to recognise and protect Indigenous languages. But those who migrated to New York in the 1980s and early 1990s did not benefit from these developments.

10 In one recent example, the Mayor's Office for Immigrant Affairs produced advertisements for a municipal identification card in Mixteco. See https://www.youtube.com/watch?v=XJqOhm5 S1oY&t=29s.

tion (2.6), although this must be understood as merely the first step towards a more detailed picture.[11]

2.1 Work

Again and again, we find Spanish to be the preferred medium of communication even in social domains that would have been amenable to Mixtec use in the hometown. AA, a 26-year-old from Cuautipan, a majority monolingual Mixtec town of roughly 30,000 people, works with five other Mixtec speakers from Guerrero in a restaurant kitchen yet he reports that they never use Mixtec in the workplace. In contrast, Mixtec speakers working the fields of Guerrero would rarely if ever communicate in Spanish showing that even between interlocutors with similar origins, we cannot talk about an undifferentiated domain of "work", as the fields produce entirely different conditions from a restaurant kitchen in New York City. The former context is where family members and townmates congregate to undertake a form of labour that has been passed down from generation to generation. The latter is a new and often unfamiliar context for those coming from Guerrero. Despite many New York City kitchens today being populated entirely by Indigenous Mexican labourers from Guerrero and Puebla, they are typically supervised by people of different origins. As we return to below, the mere potential of being overheard by outsiders appears to be a powerful factor in language choice. At the same time, we cannot completely discount the possibility that differences in hometown pose difficulties in communication but the fact that so many Mixtec speakers hail from the area around Tlapa de Comonfort makes this an unlikely cause for what appears to be a strong preference for Spanish in the workplace.

2.2 School

Education had already been cemented within the domain of Spanish when most of our interviewees were coming of age in Guerrero and only a few were taught to read and write in Mixtec, although this is becoming increasingly common as bilingual education expands. As already mentioned in section 1.2.2, Mixtec pa-

---

[11] Note that the information reported here is almost entirely self-reported on behalf of the interviewees. Follow up work should employ participant observation across these domains to understand aspects that may not emerge forthrightly in interviews.

rents generally do not state their mother tongue in school language surveys that specifically seek such information (both in New York City as well as in the Californian contexts discussed by Pérez et al. 2016). This is most likely carried over from their own experiences with schooling. Not only is Indigenous identity not offered on request, it is often actively hidden and occasionally suppressed from within the family. JS, a Mixtec woman with a son in the public school system related to us the following:

(1) Just three or four days ago, I was arguing with my brother because one of Irwin's [son] teachers came to our house and I began speaking with him and my brother yelled at me. "Why are you yelling at me?" He said, "Aren't you embarrassed to speak dialect in front of them?" "It doesn't matter," I said to him. First of all, it's visible [that you're Indigenous]. My brother got annoyed with me a little. What I always tell my brother is, "You try to speak in Spanish, but what happens? Your Spanish is not correct." I tell him. There's always a point or an accent missing, I tell him. I always tell him and he gets more annoyed with me.[12]

Note that the mere act of speaking Mixtec in the presence of a school teacher made the interviewee's brother anxious and led him to police his sister's language use within the home. This type of behaviour cannot be understood independently from the long colonial and post-colonial policy of punishing children for speaking their mother tongues within the school grounds. The picture that emerges from the interviews is one in which Mixtec speakers need a good excuse for using the language in earshot of outsiders. SG, a 38-year-old woman from a small town in the Metlatonoc region who grew up monolingually, is proud to have a command of her language and even wishes to pass it on to her children, yet she states:

(2) I only speak it [Mixtec] with my mother. They hear me. I'm not ashamed to speak it because I speak it in front of people with my mother even if they don't understand me. I say that I'm speaking with my mother.

Note that SG is prepared to counter her hypothetical critics; she is speaking to her monolingual mother and thus has no choice but to use Mixtec even if that excludes the others around her. We return to this point in more detail below in section 3.

---

[12] See https://www.youtube.com/watch?v=huMtG6v1YcQ for context.

2.3 Religion

Most Mixtec families are Catholics, although there is a growing number of Evangelicals both in Mexico and in New York City. O'Connor's (2016) study of Mixtec Evangelical Protestants does not find a clear link between language and religion in the Oaxacan towns she examines, although she does not elaborate on language use within church ceremony. On one hand, Mixtec Catholics can be said to be more traditional, for example, in typically honouring the town fiestas, patron saints, and rendering their services for *tequio*, village-based corvée labour. From this perspective, we might expect active membership in the Catholic church to correlate with higher use of Mixtec as these both represent culturally conservative features. On the other hand, it is largely through the Summer Institute of Linguistics that Protestantism has made inroads into Indigenous Mexican communities and this organisation is centered around Indigenous language literacy (for the ultimate purposes of Bible translation and proselytisation). Thus, Mixtec Protestants are more likely to have encountered their language in writing in religious contexts. However, it seems the question of religious domains is moot in New York City, as neither religion appears to offer a space for Mixtec language. Despite the large numbers of Mixtecs who attend Catholic services in the city, there has never been an effort to cater to this community linguistically on the part of the church. The Evangelical Protestant churches that Mixtecs attend, on the other hand, are operated in Spanish and cater to congregations with origins not only in Mexico but also Puerto Rico, the Dominican Republic and Latin America. While we did not investigate frequency of church attendance in our interviews, none of the interviewees reported using Mixtec in any religious function. Rather, all religious functions are carried out in Spanish.[13]

2.4 Healthcare

In the domain of healthcare, the many Mixtec speakers who only have a basic knowledge of Spanish struggle to communicate their needs to healthcare providers. New York City hospitals provide interpretation in-person and through the telephone, but we only encountered a single Mixtec speaker who availed of these services. More often, we heard stories of misunderstanding and a feeling that lan-

---

[13] The Jehovah's Witnesses are the one religious organisation which does proselytise in Mixtec (using translated tractates) but there do not seem to be many Mixtec adherents in New York. Barchas-Lichtenstein (2013) describes the complex linguistic dynamics of Jehovah Witness adherents in another Indigenous community of southern Mexico.

guage barriers prevented Mixtecs from receiving proper care. The entire notion of patient rights and language rights in healthcare is poorly disseminated and appears unfamiliar to local Indigenous immigrant communities. As a result, anyone who can communicate with even the smallest amount of confidence in Spanish elects to use Spanish in healthcare contexts, assuming this is their only option. This, in turn, results in an apparent lack of demand for Indigenous language interpretation and a general lack of attention to Indigenous populations on the part of health agencies and healthcare providers. Consequently, there is a sense of resignation in the face of language barriers in this setting. "Sometimes we understand the doctors and sometimes we don't," as SG put it.

2.5 The home

The home is perhaps the most complex language domain of all and certainly the most crucial for the survival of the language in diaspora. Within the home, we can immediately identify telephone conversations with family in Mexico as the only consistent source of Mixtec for children. In most cases, the parental generation of Mixtec migrants speak little to no Spanish and thus conversations with elder generations are conducted entirely in Mixtec. This was recognised by all interviewees as their primary use of the language in New York, especially now that it is relatively easy and cheap to place calls to Guerrero (as opposed to 15 years ago). Children who have any familiarity with the language are forced to use it on the telephone with grandparents who do not speak Spanish. However, as would be expected, children raised in Spanish are not able to pick up the language from conversations between their parents and other family members. Thus, the telephone appears to serve as a reinforcement for those children with a basic grasp of the language but never a source of Mixtec linguistic competence on its own.

It remains unclear whether language choice in telephone conversations is affected by migration. Some interviewees did report switching to Spanish when talking on the phone with family members, whether in the United States or Mexico, with whom they previously used to speak Mixtec. SG states:

(3) In New York I know very few people [from my town]. My cousins are two and there are maybe about 20 others that I know here but in Florida, Virginia, Los Angeles, San Diego, I have relatives who are there. Yes, we connect but we always speak Spanish. We don't communicate in Mixtec. I don't know why.

In most cases, Mixtec speakers were married to fellow Mixtec speakers, although not necessarily from the same town. One can compare Velasco's (2014) study, in which, out of 23 Mixtec speaking mothers in New York, 21 were married to Mixtec-speaking men. However, in neither her study nor the present one do we find strong evidence that the presence of two Mixtec-speaking parents at home ensures any level of child-directed speech in Mixtec. Velasco (2014: 96) reports:

> In families in which both parents speak Mixteco, this is the language used by the couple with friends and relatives who are all part of the same generation and who speak Mixteco as their first language. However, even these couples, both of whom are Mixteco speakers, seldom use Mixteco with their children. This language shift does not seem to be propelled by the children, as is usually the case with second-generation immigrants, but by the parents themselves. Children born in New York to Mixteco parents are not consistently addressed, or spoken to, in Mixteco.

One of the most interesting and consequential challenges here is understanding the determinants of language choice in child-directed speech at home. First of all, there are the lasting effects of discrimination that all speakers related to us (examined further below). Secondly, there is the notion that Mixtec is not a practical language for socio-economic advancement in New York. Thirdly, the time spent between parents and children may simply be insufficient for acquisition of the parents' mother tongue. In many cases, both parents work or, if only one parent is working the other parent may be too occupied with the business of providing for their children to be able to engage with them sufficiently. In many of the families we have interviewed and observed, television, smart phones and other devices play a large role in keeping children entertained when caretakers are stretched too thin. Although there are often opportunities to play with siblings and cousins, it is only the parental generation that has a full command of Mixtec.

FC, a 49-year-old near monolingual Mixtec speaker, consciously points to this as an explanation for why he must speak Spanish to his children:

(4) In our town where we were born, we speak the language day and night because they're all Mixtec. I speak Mixtec the most because I grew up with it. I speak very little Spanish, broken Spanish. [I use Mixtec] with my sister in Mexico when I call them. I speak to my wife in Mixtec a little bit. I speak to my kids very little and in Spanish because I don't really see them. They go to school [in the morning]. In the afternoon is when I see them. Just a little bit because then they go to sleep. If they spoke to me in Mixtec, I would speak to them in Mixtec. [. . .] If they start speaking with me in Mixtec, I would speak with them in Mixtec.

SG echoes a similar state of affairs in describing her attempts to communicate in Mixtec with her children:

(5) I speak sometimes [Mixtec], I taught some words to my daughters. But it is difficult, for example, the one who is 12 years old, she no longer pays attention to me, because I was not with her when she was little. [At that time] I was working hard, so when I got home what I wanted was to rest and there wasn't much communication.
The normal thing in the town is that one goes out when the sun rises and works and when the sun goes down one goes home to rest and here there is no time for a person to work like that. There are many different [shifts]. Some work in the morning, another in the afternoon, another at night. There is never a time to communicate.

Indeed, when asked what the primary challenge of living in New York was, SG answered:

(6) Here it is perhaps the time. That is, a mother and father don't have time to dedicate to their children like before.

The possibilities for language transmission are severely limited by the grueling socio-economic reality Mixtec migrants face. When asked to sum up Mixtec living conditions in New York, Maximiliano Bazan pointed immediately to isolation and the virtual enslavement imposed on the community by their working conditions. It was particularly surprising to find many cases where children and parents do not share any common language in which both are truly comfortable. It is not uncommon in immigrant households of all national origins for children to have only a passive knowledge of their parents' language and for the parents to have a minimal command of the language of wider communication but in families such as FC's, the parents are only comfortable in Mixtec. FC's wife learned more Spanish than him in New York while FC himself claims to only speak "very little broken Spanish". The children, however, are said to not only lack basic comprehension of Mixtec but also to lack Spanish:

(7) Although it's me that can't speak Spanish or English, but my kids that were born here also can't speak Spanish. They speak English. With the kids, Mixtec is no longer there. They can't speak it. When I talk to my wife, they don't pay attention, they're away from us, they don't pay attention. [My wife] doesn't speak [to them in English]. She speaks a little bit [of Spanish], she

learned a little bit more than me. Yes, she learned a little bit more than me. When she first came with me, she couldn't speak Spanish at all.

The home situation described above by FC approaches a pidginisation scenario (cf. Thomason 2001): the parents speak to their children in a language they learned only recently, as adults; the children, on the other hand, are English dominant and only have a passive knowledge of Spanish. Thus, neither party is fully comfortable in the household lingua franca, potentially affecting the nature of intergenerational communication in the family. Children in these circumstances furthermore often face difficulties in school due to perceptions of their command of English and Spanish, as well as being reflexively misclassified as Spanish speakers. A serious understanding of these outcomes is of the utmost importance not only to the future of the Mixtec language in New York but to the future of the youth who are caught in this pernicious grey area.

2.6 Written communication

As mentioned above, only a very small number of Mixtec speakers in New York have any real experience reading or writing the language, as Indigenous language literacy has only been recently introduced into the Mexican school system and is still implemented very unevenly. Many Mixtec migrants arrive in New York with only basic Spanish literacy or no Spanish literacy at all depending on their primary school education. Migrants under 40, who typically make frequent use of social media, appear to have become more literate in Spanish in New York, most likely through the regular use of these electronic means. While all the interviewees made some use of platforms such as Facebook, WhatsApp and other messaging services, they solely employed Spanish in these domains. Those who employ Mixtec on social media are dedicated language activists most of whom are Oaxacans living in Mexico or California.

3 Discrimination, alienation, and the mestizo gaze

Few forms of discrimination are more overt and unambiguous than name calling, and there are myriad denigrating terms deployed against Indigenous Mexicans. The discrimination experienced by Mixtecs, even as manifested by name calling, comes partly from fellow community members who have internalised the racist attitudes of the surrounding society, as well as from outsiders. SQ, for instance, reports Mixtecs disparagingly calling each other *indio*:

(8) We go through that a lot back home, even Mixtecs do that. Racism. Yes. That's what they call racism. I don't know what's going on with our community because they do it with their own kind. I went through it. Sometimes when we leave and go to another country, and we might not know who the people are, but they could say, who is this *indio*? And that is already racism. Our own people would do it.

But discrimination is not typically produced or perceived with such little ambiguity. One common theme affecting public language use that emerged not only from our Mixtec interviewees but also from the other five Indigenous groups included in the larger project (see section 1) can be referred to as "the mestizo gaze". Two representative examples from our interviews serve to illustrate:

(9) ZC: My own sister feels ashamed to speak like that in public places. She feels ashamed because they look at her.

(10) AA: We get embarrassed because when other people come, they look at us. They look at us. Some of them, they don't say anything, they just pass by, because other people have their own language. Sometimes we do the same thing. We look at them when they speak their language, because they speak a different language. It's their language. We feel the same thing. When I'm on the streets and I speak, and they look at me I feel that a little. Yes, they look at you. They listen to you. They can hear what you're talking about.

This theme is also reflected amply in Menchaca Bishop and Kelley's (2013) study of Mixtec and Nahuatl women in New York City, as exemplified by one of their interviews:

(11) Sometimes, when I ride the subway with my country-people, we speak Mixteco and the people in the train stare at us as if saying, "What could it be that they are speaking?" But no, they give us dirty looks, but I don't care. Yes, they look at us as if they are saying, "indios!" (Menchaca Bishop and Kelley 2013: 105)

A common assumption appears throughout the interviews but is only rarely substantiated overtly in the narration: the mestizo gaze is always perceived as belittling or disparaging rather than as innocent curiosity. It is impossible to ascertain

6 The Mixtec language in New York: Vitality, discrimination and identity — 163

how much of these perceptions represent accurate readings of an ambient anti-Indigenous racism in New York and how much it is coloured by the traumatic racism experienced in Mexico. What seems clear is the widespread interpretation of public staring as a belittling stance and the concomitant effects on public language use.

A peculiar phenomenon not reported elsewhere and perhaps unique to New York is the reference to Mixtec as "Chinese". While in some languages "Chinese" can be a common stand-in for anything unfamiliar (cf. "Greek" in American English), the particular pairing of Mixtec with Chinese, which we did not encounter with other Indigenous languages, may not be completely arbitrary. First, various Chinese languages are spoken widely throughout the city and thus the sounds of Chinese, broadly speaking, are very identifiable to most New Yorkers both young and old. Second, Mixtec and Chinese are very saliently tone languages and bear some surface similarities in their phonotactics. The transference of the term Chinese to Mixtec by outsiders, on its own, may thus have been unremarkable. What is surprising is that several Mixtec parents reported that this unfortunate usage has been adopted by their own children, as one young mother commented:

(12) I speak Spanish to her [my daughter] because I've spoken Spanish with my husband since we met, but my mother-in-law does speak Mixtec to her and sometimes she understands a little of what's spoken to her. [. . .] Now when I want to speak to her in Mixtec she says that I speak Chinese. She says, "That's not Mixtec. That's Chinese!" and that she no longer wants to speak Mixtec. When I speak Mixtec she teases me. She says "No mommy, that's not Mixtec; that's Chinese."

Another mother participating in the same group discussion corroborated this on the basis of her son:

(13) Also as she says, children say we speak Chinese. My son, the other boy, is 8 years old and says that I should learn to speak in English because he does not want to speak in Spanish and Mixtec. He just wants to speak in English. "You have to learn English to speak to me because I don't want to speak Spanish or Mixtec, because that Mixtec is Chinese," says my son.

This appears as the ultimate act of alienation; not only is the language rejected as a means of communication, the mere identity of the language is distorted beyond recognition (cf. Ruiz and Barajas 2012). Although ironically coming from a child of two Mixtec parents who has no ulterior political motives, statements such as these fit into a larger pattern of denying the existence of Indigenous languages back home.[14]

In the face of the language policing, discrimination and alienation that speakers are subjected to, it must be emphasised that the vast majority of our interviewees never claimed to be ashamed to speak their languages outside of the workplace despite reporting that they often feel like objects of curiosity and suspicion in such instances. I return to this apparent paradox in the conclusion.

4 The value and future of the language in New York

What can be prognosticated about the future of the Mixtec language in New York? Firstly, militating against its survival are grueling economic circumstances which radically reduce the meaningful hours that parents can spend with their children. Beyond this, we find two conflicting discourses with regard to whether Mixtec *should* be passed down to children outside of the Mixtec homeland in the first place. Many Mixtec parents speak of the importance of the language but, simultaneously, many still view Indigenous languages as a possible impediment to learning English and Spanish.[15] Since there are few if any countervailing forces that encourage parents to use Mixtec with their children, the misconception of children being confused by multilingual input persists across time and space despite all evidence to the contrary.

Not all Mixtec parents in New York who speak solely in Spanish to their children do so out of an ideological motivation. Some of our interviewees, in fact, express regret that Spanish has become the default language of the home despite

---

14 Velasco Ortiz (2005: 70) cites a Mixtec interviewee who recalls the erasure of her identity and language within the local school: "Tlacotepec was a parochial and municipal center; therefore the Church and educational programs came to disturb us. Both played a part in destroying the Indigenous language. I remember when we were in Tlacotepec's school, the teacher said to us, 'You are not Indigenous . . . here there are only mestizos.' The Indigenous language was the loser."

15 This misconception is often reinforced by educators and speech pathologists. Pérez Báez (2013: 39) discusses a case in which a speech pathologist, visiting a multilingual Zapotec household in Los Angeles where a child was feared to be developmentally delayed, recommended to the mother that she stop speaking Zapotec to her child. There seems to be a real gap deserving further study in how the field of speech pathology presents an officially progressive stance towards multilingualism in the home and "the facts on the ground", as evinced by many similar reports.

their desires to pass down the language. However, for many who do actively avoid passing down the language, this appears as intergenerationally reproduced behaviour. Dauenhauer and Dauenhauer (1998), among others, discuss how parents who have been punished for speaking their Indigenous language in school find it exceedingly difficult to overcome their trauma and speak to their own children in their mother tongue. This was also reflected in our interviews. MB, a 37-year-old domestic worker with three children, explained how her husband's father forbade his wife to speak Mixtec in the home because "he did not want his children to learn *dialecto indio*." As a result, not only does her husband lack the ability to speak Mixtec, he also reproduces the same attitudes towards their children in New York, as MB herself is a fluent Mixtec speaker who would speak to their children in the language were it not for her husband. A trauma inflicted by a far removed grandparent in Guerrero thus continues to play out in New York many decades later (see Perry 2009: 66 for a very similar case).

In asking the interviewees about the value of their children knowing Mixtec, practical concerns often outweighed issues of identity. In circumstances where expressions of culture and identity have become a luxury this should not be surprising, yet several interviewees shared interesting responses to this line of questioning. After explaining that Mixtec is necessary for communication with the elders, who are still largely monolingual in many areas of Guerrero, AA goes on to say that there is also a kind of sharing that occurs when Mixtecs of different towns congregate:

(14) We can say that, because people come from different towns, when they start talking to each other, they will tell stories and talk about things. You know, "we speak this way, they speak that way," but they gather. So we can't let it disappear.

AA, uniquely among our interviewees, posits the idea that informal dialect comparison itself ("we speak this way, they speak that way") is a positive experience, presumably as a unifying intellectual exercise, which could clearly not continue without the language being actively spoken. Another view is expressed by Maximiliano Bazan, who sees language as the last remnant in a long colonial process of deculturation:

(15) As you know, before the Spaniards, we did have plenty of things. We had land. We had everything. Now the only thing we have left is our language, our culture, traditions, things like that. If the language dies, well, I believe everything is going to die, including us.

This is more than metaphorical in the Mexican context, where command of an Indigenous language is precisely what determines one's official status as Indigenous or mestizo in the state's classification system. Under this system, a Mixtec town that shifts to Spanish has effectively ceased to be Mixtec. Similarly, on the level of the family, a couple may emigrate from Guerrero as Mixtecs and return decades later from New York as mestizos.

The popular and academic discourse around language endangerment (Nettle and Romaine 2000; Harrison 2007; Evans 2011, *inter alia*) often points to the loss of ritual, traditional song, oral literature and environmental knowledge as some of the most dire consequences of language loss. None of these themes, however, were mentioned by any of our interviewees. Indigenous ritual, song, and oral literature were largely driven underground and eliminated by the Spanish in their mission of total subjugation. Today, cultural production and spirituality are largely channeled through a syncretic Catholicism which still dominates much of rural Mexican society. In most areas in the Mixtec homeland, it appears that Indigenous rituals carried out in the Mixtec language only remain among traditional healers and those who petition the traditional deities for rain and a successful harvest.[16] Most of our interviewees, despite being dominant in Mixtec, were unable to recall traditional songs in their mother tongue from back home and there was no reported use of Mixtec in any explicitly spiritual-cultural sphere in New York. Folk stories and traditional trickster tales, on the other hand, have been preserved far better, although none of our interviewees volunteered these genres as part of an endangered cultural heritage that would be lost as a result of language shift. Nonetheless, Mixtec-speaking interviewees did not hesitate to state their strong attachment to their mother tongue claiming that, as an Indigenous language and as the language of their parents, it could not be traded away and should not disappear. And yet these powerful motives may not be sufficient given the utilitarian orientation of the New York based community.

5 Conclusion

I began by noting New York's hidden linguistic diversity; despite decades of surveying, over 500 languages had gone completely uncounted. Among the uncounted are dozens of Indigenous Mexican communities. Some, like Cuicatec, are

---

[16] Jonathan Amith and Rey Castillo García have documented several examples of such rituals as part of the Guerrero Mixtec Language Documentation Project (https://elar.soas.ac.uk/Collection/MPI492067).

only represented by a handful of speakers in the city while others, like Mixtec, by a population of thousands. And yet Mixtec in New York is a language hidden in plain sight; the first-hand accounts reported on here begin to shed light on why. A combination of historical trauma, ongoing discrimination and economic pressures conspire to suppress the use of Mixtec in public and prevent the transmission of Mixtec to the next generation.

As emphasised by Pérez Báez (2013: 31), the impact of diasporic Indigenous communities on the survival of their languages is understudied and of increasing importance. In addition to the survival of the language in diaspora, we must also consider the linguistic effects of diasporic population returning to the hometown either to visit or settle (Pérez Báez 2013; 2014). Clearly, the diaspora Mixtecs will play a large role in the survival of their language as their traditional homeland continues to lose its young people due to ever increasing economic pressures.

There is an apparent paradox in the picture I have presented here which is worth highlighting. On the one hand, all New York Mixtecs we have interviewed claim pride in their linguistic heritage and feel strongly that the Mixtec language must survive. On the other hand, their patterns of language use do not indicate significant language loyalty. How can these facts be reconciled? I believe the factors at play which conspire to suppress the use of Mixtec in New York can be distilled to the following (with possible further reduction):[17]

(i) an ideology of accommodation which leads many speakers to prefer Spanish in the presence of outsiders[18]
(ii) the historical destruction of exclusively Mixtec language domains
(iii) a pragmatic view of language choice in the diaspora
(iv) the fear of ridicule and discrimination

None of these powerful factors are incompatible with a feeling of pride and a desire for the language to continue. Kulick's (1992) well-known study of the Gapun shows how a community's attitudes towards (and perception of) their language use can diverge widely from their actual quotidian linguistic practice. Mixtec New Yorkers, on the other hand, do not seem to entertain many illusions about their language use and their difficult linguistic situation embedded within the surrounding Hispanophone and Anglophone society. The differences between life in Guerrero, where resources were few but working hours finite, and New York,

---

[17] Note that while these factors are distinguishable from each other, none are truly independent; most if not all result directly from the Indigenous experience under colonialism.
[18] Although, accommodation to younger community members can clearly play a major role, as well. Pérez Báez (2013, 2014) argues that accommodation to younger, US born Zapotecs is accelerating language shift to Spanish in the community of San Lucas Quiaviní, Oaxaca.

where time is the rarest commodity, are apparent to all. The consequences of work schedules on child rearing and language transmission are just as obvious. The paradox is thus merely apparent. Mixtec language loyalty may be considerable, but the forces arrayed against it are far more powerful. Language loyalty can be seen to emerge in unexpected places, as in confrontations with the perpetual curiosity that Indigenous Mexican languages in New York elicit in bystanders. MC, a young Mixtec mother from the Bronx, related the following subtle expression of resistance in such an encounter:

(16) Me and my sister were speaking Mixtec in the street and a lady came up to us and asked "What are you speaking? Is it English? It can't be English because I don't understand it!" And my sister said, "'Of course it's English. But it's our English!"[19]

Not only does MC position Mixtec on par with English as a language rather than a *dialecto*, overturning an enduring false dichotomy, she also puts Mixtec on par with English as yet another language of New York, a city where everyone has their "English". It is perhaps in these miniature skirmishes that language loyalty is hashed out most clearly, rather than in the pressured and historically fraught context of child-directed language.

There are deeper questions of ideology here for which our data are insufficient. For instance, what is the Mixtec view of language acquisition and socialisation? Pérez Báez (2013: 37) reports that Zapotec speakers of San Lucas Quiaviní believe children are born speaking the language of the land, a view which simultaneously explains why Zapotec children born in Los Angeles do not speak the language and assuages any fears of language loss in the hometown. Although our interviews attempted to get at the relation between land and language, we were only able to scratch the surface. A perhaps more glaring lacuna in our study regards how Mixtecs perceive success in New York. Beyond a basic desire for comfort and stability common to all, our interviews offer little insight into how the current Mixtec diaspora envisions "the good life" and how much it depends on aspirations for personal achievement in New York, as opposed to commitments to the hometown. Aspirations are of course in flux as migrants lay down deeper roots, so there may be no overarching patterns here. Nonetheless, a family's perceived connections and long-term obligations to the hometown may very well have consequences for their language use in the diaspora. These are all fruitful directions for future research.

---

19 See https://www.youtube.com/watch?v=1RYoJunu7a0.

Finally, I hope to have drawn attention to the hardship experienced by Indigenous children raised in an L2 Spanish context by parents coerced out of speaking to them in their mother tongue, whether explicitly or implicitly.

Despite the challenges discussed, the picture offered here should not be seen as an ineluctable march towards oblivion. Many cities outside the US are taking an increasingly active role in facilitating multilingualism among their immigrant communities and New York has now begun to acknowledge the importance of Mixtec, as well. As a small example, in 2020, for the first time anywhere in the US, as far as I am aware, a Mixtec language advertisement was produced by an official branch of city government. The Mayor's Office of Immigrant Affairs featured three Mixtec speakers promoting a new municipal identification card and speaking about the importance of belonging. The city-funded study that formed the basis of the material cited here is another such example. By addressing the root causes of the language's invisibility, including the severe economic challenges faced by its speakers, there is yet hope that Mixtec can survive alongside the many varieties of Italian, Chinese, Yiddish, and other major heritage languages established in New York during the twentieth century.

References

Amith, Jonathan D. 2005. *The Möbius Strip: the spatial history of colonial society in Guerrero, Mexico*. Stanford: Stanford University Press.

Barchas-Lichtenstein, Jena. 2013. "When the dead are resurrected, how are we going to speak to them?": Jehovah's Witnesses and the use of Indigenous languages in the globalizing textual community. PhD thesis, University of California Los Angeles.

Campbell, Eric W. 2017. Otomanguean historical linguistics: past, present and prospects for the future. *Language & Linguistics Compass* 11(4). e12240.

Campbell, Lyle. 1997. *American Indian languages: the historical linguistics of Native America*. Oxford: Oxford University Press.

Cohen, Jeffrey H. 2004. *The culture of migration in Southern Mexico*. Austin: University of Texas Press.

Dauenhauer, Nora Marks & Richard Dauenhauer. 1998. Technical, emotional, and ideological issues in reversing language shift: examples from Southeast Alaska. In Leonore A. Grenoble & Lindsay J. Whaley (eds.), *Endangered languages: language loss and community response*, 57–98. Cambridge: Cambridge University Press.

Dürr, Michael. 1987. A preliminary reconstruction of the proto-Mixtec tonal system. *Indiana* 11. 19–61.

Evans, Nicholas. 2011. *Dying words: endangered languages and what they have to tell us*. Hoboken: John Wiley.

Fishman, Joshua A. 1965. Who speaks what language to whom and when? *La Linguistique* 1(2). 67–88.

Fishman, Joshua A. 1972. *The sociology of language: an interdisciplinary approach to language in society*. Rowley: Newbury House.

Gálvez, Alyshia. 2018. *Eating NAFTA: trade, food policies, and the destruction of Mexico*. Oakland: University of California Press.

Garcia, Ofelia & Joshua A. Fishman. 2002. *The multilingual Apple: languages in New York City*. Berlin/New York: Mouton de Gruyter.

Hangen, Susan & Luna Ranjit. 2010. *Snapshots of the Nepali-speaking community in New York City: demographics and challenges*. New York: Adhikaar.

Harrison, David K. 2007. *When languages die: the extinction of the world's languages and the erosion of human knowledge*. Oxford: Oxford University Press.

Hernández Corchado, Rodolfo. 2014. My people is a people on its knees: Mexican labor migration from the Montaña region and the formation of a working class in New York City. PhD thesis, City University of New York.

Holmes, Seth. 2013. *Fresh fruit, broken bodies: migrant farmworkers in the United States*. Berkeley: University of California Press.

Jansen, Maarten & Gabina Aurora Pérez Jiménez. 2011. *The Mixtec pictorial manuscripts: time, agency and memory in ancient Mexico*. Leiden/Boston: Brill.

Josserand, Judy Kathryn. 1983. Mixtec dialect history: proto-Mixtec and modern Mixtec text. PhD thesis, Tulane University.

Kaufman, Daniel & Ross Perlin. 2018. Language documentation in diaspora communities. In Ken Rehg & Lyle Campbell (eds.), *Oxford handbook of endangered languages*, 399–418. Oxford: Oxford University Press.

Kulick, Don. 1992. *Language shift and cultural reproduction: socialization, self, and syncretism in a Papua New Guinean village*. Cambridge/New York: Cambridge University Press.

Longacre, Robert E. 1957. *Proto-Mixtecan*. Bloomington: Indiana University Research Center in Anthropology, Folklore, and Linguistics.

Macaulay, Monica A. 1996. *A grammar of Chalcatongo Mixtec*. Berkeley: University of California Press.

Martino-Velez, L. 2010. Mixtecos in New York: Language and identity. Paper presented at Mano a Mano: Mexican Culture Without Borders, 17 April, New York.

Massey, Jacob S., Douglas S. Rugh, & Karen A. Pren. 2010. The geography of undocumented Mexican migration. *Mexican studies. Estudios mexicanos* 26. 129–152.

Menchaca Bishop, Laura & Prema Kelley. 2013. Indigenous Mexican languages and the politics of language shift in the United States. In Carol Benson & Kimmo Kosonen (eds.), *Language issues in comparative education*, 97–113. Rotterdam/Boston/Taipei: Sense Publishers.

Nettle, Daniel, & Suzanne Romaine. 2000. *Vanishing voices: the extinction of the world's languages*. Oxford: Oxford University Press.

Nolan, Rachel. 6 January 2020. A Translation crisis at the border. *The New Yorker*.

O'Connor, Mary I. 2016. *Mixtec Evangelicals: globalization, migration, and religious change in a Oaxacan Indigenous group*. Louisville: University Press of Colorado.

Pérez, William, Rafael Vázquez & Raymond Buriel. 2016. Zapotec, Mixtec, and Purhépecha youth: multilingualism and the marginalization of Indigenous youth in the United States. In Samy Alim, John Rickford, Arnetha F. Ball (eds.), *Raciolinguistics: how language shapes our ideas about race*, 255–272. Oxford: Oxford University Press.

Pérez Báez, Gabriela. 2013. Family language policy, transnationalism, and the diaspora community of San Lucas Quiavinî of Oaxaca, Mexico. *Language Policy* 12(1). 27–45.

Pérez Báez, Gabriela. 2014. Determinants of language reproduction and shift in a transnational community. *International Journal of the Sociology of Language* 227. 65–81.

Pérez-Rodríguez, Verónica. 2016. Terrace agriculture in the Mixteca Alta Region, Oaxaca, Mexico: ethnographic and archeological insights on terrace construction and labor organization. *CAFE: Culture, Agriculture, Food, and Environment* 38(1). 18–27.

Perlin, Ross & Daniel Kaufman. 2019. *Map of the languages of New York City*. New York: Endangered Language Alliance.

Perry, Elizabeth. 2009. The declining use of the Mixtec language among Oaxacan migrants and stay-at-homes: the persistence of memory, discrimination, and social hierarchies of power. *CCIS Working Paper* 180.

Ruiz, Nadine T. & Manuel Barajas. 2012. Multiple perspectives on the schooling of Mexican Indigenous students in the U.S.: issues for future research. *Bilingual Research Journal* 35(2). 125–144.

Sicoli, Mark A. 2011. Agency and ideology in language shift and language maintenance. In Tania Granadillo & Heidi A. Orcutt-Gachiri (eds.), *Ethnographic contributions to the study of endangered languages*, 161–176. Tucson: University of Arizona Press.

Smith, Robert. 2005. *Mexican New York: transnational lives of new immigrants*. Berkeley: University of California Press.

Stephen, Lynn. 2007. *Transborder lives: Indigenous Oaxacans in Mexico, California, and Oregon*. Durham: Duke University Press.

Terreciano, Kevin. 2001. *The Mixtecs of colonial Oaxaca: Ñudzahui history, sixteenth through eighteenth centuries*. Stanford: Stanford University Press.

Thomason, Sarah G. 2001. *Language contact: an introduction*. Edinburgh: Edinburgh University Press.

Torrens, C. 28 May 2011. Some NY immigrants cite lack of Spanish as barrier. *UTSanDiego.com*.

Velasco, Patricia. 2010. Indigenous students in bilingual Spanish–English classrooms in New York: a teacher's mediation strategies. *International Journal of the Sociology of Language* 206. 255–271.

Velasco, Patricia. 2014. The language and educational ideologies of Mixteco-Mexican mothers. *Journal of Latinos and Education* 13. 85–106.

Velasco, Patricia & Bobbie Kabuto. 2019. Transgenerational reading practices: a case study of an undocumented Mixteco family, in Elizabeth Ijalba, Patricia Velasco & Catherine J. Crowley (eds.), *Language, culture and education: challenges of diversity in the United States*, 139–158. Cambridge: Cambridge University Press.

Velasco Ortiz, M. Laura. 2005. *Mixtec transnational identity*. Tucson: University of Arizona Press.

Zylstra, Carol. 2012. *Gramática del Tu'un Savi (la lengua mixteca) de Alacatlatzala, Guerrero*. Mexico City: Instituto Lingüístico de Verano/Summer Institute of Linguistics.

Chloé Diskin-Holdaway
7 Second language identities among recently-arrived migrants in Dublin, Ireland

1 Introduction: The sociolinguistics of globalisation

There are estimated to be 272 million migrants in the world today (International Organization for Migration 2019: 2). This has far-reaching ramifications for how we conceptualise language contact in urban spaces, with "superdiversity" – the ongoing, multi-layered nature of migration, where new migrants settle alongside more traditional, long-standing migrant communities – becoming the norm in the majority of the world's megacities (Vertovec 2006). These new patterns are considered to be fluid, tenuous and increasingly temporary, with migrant identities becoming more fragmented, moving away from conventional notions of the "immigrant" to more fine-grained identifications, such as "economic migrant", "international student", "expatriate", "short-term sojourner", etc. (see Leung 2017). This has led to more nuanced interpretations of transnationalism, where transnationalism can involve both the physical movement of people, and a sentiment of transnationalism *in situ* – a "transnational subjectivity" (Dahinden 2009).

The role of language in globalisation, and the unsettling of its boundaries within particular sociolinguistic landscapes, has garnered scholarly attention (see e.g. Blommaert 2010). Since it is no longer possible to speak of identity as fixed, static or immutable, it is also no longer viable to view language as a fixed entity; but rather as a "repertoire" (Blommaert 2010) or "constellation" (Eckert 2008) of potential linguistic and semiotic resources. Having a sophisticated set of linguistic resources is becoming increasingly important in the context of migration, particularly in contexts where there are high degrees of multilingualism and pluricentricity. This set of resources can be exploited for the construction and maintenance of a new identity that is specifically tied to language practices – in other words, a second (or subsequent) language identity.

Bucholtz and Hall (2004: 369) write that language is one of the most flexible and pervasive resources available in the cultural production of identity. They claim that identity is often established through notions of sameness and difference, or a process of what they term *adequation* (the pursuit of socially-recognised sameness) and *distinction* (the production of salient difference) (Bucholtz and Hall 2004:

383–384). This process can be identified in interactions between individuals as they negotiate their identity through language, and in their metalinguistic discourse; specifically, how they delineate the degree of similarity and difference between their own language identity and that of others. Wortham (2006) argues that social identification occurs not only over decades and lifespans, but within event-level interactions, sometimes only minutes in length. While second language (L2) speakers are largely absent from these aforementioned perspectives, other work has given greater insight into the role of attitudes and ideologies in the formation of L2 identities in a transnational context (see Block 2007; De Costa 2012). Language ideologies, a set of beliefs about languages and their speakers, or a "cultural system of ideas about social and linguistic relationships" (Irvine 1989: 255), are an important component of the formation of these L2 identities, particularly in a pluricentric context.

This chapter will focus on a group of recently-arrived migrants from Poland and China to the city of Dublin in Ireland, who are faced with challenges in the reinterpretations of their identities. They must negotiate a new sociolinguistic landscape, encountering local ideologies about Dublin English (DubE) and coming to terms with them as L2 speakers of English in a new environment. In line with Bucholtz and Hall's (2004) view of identity, the paper will focus on three main elements: (1) *distinction*, or the production and experience of salient difference experienced by migrants when encountering DubE; (2) *adequation*, or the pursuit of sameness between DubE, prior experiences with learning English, and the first language (L1); (3) *local sociolinguistic ideologies* about DubE and how they are reflected and refracted by migrants. These themes are explored in an effort to address four main research questions (see below) about what is inherited, adopted, rejected or transformed in the process of becoming a migrant and how this ties into the establishment of a second or further language identity. The analysis will aim to move forward from Bucholtz and Hall's conception of an arguably "tight if not perfect identity" (Lempert 2014: 382) to a view of identity that is fluid, incomplete and in constant negotiation with an assemblage of surrounding discourses and context.

The research questions this contribution attempts to answer are thus: To what extent do Polish and Chinese migrants in Dublin

(1) . . . experience difference and disjuncture between their prior skills in English and the variety of English they encounter in Dublin (DubE)?
(2) . . . draw parallels or pursue sameness between their prior language experience and DubE?

(3) . . . reflect and refract local sociolinguistic ideologies surrounding DubE and its pluricentricity?

and

(4) How do these issues relate to the formation of a second language identity in a new environment?

2 Methodology

2.1 Data and participants

The research questions will be addressed by means of a discourse analysis of a series of one-on-one semi-structured interviews conducted by the author with eleven migrants of Polish and Chinese origin in 2012, as part of a broader sociolinguistic (variationist) study (see Diskin 2017). This subset of eleven migrants was specifically selected as it was considered, in terms of the range of attitudes and beliefs that came through in the interviews, to be representative of the larger sample as a whole. The participants were in their 20s and 30s and had all moved to Dublin as adults, with lengths of residence ranging from one to seven years.

The participants were interviewed using the method of the sociolinguistic interview (Labov 1972). The interviews lasted between one and three hours and were loosely structured, resembling a chat, and the interviewer aimed to allow the participants to relax into the conversation by making minimal interruptions. There was a list of question modules, which mostly concerned the participants' daily lives and interests, available to the interviewer; however, this was only used as a guide and was not visible to the participants. At least one question was designed to elicit language attitudes and ideologies about Irish English (IrE) and/or DubE. It was at times posed directly, e.g. "Do you think that the way we speak English here is different to the way you learnt English in school?"; whereas at other times the topic arose naturally or following a related question, such as "Do you remember the first day you arrived in Dublin?" While the data is not, strictly speaking, "naturally-occurring" data (see Bucholtz and Hall 2004), the open nature of the questions asked means that the responses still constitute spontaneous speech, with the interviewer in a position to follow up and invite elaborations on themes relating to language and identity, which was one of the aims of the broader study.

2.2 A discourse-analytic approach

The discourse analytic approach adopted here is in line with that of Paltridge (2006: 9), who defines discourse analysis as "[. . .] a view of language in use; that is, how, through the use of language, people achieve certain communicative goals, perform certain communicative acts, participate in certain communicative events and present themselves to others". This approach can provide a framework for understanding qualitative analysis not just as descriptive, but as analytical, with a firm basis in the belief that talk is socially embedded, and reflects rooted convictions or ideologies. Discourse analysis "emphasises the way versions of the world, of society, events, and inner psychological worlds are produced in discourse" (Potter 2004: 202, cited in Silverman 2011: 301). By viewing discourse analysis as an analysis of what people do, through the medium of text and/or talk, and as embedded in social practices, it is possible to apply it to the semi-spontaneous interview data collected for this study.

Discourse analysis also emphasises the notion of social constructivism, whereby discourse is both constructed by its speakers and the interactional context, and constructive, in the sense that the very act of "doing" discourse reiterates and stabilises versions of the world (Potter and Hepburn, 2008: 277, cited in Silverman, 2011: 302). The present analysis acknowledges that the participants are not only expressing views, but they are simultaneously creating and reifying them, and subsequently being challenged by them. They are also, in the spirit of Bakhtin's *heteroglossia* (see Bakhtin 1981) expressing the views of others, through indirect and direct means, and in doing so, are "discerning the significance of their experience" (Ochs and Capps 2001: 2). What they choose to convey, perform or draw attention to about local sociolinguistic knowledge is reflective of the inherent *citationality* of these 'facts' (Nakassis 2013) and, as such, are part of their socialisation as both locals and outsiders, or transnationals, in the context of a global city, but also on a moment-by-moment basis (Wortham 2006).

3 Background: Recent migration to Dublin and Ireland

The Republic of Ireland (RoI) has long been known as a country of large-scale outward migration, with a notable Irish diaspora present in the UK, the US and Australia. However, since the economic boom or "Celtic Tiger" years of the late 1990s and early 2000s, there has been a reversal in these trends, with the country bearing witness to notable inward migration, particularly during the period 2006–2012, when there was a 143% increase in the number of migrants (CSO 2012: 7). While this growth has reached a plateau over subsequent years, the 17.3% of the population that are currently classed as "non-Irish" (CSO 2016: 46) has led to a significant shift in the nation's identity from a country that was predominantly monocultural to one that is multicultural, and, by extension, multilingual. The city of Dublin, as the capital, is a hub for both international and national (domestic) migration. It is by far the largest city on the island, with a population of 1.1 million at the time of the 2011 Census (CSO 2011: 13). As a consequence, it is a focal point for language contact between speakers of different varieties of IrE, as well as L2 speakers of English from a diversity of backgrounds.

3.1 Polish migration to Dublin and Ireland

Since 2006, Polish nationals represent the largest non-Irish group (in terms of nationality) in RoI, with a population of 122,515 or close to 3% of the Irish population (CSO 2016). Furthermore, the Polish population increased by 94% between 2006 and 2012, exhibiting the most growth of any non-Irish group during the post-2008 economic recession (CSO 2012: 7). Polish migration to RoI has been somewhat unusual in its distribution, as it has not been solely concentrated in large urban areas. Poles are the only nationality apart from UK nationals to be recorded as living in every town in the country; nonetheless, while only 29% of Poles live in the Dublin urban area, it is still the most popular destination (CSO 2008: 28; CSO 2016). There are notably high concentrations of Poles living in Dublin's northern and western suburbs, which are experiencing overall growth and expansion in population in the city. A quarter of the Poles interviewed for the present paper were residing in the north-western suburb of Ashtown, a neighbourhood that was undergoing extended development in the mid-2000s, with a rapid proliferation of apartment buildings and other services and amenities. At the time of data collection, the neighbourhood had earned itself the affectionate nickname, at least among its Polish residents, of "Polishtown". At the time of writing, however, a number of apartment buildings in the area had been taken over by the National Asset Management Agency (NAMA), who deal with non-performing property loans (usually from developers) acquired from Irish banks. This led to an overall feeling of insecurity in the area and a number of the participants have since moved to other neighbourhoods.

3.2 Chinese migration to Dublin and Ireland

Migration from mainland China to Ireland is a very recent phenomenon, starting in the early 2000s. In terms of demographics, 67% of Chinese nationals live in the Dublin area and 95% live in an Irish urban area (CSO 2008: 48). According to the 2011 census, the Chinese were the third most numerous of the "Asian" nationalities (the term used in the census) after Indians and Filipinos (CSO 2012: 7). Similar to the distribution of Polish migrants, Asian migrants are concentrated in Dublin's northern and western suburbs. However, there is also a concentration of Asian nationals in the core of the city centre in Dublin; an area with a relatively low socioeconomic index (Haase 2008). Chinese migrants have visibly contributed to the cultural and linguistic landscape of Dublin city, with the growth of unofficial Chinatown areas in the city centre, on Capel Street and Parnell Street East (Figure 1).

Figure 1: Parnell Street East in Dublin's city centre: one of the city's two unofficial 'Chinatowns' (Photo: Chloé Diskin-Holdaway).

4 The pluricentricity of English(es) in Dublin and Ireland

Irish English (IrE) is the oldest contact variety of English in the world at around 800 years old (Hickey 2012). It has a long history of dissociation from British English (BrE), which has led to its perception as being markedly different from any other variety of English (Hickey 1999, 2012). There has been a certain reticence among the Irish about accepting the English language (rather than the Irish language) as a "legitimate carrier of Irish culture, traditions and identity" (Migge 2012: 312). However, due to ongoing shift from Irish to English as the majority language on the island (although both are official languages of RoI), varieties of IrE, including DubE, have become strong indicators of Irishness.

Furthermore, there are high degrees of regional variability in IrE and a consensus that there is an absence of an "endogenous standard" or "neutral" variety (Moore 2011: 230; see also Diskin 2016; Hickey 2007). Indeed, it could be said that Irish identity is closely linked to this linguistic heterogeneity, with regional identity linked strongly to the counties on the island – 26 in RoI and 6 in Northern Ireland – and often ascertained and reinforced through the dialect (variety) that is spoken there ("Dublin" refers to both the city and its county, but, due to the small size of the county, little difference is made dialectally between the former and the latter). Migrants who move to Dublin from elsewhere are inevitably exposed to this linguistic heterogeneity, through living and working in the city and coming into contact with speakers of DubE (along with other varieties of IrE and a host of L2 Englishes). The particular status quo of IrE as inherently pluricentric can have implications for these migrants, who may find that their prior experience with "standard" English within the formal education system is at odds with the English(es) they encounter upon arrival in Dublin (Diskin and Regan 2017; Migge 2012).

Previous research has shown that "standardness" in language, although essentially an abstraction, is often equated with the language heard in the media or appearing in standardised textbooks (Lippi-Green 1997). For many non-native speakers in particular, both BrE and American English (AmE) are often taken as the *de facto* standards or targets for "correct" English (Diskin and Regan 2017; Matsuda and Matsuda 2010). This can particularly be the case for migrants with prior high proficiency in English, who can feel that their cultural, economic and linguistic capital does not transfer to the Irish context (see Diskin and Regan 2017). Coupled with the fact that many educated migrants have to contend with working in jobs for which they are overqualified (see Kobiałka 2016), this social and linguistic disjuncture can have implications for integration, with migrants experiencing difficulty in gaining ingroup membership to Irish social networks.

The varieties of English spoken in Ireland's capital, Dublin, are distinct, and instantly recognizable by Irish people. DubE is generally believed to have at least three sub-varieties, predominantly demarcated along socioeconomic lines (see Hickey 2005, Lonergan 2013), which align geographically with three main areas of the city and their location vis-à-vis the River Liffey: the Southside, the Northside, and the Inner City (see Figure 2). The Northside is generally accepted to be less affluent than the Southside, which has a reputation for being wealthy and "posh". The Inner City, which comprises of neighbourhoods both north and south of the river, is viewed as the most deprived, but also the most "authentic" and "traditional" part of the city. The Inner City dialect is reportedly less rhotic than other varieties of DubE (and IrE); it maintains a distinction between the vowels in NURSE and TERM; and has a neutralised contrast between [t, d] and [θ, ð] (Lonergan 2013: 337). Unlike some DubE varieties, which have a FOOT-STRUT merger, Inner City speakers tend to keep these vowels distinct, by having a FOOT that approaches the vowel in GOOSE. The Southside variety is characterised by high realisations of THOUGHT and fronted GOAT onsets, and an increasing tendency towards a flapped /t/ (Lonergan 2013: 340). Both the Northside and Southside varieties have merged, central realisations of NURSE and TERM; some Northside men also have lower realisations of THOUGHT (Lonergan 2013: 341). Furthermore, for Northsiders and Southsiders, CHOICE has a much higher onset than PRICE, but for inner city Dubliners the two appear to be merged (Lonergan 2013: 341).

There are, however, exceptions to the strict socio-demographic demarcations of North, South and Inner City (Figure 2). Urban redevelopment and regeneration projects, as well as the general expansion of the city, have resulted in a re-allocation of the wealth in these areas, with prime real estate being developed in the Inner City, for example, along with more deprived areas, such as Tallaght, expanding on the periphery of the traditionally more affluent Southside. Furthermore, some high-income neighbourhoods on the Northside, particularly the Howth peninsula, have long been an exception to the reputation of the Northside as being working class. Nonetheless, the traditional tripartite division of the city remains locked within the imagination of its inhabitants and being a "Northsider", "Southsider", or being from the Inner City is an important and generally overt identity marker. A Bulmers cider advertisement, located near Connolly Station in Dublin (Figure 3), gives an indication, via an obvious play on words, of the rootedness of the Northside/Southside distinction in the collective identity of the city.

7 Second language identities among recently-arrived migrants in Dublin, Ireland — **181**

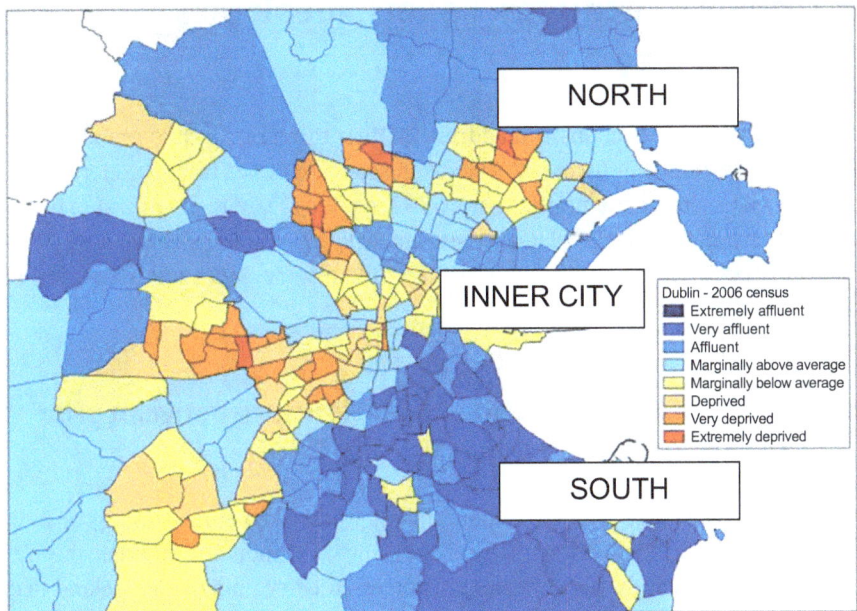

Figure 2: City of Dublin: Socioeconomic stratification. Map reproduced with permission from John Lonergan (Lonergan 2013), based on composite index by Haase (2008) and boundary files provided by Ordnance Survey Ireland. "North", "South" and "Inner City" labels added by author.

Figure 3: Bulmers advertisement on Dublin Area Rapid Transit (DART) bridge near Connolly Station, Inner City (Photo: Chloé Diskin-Holdaway).

5 Findings: Attitudes, beliefs, ideologies and identity

The following three sections will address the first three research questions of the paper (see section 1) in turn, by focusing on select examples from the eleven participants selected for the present study: Ya Ling, Eliza, Xiuying, Agnieszka, Irena, Aleksander, Marcin, Paweł, Janusz, Igor and Michał. It will conclude with a discussion section on the implications of these findings for the conceptualisation of an L2 identity (research question 4).

5.1 Experiences of distinction and disjuncture between prior skills in English and DubE

In the semi-structured interviews, participants were asked either directly or indirectly about the local accent or "way of speaking" in Dublin and whether this differed to the English they had been accustomed to before moving to Ireland (e.g. excerpt (3), lines 1–3). The majority immediately commented (or agreed) that they found the Irish or Dublin accent to be noticeably different to the kinds of English accent they were used to prior to moving to Ireland.

(1) **Ya Ling**[1]
1   Some words it's- never, you- I would never seen them from textbook.

(2) **Eliza**
1   You know and it was very um funny
2   Because um I always
3   Uh I don't::
4   My English was very bad because um
5   You know it's different
6   When you um learning alone from book
7   And it's different when you confronted with um life

---

[1] Transcription convention (based on Goodwin (1990)):
- Sudden cut-off of current sound
: Lengthening
(.) Short silence
(h) Breathiness, laughter.

8		Yeah so and um Irish languages
9		Different than um British
10		So when I was here I understood nothing.

(3) **Xiuying**

1	Chloé	When you came to Ireland
2		Did you find that like [people] speak differently
3		To the way you learnt English in China?
4	Xiuying	I think the accent (.) yeah
5		Because in China we are taught uh (.)
6		More like US English
7		Yeah::
8		Uh (.) but the accent
9		Yeah but accent in Ireland is (.) different

There was an overall perception that IrE was strange, "different" (excerpt (2), lines 5, 7, 9; excerpt (3), line 9), "funny" (excerpt (2), line 1), and as a result, difficult to learn and understand (excerpt (2), line 10), particularly when first arriving in Ireland. These adjectives and qualifiers were used covertly in comparison to a perceived "standard", and often covertly by comparison to a book, textbook or dictionary (excerpt (1); excerpt (2), line 6). These adjectives and qualifiers were also used to make overt comparisons between IrE and both BrE (excerpt (2), line 9) and AmE (excerpt (3), line 6). It is noteworthy that almost all of the migrants interviewed made an explicit comparison between IrE and these "textbook" varieties, with the implication that there is a mismatch between them. In so doing, the migrants tended towards *distinction* (emphasising difference), rather than *adequation* (emphasising sameness) in their articulations of views towards IrE. It is also noteworthy that participants such as Eliza in excerpt (2) stressed that "textbook" English, even if it represents a "standard" is not the same as being "confronted with [. . .] life" (line 7), alluding to the fact that prestigious varieties, such as BrE (line 9), may not be good preparation for functioning in day-to-day interactions in Dublin. Her explicit description of IrE as "Irish languages" (line 8) also shows an acknowledgement of IrE as idiosyncratic and something that can be viewed as distinctly different to varieties such as BrE.

5.1.1 Language shock

The process of distinction was also visible in the discrepancy between the prior learning of English and a "shock" encounter with IrE upon arrival in Dublin, which emerged as a common experience. The concept of "language shock" was first reported by Schumann (1978) in reference to the degree to which psychological (as well as social) distance can affect (or inhibit) the acquisition of an L2.

(4) **Agnieszka**
1	I moved in with uh people (.)
2	From uh West Cork and Kerry
3	So's another one (h)
4	Another just like uh you know::
5	Kind of a cold shower
6	Ah and I remember
7	Actually myself sitting there you know
8	Uh in our kitchen
9	With all of them
10	Uh you know (.)
11	Just drinkin tea in the evening and so on
12	And (.) uh (.) same story wou-would happen
13	As it does with uh my Dublin guys now
14	That I will just sit there
15	Not saying a word
16	Because my brain was just like (.)
17	Trying to proceed all this information
18	That was just thrown into me
19	And with all this funny accents
20	And you know people from Kerry
21	They are especially (.) uh (.) there are
22	Particularly known for that (.)
23	So I was sitting there
24	And I was like 'Oh my goodness(h)'
25	You know?
26	So (.) yeah::
27	Every so often they would just (.)
28	Like ask me a question
29	And I would be
30	Still kind-of trying to catch up with the conversation
31	I was "oh what"
32	So (.) yeah.

In excerpt (4), Agnieszka describes the language shock she experienced when she first moved in with housemates from Cork and Kerry (two counties in the south/

south-west of Ireland) as a "cold shower" (line 5) and she explicitly contrasts this with the city of Dublin and "my Dublin guys" (line 13), which is indicative of her sense of place in Dublin. However, this is also contrasted with an overall sentiment of being behind ("trying to catch up" – line 30) or out of her depth. She describes the Cork/Kerry variety spoken by her housemates as "funny" (line 19). It is ambiguous as to whether she intended this evaluation as strange or humorous; it is possible that she intended both. She also describes the processing overload she experienced in these first months ("my brain was just like (.) trying to proceed all this information" – lines 16–17) and describes the experience as stupefying: "I was 'oh what?'" (line 31). Overall, she also denotes IrE as something different, and out of the ordinary. She attempts to account for her difficulty in comprehension by claiming that people from Cork and Kerry are "particularly known" (line 22) for their strong accents, which also shows her awareness of regional variation in Ireland. Nonetheless, she goes on to say that she has similar experiences of miscomprehension with her current housemates, who are from Dublin (line 13).

Agnieszka's experience is indicative of an ideology that IrE and DubE are distinctive – they differ from the abstract concept of "English" that is learned in school. The implied repetition of such scenarios ("same story would happen" – line 12) and the habitual aspect of the narrative ("They would just like ask me a question" – lines 27–28 / "I would be still kind-of trying to catch up" – lines 29–30) indicate firstly that such experiences are commonplace, and secondly that these experiences are generally familiar for migrants in a new environment, which is part of the experience of becoming a migrant and establishing a migrant/L2 identity.

(5) **Irena**
1   Here people speak completely different
2   And faster
3   And that was another (.)
4   Actually for me to learn (.)
5   And was-it was a nightmare at the beginning
6   I didn't understand anything

This language shock was echoed by Irena in excerpt (5), who termed her initial encounters with IrE a "nightmare" (line 5). She also drew on the markedness of IrE as "completely different" (line 1), as well as its perceived elevated speech rate (line 2). This experience, she later reports, led her to feel alienated from the majority of her native Dublin classmates at a college course she was attending in Dublin, particularly during the first two years. Throughout her interview, she communicated a degree of frustration with the fact that she felt that prior to moving to Ireland (she worked as an au pair in the south-east of Ireland for a year before moving to Dublin), she had believed her standard of English to be quite proficient. Though she had come to view Dublin as her home in many ways, she had not reconciled this linguistic disjuncture in the five years living there. Not long after the interview, she returned to live in Poland permanently.

5.2 Drawing parallels: Adequation and the pursuit of sameness

The selected examples in the previous section might lead us to believe that all the migrants in this study were in a state of shock upon encountering IrE. However, a number of them managed to reflect on these situations of language contact and recast them in a positive or transformative light. Indeed, among three of the Polish migrants in particular, a discourse emerged that the English language was fundamentally "easier" to learn than other languages (including, in some cases, their L1), and in so doing, pursued "sameness", rather than "difference" in the construction of their L2 identities. This emphasis on "sameness" can be indicative that these migrants sought to be assimilated into their new environment, by focusing on making the L2 experience easy, rather than difficult. In addition (or alternatively), it may indicate that they had not been exposed to the same ideologies of "standardness" and "textbook English" as the participants in the previous section; or that they did not subscribe to them.

(6) **Aleksander**
1	English is much easier to-to pronounce than Polish
2	In many cases::
3	In many cases (.) but uh
4	This is why probably it becomes so popular (.)
5	Uh because it's so (.)
6	You know (.) fast
7	Polish is not that fast.

(7) **Marcin**
1	Probably he [my son] kept Irish- the English words if::
2	Much easier like you know.
3	If you have a choice (.)
4	'Samochód' or 'car'
5	So the shorter and quicker

7 Second language identities among recently-arrived migrants in Dublin, Ireland — 187

(8) **Paweł**

1	But uh English language (.)
2	It's so-it's so nice (.)
3	It's so friendly.
4	Because even if you don't know the word (.)
5	You-you can know a part of it
6	Y-you know
7	So-so it makes it easier
8	Because in-in Poland
9	Uh: in Polish language
10	Which I think it's one of the most difficult ones
11	Because I try to learn this-this- this
12	And this language
13	And it was always easier for me than Polish (.)
14	My own language
15	At school (.) oh no
16	I mean like ((makes "pff" sound))
17	No (.) you can have the grammar
18	The-the grammar that you have
19	That's like (.) come on
20	Seriously (.) you-you have::
21	You have it straight
22	It's there (.) you know?
23	For-for-for-for the rules that we have
24	It's:: I think someone
25	Mm one day uh
26	Sat there and (.) and
27	And said "Oh let's make this language difficult"

Aleksander describes noticing an elevated speech rate in English as compared to Polish (excerpt (6), lines 5–7). However, this does not necessarily contrast with the view that (Irish) English is "too fast" to understand, as expressed by Agnieszka and Irena. Aleksander's reasoning is that the inherent structure of the English language lends itself to being spoken quickly, and that it is "easier to pronounce" than Polish (excerpt (6), line 1). It is also noteworthy that both he and Paweł appear to be referring to the English language in general (excerpt (6), line 1; excerpt (8), line 1), rather than IrE *per se*. Thus, in contrast to the participants in the previous section, they do not draw particular attention to the fact that IrE or DubE is particularly different as compared to the more abstract notion of "English". For

Marcin in excerpt (7), it is less clear whether he makes a distinction: his false start (line 1) may indicate that he views IrE (what he terms "Irish") as different from an unmarked "English"; or on the contrary, that he views the terms as interchangeable.

At a later stage in his interview, when speaking about his daughter, who he describes as "bilingual" in Polish and English (a status that he does not ascribe to himself due to his later acquisition of English), Aleksander states that although the language of their household is exclusively Polish, she frequently inserts English words into her speech. He accounts for this highly common bilingual activity by stating that it is "quicker" to say English words as they are shorter and the phonemes are less complex. The same view is expressed by Marcin, who explained that the Polish word for 'car' is *samochód*, which is not as short and efficient as 'car' (excerpt (7), lines 3–5), and thus his bilingual son may choose to use the English word when speaking with him in Polish. While this reasoning has some truth, what is more relevant for the purposes of the present discussion is the fact that neither Aleksander nor Marcin draw explicitly on dialectal/varietal differences in their reflections on migration and language contact; and, even if they are aware of such differences (excerpt (7), line 1), they are certainly not cast in a deficit frame. Indeed, by focusing on the relative ease with which English can be learned as compared to Polish (a view which is particularly surprising considering Polish is their L1), they indicate that English has been a welcoming language for them; and that, by extension, Ireland (at least linguistically speaking) has been a welcoming place for them also. This differs starkly to the views and experiences of Irena (excerpt (5)) in particular.

Paweł's views echo those of Aleksander and Marcin, where in excerpt (8) he states that he considers English to be easier to learn than Polish, despite the fact that Polish is his native language (lines 13–14). He explains this by the flexibility of English morphology (lines 4–5) and the comparatively "difficult" grammar in Polish, towards which, with a dismissive "pfff" (line 16), he projects a stance that it is so complicated it is not worth explaining to the interviewer. Paweł also projects an affective stance towards (Irish) English, denoting it as "friendly" (line 3). This may reflect his stance towards the speakers of IrE (the Irish) themselves, as ideologies about speakers often go hand-in-hand with ideologies about the languages they speak (Lippi-Green 1997). However, speakers also tend to rate stigmatised varieties highly in terms of likeability, but not in terms of standardness (Preston 1999). Thus Paweł's view of (Irish) English may not necessarily be reflecting a view of this variety as "standard". Nonetheless, Aleksander, Marcin and Paweł all display a different view towards IrE than exhibited in the previous section, which is essentially more positive, but also less divisive in terms of how it carves out different kinds of Englishes. Interestingly, the differing assessments of

IrE and its relative difficulty, markedness and speed does not correlate with these migrants' proficiency in English or length of residence in Ireland (see Diskin and Regan 2017 for an extended discussion). Through these reflections on English language use and bilingual practices, these participants do not appear to have been "shocked" by IrE or DubE, which is significant for the positioning of their L2 identities. The English language in Ireland has provided a welcoming space for them to carve out a new space for themselves, and they do not appear to be burdened by the standard language ideologies that emerged in the discourse of Irena, Agnieszka, Ya Ling and Xiuying.

5.3 Reflecting and refracting local sociolinguistic ideologies

Previous research has indicated that L2 speakers can replicate, reallocate, or resist local patterns of sociolinguistic variation in a migrant context (see Diskin and Levey 2019; Drummond 2012, Meyerhoff and Schleef 2012), and that this behaviour is closely linked to these speakers' identities and beliefs about language, which can be called into question or re-evaluated in the migrant context. In other words, "systematic beliefs" about language affect how language is used, adopted and re-shaped in the process of the formation of an L2 identity, which itself is far from immutable and static (see Block 2007; De Costa 2012). These beliefs can emerge and be negotiated in language as performance, whereby assessments are embedded into the structure and significance of speech itself (Bauman and Briggs 1990: 69). This section will examine the degree to which, in a number of key moments or performances, the participants aligned with local ideologies about the inherent pluricentricity of DubE and IrE. The analysis shows how prestige and ideologies of "standardness" from the ambient sociolinguistic landscape are reflected or refracted, or at times *entextualised* (Urban and Silverstein 1996), to come across as "normal" and "authoritative" ways of talking about local accent and identity.

(9) **Irena**
1	Irena	She's from Portarlington
2		She spoke much slower than everybody else
3		Just perfect (.) perfect
4		Yeah
5	Chloé	Mm hm
6	Irena	Mm
7	Chloé	So::

8		What was her accent like compared to say the kind of Dublin accent
9	Irena	Uh she spoke the s- mm
10		Very calmly you know and (.)
11		Um (.) just much slower
12		You know?
13		Um (..)
14		I think that's what it was (.)
15		You know (.) maybe the countryside
16		The life is just so much slower over there
17		Everybody's a lot more relaxed
18		And that's why they don't have to speak so (.) you know (.) so fast
19	Chloé	Yeah
20	Irena	So maybe that's what it was
21		But then another friend of mine (.) from Kildare
22		And he speaks you know very slowly as well
23	Chloé	Mm-hm
24	Irena	And clearly (.) so it's perfect
25	Chloé	Mm
26	Irena	Yeah
27	Chloé	So you think the speed thing is particularly Dublin==
28	Irena	[Could be
(29		=Or Tallaght (.) or?
30	Irena	Mm
31	Chloé	Were the group from all parts of Dublin or?
32	Irena	Yeah all- yeah
33		The fastest speaker was from the Inner City
34		(h)(h) yeah
35		Nobody could understand her though
36		(h)(h) Not just me!

In excerpt (9), Irena compares two friends of hers – one from the small town of Portarlington in County Laois and another from county Kildare – who speak "much slower than everybody else" (line 2), to a classmate from Dublin's Inner City, who speaks the "fastest" of anyone she knows (line 33).[2] She concludes that

---

[2] Portarlington in County Laois is approximately 80 kilometres from the city of Dublin. Although it is becoming increasingly common to live in Portarlington and commute to Dublin, the former

life is "slower" and "more relaxed" in the "countryside" (lines 16–17; it is implied that this is County Laois and County Kildare) and that this way of life is reflected in the speech rate of its inhabitants. In creating this distinction, she implies that life in the capital is more fast-paced and that its inhabitants as a result speak more rapidly than their rural counterparts.

While on the surface appearing to be a reflection on speech rate and intelligibility in IrE, Irena's affective evaluation is very clear: the countryside accent is "perfect" (lines 3, 24); whereas the Inner City (line 33), an area which is subject to high levels of stigma (Hickey 1999, 2005; Lonergan 2013), represents an undesired variety of DubE, at least in the sense that, to Irena, it is incomprehensible and, as a consequence, impermeable. Irena's laughter in lines 34–36 is perhaps indicative of the frustration or embarrassment felt in these situations where she could not understand her classmate and she attempts through this retelling to recruit the rest of her class into the same shared experience ("Nobody could understand her though / Not just me!" – lines 35–36). It should also be noted, however, that Irena reports that for the first two years of her university program in Dublin, the girl from Portarlington had been her only friend. This friendship may also account for the more positive evaluation of the girl's speech – a detail that again points to the multi-layered nature of speech perception and language attitudes, where it becomes difficult to disentangle beliefs about speakers from beliefs about their language use, especially in self-reported metalinguistic commentaries such as those elicited in this study.

The urban-rural divide in IrE was commented upon by a number of the other migrants; however, it did not always directly echo Irena's views and experiences, who indicated a strong preference for rural varieties. This preference was specific to her experience, as her exemplar of an "urban" DubE was the Inner City variety. While she appears to be replicating local ideologies of Inner City DubE as stigmatised, she does not appear to have other varieties of DubE, including the more commonly desirable Southside DubE, as viable alternatives. As such, she turns to the next available opposition to Inner City DubE from her pool of language experiences, which is the English spoken in Kildare and Laois. This is not the same set of ideologies that a native speaker of IrE, born and raised in Ireland, would have. The sets of beliefs held by a native IrE speaker would also be somewhat variable, of course, but arguably more predictable and consistent.

---

is still considered to be a rural area in the Midlands, with a markedly different dialect to DubE. County Kildare is approximately 60 kilometres from Dublin city, and is increasingly becoming part of the wider Dublin commuter belt.

(10) **Janusz**
1   [In Portlaoise] I couldn't understand a s**t what they talking to me

(11) **Igor**
1   But I like talking accent of uh-uh Dublin
2   Because everybody talking very clearly
3   If I go to the shop
4   No problem with the accent

For Janusz and Igor, they experienced the opposite to Irena, where Janusz reported having no difficulties with his Irish colleagues in Dublin; however, when he started to travel for work purposes, he was stupefied by the variety he heard in the regional town of Portlaoise (excerpt (10)), which is in direct opposition to Irena's view that speakers from "the country" are easier to understand (excerpt (9)). Igor stated that he found DubE to be "clear" and easy to understand (excerpt (11), line 2) and later stated that the accent in Cork was more "different". These different and at times diametrically opposite views of Dublin city vs country dialects among some of the participants illustrates that the ideological construction of stances towards language varieties are rooted in personal experience (or lack thereof) and can differ from mainstream ideologies about language variation.

    Among other participants, DubE was also subject to overt scrutiny, with the Northside and Inner City, as well as specific Northside neighbourhoods such as Ballymun, Finglas, Mulhuddart and Tallaght, being the areas most frequently cited as having an accent that is difficult to understand. This is very similar to native speakers' views of the social stratification of Dublin and the negative perception of "local" Northside DubE (Diskin 2016; Hickey 1999; Lonergan 2013). For example, Ya Ling, when prompted, said that the "strong" accent was spoken on the Northside of Dublin and that there were "two boys" in her class at university who "spoke this way" and who she could not understand. However, the participants focused more on neighbourhoods they were familiar with, such as e.g. Eliza, who spoke at length about the fact that she could not understand anyone in Mulhuddart, which was also where she was working at the time.

(12) **Michał**
1   Chloé   And what-what does the Irish accent sound like?
2   To you?
3   Michał   Um (.) the Irish or uh Dublin accent?
4   Chloé   Say, Dublin

5	Michał	Dublin
6		A lot of uh::
7		"oo" (([u]))
8		Uh::
9		Uh::
10		A lot of uh::
11		Hm;;;
12		It's hard to describe (.) you know (h)(h)
13	Chloé	(h)(h) yeah
14		Is it very fast?
15	Michał	Fast (.) it is fast yeah
16	Chloé	And did you- do you notice a difference
17		Between like different parts of Dublin?
18		Different ways of speaking?
19	Michał	I no- I can't notice that (.) no
20	Chloé	Generally just sounds the same?
21	Michał	Yeah

Excerpt (12) is an extract from a more extended discussion by Michał about DubE. It is clear that he views IrE and DubE as separate, as he asks for clarification with the interviewer/author when she asks him about the Irish accent ("Um the Irish or uh Dublin accent?" – line 3). He reports that he has noticed that local realisations of the FOOT or STRUT vowel (what he describes as the "oo" sound – line 7) are a marked feature of DubE, and differ to the Polish pedagogical model of this vowel, taken from British English (see Kobiałka 2016 for how IrE vowels are typically re-interpreted according to Polish phonology). Michał has indeed noticed with some degree of accuracy that in more stigmatised varieties of DubE, such as the Northside and Inner City varieties, there is a more fronted GOOSE vowel; and in some cases, a FOOT that approaches the vowel in GOOSE (see also Section 4). However, it may also be a reallocation of the variable input he is receiving for the STRUT vowel. As reported by Hickey (2004: 4), there are two realisations for this vowel in DubE: [ʌ̈] for "mainstream" DubE (typically Northside or Southside); and [ʊ] for "popular" DubE (Inner City), which is typically stigmatised, and a feature that is above the level of conscious awareness. Indeed, Michał himself reports an inability to recognise different varieties of DubE (lines 19–21), and admits that it is hard to describe (line 12), thus recognising that his summary ("[there is] a lot of 'oo'" – lines 6–7) is somewhat lacking. It is nonetheless noteworthy that he is being suitably cautious, and has not adopted the local, somewhat divisive, oversimplified view of DubE as stereotypically "Northside vs Southside" – a distinction and imagined isogloss, or linguistic boundary, that is often so intrinsic to Dubliners' identities (see Diskin 2016), but that does not necessarily reflect the linguistic reality, where Northside and Southside DubE are becoming increasingly difficult to clearly delineate (Lonergan 2013).

6 Conclusion: L2 identities and pluricentricity

This contribution has explored the attitudes, beliefs and ideologies held by eleven migrants, all recent arrivals to the city of Dublin, towards DubE and IrE. A discourse analysis was conducted with the broader aim of gaining greater insight into the complex process of adoption, reallocation and resistance to (local) language ideologies in the migrant context. Drawing on Bucholtz and Hall's (2004) concept of a language identity consisting of a dual process of pursuing *distinction* (difference) and *adequation* (sameness), the first two research questions ("To what extent do Polish and Chinese migrants in Dublin experience difference and disjuncture between their prior skills in English and DubE?" and "To what extent do they draw parallels or pursue sameness between their prior language experience and DubE"?) sought to shed light on these processes, as part of the formation of migrants' L2 identities in Dublin. Findings showed that a number of migrants experienced IrE as a "shock" to the system and emphasised its difference vis-à-vis other more "standard" varieties of English, such as BrE and AmE. In this sense, IrE for these migrants appeared to be lacking "currency" in an imagined linguistic marketplace (Bourdieu 1991), and was the source of feelings of dissonance and mismatch, rather than harmony. However, for other migrants, no such distinctions were drawn, and there was an emphasis on the "easy" and "friendly" nature of the experience of learning English; of being bilingual; and, for some, having bilingual children. However, this cohort did not tend to report on IrE or DubE specifically, raising questions about the degree to which they had full indexical access to the assemblage of discourses and ideologies that make up the ambient sociolinguistic landscape of Dublin, which they are navigating as L2 speakers. The analysis in section 5.3 in particular showed that these pathways of indexical access are strongly influenced by migrants' personal experiences in their new environment.

The third research question attempted to address this issue of indexical access more directly, by focusing on the degree to which local ideologies about DubE specifically were being rejected, replicated or reallocated by these migrants. Analyses showed that participants expressed views about urban and rural varieties of IrE, and varieties relating to specific areas of Dublin, that were very much tied to their personal experiences and, consequently, their L2 identities (the fourth research question). Others displayed a sensitivity to local variability, such as that found in the vowels in FOOT/STRUT/GOOSE, but admitted themselves that they were not fully adept at picking up varietal differences in their L2. This indicates that newcomers may overlook, ignore, but also reject or transform local sociolinguistic ideologies. This has implications for the future shaping of the sociolinguistic landscape in diverse, multi-layered and globalised areas. Since migration is becoming the norm in the majority of the world's urban areas, language contact and language variation and change will be increasingly influenced by the presence of multilingual speakers, and shaped by the experiences of those whose identities are complex and multifaceted.

References

Bakhtin, M.M. 1981. *The dialogic imagination: four essays*. Austin: University of Texas Press.
Bauman, Richard & Charles L. Briggs. 1990. Poetics and performance as critical perspectives on language and social life. *Annual Review of Anthropology* 19. 59–88.
Block, David. 2007. *Second language identities*. London/New York: Continuum.
Blommaert, Jan. 2010. *The sociolinguistics of globalization*. Cambridge: Cambridge University Press.
Bourdieu, Pierre. 1991. *Language and symbolic power*. Cambridge: Polity Press.
Bucholtz, Mary & Kira Hall. 2004. Language and identity. In Alessandro Duranti (ed.), *A companion to linguistic anthropology*, 369–394. Malden: Blackwell.
CSO (Central Statistics Office). 2008. *Non-Irish nationals living in Ireland*. https://www.cso.ie/en/census/census2006reports/non-irishnationalslivinginireland/ (accessed 24 April 2019).
CSO (Central Statistics Office). 2011. *This is Ireland: highlights from census 2011, part 1*. https://www.cso.ie/en/media/csoie/census/documents/census2011pdr/Census_2011_Highlights_Part_1_web_72dpi.pdf (accessed 26 August 2019).
CSO (Central Statistics Office). 2012. *Profile 6: migration and diversity*. https://www.cso.ie/en/census/census2011reports/census2011profile6migrationanddiversity-aprofileofdiversityinireland/ (accessed 24 April 2019).
CSO (Central Statistics Office). 2016. *Census 2016 summary results, part 1: full summary*. https://www.cso.ie/en/media/csoie/newsevents/documents/census2016summaryresultspart1/Census2016SummaryPart1.pdf (accessed 24 April 2019).
Dahinden, Janine. 2009. Are we all transnationals now? Network transnationalism and transnational subjectivity: the differing impacts of globalization on the inhabitants of a small Swiss city. *Ethnic and Racial Studies* 32(8). 1365–1386.
De Costa, Peter. 2012. Constructing SLA differently: the value of ELF and language ideology in an ASEAN case study. *International Journal of Applied Linguistics* 22. 205–224.
Diskin, Chloé. 2016. Standard language ideologies in multicultural Ireland: a case study of Polish and Chinese migrants in Dublin. In Vera Regan, Chloé Diskin & Jennifer Martyn (eds.), *Language, identity and migration: voices from transnational speakers and communities*, 287–326. Oxford: Peter Lang.

Diskin, Chloé. 2017. The use of the discourse-pragmatic marker 'like' by native and non-native speakers of English in Ireland. *Journal of Pragmatics* 120. 144–157.

Diskin, Chloé & Vera Regan. 2017. The attitudes of recently-arrived Polish migrants to Irish English. *World Englishes* 36(2). 191–207.

Diskin, Chloé & Stephen Levey. 2019. Going global and sounding local: quotative variation and change in L1 and L2 speakers of Irish (Dublin) English. *English World-Wide* 40(1). 53–78.

Drummond, Rob. 2012. Aspects of identity in a second language: ING variation in the speech of Polish migrants living in Manchester, UK. *Language Variation and Change* 24(1). 107–133.

Eckert, Penelope. 2008. Variation and the indexical field. *Journal of Sociolinguistics* 12(4). 453–476.

Goodwin, Marjorie Harness. 1990. *He-said-she-said: talk as social organization among Black children*. Bloomington: Indiana University Press.

Haase, Trutz. 2008. *New measures of deprivation in the Republic of Ireland*. Dublin: Pobal.

Hickey, Raymond. 1999. Dublin English: current changes and their motivation. In Paul Foulkes & Gerard Docherty (eds.), *Urban voices: accent studies in the British Isles*, 265–281. London: Edward Arnold.

Hickey, Raymond. 2004. *A sound atlas of Irish English*. Berlin: Mouton de Gruyter.

Hickey, Raymond. 2005. *Dublin English: evolution and change*. Amsterdam: John Benjamins.

Hickey, Raymond. 2007. *Irish English: history and present-day forms*. Cambridge: Cambridge University Press.

Hickey, Raymond. 2012. Standard Irish English. In Raymond Hickey (ed.), *Standards of English: codified varieties around the world*, 96–116. Cambridge/New York: Cambridge University Press.

International Organization for Migration. 2019. *World Migration Report 2020*. Geneva: United Nations.

Irvine, Judith. 1989. When talk isn't cheap: language and political economy. *American Ethnologist* 16(2). 248–267.

Kobiałka, Ewa. 2016. Language, identity and social class among Polish migrants in Ireland. In Vera Regan, Chloé Diskin & Jennifer Martyn (eds.), *Language, identity and migration: voices from transnational speakers and communities*, 191–216. Oxford: Peter Lang.

Labov, William. 1972. *Language in the inner city: studies in the Black English vernacular*. Philadelphia: University of Pennsylvania Press.

Lempert, Michael. 2014. Imitation. *Annual Review of Anthropology* 43. 379–395.

Leung, Maggi W. H. 2017. Social mobility via academic mobility: reconfigurations in class and gender identities among Asian scholars in the global north. *Journal of Ethnic & Migration Studies* 43(16). 2704–2719.

Lippi-Green, Rosina. 1997. *English with an accent: language, ideology and discrimination in the United States*. London: Routledge.

Lonergan, John. 2013. An acoustic and perceptual study of Dublin English phonology. PhD thesis, University College Dublin.

Matsuda, Aya & Paul Kei Matsuda. 2010. World Englishes and the teaching of writing. *TESOL Quarterly* 44(2). 369–374.

Meyerhoff, Miriam & Erik Schleef. 2012. Variation, contact and social indexicality in the acquisition of (ing) by teenage migrants. *Journal of Sociolinguistics* 16(3). 398–416.

Migge, Bettina. 2012. Irish English and recent immigrants to Ireland. In Bettina Migge & Máire Ní Chiosáin (eds.), *New perspectives on Irish English*, 311–326. Amsterdam/Philadelphia: John Benjamins.

Moore, Robert. 2011. Overhearing Ireland: mediatized personae in Irish accent culture. *Language and Communication* 31. 229–242.

Nakassis, Constantine V. 2013. Citation and citationality. *Signs and Society* 1(1). 51–77.

Ochs, Elinor & Lisa Capps. 2001. *Living narrative: creating lives in everyday storytelling*. Cambridge: Harvard University Press.
Paltridge, Brian. 2006. *Discourse analysis*. London: Continuum.
Potter, Jonathan. 2004. Discourse analysis as a way of analysing naturally-occurring talk. In David Silverman (ed.), *Qualitative research*. 2nd ed., 200–221. Thousand Oaks: Sage.
Potter, Jonathan & Alexa Hepburn. 2008. Discursive constructionism. In James A. Holstein & Jaber F. Gubrium (eds.), *Handbook of constructionist research*, 275–293. New York: Guildford Press
Preston, Dennis. 1999. A lanquaqe attitude analysis of reqional U.S. speech: is northern U.S. English not friendly enough? *Cuadernos de Filología Inglesa* 8. 129–146.
Schumann, John. 1978. The acculturation model for second language acquisition. In Rosario C. Gingras (ed.). *Second language acquisition and foreign language teaching*, 27–50. Arlington: Center for Applied Linguistics.
Silverman, David. 2011. *Interpreting qualitative data*, 4th ed. London: Sage.
Urban, Greg & Michael Silverstein. 1996. *Natural histories of discourse*. Chicago: University of Chicago Press.
Vertovec, Steven. 2006. The emergence of super-diversity in Britain. *ESRC Centre on Migration, Policy and Society Working Paper* 25.
Wortham, Stanton Emerson Fisher. 2006. *Learning identity: the joint emergence of social identification and academic learning*. Cambridge: Cambridge University Press.

Claudia Maria Riehl and Sara Ingrosso
8 "The northernmost city of Italy": Italian immigrants in Munich

1 Introduction

In recent years, Munich, the third most populous city in Germany, has received huge numbers of immigrants from all over the world. Their reasons for moving to Munich are extremely heterogeneous and they range from political refugees to highly qualified employees in multinational companies. Over the past 70 years since World War II, the numbers of immigrants have grown steadily. In 1950, foreign citizens made up only 4% of Munich's population, but after the first arrivals of so-called "guest-workers"[1] in the 1960s, they constituted 17.2% in 1973 and 21.6% in 1996 (including refugees of the Kosovo War after 1991). The numbers have continued to increase over the past 20 years (see Figure 1), including the arrival in 2015 of about 14,000 refugees mainly from Afghanistan, Syria, Nigeria, Iraq, Somalia, and Pakistan.

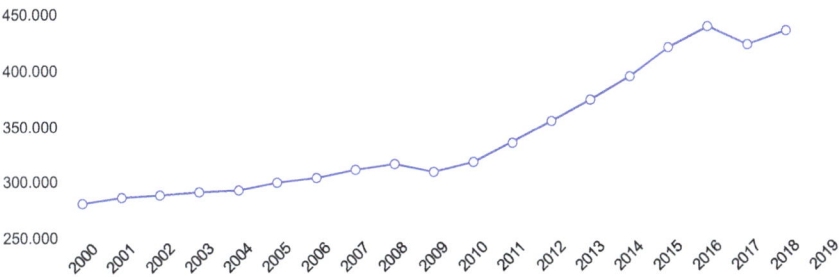

Figure 1: Non-citizens of Germany in Munich from 2000 to 2018 (source: Statistisches Amt München 2022).

At present, 28.1% of the population of Munich are not German citizens (Statistisches Amt München 2022). This figure, however, does not include inhabitants with a so-called *Migrationshintergrund* ('migration background', i.e. people who

---

[1] The migration of foreign workers to Germany as a result of recruitment agreements was officially conceived as temporary, and they were therefore called *Gastarbeiter* ('guest-workers'). This term was introduced in the early 1960s and was used until the mid-1970s (Wengeler 1995: 716–717).

https://doi.org/10.1515/9781501511974-009

themselves or at least one of their parents did not acquire German citizenship by birth) nor ethnic Germans from Eastern European countries. If these citizens are included, the proportion of inhabitants having a cultural or linguistic background other than German exceeds 40% (Isurin and Riehl 2017).

Among the different ethnic groups, immigrants from Turkey and Croatia represent the largest in size both in Germany and in Munich (around 38,000 persons each in the latter) followed by immigrants from Italy and Greece. In this context, the Italian community in Munich, which encompasses around 28,000 individuals, is of particular interest for four reasons. First, and in contrast to the aforementioned communities, Italian migration to Munich has historical roots dating back to the 17th century. A continuous presence of seasonal workers from Italy has been documented since the 19th century. Secondly, among post-war migrants, the Italian community enjoys relatively high prestige in Munich. This is due to the city's geographical proximity to Italy and the Italian cultural presence produced by numerous local Italian restaurants and bars. As a consequence, Munich is often called "the northernmost city of Italy". Thirdly, the Italian community has grown rapidly in the last ten years due to so-called "newcomers" who arrived in the wake of the economic crisis in Southern Europe. Furthermore, the Italian community faces a rather complex linguistic situation since many post-war arrivals spoke various local and regional Italian dialects that are rather dissimilar to Standard Italian.

Thus, in this chapter we will investigate language use and language repertoires of three different groups of Italian immigrants: the "guest-worker generation", "second and third generation" and "newcomers".

Against this background, we address the following questions:

(1) Is there enough homogeneity among Italians in Munich both from a sociodemographic and linguistic perspective that we can speak of an "Italian community"?
(2) In what way do second- and third-generation speakers differ from first-generation immigrants concerning the use of linguistic varieties?
(3) In what way do linguistic repertoires of the traditional generation of individuals who arrived in Munich as *Gastarbeiter* (between 1955 and 1973) and their offspring differ from those of the newcomers?

To approach these questions, we first give an historical overview of the different phases of migration and their specific settings in Munich from the 1950s to the 2010s. We then discuss the sociolinguistic characteristics of the different groups of Italian immigrants. Finally, we analyse their language use and the characteristics of their language repertoire based on a Munich-specific corpus.

2 The Italian community in Munich: Historical and sociolinguistic background

Human mobility and trade relations between Munich and Italy are not only due to geographical closeness, but also to significant historical and cultural exchanges. These relations did not arise in recent times, but date back to earlier centuries: during the Baroque period (17th-18th centuries), the presence of Italian architects, bricklayers, and musicians in the Bavarian courts was already influencing the arts and the urban structure of the city. As a consequence, the Italian language enjoyed considerable prestige and was recognised, along with French, as a language of culture, as it was used by Bavarian courtiers and by the local bourgeoisie (Rieder 2004: 1).

In the 19th century, seasonal workers from the region of Veneto moved to Munich as ice-cream-makers (Campanale 2006: 45–46), while the majority of seasonal workers came from the neighbouring region of Friuli (Del Fabbro 1996: 283). Major phases of migration, however, started after World War II in three different periods: the guest-worker generation (1955–1973), labour migration between 1974 and 2010, and the newcomers (since 2010).

2.1 The guest-worker generation (1955–1973)

The 1955 bilateral agreement on the recruitment of foreign workers between the Republic of Italy and the Federal Republic of Germany was signed not only because of the need for workers in German industries, but also with the aim of reducing Italian unemployment, especially in the southern regions of Italy (Pichler 2008: 249). The agreement resulted in an increase in arrivals of Italian workers, who were more widely employed in manufacturing and in the construction sector. Munich played a very important role as all trains transporting the recruited workers from Southern European countries, including Italy, terminated at Munich Central Station. In 1956, 1,999 Italians were registered in Munich, and by the end of 1963 their number had risen to 20,471 (Statistisches Amt München, personal communication). This process was reinforced by the signing of the Treaties of Rome in 1957, which guaranteed freedom of movement for workers in the then European Economic Community (Leuzzi 2011: 171–172). In December 1974, the number of Italian citizens registered in Munich reached its peak with 29,985. This was mainly a result of the growing demand for workers to build the infrastructure for the Olympic Games in 1972, including the first underground railway line in Munich (Prontera 2015: 211). However, the 1973 oil crisis brought an end to the structured recruitment of foreign workers (*Anwerbestopp* 'recruitment freeze') and signalled the beginning of a new era.

2.2 Migration between 1974 and 2010: A period of changing migration patterns

The years between 1974 and 1985 represented an intermediate phase of qualitative change and quantitative stabilisation of the Italian population. While the recruited workers from the previous phase were mostly men, family reunions starting from the 1970s led to an increasing number of Italian women being registered (Prontera 2015: 210–211). A further transformation in this decade concerned the decline in work in the industrial sector, which was matched by growing employment in the hospitality sector and the arrival of qualified professionals who were employed in the tertiary sector (Rieder 2004: 7).

The late 1980s and the 1990s were also characterised by a qualitative change. New student exchange projects, such as Erasmus, a student exchange program first funded by the European Union (EU) in 1987, as well as the progressive lifting of borders and increased freedom of movement within the EU, boosted by the Maastricht Treaties, contributed to the development of a new European mobility (Pichler 2017: 87) and to new arrivals resulting from the internationalisation of the labour market.

2.3 Newcomers (2010–present): The mobility generation

Since the end of the 2000s, Munich has experienced a renewed phase of arrivals from Italy, characterised by extremely complex dynamics and different drivers. Their qualitative characteristics are difficult to generalise, but they originate in economic and cultural mobility (Ingrosso 2017b: 120). In this regard, Pichler (2011: 291) states that the term "migration" no longer appropriately describes the contemporary state and therefore introduces the terms "mobility" and "new mobility".

The increasing internationalisation of the labour market has led to professional mobility of members of international organisations employed in various professional fields (Cumani 2011: 5). Growing opportunities within EU projects have resulted not only in the mobility of skilled professionals, but also of young students and researchers studying or working at local universities (Pugliese 2015: 30) and numerous research centres, such as the European Southern Observatory, the *Max Planck Gesellschaft*, and the *Fraunhofer Institut*. Mobility within the EU also increased due to changing labour market conditions and socio-economic developments (Minneci 2015: 173–174; Pugliese 2015: 37). Hence, it is no coincidence that the rise in new arrivals from Italy to Munich took place at the same time as the economic and political crisis in Southern Europe, which led to unemployment, difficult and precarious working conditions, and reduced wages in the countries located there. Furthermore, it affected both young people and adults regardless of their educational qualifications (Tirabassi and Del Pra' 2014: 12).

2.4 The Italian population in Munich today

From a quantitative point of view, it is difficult to give an exhaustive picture of the actual presence of Italians in Munich, in particular because of the lack of border controls within the EU and the absence of temporary residence permits (Tirabassi and Del Pra' 2014: 23–24).[2] In other words, statistics cannot provide an exact representation of current migration (Valisena 2016: 174). According to numbers provided by the *Statistisches Amt München*, which are based on municipal registrations (the so-called *Anmeldung*), significant increases have been recorded in recent years, with an annual growth of around 1,000 arrivals from Italy between 2010 and 2016. As a result, the number of registered Italians grew by 7,238 people in that same timeframe to reach 28,276. However, the most recent data show a slight decrease, with 27,821 people with Italian citizenship registered at the end of 2018 (see Figure 2).

As outlined in sections 2.1 and 2.2, and illustrated in Figure 2, in the early 1960s the Italian population grew exponentially, then its number slightly decreased in the 1980s and settled at around 20,000 people until the first decade of the 21st century, before growing again after 2010.

From a qualitative point of view, the Italian population in Munich is highly heterogeneous (Cumani 2011: 4), both socially and professionally. Data provided by the Italian Consulate General in Munich (personal communication, October 15, 2018)[3] document an extremely diverse professional distribution of Italians in Munich.[4] However, within the last decade, the number of skilled workers has increased. While in 2011 over a quarter of Italians in Munich (26.05%) were employed as labourers (Cumani 2011: 4), in 2018 they tended to work instead as clerks and employees (24.62%) or in the hospitality/hotel industry (14.42%), while the proportion of

---

[2] Nevertheless, registration with the municipal office is compulsory within 14 days of arrival and registration with the consular registry of Italians resident abroad (AIRE) must be completed within a year (Ingrosso 2017a: 41, 2017b: 119).
[3] We thank Dott. Renato Cianfarani, Italian Consul General in Munich from 2015 to 2019, for making the data of the consular registers available for our research.
[4] These statistics unfortunately give only a partial image of the numbers, since they are based on optional information given by 14,445 people while entering or updating their data in the Consular register AIRE. Data from the Municipality of Munich do not provide such information.

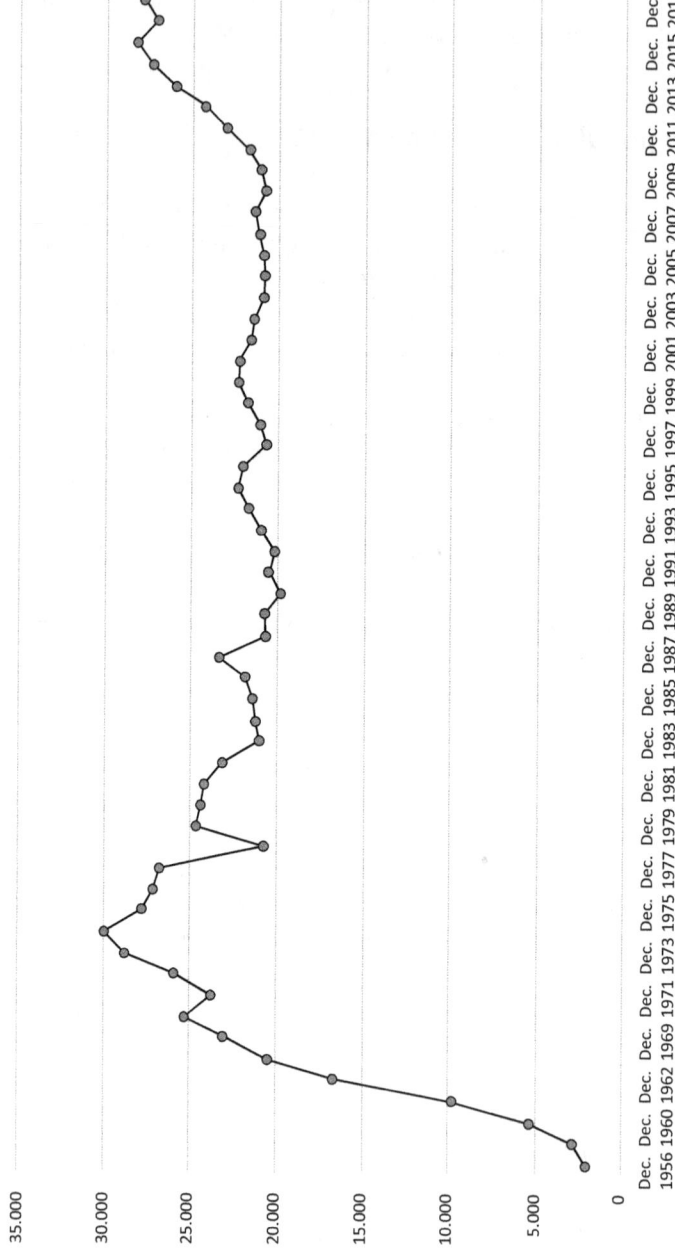

Figure 2: Italian population in Munich from 1956 to 2018 (source: Statistisches Amt München, personal communication).

workers had decreased (14.75%). A significant number of Italian students also live in Munich (7.85%).

Regarding the regions of origin of the Italian population in Munich, most come from Southern Italy.[5] As illustrated in Figure 3,[6] these include the regions of Sicily (13.91%), Campania (10.97%) and Apulia (10.31%). Very few Italians are from Umbria (0.57%) and Valle d'Aosta (0.05%). On the other hand, the numbers of immigrants from the Northern regions of Trentino/Alto Adige (9.50%) and Veneto (6.78%) are comparatively high. This can be explained by the geographical closeness between Munich and these areas.

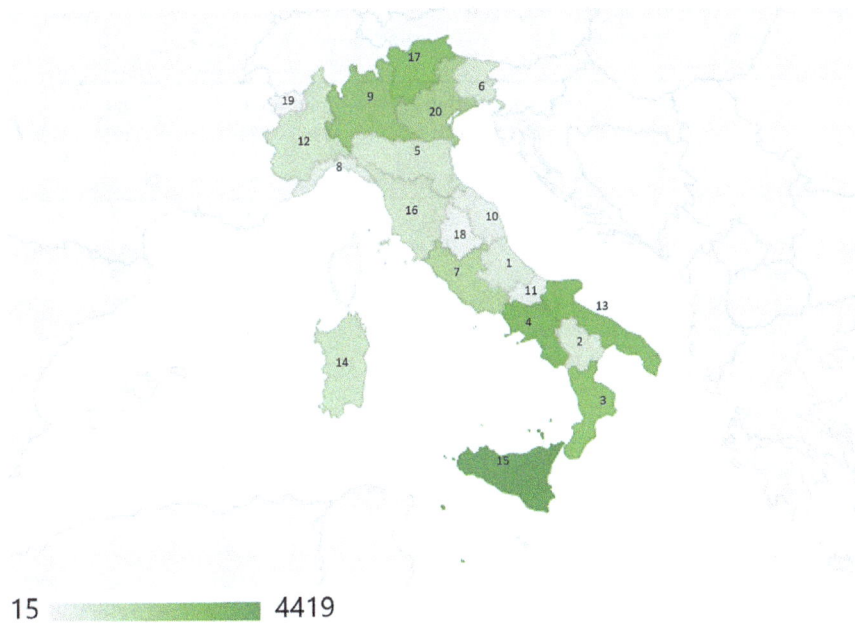

Figure 3: Regions of origin of the Italian population in Munich on October 15, 2018 (Ingrosso 2019b: 32; numbers refer to the areas listed in Table 1).

When considering the time of arrival, it can be observed that people who arrived at the time of the recruitment agreements between 1956 and 1973 came predominantly from Southern Italy (16.42% from Sicily, 14.45% from Campania, and 9.36% from Apu-

---

5 These figures are based on the last city of residence in Italy before registering in the AIRE register (Consulate General of Italy in Munich, personal communication, October 15, 2018).
6 The statistics are based on absolute figures of the consular data. The population density of the regions of origin could not be considered in the present analysis.

lia), whereas the percentage of those coming from Northern Italy (except Trentino/ Alto Adige with 13.3%) was much lower (5.25% from Veneto and 2.63% from Lombardy). In contrast, the numbers differ significantly for the newcomer population, who moved to Munich between 2010 and 2018. Although arrivals from the Southern Italian regions – especially from Sicily (10.47%) and Campania (7.58%) – are still numerous, there is a considerable increase in arrivals from Northern Italy. Most newcomers come from Lombardy (14.30%) followed by those from the neighbouring regions Trentino/Alto Adige (11.72%) and Veneto (8.93%). These data are summarised in Table 1.

Table 1: Regions of origin of the Italian population in Munich on 15 October 2018 (data source: Consulate General of Italy in Munich, personal communication, 15 October 2018).

No.	Region of origin	Italian population in Munich 2018		migrated 1956–1973		migrated 2010–2018	
		N	%	N	%	N	%
1	Abruzzo	735	2.31%	14	2.30%	206	2.08%
2	Basilicata	774	2.44%	21	3.45%	144	1.45%
3	Calabria	2,987	9.41%	55	9.03%	478	4.82%
4	Campania	3,483	10.97%	88	14.45%	752	7.58%
5	Emilia Romagna	877	2.76%	6	0.99%	418	4.21%
6	Friuli Venezia Giulia	847	2.67%	17	2.79%	325	3.28%
7	Lazio	1,862	5.86%	22	3.61%	860	8.67%
8	Liguria	472	1.49%	6	0.99%	157	1.58%
9	Lombardia	2,700	8.50%	16	2.63%	1,419	14.30%
10	Marche	492	1.55%	13	2.13%	217	2.19%
11	Molise	293	0.92%	14	2.30%	43	0.43%
12	Piemonte	1,046	3.29%	7	1.15%	473	4.77%
13	Puglia	3,275	10.31%	57	9.36%	627	6.32%
14	Sardegna	1,152	3.63%	38	6.24%	255	2.57%
15	Sicilia	4,419	13.91%	100	16.42%	1,039	10.47%
16	Toscana	979	3.08%	15	2.46%	377	3.80%
17	Trentino Alto Adige	3,016	9.50%	81	13.30%	1,163	11.72%
18	Umbria	182	0.57%	7	1.15%	78	0.79%
19	Valle D'Aosta	15	0.05%	0	0.00%	4	0.04%
20	Veneto	2,153	6.78%	32	5.25%	886	8.93%
	Total	31,759[7]	100%	609	100%	9,921	100%

---

[7] According to Consulate statistics, the Italian population in Munich consisted of 32,702 people on 15 October 2018. Among them, 31,759 people were born in Italy. The fact that consular figures are higher than those provided by the Municipality of Munich results from a lack of communication between the Italian population and the consular district, as people who relocate from Munich do not necessarily inform the Consulate where they had registered.

In the following, we describe the sociolinguistic and linguistic characteristics of the different groups of Italian origin. First, we provide some general information on the current sociolinguistic background of the Italian community in Munich (Section 3). Then we analyse a Munich-specific corpus on language use and linguistic characteristics (Section 4). In doing so, we aim to provide insights into the language practices and repertoires of the different Italian migration groups.

3 Sociolinguistic characteristics of the Italian community

Due to its profound socio-demographic heterogeneity, the Italian population in Munich also presents highly different linguistic constellations. Their linguistic repertoires are characterised by strong individual features and differ also in communicative practices from speaker to speaker (Krefeld 2006: 236–237). Although there is no longitudinal linguistic study focusing on the Italian population in Munich, the investigations conducted by Krefeld (2004, 2006) and Krefeld and Melchior (2008) convey substantial insights into the language use and linguistic characteristics of the local Italian community, which are corroborated by our recent data (see Section 4).

3.1 The guest-worker generation and their offspring

With regard to the guest-worker generation (see Section 2.1) and their offspring (i.e. second and third generation heritage speakers), there are no common features of linguistic behaviour. According to Krefeld and Melchior (2008: 14–16) the linguistic repertoire of the traditional first generation is characterised by a high prevalence of regional dialect, as well as by a limited knowledge of Standard Italian, especially with regard to speaking and writing. Moreover, the dialect represents their L1 and only after their arrival to Germany did they acquire (limited) knowledge of Standard Italian, which took the role of a vehicular language when interacting with compatriots coming from other dialectal areas in Italy (Berruto 1991: 62; D'Agostino 2012: 18). Nevertheless, the Italian dialects have been maintained and are still used to communicate with fellow citizens from the same geographic area (Krefeld and Melchior 2008: 14–15). Unfortunately, there is a lack of studies on Italian dialects in Germany: linguistic studies in the 1970s and the

1980s focused on the acquisition of the German target language, while the development of the first language and the entire linguistic repertoire of the Italian workers received only marginal attention. However, due to the high number of immigrants from Southern Italy, it can be assumed that Southern Italian dialects played a major role.

The inclusion in the host community from social, communicative, and family[8] perspectives inevitably leads to linguistic integration, which may be characterised by attrition or even loss of competency in Standard Italian and dialect (Krefeld and Melchior 2008: 14–15). This mainly holds for the offspring of first-generation immigrants, i.e. second- and third-generation speakers, for whom the dominant language in daily conversation is German. Although these dynamics are persistent, language use and language choice are dependent on individual preferences and attitudes. The observations by Krefeld and Melchior (2008) are corroborated by data obtained in a recent project on multiliteracy in migrant communities (see Riehl 2020).

Against this background, ongoing contact with the country of origin through geographical closeness might enhance the maintenance of the Italian language and culture and the sense of *italianità* 'Italianness' (Allemann-Ghionda 2005). In addition, the Italian group has relatively high prestige in the host society (Di Salvo and Moreno 2017: 6). This is also reflected in the communicative behaviour of native Germans. In contrast to other immigrant languages, native Germans sometimes use Italian when talking to members of the Italian migrant community. This especially holds for greeting formulas in Italian (e.g. *buongiorno* 'good morning') in opening or closing phases of an interaction (Barberio and Ingrosso 2019: 64).

With regard to the third generation, Krefeld (2004: 50) observes a polarisation of competence profiles. Due to an emerging desire to identify with their language and culture of origin in a situation of extraterritoriality, some third-generation speakers show a basilectal reorientation (*basilektale Rückorientierung*), i.e. a redialectalisation, which is contrary to the development in the home country where a shift from dialect to Standard Italian is ongoing. Other third-generation speakers acquire the Italian language (through tutored instruction) only in adulthood or revitalise an already attrited variety of the Italian variety they had acquired in childhood.

This development also results from the limited access to Italian language education in Munich. This involves in the first instance some afterschool programs organised by the Italian Consulate General, mainly in primary schools. Additionally, Munich hosts ten academically oriented high schools (*Gymnasiums*) where

---

[8] According to the *Statistisches Amt München*, the highest incidence of intermarriage is between German and Italian citizens.

Italian is taught as a third foreign language (after English, French or Latin). However, as teaching of the third language starts only in grade 10 and these classes are designed for foreign language learning, they are not suitable for L1 speakers. Moreover, these opportunities are restricted to the intellectual elites attending the *Gymnasiums* (Barberio 2019: 12). Furthermore, there are two private schools, the *Leonardo da Vinci-Schule* founded in 2013 (a primary school that only recently started offering secondary education) and the *European School Munich* which offers bilingual programs in various European languages, including Italian. However, the number of places is limited to children of employees of the European Patent Office in Munich, the EU, and the staff of the school.[9] Thus, only a small group of second- and third-generation speakers has access to L1 Italian literacy in the school system.

3.2 The newcomer population: Linguistic complexity and individual aspects of multilingualism

The heterogeneous socio-professional composition of the newcomer population (see Section 2.3) has led to extremely divergent sociolinguistic dynamics that are not attributable to a single model and are influenced by individual communicative networks of the speakers.

However, some common patterns can be observed. First, all newcomers – especially young professionals – have high competency in Standard Italian since their entire educational career (including university) has been in this language. Their competence in their dialect of origin no longer typically represents the language of first socialisation in the place of origin (Ingrosso 2019a: 403; Krefeld and Melchior 2008: 17). Regional differences also come into play: in the region of Trentino/Alto Adige, students have access to lessons in German even in primary school, in the bilingual province of Bolzano German lessons are even compulsory from the first grade (Consiglio della Provincia Autonoma di Trento 2015: art. 19). This means that newcomers from this area are already able to communicate in German upon their arrival. The linguistic repertoires of the newcomers are also characterised by an internationalisation of communicative spaces and by the increased use of English as a vehicular language, in particular among highly skilled new arrivals, who are employed in specific professional fields such as education or technology (Ingrosso 2017b: 125). Nevertheless, since English language lessons

---

9 https://esmunich.de/en/home.html (accessed 24 October 2020).

are mandatory in Italian schools (Ministero dell'Instruzione dell'Università e della Ricerca 2004: art. 5) it can be assumed that newcomers, regardless of their socio-professional context, possess at least some basic knowledge of the English language (Ingrosso 2019a: 403).

4 Language use and linguistic characteristics of the Italian migrant population

Given the sociolinguistic situation of the Italian population living in the Bavarian capital, this section provides evidence of the language use and linguistic characteristics of the diverse groups and generations based on a corpus of Munich-specific data. It consists of:

1. Free spoken data published by Krefeld (2004) from first-, second-, and third-generation heritage speakers of Italian (30 subjects from Munich and two other smaller towns in Bavaria; Krefeld 2004) [= KRE]
2. Spoken and written data collected by Riehl et al. within the research project *Mehrschriftlichkeit* ('multiliteracy') between 2013 and 2016 from 62 second-generation heritage speakers of Italian in Munich (9th and 10th graders, mean age 14.9; see Riehl 2020, Barberio 2019). The corpus encompasses a semi-structured interview of 20–30 minutes length and a narrative and argumentative text in L1 Italian for each respondent [= MULT_S – spoken data; MULT-W – written data]
3. Spoken data from radio interviews conducted with guest-workers in the early 1960s as part of the radio program *Buon Giorno, Collega!* This program for Italian guest-workers was broadcast in Italian by the *Bayerischer Rundfunk* (see Ingrosso 2019a) [= BRI][10]
4. Spoken data based on language biographical interviews collected by Ingrosso (2017b, 2019a, 2019b) carried out with twenty Italian newcomers, aged between 25 and 35, who had recently settled in Munich [= NEW]
5. Written data taken from WhatsApp chats with twenty young Italian newcomers in Munich (Barberio and Ingrosso 2019) [= WAPP]

---

[10] We thank the *Bayerischer Rundfunk* for the opportunity to consult their historical archive and for the permission to cite the excerpts.

4.1 Linguistic characteristics of the guest-worker generation

The linguistic behaviour of the guest-worker generation and their offspring has been analysed since the 1970s. The first studies focused on the acquisition of German as a foreign language and whether the so-called *Gastarbeiterdeutsch* ('German of guest-workers') represented some kind of pidgin variety.[11] Most of the guest-workers did not attend German language classes but acquired the language in a natural context through face-to-face interactions in their daily life. Their utterances in German were characterised by simplified structures, e.g. sentences without subject or verb complex, lack of articles, attributes, pronouns, prepositions, copula, and auxiliaries (Bierbach and Birken-Silvermann 2003: 3; Riehl 2014b: 129–135). Since no longitudinal studies were conducted with the first generation of Italian immigrants in Munich, it can only be hypothesised that these observations – which have been documented in other German urban areas – also hold for the Italian population in the Bavarian capital. As a result of the academic interest in the acquisition of the German target language, the development of the first language and the entire linguistic repertoire of the Italian workers have only been marginally analysed. As a consequence, an extensive linguistic corpus comprising spontaneous speech recorded with the first generation of Italians is lacking (Ingrosso 2019a: 396).

However, our sub-corpus of radio interviews with Italian guest-workers shows phenomena of lexical transfer from German, mainly German equivalents of Italian lexemes that are integrated into the Italian language system to denote new communicative practices and activities in Germany. This is exemplified by example (1), from an interview with an Italian guest-worker settled in Munich recorded on 26 January 1963.

(1) *dunque io dico che un pomeriggio così organizzato dalla caritas verbànde di Monaco penso ch_è una buona occasione per trovarsc tutt riuniti*
'Well, I say that such an afternoon organised by the Caritas Verband ('the Caritas association') of Munich I think that's a good opportunity to all meet up together'
[= BRI] (Ingrosso 2019a: 399)[12]

---

[11] Whether the rudimentary German spoken among the guest-workers coming from different countries represented a sort of pidgin was for example researched by Clyne (1968) and within the research project *Pidgin-Deutsch* (Klein 1975). The results did not prove the emergence of a pidgin variety but highlighted that *Gastarbeiterdeutsch* should rather be considered a learner variety because of its variation and continuous development (Riehl 2014a: 115–116).
[12] This and the following translations were generated by the authors of this contribution.

Example (1) demonstrates the influence of both the German language and the Italian dialect substrate.[13] The phrase *dalla caritas verbànde* ('by the Caritas association') represents a lexical transference that is integrated into the system of the Italian language. The use of the Italian feminine article *la* instead of the German masculine article (*der Verband* 'the association') is due to a process of integration from the word *Caritas* that also exists in Italian (*la Caritas*). Moreover, the epithetic addition of a vocalic sound at the end of the German word *Verband* [ferbandə] is a typical characteristic of Italian speakers that systematically occurs in words ending in a consonant (Huszthy 2013: 178).

The corpus also shows elements that denote a particular register of the Italian language which is very close to the dialect and has been defined as *italiano popolare* (lit. 'popular Italian') or *italiano dei semicolti* (lit. 'Italian of the semieducated'). This term refers to "il tipo di italiano imperfettamente acquisito da chi ha per madrelingua il dialetto" ('the kind of Italian language which has been imperfectly acquired by a person whose mother tongue is the dialect') (Cortelazzo 1972: 11). This includes mainly transferences from the respective dialect at the phonological, morpho-syntactical, and lexical levels, and also simplification strategies which do not occur in the dialect (e.g. phonological assimilation, lacking agreement, generic use of possessive pronouns, generic use of the subordinating conjunction *che* etc.) (Masini 2003: 54–60). In example (1) a phonological adaption of the *italiano popolare* appears in the phrase *trovarsc tutt* (instead of *trovarci tutti* 'all meet up'): the fricative /ʃ/ replaces the affricate /tʃ/, denoting a simplification of a composite articulation (Tuttle 1997: 28) and elision of the expected vowel ending *i*.

In other broadcast excerpts, we find typical lexical transfers which result from the L2 German, as in example (2).

(2)   *poi ci sono i capi squadra e gli scèffe di gisìng*
      'There are the team leaders and supervisors from Giesing'
      [= BRI] (Ingrosso 2019a: 398)

Usually the transferences from the L2 are phonologically and morphologically integrated into the system of the Italian language. They include toponyms (*gisìng*, i.e. Giesing, a district in Munich) and expressions used in daily life as well as in the professional domain (*sceffé*, German 'Chef' = 'supervisor').

---

13 Due to the fact that this segment has been extrapolated from a radio interview and we have no metadata of the speaker, we cannot reconstruct his demographic background.

4.2 Linguistic behaviour and characteristics of the second- and third-generations

In contrast to the first generation, second-generation speakers were born in the host country and/or spent the major part of their school career in Germany (Krefeld 2004: 61–62). Since these speakers have usually grown up with an Italian dialect, they acquire Standard Italian mainly via television or through written communication with family members in Italy (Krefeld 2004). Few speakers attend lessons in Standard Italian, since the possibilities in Munich are relatively restricted (see Section 3.1). Typical utterances of second-generation speakers consist of a mixture of the Italian vernacular (*italiano popolare*), the dialect of origin, and German vernacular. Krefeld (2004: 66) characterises this type of language mixing as "*italiano popolare di stampo tedescheggiante*" ('Italian vernacular with a Germanising imprint'). A typical characteristic of this linguistic repertoire is the high amount of variation in morphological forms between dialect and the spoken standard. The following excerpt (3) from an interview with a thirteen-year-old second-generation speaker is a typical example for this language mix.[14]

(3) *ieri mia mamma ci ha dato trenta marchi . **samo** andati a* **Rummel** [. . .] *. e poi . **samo** andato nel . ?***Auto-Scooter*** *. abbiamo . mio fratello è andato un'altra macchina . io sono andato un **attro** . abbiamo cercato di . ehm . sbattere .* **andere Kinder** *e . e poi . qu'**attro** bambino c'ha . ha tozzato mio fratello e io ho **tozzato a lui** ed dopo . dopo cinque minuti è finito . **samo** andato nel .* **Weltwasserbahn** [. . .] *e si . tutta .* **Wasser** *. esce fuori esce.*

'Yesterday my mum gave us thirty marks . we went to the funfair [. . .] . and then . we drove . ? bumper cars . we have . my brother drove another car . i drove another . we were trying to . ehm . to bump . other children and . and then . this other child bumped into my brother and I bumped into him and after . after five minutes it was over . we went to the . world water slide [. . .] and yes . all . water . came out came.'
[= KRE] (Krefeld 2004: 65)

In example (3) variation between Neapolitan dialect and Standard Italian is expressed in the use of different morphological forms, e.g. *attro – altro* 'other'; *samo – siamo* 'we are', and variation in morpho-syntactic constructions, e.g. align-

---

14 Transcription conventions according to the original, full-stop refers to pause.
   In this and all following excerpts the different linguistic varieties are marked with the following font types: Italian = *italics*; German = **bold**; dialect = ***italics bold***; English = plain.

ing the direct object using the preposition *a* (*ho tozzato* **a** *lui*) as in the dialect or without preposition (*ho tozzato mio fratello*) as in Standard Italian. We also find variation in subject-verb agreement: a lack in agreement (*samo andato*), typical for *italiano popolare*, in alternation with correct agreement (*samo andati*). Moreover, there are typical lexical insertions referring to German leisure attractions (*Rummel, Weltwasserbahn*) and everyday life (*andere Kinder*).

Speakers of the third generation typically develop a type of mixed language, which characterises migrant communities and forms part of their bilingual identity (Riehl 2018: 49), as in example (4):

(4) *Eh eh eh sì, per fa'* la **Kosmetikerin** *ci vuole il ehm il* **so'n Pass, ich glaub** *per fare la,* **du musst halt in die neunte gehen***, e se poi ce la fai* **kannst du des so mit'm Pass schaffen.**
'Uhm, uhm, uhm yes, to become a beautician, you need the uhm the type of a pass, I think, to become, you have to attend the ninth (grade), and then, if you make it, you can succeed with this kind of pass.'
[= KRE] (Student, third generation, 11 years old, from Krefeld 2004: 100)

A characteristic of this mixed variety is that the main information such as *Kosmetikerin* ('beautician'), *so'n Pass* ('type of pass'), *in die neunte gehen* ('attend the ninth grade') is rendered in German, while catch-all terms (e.g. *fare* 'to do') and frequent colloquial formula such as *ci vuole* ('it is necessary') and *ce la fai* ('you make it') appear in Italian. This type of speech is a communicative routine typical for plurilingual speakers which emerges in the second generation and is transmitted to the next generation (Riehl 2018: 49); this behaviour is not specific to Italian heritage speakers.

A phenomenon indicating that the Italian language is acquired only in the family domain and restricted to routine patterns and everyday vocabulary is frequent code-switching without any apparent conversational function. This means code-switching is not used as a conversation cue, e.g. marking quotations, expressing attitudes or commenting utterances, or marking meta-communicative utterances (Auer and Eastman 2010), but is instead provoked by lacunas in the Italian mental lexicon which are either filled by lexical transfer or a complete switch to L2, as illustrated by example (5).

(5) **Mm, genau.** *Uno è così* [gestikuliert], *e noi dobbiamo ehm* **entweder** *ehm* **Überschlag nach hinten machen oder nach vorne.**
'Um, exactly. One is like this [gesticulates], and we must uhm either uhm do a somersault forwards or backwards.'
[= KRE] (Student, third generation, 11 years old, from Krefeld 2004: 101)

In this example it becomes obvious that the speaker who is commenting on an activity in physical education not only lacks the Italian equivalent for *Überschlag* ('somersault'), but also has difficulties communicating the complete activity (to do a somersault forwards or backwards) in Italian since this activity is part of the school language domain, i.e. German. The switch is accompanied by hesitation markers such as *uhm* indicating that the speaker is making an effort to express the content in Italian (as proposed by the monolingual interview setting), but finally gives up and switches to German instead.

Although these examples are rather typical for third-generation heritage speakers in general, it also reflects the specific situation in Munich where the possibility of acquiring the heritage language at school is rather restricted and many speakers acquire their heritage language only in the family domain (see Section 3.1).

The speech of second- and third-generation speakers exhibits both typical processes of language contact and simplification strategies based on incomplete acquisition (Montrul 2008, 2016). Language contact processes appear mainly in the lexicon – similar to migrant settings in general (Riehl 2019). This especially holds for cultural borrowings (example 6a) and words denoting institutions or locations of the immediate environment (6b).

(6) a. *è venuta mamma, ha portato i* **Nikoläuse** *così piccolini.*
  'Mummy has come, she brought the Nikoläuse, so small.'
  [= KRE] (Student, second generation, 11 years old, from Krefeld 2004: 104)
  b. *Era la* **achte Klasse.**
  'It was the eighth grade.'
  [= MULT_S] (Student, second generation, 15 years old)

While in (6a) the speaker refers to a feature of German traditional culture (small figures of Saint Nikolaus made of chocolate which are distributed on 6 December), (6b) denotes a year level within the German school system. In contrast to the first-generation speakers in example (1), these loans are not integrated phonologically and morphologically into the system of the Italian language.

Besides these typical instances of matter borrowing (Matras 2020), we find semantic restructuring which refers to the "partial modification of already existing language-mediated conceptual categories" (Jarvis and Pavlenko 2008: 160). Semantic transference occurs mainly with cognates (etymologically related words in different languages) or otherwise homophonous lexemes (Clyne 2003; Riehl 2014a, 2014b). In these cases, speakers adopt the L2 meaning for similar sounding words (sometimes with completely different roots) in Italian. Examples from our corpus include *regalo* (Italian 'gift') which borrows the meaning of German *Regal* ('shelf'), *rosino* (Italian 'little rose') which suggests the German *Rosine* ('raisin'), *mappa* (Italian 'map') which takes on the meaning of German *Mappe* ('folder') (Krefeld 2004: 73), and *nota* (Italian 'note') which adopts the meaning of German *Note* ('mark') (MULT_S). These examples support the assumption that phonologically similar words are interconnected in the mental lexicon *independently* of the language subset to which they belong (Riehl 2010).

Another type of restructuring is the use of semantically similar words or the use of neologisms, which Clyne (1981: 38) calls linguistic alienation (*sprachliche Entfremdung*): This especially applies to the creation of new words using well-known word formation patterns in Italian. The following examples are taken from our corpus of written texts by bilingual 9th and 10th graders in Munich: *bizzarezza* (*una cosa bizzara* 'a bizarre thing'), *paccone* (*un grande pacco* 'a big parcel') (MULT_W; Barberio 2019: 148).

Other language contact phenomena include transfer of collocations (*fa senso* – lit. 'it makes sense' instead of *ha senso*, MULT_S), transfer of phrasemes (*andare fuori* – lit. 'go out' instead of *uscire*) or the pragmatic use of *così* analogous to the German particle *so* which is used as a hedge (*era meglio a scuola e così*, lit. 'she was better at school and so' [meaning: 'and similar things']) (Krefeld 2004: 77–80).

Besides these contact-induced changes, we find internal processes of language change which are a common phenomenon in language attrition and language shift, i.e. simplification processes of the grammatical system (Riehl 2019). This mainly holds for the gradual reduction of morphological structures. A typical phenomenon in migrant varieties of Italian is the lack of differentiation between different types of articles, such as the variant masculine articles *lo* (Sg.) or *gli* (Pl.) the use of which is limited to specific phonological contexts (after vocal or *s* + consonant), where their more general equivalents, *il* and *i*, should not appear. Thus, in second- and third-generation speakers' utterances, the following combinations occur, even in our written corpus: *il stesso typo* (instead of *lo stesso*), *i studenti* (instead of *gli studenti*), *i stranieri* (instead of *gli stranieri*) (MULT_W; Barberio 2019: 145–146). These examples show that under the conditions of language acquisition in a migrant context, a complex phonotactic rule (*il* -> *lo* and *i* -> *gli* before *s impurum*) is not acquired (Krefeld 2004: 69). Similar examples for reduction of polymorphological structures are found in verb inflection paradigms: *diciono* (instead of *dicono* 'they say') based on other parts of the same paradigm, e.g. *dice*, *diciamo* (Krefeld 2004: 69), *leggio* (instead of *leggo* 'I read'), similar to *leggi*, *leggiamo* (MULT_S). This strategy is used to optimise the consistency of forms within paradigms (Krefeld 2004: 69).

4.3 Linguistic behaviour and characteristics in the newcomer group

The sociolinguistic characteristics of Italian newcomers shaped by multilingualism (see Section 3.2) also become evident in their communicative behaviour. On the one hand, contact with the German target language leads to transference from German into Italian, as demonstrated in example (7). On the other hand, the newcomers – especially the highly skilled ones – act in a communicative space which is characterised by the increasing use of English, mainly in interaction with speakers who speak neither German nor Italian.

Primarily, we find phrases and terms adopted from German as a consequence of the specific migratory context:

(7) *ho iniziato da poco come [. . .]* **freiberufliche** *in realtà* **archeologe** *quindi adesso ho iniziato con la* **steuernummer** *insomma a lavorare adesso collaboro anche un istituto (.) una* **kulturverein** *italiana (0.73) sempre con [. . .] con lo* **steuernummer** *fai ritenuta (.) non ritenuta d_acconto insomma si fa la (.) si fanno le* **rechnung**.
'I recently started working as freelance actually archaeologist, so I started working with the tax number so to say and now I also collaborate with an institute, an Italian cultural association. Again with the tax number you make a withholding . . . not a withholding so to say you make the you make the invoices.'
[= NEW]

Example (7) was collected from a 33-year-old female speaker who moved to Germany in 2013. In this excerpt, the numerous lexical transferences of nouns, the most prominent word class which is affected by borrowing (Matras 2020: 169; Riehl 2014a: 108–109), all describe bureaucratic activities that she had to tackle. Despite the systematic use of lexemes taken from the contact language, their morphological integration shifts. The speaker refers twice to *steuernummer* ('tax number'); first, she uses the Italian feminine article *la*, which corresponds to German *die Steuernummer*, shortly after she utters *lo steuernummer*, suggesting an adaptation of the Italian masculine gender *il numero* ('the number'). Moreover, the morphological integration of *Rechnung* ('invoice') is limited to the use of the Italian definite plural article *le*. The noun itself appears as a bare noun, neither adopting the Italian plural suffix *-e* nor the German plural morpheme *-en*. Gender is also only partially rendered, as the speaker describes herself as *freiberufliche archeologe*, combining the adjective form which would be used to indicate the feminine gender with the masculine form of the noun *Archäologe* (archaeologist) instead of the feminine form *Archäologin*.

In contrast to the first generation of guest-workers (see Section 4.1), lexemes are phonotactically not integrated into the Italian system (by adding an epithetic-*e*). This can be explained by the higher level of education of this particular group and their higher skills in German, since all of the subjects interviewed in the study attended a German language course after their arrival.

The linguistic repertoire of the Italian newcomers in Munich[15] is not limited to Italian and German. In particular, increasing internationalisation also leads to contact with English, which becomes part of their linguistic repertoire. This is shown in examples (8a) and (8b), taken from two different speakers of the same corpus, who obtained their first job in Munich without knowledge of German and used both English and German at work.

(8) a. *fare una* [. . .] application
     'to send an application'
   b. *mandavo sempre applicazioni in inglese.*
     'I used to send applications in English.'
   [= NEW] (Ingrosso 2019a: 399)

Here it is noticeable how the same concept may be expressed through different kinds of transference, varying from speaker to speaker. Example (8a) shows a lexical transfer, as the substantive *application* is integrated into the Italian utterance through use of the feminine article *una*. Example (8b), however, is a case of semantic transference. There is no lexical integration, but the Italian noun *applicazione* ('practice', 'attribution', 'execution') adopts an additional meaning, i.e. 'job application'. Here, the same restructuring processes occur as demonstrated in Section 4.3. Interestingly, however, the source language is not German as in the examples above, but as part of the whole linguistic repertoire, the semantic transfer comes from L2 English.

Other interesting data documenting the multilingual communicative practices in the newcomer community are found in our corpus of WhatsApp messages. All subjects hold a university degree from an Italian university, reported speaking Standard Italian as their first language, and make limited use of their dialect of origin (Barberio and Ingrosso 2019: 61–62). Typically, in computer-mediated con-

---

15 Whether these characteristics can be found in other urban settings in Germany or in German-speaking cities requires further research.

versation, speakers use their whole language repertoire, often in a playful way (Androutsopoulos 2015).

(9) a. M26IT_P: *Birra domenica sera?* ('Beer on Sunday night?')[16]
 F27IT_P: Idk *domenica è troppo lontana* ('I don't know, Sunday is too far away')
 F27IT_P: **Es tut mir leid**!!! ('I'm sorry!!!')
 b. F27IT_P: Get over it *e fatti la tua vita* ('Get over it and enjoy life')
 M26IT_P: *È quello che faccio* ('That's what I do')
 M26IT_P: *Ma poi fa ste* **cagate** ('But then she makes bullshit')
 M26IT_P: *E mi risale l'odio* ('And I get angry')
 M26IT_P: **L murt ca ten** ('damned')
 [= WAPP] (Barberio and Ingrosso 2021: 317)

Example (9a) shows an interaction where speakers switch between the first language Italian, German (*Es tut mir leid*), and English (*Idk*, acronym for *I don't know*). The complexity of the repertoire also becomes evident in example (9b), where code-switching takes place not only from Italian to English (*get over it*) but also between Standard Italian and the Apulian dialect of origin of the speaker (*cagate* 'bullshit', *L murt ca ten* 'damned', lit. 'may your death relatives/ancestors be damned'). However, in contrast to the guest-worker generation and their offspring, the newcomers use dialectal expression only in formulaic expressions (mostly with emotional connotations).

5 Discussion: Is there a 'Comunità Italiana' in Munich?

With regard to our first research question, our analysis has shown that the Italophone community in Munich is composed of heterogeneous groups, based on the socio-demographic perspective, the region of origin, linguistic repertoire, and language practices. From a socio-demographic perspective, the professional qualifications of Italian immigrants range from unskilled workers to highly qualified academics. The regions of origin have also shifted from an overwhelming percentage of people coming from Southern Italian regions (Sicily, Campania, Apulia)

---

16 In examples 9a and 9b, M26IT_P refers to a man, aged 26, Italian native speaker, coming from Apulia and F27IT_P refers to a woman, aged 27, Italian native speaker, coming from Apulia.

in the 1960s to 1990s to a higher influx of people from northern parts (Lombardy, Veneto, Trentino/Alto Adige) in the new millennium. For this reason, the term "community" itself can be questioned, as it should indicate a common membership and a sense of belonging (Ingrosso 2017a: 43) and does not take into account such complexity.

The socio-demographic and regional diversity also has an impact on the linguistic repertoire of the speakers. Speakers with no or low education coming to Munich in the post-war period from rural regions, especially from the South, usually had little or no command of Standard Italian, but only of their respective dialect and the register of *italiano popolare*. Educated speakers on the other hand master Standard Italian and to a lesser extent the regional dialect (Krefeld 2016: 270). Moreover, speakers holding a degree of higher education typically have a strong command of the English language. Access to German in the country of origin also depends on the respective region. Newcomers from Trentino/Alto Adige already have some competence in German on arrival while others have to resort to English first and attend German language classes once in Munich.

Referring to our second and third research questions, namely the way the linguistic repertoire of the different generations of the Italian-speaking population in Munich differs, we found that diverse initial situations lead to a complex setting of linguistic repertoires: Primarily, the Italian community is characterised by polyglossic use of L1 repertoires (dialect, *italiano popolare*, Standard Italian). The guest-workers who came from Southern Italy still use their dialects of origin and have a limited command of Standard Italian. Since they have transmitted their respective dialects to the younger generations, speakers of the second and third generation often preserve a deep dialectality in their heritage language which conspicuously differs from the vernacular used by their peers in the homeland. Due to limited opportunities to acquire Standard Italian at school (see Section 3.1), the vast majority of second- and third-generation speakers do not acquire (elaborate) literacy in their heritage language. Thus, their linguistic repertoire will be reduced to the respective regional dialect and the vernacular (*italiano popolare*) on the one hand and various varieties of German on the other. In contrast to the first generation, their Italian registers are increasingly influenced by contact with German and reduced to more generic or formulaic use mainly in the family domain (see example 4).

Contrary to this "old" community, the newcomers only partially demonstrate polyglossic use of Italian. Many of them have Standard Italian as their L1 and only a limited (or passive) competence of the dialect of origin, which they use only in formulaic expressions or to express a certain communicative function (see example 9). In contrast, the majority of newly arrived Italians use a multilingual repertoire. This is not only reflected in the communicative use of L2 English but also in transfer processes from English into Italian (example 8). Thus, also from a linguistic point of view, the Italian group is highly heterogeneous and has not developed its own extraterritorial variety of Italian.

6 Conclusion

As demonstrated in this contribution, the Italian community in Munich shows some peculiarities. First, continuous contact with the country of origin through geographical closeness enhances the maintenance of Italian language and culture. Second, the Italian group has relatively high prestige in the host society, which leads to a general acceptance of the Italian language and culture in the public sphere. The Italian migrant group is characterised by an extreme heterogeneity not only in socio-demographics and education (which also holds for other immigrant groups from Southern Europe), but also in their linguistic repertoires ranging from a polyglossic use of the Italian language to a multilingual repertoire including Standard Italian, German, and English.

In this respect, the language use in the Italian community reflects the dynamics of multilingualism and multiculturalism in European metropoles in the first decades of the 21st century, which are shaped by past and present transmigration, a high professional diversity and multilingual repertoires.

References

Allemann-Ghionda, Cristina. 2005. Le ragioni dell'insuccesso dei ragazzi italiani nel sistema scolastico tedesco e le possibili soluzioni. *Studi emigrazione: International Journal of Migration Studies* 42. 245–258.

Androutsopoulos, Jannis. 2015. Networked multilingualism: some language practices on Facebook and their implications. *International Journal of Bilingualism* 19(2). 185–205.

Auer, Peter & Carol M. Eastman. 2010. Code-switching. In Jürgen Jaspers, Jan-Ola Östman & Jef Verschueren (eds.), *Society and language use*, 84–112. Amsterdam/Philadelphia: John Benjamins.

Barberio, Teresa. 2019. Schreiben in zwei Sprachen: Argumentative und narrative Texte bilingualer italienisch-deutscher Schülerinnen und Schüler. PhD thesis, Ludwig-Maximilian University Munich.

Barberio, Teresa & Sara Ingrosso. 2019. „Ora ho una super geiles neues Fahrrad ☺": Sprachkontaktphänomene am Beispiel italienisch-deutscher Chats. *JournaLipp* 6. 57–69.

Barberio, Teresa & Sara Ingrosso. 2021. Chat plurilingue tra scrittura e oralità. In Teresa Gruber, Klaus Grübl & Thomas Scharinger (eds.), *Was bleibt von Nähe und Distanz? Mediale und konzeptionelle Aspeke sprachlicher Variation*, 305–324. Tübingen: Narr.

Berruto, Gaetano. 1991. Note sul repertorio linguistico degli emigrati italiani in Svizzera tedesca. *Linguistica* 31. 61–79.

Bierbach, Christine & Gabriele Birken-Silvermann. 2003. Deutsch – italienischer Sprachkontakt. In Sandro Moraldo (ed.), *Tendenzen der deutschen Gegenwartssprache*. Bologna. https://madoc.bib.uni-mannheim.de/6825/ (accessed 8 June 2019)

Campanale, Laura. 2006. I gelatieri veneti in Germania: un'indagine sociolinguistica. *AltreItalie* 33. 45–64.

Clyne, Michael G. 1968. Zum Pidgin-Deutsch der Gastarbeiter. *Zeitschrift für Mundartforschung* 35(2). 130–139.

Clyne, Michael. 1981. *Deutsch als Muttersprache in Australien. Zur Ökologie einer Einwanderersprache*. Wiesbaden: Steiner.

Clyne, Michael. 2003. *Dynamics of language contact: English and immigrant languages*. Cambridge: Cambridge University Press.

Consiglio della Provincia Autonoma di Trento. 2015. *Lo statuto speciale per il Trentino – Alto Adige*. https://www.consiglio.provincia.tn.it/news/web-radio/archivio/Mp3/statuto%20speciale%20annotato.pdf (accessed 10 October 2019)

Cortelazzo, Manilo. 1972. *Avviamento critico allo studio della dialettologia italiana*. Vol. 3. Pisa: Pacini.

Cumani, Claudio. 2011. *La comunità italiana in Baviera*. Munich: COMITES. http://www.cumani.eu/pubblicazioni/2011-italiani_in_baviera.pdf (accessed 15 May 2019)

D'Agostino, Mari. 2012. *Sociolinguistica dell'Italia contemporanea*. Bologna: Il mulino.

Del Fabbro, René. 1996. *Transalpini: Italienische Arbeiterwanderung nach Süddeutschland im Kaiserreich 1870–1918*. Osnabrück: Rasch.

Di Salvo, Margherita & Paola Moreno. 2017. Introduction: for the state of the art on linguistic studies of Italian communities worldwide. In Margherita di Salvo & Paola Moreno (eds.), *Italian communities abroad: multilingualism and migration*, 1–18. Newcastle upon Tyne: Cambridge Scholars Publishing.

Huszthy, Bálint. 2013. L'accento straniero degli italiani: esiste un "accento italiano" comune? *Verbum Analecta Neolatina* XIV. 167–181.

Ingrosso, Sara. 2017a. Italian newcomers to Germany and cultural identity. *AEMI-Journal* 15. 40–50.

Ingrosso, Sara. 2017b. Nuove mobilità e plurilinguismo: il caso di Monaco di Baviera. *AltreItalie* 55. 118–135.

Ingrosso, Sara. 2019a. Da "Gastarbeiter" a "expat". Micro-diacronia linguistica nello spazio urbano di Monaco di Baviera. In Roger Schöntag & Stephanie Massicot (eds.), *Diachrone Migrationslinguistik: Mehrsprachigkeit in historischen Sprachkontaktsituationen. Akten des XXXV. Romanistentages in Zürich, 8–12 Oktober 2017*, 385–410. Berlin: Peter Lang.

Ingrosso, Sara. 2019b. Sprachbiographische Erzählungen junger Italiener in München: Postmoderne Migrationsformen aus linguistischer Perspektive. PhD thesis, Ludwig-Maximilian University Munich.

Isurin, Ludmila & Claudia M. Riehl. 2017. Introduction. In Ludmila Isurin & Claudia M. Riehl (eds.), *Integration, identity, and language maintenance in young immigrants: Russian Germans or German Russians*, 1–10. Amsterdam/Philadelphia: John Benjamins.

Jarvis, Scott & Aneta Pavlenko. 2008. *Crosslinguistic influence in language and cognition*. London: Routledge.

Klein, Wolfgang. 1975. *Sprache und Kommunikation ausländischer Arbeiter*. Kronberg: Scriptor.

Krefeld, Thomas. 2004. *Einführung in die Migrationslinguistik: von der "Germania italiana" in die "Romania multipla"*. Tübingen: Narr.

Krefeld, Thomas. 2006. Chicago di Baviera? Repertori, reti e spazio urbano. In Nicola de Blasi & Carla Marcato (eds.), *La città e le sue lingue: repertori linguistici urbani*, 223–242. Naples: Liguori.

Krefeld, Thomas. 2016. Profilo sociolinguistico. In Sergio Lubello (ed.), *Manuale di linguistica italiana*, 262–274. Berlin: de Gruyter.

Krefeld, Thomas & Luca Melchior. 2008. La Germania Italiana oggi. *Bollettino della Società di Linguistica Italiana* XXVI. 9–26.

Leuzzi, Vito Antonio. 2011. L'emigrazione meridionale di massa ed una nuova meta: la Germania. In Giulio Esposito & Vito Antonio Leuzzi (eds.), *Puglia/Europa: percorsi migratori 1946–1973*, 171–204. Bari: Edizioni dal Sud.

Masini, Andrea. 2003. L'italiano contemporaneo e le sue varietà. In Ilaria Bonomi, Andrea Masini, Silvia Morgana & Mario Piotti (eds.), *Elementi di linguistica italiana*, 15–86. Rome: Carocci.

Matras, Yaron. 2020. *Language contact*. 2nd ed. Cambridge: Cambridge University Press.

Ministero dell'Istruzione dell'Università e della Ricerca. 2004. *Decreto legislativo 19 febbraio 2004, n. 59*. https://archivio.pubblica.istruzione.it/riforma/allegati/dl190204.pdf (accessed 15 May 2019).

Minneci, Fabiana. 2015. If there were a "highly skilled red octopus"? The case of Italian highly skilled mobility at times of crisis. *Economics and Sociology* 8. 170–182.

Montrul, Silvina. 2008. *Incomplete acquisition in bilingualism: re-examining the age factor*. Amsterdam/Philadelphia: John Benjamins.

Montrul, Silvina. 2016. *The acquisition of heritage languages*. Cambridge: Cambridge University Press.

Pichler, Edith. 2008. Community, Milieus und Schulkarrieren am Beispiel der italienischen Bevölkerung in Berlin. In Felicitas Hillmann & Michael Windizio (eds.), *Migration und städtischer Raum. Chancen und Risiken der Segregation und Integration*, 247–259. Opladen/Farmington Hills: Budrich UniPress.

Pichler, Edith. 2011. Die Italiener in Berlin und ihr Selbstverständnis als neue Europäer. In Roberto Sala & Oliver Janz (eds.), *Dolce vita? Das Bild der Italiener in Deutschland*, 277–294. Frankfurt am Main/New York: Campus Verlag.

Pichler, Edith. 2017. Germania: Migrazioni, euro-mobilità interna e cittadinanza Europea. In Immaccolata Amodeo, Christiane Lierdmann, Edith Pichler & Matteo Scotto (eds.), *Why Europe? German-Italian reflections on a common topic*, 87–92. Stuttgart: Steiner.

Prontera, Grazia. 2015. Donne italiane e politica a Monaco di Baviera. In Stefano Luconi & Mario Varricchio (eds.), *Lontane da casa: donne italiane e diaspora globale dall'inizio del Novecento a oggi*, 207–232. Turin: Accademia University Press.

Pugliese, Enrico. 2015. Le nuove migrazioni italiane: il contesto e i protagonisti. In Iside Gjergji (ed.), *La nuova emigrazione italiana: cause, mete e figure sociali*, 25–38. Venice: Edizioni Ca'Foscari.

Rieder, Maximiliane. 2004. *50 Jahre Anwerbung zwischen Deutschland und Italien: Italienische 'Gastarbeiter' und Unternehmer in Bayern und München*. https://www.muenchen.de/rathaus/dam/jcr:78f9e607-e6b2-452e-a975-1270672d11dc/mb050301.pdf (accessed 15 May 2019).

Riehl, Claudia M. 2010. Mental representation of bilingualism. *Wiley Interdisciplinary Reviews: Cognitive Science* 1(5), 750–758.

Riehl, Claudia M. 2014a. *Mehrsprachigkeit: eine Einführung*. Darmstadt: WBG.

Riehl, Claudia M. 2014b. *Sprachkontaktforschung: eine Einführung*. Tübingen: Narr.

Riehl, Claudia M. 2018. Mehrsprachigkeit in der Familie und im Lebensalltag. In Anne-Katharina Harr, Martina Liedke & Claudia M. Riehl (eds.), *Deutsch als Zweitsprache: Migration – Spracherwerb – Unterricht*, 27–60. Stuttgart: Metzler.

Riehl, Claudia M. 2019. Language contact and language attrition. In Monika Schmid & Barbara Köpke (eds.), *Handbook of language attrition*, 314–328. Oxford: Oxford University Press.

Riehl, Claudia M. 2020. Multiliteracy in heritage language speakers: the interdependence of L1 and L2, and extra-linguistic factors. *Heritage Language Journal* 17(3). 377–408.

Statistisches Amt München. 2022. *Indikatorenatlas München*. https://www.mstatistik-muenchen.de/indikatorenatlas/atlas.html?indicator=i63&date=2019 (accessed 19 May 2022)

Tirabassi, Maddalena & Alvise Del Pra'. 2014. *La meglio Italia: le mobilità italiane nel XXI secolo*. Turin: Accademia University Press.

Tuttle, Edward. 1997. Palatalization. In Martin Maiden & Mair Perry (eds.), *The dialects of Italy*, 26–31. London: Routledge.

Valisena, Daniele. 2016. From migrations to new mobilities in the European Union: Italians in Berlin between anomie and multi-situated identity. *AEMI-Journal* 14. 174–181.

Wengeler, Martin. 1995. Multikulturelle Gesellschaft oder Ausländer raus? Der sprachliche Umgang mit der Einwanderung seit 1945. In Georg Stötzel & Martin Wengeler (eds.), *Kontroverse Begriffe: Geschichte des öffentlichen Sprachgebrauchs in der Bundesrepublik Deutschland*, 711–750. Berlin: de Gruyter.

Part 3: **Language across time and space**

Peter Trudgill and Jane Warren
9 Norwich across time: A city of strangers

1 Introduction

The current era is characterised by increasing global mobility, with greater numbers of people from a wider range of countries and language backgrounds coming into contact. Transnational movements of people are intensifying due to a whole range of economic, political and social conditions, including "invasion, colonization, slavery, religious mission, persecution, trade, conflict, famine, drought, war, urbanization, economic aspiration, family reunion, global commerce and technological advances" (Blackledge and Creese 2018: xxii). People's migration itineraries and their insertion into host societies are also changing, exemplified in the UK by discussions about the status of EU nationals now that the UK has left the EU, or the initial five-year "leave to remain" status granted to successful asylum seekers. The term "super-diversity" was coined to describe the changing patterns of migration in Britain over the last two decades or so, which are creating new forms of contact and segregation (Vertovec 2007).

These new patterns are particularly salient in the UK's major urban areas, but it is worthwhile reflecting on smaller cities where cultural and linguistic diversity appears more muted, at least at first sight and sound. Norwich, capital of the county of Norfolk in East Anglia, is one such city.[1] Up until recently, Norwich has been stereotyped as isolated, cut off from the rest of the UK by its location, poor transport connections and comparative lack of industrialisation, its population largely monocultural, Protestant, white English. Norfolk's self-deprecating "Normal for Norfolk" tag for what outsiders might consider odd behaviours and customs, and its traditional motto of "Do different", point to a self-awareness of and a certain pride in the county's distinctiveness and isolation from the rest of the country, at least in the recent past.

A closer look at Norwich reveals, perhaps not unsurprisingly, a complex and nuanced picture of migration, reconfiguring the city at different times and in different ways. In both the later medieval period and the 16th century, Norwich was one of the largest towns in England. Greater Norwich is now ranked only 31st among

---

[1] East Anglia is a geographical area in the East of England, comprising the counties of Norfolk, Suffolk and Cambridgeshire.

https://doi.org/10.1515/9781501511974-010

England's cities.[2] However, this rather "out of the way" place is inevitably caught up in the currents and eddies of present-day global mobility. In Norwich schools, despite the city's size (about 140,000 inhabitants) and geographical location, there are at least 117 languages other than English spoken. Compare this current situation to that of the 16th century, when immigrants from the Low Countries settled in Norwich. By the late 1500s, Dutch and French speaking immigrants made up nearly 40% of the city's population. They were known as *Strangers* – a word that in Norwich at the time applied to anyone who was not part of the city community (Meeres 2012: 35).

This chapter investigates how and to what extent Norwich in past and current configurations is a site of multilingualism and diversity. It examines three periods in the city's history when it experienced major linguistic change resulting from transnational population movements: the medieval period, the 16th century, and the present day. The chapter is framed by the following research questions:

(1) What are the motivations of the new linguistic groups arriving in Norwich in each of the three periods?
(2) How is the multilingualism of each period characterised, and to what extent have speakers of languages other than English left their mark on the city?

The different historical periods examined require different theoretical frameworks. The analysis of the medieval period and the 16th century takes an historical sociolinguistic approach, examining language contact phenomena in the evolution of the English language in Norwich and East Anglia (see Trudgill 2021). The two periods illustrate some of the wide-ranging linguistic consequences of language contact, which vary according to the prevailing sociolinguistic context (Trudgill 2011, 2016). Each period's distinct migration, settlement, and language contact patterns are discussed, followed by the resulting impact on the English language of the time, including the naming of Norwich streets, districts and settlements.

The exploration of the present day also takes into account the migration and language context and signage in the city. It draws on the methodology used by Matras and Robertson (2015) in their study of multilingualism in Manchester, which triangulates quantitative datasets, observational data and ethnographic interviews. This chapter focuses on the first two elements. Firstly, it uses three datasets – the National Census, the School Census, and requests received by local translation and interpretation service INTRANS – to form a picture of who speaks

---

[2] The city is more important than its size might suggest. The nearest place to Norwich that is bigger than Norwich is London, and Norwich was one of only 14 towns and cities to have an English Premier League football team in the 2021–22 season.

which languages in Norwich. Secondly, it adopts a linguistic landscape approach to explore the extent to which the city's multilingual population is visible in the languages displayed in public spaces, taking as its observational data "publicly visible bits of written language: [adverts], road and safety signs, shop signs, graffiti and all sorts of other inscriptions in the public space, both professionally produced and grassroots" (Blommaert and Maly 2014: 2).[3] Shop signs and advertisements in particular, including their visual aspect and the images that can accompany them, also help to "sell [a] neighbourhood as a whole" and contribute to "the establishment of social differences and spatial boundaries" (Papen 2015: 22).

2 Medieval multilingual Norwich (865–1200)

Norwich was multilingual for much of its early history. It is likely that there was some survival of Brittonic Celtic for several generations after the arrival of the Germanic-speaking Anglo-Saxons in the area where the city now stands. One possible indication of this linguistic survival is the name of the area of central Norwich known as Coslany, one of four original settlements around which Norwich gradually formed (the other three being Conesford, Westwic and Norðwic). The older pronunciation was /k'âzni/, more recently /k'âzlëni/. Coates and Breeze (2000) argue that this name derives from a Late British form *köslönnī*, from Early British *ko-slunn-ijā*, which was ancestral to Modern Welsh *cystlynedd*, 'kindred, affinity, alliance'. It probably signified a 'place where people live together, community': a good translation might be 'The Kindred' or 'The Alliance'. Coates and Breeze suggest that the name was adopted by Old English speakers around 550 AD as the name of "a place of some significance in the geography of Celtic eastern Britain" (2000: 158).

Much more significant for Norwich multilingualism, however, was the arrival, with the Great Viking Army which invaded East Anglia in 865, of Old Danish. Large-scale Viking settlements subsequently took place in England during the 9th and 10th centuries, leading to many eastern and northern areas of the country containing a heavily Scandinavian or Scandinavianised population, as famously witnessed by the hundreds of Old Norse place-names.[4] The number of

---

[3] See e.g. Gorter and Cenoz (2017) for an overview of the range of research undertaken in linguistic landscape studies relating to multilingualism.
[4] The Viking settlers in Norwich were Danes. Their language, Old Danish (800 AD to 1525), developed out of a dialect of Old Norse, a North Germanic language spoken by inhabitants of Scandinavia. In this chapter, we use Old Danish to refer to the language that arrived in Norwich, and Old Norse when referring to the Scandinavian parent language, and when citing authors who refer to Old Norse.

Scandinavians who actually arrived and settled in Britain is unknown and the subject of considerable controversy (Härke 2002; Holman 2007). But from about 890 onwards, East Anglia became officially part of the Danelaw – the area of England which had been signed over to the Danes by Alfred, the King of Wessex. After the Anglian defeat, parts of East Anglia were "shared out to Danish Viking soldiers, who were thereby transformed into settlers" (Nielsen 1998: 167); and large numbers of further settlers subsequently arrived, in a secondary wave from Denmark. In spite of the fact that the Danelaw came back under English control in 917, very large numbers of Danes stayed on in East Anglia; and there was considerable influence from Danish culture on the English: archaeological finds "demonstrate the clear impact Viking forms of culture exerted in East Anglia" (Pestell 2013: 255).

The Danes established a very considerable presence in Norwich, which they actually ruled from 870 to about 925 (Campbell 1975). The urban Scandinavian-speaking community may also have been reinforced in 1016, when Cnut of Denmark became king of England, although after his conquest Cnut paid off his soldiers, many of whom went back home again to Denmark. According to Shelley (2015), however, South Conesford may have been an important Anglo-Danish garrison port during Cnut's reign (1016–1035). Ayers (2004: 5) says that Danish settlement in Norwich fostered urbanisation and that there is "considerable evidence from the 10th century and later to imply a strong and sustained Anglo-Scandinavian presence". The main zone of Danish settlement seems to have been in Coslany, to the north of the River Wensum in the area around Colegate, Cowgate, Fishergate and what is now Magdalen Street but which was known to the Danes as Fibriggate 'Fye Bridge Street'.

According to Sandred (2001: 45), "the Scandinavian impact on the language [of East Anglia] must have been considerable". The original parent language of Old Danish, North Germanic, was a close relative of West Germanic; and many linguists postulate an earlier language which was ancestral to both, Northwest Germanic. This would not have split up into North Germanic and West Germanic until around 450 AD (Kuhn 1955). It is therefore quite possible that English-speakers and Danish-speakers in Norwich were still able to understand one another reasonably well during the 9th, 10th and 11th centuries even without necessarily becoming particularly bilingual as individuals. According to Townend (2005), there is plenty of evidence to suggest that there was a considerable degree of mutual intelligibility. He cites numerous examples of contacts between Old Norse and Old English speakers where the individuals involved use language to make treaties, buy land, negotiate contracts and marriages, and settle disputes – to the extent that it is impossible to imagine that they could have done this if they had not been able understand one another to a fair degree. No interpreters or translators are ever mentioned, as is often the case when other comparable situations involving other languages are being described.

Bidialectalism, then, might well be a better description for the situation in 10th-century Norwich than bilingualism. It was probably mostly passive bidialectalism, however. Townend (2005: 183) argues that the situation was one of *adequate intelligibility*, meaning "amongst other things, the ability to understand individual words, if this ability was sufficiently widespread and sufficiently successful to permit face-to-face and day-to-day transactions, and so to preclude the need for one or both of the speech communities in the Danelaw to become bilingual, or for interpreters to be habitually used for the purposes of Anglo-Norse communication".

Parsons (2006: 175) writes that "we are very poorly informed on the crucial question of how long Norse survived anywhere in eastern England". But Townend (2005) suggests that Old Norse probably died out in northern England in the 1200s. It is therefore likely that Old Danish as such had disappeared from East Anglia, which was less heavily Scandinavianised than the north, before that. But it is not at all unlikely that Old Danish, or at least an anglicised contact-form of the language, did continue to be spoken in Norwich during the 12th century (Dance 2012; Parsons 2001; Kisbye 1982), although speakers of Old Danish did eventually abandon it in favour of English. However, this was an English which by then, as a consequence of English-Danish bilingualism/bidialectalism, had become considerably Norsified, to the extent that "abandon" is probably not the most appropriate word. In view of the at least quasi-dialectal nature of the relationship between Old English and Old Danish, we would do better to think of the descendants of the Viking invaders as gradually modifying their Old Danish over the generations in the direction of Old English. Then, if Old English speakers in bilingual Norwich also gradually modified their dialect in the direction of Old Danish, there would have come a point where the two became no longer distinguishable.

Emonds and Faarlund (2014) claim that the Germanic language which eventually emerged out of language contact in early medieval eastern England between Old English and Old Norse was in fact not Norsified English but Anglified Norse – a Scandinavian language heavily influenced by Old English. Modern English, they argue, should therefore be considered to be a Scandinavian language. They argue their case using mainly syntactic data, citing the Norse character of a number of Middle English syntactic constructions as compared to Old English. They point out, for example, that van Riemsdijk (1978) makes the strong claim that the only languages in the world which permit grammatical constructions with fully developed preposition stranding[5] are, firstly, members of the North Germanic language family and, secondly, English: Danish *reven ble skutt på* [fox-the was shot at] is

---

5 In *The boy I gave it to*, the preposition *to* is said to be "stranded" at the end of the sentence, as opposed to in *The boy to whom I gave it.*

entirely paralleled by English 'The fox was shot at' (Holmberg and Rijkhoff 1998). According to Emonds and Faarlund (2014), most languages disallow this construction completely; and West Germanic Dutch allows it only under very restrictive conditions – which was also the situation in Old English.

However, in view of the scenario we have outlined above of the gradual melding of the two Germanic dialects into one, the opposition between Anglified Norse and Norsified English would seem to be a distinction without much of a difference. Le Page and Tabouret-Keller (1985) pointed out that languages can be sociolinguistically more or less *focussed* or *diffuse*. In diffuse linguistic communities, little codification has taken place; there is little agreement about norms; little concern for demarcating the language variety from others; and relatively little importance is accorded to what the language is called. In focussed communities, codification has taken place; there is a high degree of agreement about norms; speakers show concern for demarcating their language variety from others; and there is agreement about the language's name.

We can suppose that Viking Age Norwich was a much more linguistically diffuse than focussed place. People walking around the 10th-century town would have simply been speaking to each other in such a way as to ensure the best possible communication. Very few of them would have had any clear notion of the sociolinguistic situation as being one of bilingualism; and there is no reason for us to have that perception either. The single Germanic language which eventually emerged out of the linguistic contact in medieval East Anglia was descended from the language of the Danish Vikings; but it was also descended from the Old English dialects of Anglian Norfolk and Suffolk.

Nevertheless, the case for the Emonds and Faarlund scenario is strengthened by the fact that in East Anglia, as in other parts of Britain where Norse settlement was heavy, a larger number of words from Old Norse survive to this day in local speech than in English generally. Of particular importance for Norwich is the form *staithe*, from Old Norse *stǫð* 'landing stage' cf. modern Norwegian *stø*. In central medieval Norwich there were eleven landing stages called *staithes*, many in South Conesford (see below), which "throws particular light on the role of the city as an early market and port" (Sandred 2001).

As further evidence of considerable Old Danish/Old English bilingualism, we can also point to the fact that there are still many streets in Norwich whose names end in *-gate*, the Scandinavian word for 'way, street': Bishopgate, Colegate, Cowgate, Finkelgate, Fishergate, Pottergate, Mountergate, and Westlegate (see Figure 1). Sandred and Lindström (1989: 98) see a possible origin for Colegate in the Scandinavian personal name Koli; and they suggest an origin for Finklegate in the Old Scandinavian personal name Finkell (1989: 124).

Figure 1: Present-day street signs for Colegate and Pottergate, Norwich (Photos: Jane Warren).

Sandred and Lindström's research also revealed that a number of older Norwich street names ending in *-gate* have been lost. For example, Ten Bell Lane, which is on a slope leading down to the River Wensum, was known as Holgate until the 1300s, from Old Norse *holr:* they suggest that rainwater "probably washed the lane hollow" (1989: 145). St Mary's Plain was called Soutergate up until the 14th century, from Old Norse *sutari* 'shoemaker'.

Tombland, an open space by Norwich Cathedral which was the site of the Anglo-Danish market until the Norman invaders moved it, has its name from Scandinavian *tom* 'empty'.[6] And a number of other names containing originally Old Danish elements have also been lost. Timber Hill was known as Durnedale until the 1300s, with Old Danish *dal* 'valley', and Bishopgate was formerly Holmstrete, from Old Danish *holm* 'water meadow'.

Pockthorpe was a village immediately outside the Norwich city walls which became incorporated into Norwich: its name signified 'Poka's village'. Place-names ending in *-thorpe* originally indicated smaller outlying Danish villages dependent on a town: one such name is that of the Norwich suburb now known as Thorpe St. Andrew, until recently called Thorpe-next-Norwich.

Linguistically mixed names such as Bishopgate, and Pottergate – which derives from Old English *pottere* 'potter' plus *gate* – indicate that *-gate* eventually became naturalised as an English-language word, a phenomenon suggestive of individual personal bilingualism or bidialectalism in Norwich. According to Sandred and Lindström (1989: 114) the name Conesford is similarly part Old Danish, part Old English. Because the second element *ford* is certainly English, they argue, the original first element is likely to have been Old English *cyning* 'king'; though

---

6 The <b> in the modern spelling is unetymological.

on phonological grounds the modern name can only have descended from a form where Anglian *cyning* 'king' had been replaced by Old Danish *kunung*.

Further suggestive of extensive bilingualism and/or bidialectalism in Norwich are certain linguistic features typical of the medieval dialect of the city. For example, the phonological change /ht/>/t/ had occurred in Old Norse by 1050 (Schulte and Williams 2018), and it may therefore not be a coincidence that the medieval dialect of Norwich also shows very early loss of /h/ before /t/, as in spellings from the 1200s such as <caut> 'caught', <taute> 'taught', <rite> 'right'.

After the Norman conquest of England in 1066, Norwich became an even more multilingual place. In addition to speakers of Old English and Old Danish, there were now of course speakers of the newly arrived Norman French, but the Normans also brought with them from the continent large numbers of speakers of other languages, especially Flemish and Breton. The main area of Norman settlement – the "French Quarter" – was the leet (historical administrative ward) of Mancroft, by the current Market Place, including the Haymarket. Many Jews also arrived with the Normans, as well as subsequently. Sandred and Lindström (1989: 69) tell us that "the Jews of medieval Norwich dwelt in the White Lion area [by the Haymarket]. They chose this place because it was close to the Castle, in which they could take refuge in case of a pogrom. The *Scola Iudeorum*, their synagogue, was near the present Orford Place." They were probably mostly speakers of Norman French, although it might be that some of them were speakers of Ladino (Judeo-Spanish), and they appear to have remained for the most part francophone until they were expelled from Britain in 1290. They were thus distinguished from the original Norwich population by language as well as religion. The educated Jews also had a knowledge of Hebrew, as their liturgical language and language of scholarship. One of the most famous of medieval Jewish Hebrew poets lived in the city and is known to Jewish scholars today as Meir ben Elijah of Norwich (see Pim et al. 2013).

3 A city of *Strangers* (16th–18th centuries)

In the 16th century, another major linguistic event occurred in Norwich which again involved immigration from across the North Sea. King Philip II of Spain also had control over the Low Countries (which are for the most part now Belgium and The Netherlands). He was brought up in Spain and was a devout Catholic. Most of his domestic, colonial and foreign policies were focussed on stamping out Protestantism, so it was inevitable that there would be trouble in the Low

Countries where, in the northern provinces (now The Netherlands), Calvinism had taken root.

As a result of insurrection against Spanish domination and persecution, Dutch, Flemish and Walloon refugees fled to Protestant England. Many of them settled in Sandwich (Kent), London and Colchester, but by far the biggest group of refugees found their way to Norwich. They were probably attracted at least partly by an already established group of Flemish weavers who had arrived in 1565. The Mayor and Aldermen of Norwich had invited 30 "Dutchmen" and their families – no household was to exceed ten persons – to Norwich in an attempt to modernise the local textile industry, which had been lagging behind in terms of technology, design and skills: 24 Flemish and 10 Walloon master textile makers arrived and settled in Norwich. The refugees themselves, although predominantly also textile workers, included ministers, doctors, teachers, merchants and craftsmen.

By 1579 nearly 40% of the population of Norwich, which at that time was about 16,000, were native speakers of Dutch or French. This very high proportion of *Strangers*, 'foreigners', in the city did lead to a certain amount of friction, and there was at least one attempted xenophobic revolt against them; but generally, the absorption of a very large number of refugees into the population, while undoubtedly causing overcrowding, was relatively trouble-free. There were two main zones of refugee settlement. One was in the leet of Ultra Aquam, the same "Norwich over the Water" area north of the Wensum around Magdalen Street and St Mary's Plain which had formerly been the main Danish centre. The other was in the leet of Wymer, immediately opposite Ultra Aquam on the south bank of the river (Pound 2004), in the area of modern Westwick Street and St Andrew's Plain (the other medieval leets were Mancroft and Conesford).

The refugees were mostly Dutch speakers from Flanders and Brabant, but there were also French-speaking Walloons from Armentières, Namur and Valenciennes (at this period, the border with France was further south than it is today), and even some German speakers from Lorraine. According to Moens (1888), "in the first half of the 17th century, as much Dutch and French was spoken in Norwich as English", which cannot exactly have been true. However, orders for the conduct of the *Strangers* were certainly written in French in 1659, and the first books ever printed in Norwich were written in Dutch. Their printer was Anthony De Solempne, who had been a spice merchant in Antwerp and had arrived in Norwich as a religious refugee in 1567. Soon after arriving, he was operating a printing press in the parish of St Andrew in Norwich, and he produced two books in Dutch in 1568. These were "an edition of the psalms and some prayers in metre translated by Petrus Dathenus together with a catechism for the use of the Dutch Reformed Church" and "a reprint of a Dutch translation of the *Confession of Faith* drawn up by the Swiss Reformed Church and subsequently studied by some of the Dutch Calvinists" (Stoker 1981).

Norwich even produced some poets of note who wrote in Dutch (Joby 2014). The best known was Jan Cruso, who also wrote in English. He was born in Norwich in 1592 of parents who had come to the city in the 1570s from Hondschoote in Flanders, which is now in France, immediately over the border from Belgium. He is thought to have attended Norwich School, and later spent several years in London,[7] but was back in Norwich by 1620, running the family cloth business. He was also a member of the local militia, and a church elder.

According to Ketton-Cremer (1957), services in Dutch and French were maintained in the churches in Norwich that had been given over to the immigrant communities "for many decades", and the congregations remained vigorous until 1700 or so (Joby 2015). The French-speaking community in Norwich was later further strengthened by the arrival of Huguenots from France, after the revocation of the edict of Nantes in 1685; and it is clear that Norwich remained a trilingual city for 150 years, well into the 18th century. Then, "slowly but inevitably the *Strangers* became merged into the surrounding population and the community lost its separate identity" (Ketton-Cremer 1957: 128). By 1742 the congregations attending church services were small, and the churches decayed. Dutch and French finally died out of use in Norwich in the 1700s.

The large proportion of Flemish and Walloon speakers in the Norwich population undoubtedly had linguistic consequences. East Anglia is the only major area of Britain to have zero-marking on third-person singular present-tense verb forms: *he go, she like*. It has been argued (Trudgill 2002; Nevalainen et al. 2001) that this has to do with this very large-scale immigration into Norwich. As is well known, second-language learners of English often have difficulty with the irregularity of the third-person singular *-s* of Standard English and therefore omit it. Furthermore, as the language of Shakespeare shows, the 16th century was the period in the history of the English language during which northern third-person singular verb forms in *-s* were spreading south and gradually replacing the older southern forms in *-th*, with both forms occurring variably in London English. It is hypothesised here that the more-or-less simultaneous arrival into Norwich of the new *he goes* form from the north of England (see Wright 2001), and the hypothesised *he go* forms from the foreigner-English of the *Strangers*, both of them in competition with the old southern *he goeth* forms, led to a situation where there was conflict between the three forms *-th*, *-s*, and *-Ø*, in which the most regular form

---

7 Cruso's brother moved to London and had a son, Timothy, who is said to have given the novelist Daniel Defoe the idea for the name *Robinson Crusoe*.

was the one which eventually won. It subsequently spread outwards from Norwich, which was the second largest city in England at the time, to the whole of the area which the city dominated culturally and economically, namely East Anglia (see Trudgill 2002).

Another linguistic phenomenon which is widely accepted as being the result of language contact between English and Flemish in Norwich is the presence in the city of open areas which are not called *squares*, as they would be elsewhere, but *plains*. This seems rather uncontroversially to be a borrowing of Dutch *plein*: in Norwich there is a Bank Plain, St Andrew's Plain, St George's Plain, St Giles's Plain, St Mary's Plain, St Martin at Palace Plain (see Figure 2) and several more, all of which names postdate the arrival of the *Strangers* (see Sandred and Lindström 1989 for dates). And this naming tradition is continued to the present day, albeit somewhat self-consciously, in new-build areas.

Figure 2: Present-day street signs for St Martin at Palace Plain and Bank Plain, Norwich (Photos: Jane Warren).

A number of East Anglian dialect words have also been suggested (Trudgill 2003) as being of Dutch origin. Some of these date from as early as the 1400s and can clearly therefore not have arrived with the 16th-century refugees. On the other hand, *dwile* 'floorcloth, dishcloth' is not recorded until the late 1700s and so can well have arrived with the *Strangers*: Forby (1830: 101) defines it as "a refuse lock of wool" or "a mop made of them" or "any coarse rubbing rug". The *English Dialect Dictionary* (EDD) shows the word as being confined to the dialects of Norfolk and Suffolk, the area dominated by Norwich as the chief central place which linguistic innovations are most likely to have spread out from geographically. The Oxford English Dictionary suggests a derivation from Dutch *dweil* 'mop, floorcloth', which is surely correct. *To crowd* is defined by the EDD as "to push, move, shove, especially to push a wheelbarrow", with examples again only from Norfolk and Suffolk. The word probably comes from Dutch *kruien*, earlier *kruyden*, 'to push a wheelbarrow'. It is true that Old English did have a verb *crúdan* 'to push', so the case for an origin in the Low Countries cannot be entirely certain. But the fact that the meaning is very precisely 'push a wheelbarrow'[8] in both the Low Countries and in East Anglia does point in that direction, as does the fact that the English word is restricted to Norfolk and Suffolk.

Another significant linguistic group who arrived in the Norwich area during the 16th century were the Romani-speaking people, known as Roma. Romani is a language – or more accurately a group of languages – which is a member of the Indo-Aryan sub-family of Indo-European whose closest linguistic relatives, such as Hindi, Punjabi and Kashmiri, are found in the northwestern part of the Indian subcontinent (Matras 2005). According to Hancock (1984), the generally accepted date of arrival of Romani speakers in Britain is 1505 for Scotland, and 1512 for England, though Matras (2010) has it that they may have settled in Scotland as early as 1460. Fascinatingly, Töpf and Hoelzel (2005) present strong genetic evidence from excavations in Norwich for the presence of people of Romani ancestry in Anglo-Danish East Anglia as early as the 900s AD.

According to Matras (2010: 57), "much of the history of the Romani-speaking community in Britain can be traced thanks to sources that provide us both with a description of the community and with a sample of their Romani speech". One important such source is an anonymous text from 1798 known as the *East Anglian vocabulary of Romani* (Sampson 1930). Roma are well known to have had regular camping sites on Mousehold Heath in Norwich, and the novelist and travel writer George Borrow (1803–1881) took a great interest in them. He was born in Dereham, about 15 miles/25 kilometres west of Norwich, and was educated at Norwich School. He was most interested in the Romani languages (Hancock 1997) and spent time with many Roma communities in different parts of continental Europe and Britain, including on Mousehold Heath in Norwich, as famously described in his 1851 novel/memoir *Lavengro: the scholar, the Gypsy, the priest*.

4 Multilingual Norwich in the 21st century

New groups of *Strangers* are contributing to the city's present-day linguistic diversity. According to the 2011 Census for England and Wales, 12.9% of Norwich residents were not born in the UK. In 2001 the figure was 8.1%, and in 1991 5.5%, showing the relative recency of a degree of ethnic diversity. The 2011 Census also

---

8 Also, in 20th-century East Anglia, 'to pedal a bicycle vigorously'.

shows that just over ten thousand or 8% of Norwich residents reported a language other than English as their main language – their first or preferred language in Census terms (ONS n.d.).[9] This is the same as the UK average, and contrasts with 22% in London, the UK's most diverse urban area.

People from language backgrounds other than English find their way to Norwich for a variety of reasons. Among more recent factors, freedom of movement across the EU, a thriving international university community, and the UK government's refugee programmes and asylum seeker dispersal policy have all contributed to a comparatively culturally and linguistically diverse community. The 2011 Census lists 70 individual languages other than English spoken in Norwich, with regional groupings of 'other' languages that are not specified (ONS n.d.). The summer 2019 School Census, which provides data on the 'first language' spoken by pupils, gives a more complete picture: at least 117 languages are spoken by state school pupils in Norwich, and nearly one in five pupils has a first language other than English (18.4%; 3,844 of 20,856).[10]

The top five 2011 Census languages are Polish, Chinese languages, Arabic, Lithuanian and Hungarian (Table 1). Poland, Lithuania and Hungary were three of the eight central/eastern European countries – the A8 – that joined the EU in 2004. Given high rates of unemployment in their home countries, A8 nationals have been attracted to Norfolk and Norwich by job opportunities, typically in hospitality, factories, and agriculture. This pattern of migration is changing: the UK was a less attractive destination for EU migrants after the UK's referendum on EU membership in 2016. There was a 60% decline in the net migration of EU nationals to the UK from 2016 to 2018, with the largest fall among those from A8 countries looking for work (Sturge 2018). A proposed points-based immigration system may well change migration patterns in the UK still further.

The group "Chinese languages" in Table 1 includes Cantonese (121 individuals), Mandarin (118), and what the Census calls "Other Chinese languages" (1,061) – most likely responses of "Chinese" as the main language. This language group includes a large transient population of students at the University of East Anglia: in 2018–19, students from China and Hong Kong accounted for nearly three quarters of full-

---

[9] The 2011 Census was the first to ask about language use, with two new questions about respondents' "main language" and proficiency in English. There has been some debate about the validity of the new questions, promoting as they do a monolingual ideology (Sebba 2018). "Main language" can be interpreted as language of the home, language used at work, the language people speak the most, their most proficient language, or the official language of their country of origin (Matras & Robertson 2015: 299).

[10] Personal communication, Tanya Ingram, EAL Adviser, Norfolk County Council, 22 October 2019.

Table 1: Top five main languages other than English, Norwich (2011 Census).

Language	No.	%
Polish	1,480	14.71%
Chinese languages	1,300	12.92%
Arabic	585	5.82%
Lithuanian	558	5.55%
Hungarian	472	4.69%
Total main languages other than English	10,060	100%

time international students at the university.[11] In 2011, the University ward of the city had the highest percentage of residents who reported speaking a language other than English as their main language (15.4%). This is due in large part to the number of speakers of Chinese languages living there, making up nearly half (47.6%) of all residents whose main language is not English.

Arabic is an official or co-official language in countries such as Syria, Iraq and Sudan, where conflict, war and persecution have resulted in huge exoduses of people. From 2015 onwards, Syrians have been the largest group granted asylum and humanitarian protection in the UK (Sturge 2019). The UK's asylum seeker dispersal policy was designed to move asylum seekers outside London and the South East. Norwich volunteered to become an asylum seeker dispersal area in 2003 and has also been involved in UK refugee resettlement programmes.

Since 2017, a small number of Syrian refugees have been resettled in the Greater Norwich area through the government's Syrian Vulnerable Persons Resettlement Scheme. Their recent arrival in Norwich would not change the Census rankings in Table 1, but it is reflected in the increase in INTRAN interpreting and translation requests for Arabic speakers in the city (see Table 2). INTRAN is a non-profit-making partnership that provides interpreting and translation services for organisations in the East of England such as local authorities and health service organisations.[12] In 2013–14, Arabic was in ninth place, but had risen to third by

---

[11] https://portal.uea.ac.uk/documents/6207125/7112761/Facts+and+Figures+External+Report_Jan+2019.pdf/c41585bf-471f-8800-2e5f-016bff217ca5 (accessed 21 June 2019).

[12] INTRAN's interpreting and translation requests do not capture all the language needs of Norwich residents, as some will rely on family or friends. More recent arrivals and older residents would typically have more limited English skills and therefore use translating and interpreting services more often (Matras and Robertson 2015: 302). The INTRAN figures also comprise the numbers of instances of translation or interpreting requested, not the number of individuals – one individual could make a single or multiple requests.

2018–19. The top five languages requested in Norwich in 2013–14 and 2018–19 show some crossover with the 2011 Census: Polish and Lithuanian both figure in each. These groups are also relatively recent, meaning their English skills may be more limited, requiring translation or interpreting support.

Table 2: Top five main languages other than English, Norwich, translation/interpretation requests.[13]

Languages requested*	2018–19			2013–14		
	No.	%	Ranking	No.	%	Ranking
Lithuanian	1,417	15.97%	1	895	16.01%	2
Polish	1,042	11.96%	2	741	13.15%	3
Arabic	990	11.37%	3	149	2.64%	9
British Sign Language	848	9.74%	4	996	17.67%	1
Portuguese	555	6.37%	5	417	7.40%	6

*42 languages in total in 2018–19, and 37 in 2013–14.

British Sign Language is in the top five in both years, reflecting the ongoing language needs of this small population group (52 in the 2011 Census), and Portuguese moves into fifth place in 2018–19. Portugal joined the EU in 1986, and high rates of unemployment resulted in Portuguese coming to the UK – and Norfolk – looking for work from the 1990s onwards. The 2019 School Census confirms the importance of Polish, Lithuanian, Portuguese and Arabic, which are the top four first languages, other than English, of Norwich state school pupils.[14]

The 2011 Census, INTRAN, and 2019 School Census figures paint a portrait of a city that contains a diversity of languages and migration experiences. It is fairly commonplace to hear languages other than English in snatches of conversation as people pass by, but to what extent do they leave a visible trace in the city's public spaces? The history of street and settlement names has been key to exploring the linguistic background of Norwich residents in the medieval period and the 16th century. In the present-day city, official street signs are already fixed, or governed by formal naming processes that do not favour recent arrivals. How, then, do Norwich residents whose first languages are not English make their mark on the linguistic landscape of the city?

To answer this question, we return to one of the two main zones of refugee settlement in 16th century Norwich; the "Norwich over the Water" area, previously

---

13 Personal communication, Valérie Gidney, INTRAN Partnership Manager, 23 August 2019.
14 The fifth language is Malayalam, the second most common South Asian language in Norwich after Bengali (with Sylheti) (2011 Census).

the main Danish centre. Present-day Magdalen Street was the main street of Norwich over the Water and continues to be a key site of multilingualism. Since the time of the *Strangers*, it has undergone cycles of renewal and decay. It is now a mix of independent shops and small businesses, including food shops, cafes, restaurants, hair salons, and second-hand shops. It is known as the most culturally diverse street in Norwich, with business owners coming from three continents and 15 countries (Long 2016). It is located in the Mancroft ward of the city, an area where 8.6% of residents do not use English as their main language.

The multilingual urban identity of Norwich is primarily constructed through a limited amount of private sector signage. Two periods of fieldwork in Magdalen Street and adjoining Fye Bridge Street in October-November 2016 and August-September 2019 show that English was unsurprisingly the language that dominated, used in all official signage such as road and information signs, and on shop fronts. In 2019, around a fifth (18 of 100) of the businesses in the two streets displayed signs that included languages other than English, including fixed commercial shop names and signs, menus, products in shop windows, adverts and banners showing products for sale, and temporary or unofficial signage. The top five 2011 Census languages were present – Polish, Chinese, Arabic, Lithuanian and Hungarian. Also visible were Eastern/Central European languages Bulgarian, Latvian, and Romanian; established migrant languages Bengali and Hindi; French, Portuguese and Spanish, representing older EU member countries; Lingala, official language of the Democratic Republic of the Congo and the Republic of the Congo; and Turkish.

Shop signs can be classified along a continuum ranging from a primary communicative function "motivated by a practical need to convey content and information", to an emblematic one, where signs "serve primarily to attract emotional identification" (Matras and Robertson 2015: 308). Emblematic usage is reflected in restaurant names, menus, or signs that give a flavour of another culture's culinary traditions to attract mainly English-speaking customers. A Spanish restaurant, for example, described itself as a *bar de tapas*, with *Cerrado/Abierto* instead of 'Closed/Open' on the door. Signs with a primarily communicative function include commercial shop signs or adverts that use languages other than English to select certain audiences. Examples in the data collected included window banners showing food and drink products labelled in Polish, Lithuanian, Bulgarian, and Romanian, and food shops advertising Halal in English and Arabic.

Signs with a communicative function also included temporary or unofficial notices directed explicitly towards particular linguistic groups. They were monolingual or bilingual (with English), and advertised work opportunities, opening hours, or shop relocation information. In November 2016, for example, a typewritten notice in Romanian appeared on the window of an Eastern European food store run by Romanians, giving details of a firm looking for Norwich-based delivery drivers for a global online company. These are the kinds of jobs typically generated by globalisation, part of the ever-increasing movement of goods around the world, both across and within borders.

Another type of sign, with a strong emblematic function, had appeared on the same Eastern European shop window earlier in the year. During the night of 8 July 2016, shortly after the UK referendum on EU membership, the shop was subject to an arson attack. The newspaper the following day reported that "the motive is unclear but one possible line of inquiry is that the arson attack is a hate crime against the owners of the store" (Norwich Evening News 2016). Following the attack, the shop was subject to a "love bombing", with well-wishers sticking over 300 heart-shaped messages of support in English and a range of other languages on the shop's temporarily boarded up window (Pigeon-Owen 2016). The direct addressees were the Romanian shop owners and community, but the messages were also a public display of inclusion, expressing solidarity with all Norwich residents from other countries and rejecting xenophobia (see Figure 3). This was in a political context where 56.1% of the city's residents had voted to remain in the EU.

Figure 3: "Love bombing" of a Magdalen Street food shop (©2016 Archant CM Ltd Norfolk).

The public response to this incident shows that the idea of Norwich as a place of welcome continues to resonate. In 2017, the Lord Mayor and Sheriff made "Norwich – the welcoming city" the civic year's theme, "in recognition of the centuries-long local tradition of welcoming 'strangers'" (Norwich City Council 2017). They chose as charity of the year the Norwich Integration Partnership, which groups together New Routes Integration, The Bridge Plus+ and English+, supporting asylum seekers, refugees and people of black and minority ethnic backgrounds.

New Routes was established in 2004 to support the social integration of the first 30 asylum seekers dispersed to Norwich by the Home Office[15] – an echo of the 30 Flemish weavers and their families formally invited to Norwich in the 16th century to help modernise the textile industry. Since 2015, New Routes has supported over 1,600 individuals, speaking more than 60 languages between them.[16] Both New Routes and The Bridge Plus+ are located in Norwich over the Water, an area of the city that continues to attract those from language backgrounds other than English.

5 Conclusion

The approach taken here, to compare and contrast the language situation in Norwich at three distinct periods in its history, has revealed the richness and complexity of the city's past and present multilingual configurations. Firstly, the three periods illustrate different motivations underpinning the arrival of people and languages in the city. In the medieval period, invasion and colonisation – by Germanic-speaking Anglo-Saxons, then Vikings, and finally Norman French – created huge change in the linguistic make-up and landscape of nascent Norwich. These periods of conflict eventually resolved in a melding of communities and languages. In the 16th and 17th centuries, religious persecution, economic aspiration and family reunion were key factors in the arrival of the *Strangers*. They were subject to strict regulation and there was at least one attempted revolt against them, but it seems integration was relatively trouble-free.

What distinguishes the present day is not only the complex set of economic, political and social conditions in countries of origin that cause people to migrate, but also the range of countries involved, and the varied levels of support and welcome offered to new arrivals. In Norwich, migrants of all backgrounds can feel vulnerable and discriminated against, particularly given the polarised situation created by the UK's decision to leave the EU. The day after the official leaving date of 31 January 2020, typed notices appeared in the communal areas of a city block of flats. Titled "Happy Brexit Day", they warned: "We do not tolerate people speaking other languages than English in the flats. We are now our own country again and [. . .] the Queens [sic] English is the spoken tongue here" (Weaver 2020). In response, residents staged an anti-racism demonstration and put up

---

[15] The Home Office is the UK government department responsible for immigration and passports, drugs policy, crime, fire, counter-terrorism and police.
[16] Personal communication, Dee Robinson, New Routes Project Coordinator, 7 September 2019.

posters affirming everyone was welcome in Norwich, and the city council again invoked the city's tradition of welcome. These notices and the "love bombing" of the Magdalen Street shop are both examples of signs directed towards minority groups rather than being produced by them, and they illustrate how languages are used for political purposes in the city, both to exclude and to include.

Secondly, the multilingualism of each era is quite distinct. After the Norman conquest of England, Norwich would have been multilingual: speakers of Norman French, Flemish, Breton and possibly Ladino would have swelled the ranks of Old English and Old Danish speakers, who themselves would have most likely been bilingual/bidialectal by that time. By the late 16th century, refugees speaking Dutch and French made up nearly 40% of the Norwich population, which also included German and Romani speakers. Dutch and French remained community languages in the city for at least 150 years. In both periods, language contact had an impact on the development of English in Norwich and the surrounding area. As a consequence of English-Danish language contact, each language would have gradually moved towards the other to become indistinguishable, in what was a linguistically diffuse situation. In the 16th/17th centuries, it is argued that zero marking on third person singular present-tense verb forms – a trait of Norwich and East Anglian dialects – was influenced by the foreigner English of the *Strangers*.

Present-day Norwich is multilingual in the sense that nearly one in five school pupils has a first language other than English, speaking at least 117 languages. However, English continues to dominate, and most of these languages are destined to disappear due to limited numbers of speakers and a lack of any formal community language policy or provision, as well as the transience of some groups. The brief examination of a multilingual area in the city shows that languages other than English are visible to a certain extent through private sector signage, but again English is dominant. Further changes can be expected in the range of languages represented in Norwich as the consequences of the UK's decision to leave the EU become clearer.

Urban neighbourhoods can be viewed as being in perpetual motion, "with layers upon layers of historically conditioned activity taking place" (Blommaert and Maly 2014: 4). The Norwich over the Water area of the city epitomises these linguistic layers of activity across a huge stretch of time. It was the main Danish centre in the medieval period, then one of two main zones of refugee settlement in 16th/17th century Norwich, and it currently contains one of the city's most linguistically diverse streets, the commercial signage of its many independent shops establishing its identity as a multiethnic area of the city. In the two earlier periods, one of the consequences of language contact was the naming of streets and areas in the city. A key difference now is the ephemeral nature of the signs that point to residents whose first languages are not English. It is interesting to reflect on whether any physical traces will remain in 200 or 500 years of these 21st-century language communities.

References

Ayers, Brian. 2004. The urban landscape. In Carol Rawcliffe & Richard Wilson (eds.), *Medieval Norwich*, 1–28. London: Hambledon & London.

Blackledge, Adrian & Angela Creese. 2018. Language and superdiversity: an interdisciplinary perspective. In Adrian Blackledge & Angela Creese (eds.), *The Routledge handbook of language and superdiversity*, xxi–xlv. Abingdon/New York: Routledge.

Blommaert, Jan & Ico Maly. 2014. Ethnographic linguistic landscape analysis and social change: a case study. *Working Papers in Urban Language and Literacies* 133.

Campbell, James. 1975. Norwich. In Mary Lobel (ed.), *The atlas of historic towns*, 13–14. London: Scolar Press.

Coates, Richard & Andrew Breeze. 2000. *Celtic voices, English places: studies of the Celtic impact on place-names in England*. Spalding: Shaun Tyas.

Dance, Richard. 2012. English in contact: Norse. In Alexander Bergs & Laurel Brinton (eds.), *English historical linguistics: an international handbook*, 1724–1737. Berlin: de Gruyter.

Emonds, Joseph & Jan Terje Faarlund. 2014. *English: the language of the Vikings*. Olomouc: Palacký University Press.

Forby, Robert. 1830. *The vocabulary of East Anglia*. London: J.B. Nichols and Son.

Gorter, Durk & Jasone Cenoz. 2017. Linguistic landscape and multilingualism. In Jasone Cenoz, Durk Gorter & Stephen May (eds.), *Language awareness and multilingualism: encyclopedia of language and education*, 3rd ed., 233–245. Cham: Springer.

Hancock. Ian. 1984. Romani and Angloromani. In Peter Trudgill (ed.), *Language in the British Isles*, 367–383. Cambridge: Cambridge University Press.

Hancock, Ian. 1997. George Borrow's Romani. In Yaron Matras, Peter Bakker & Hristo Kyuchukov (eds.), *The typology and dialectology of Romani*, 199–214. Amsterdam: John Benjamins.

Härke, Heinrich. 2002. Kings and warriors: population and landscape from post-Roman to Norman Britain. In Paul Slack & Ryk Ward (eds.), *The peopling of Britain: the shaping of a human landscape*, 145–175. Oxford: Oxford University Press.

Holman, Katherine. 2007. *The northern conquest: Vikings in Britain and Ireland*. Oxford: Signal Books.

Holmberg, Anders & Jan Rijkhoff. 1998. Word order in the Germanic languages. In Anna Siewierska (ed.), *Constituent order in the languages of Europe*, 75–104. Berlin/New York: Mouton de Gruyter.

Joby, Christopher. 2014. Dutch poetry in Early Modern Norfolk. *Dutch Crossing* 38(2). 189–203.

Joby, Christopher. 2015. *The Dutch language in Britain (1550–1702)*. Leiden: Brill.

Ketton-Cremer, R.W. 1957. *Norfolk assembly*. London: Faber.

Kisbye, Torben. 1982. *Vikingerne i England – sproglige spor* [The Vikings in England – linguistic traces]. Copenhagen: Akademisk Forlag.

Kuhn, H. 1955. Zur Gliederung der germanischen Sprachen. *Zeitschrift für deutsches Altertum und deutsche Literatur* 86. 1–47.

Le Page, Robert B. & Andrée Tabouret-Keller. 1985. *Acts of identity: creole-based approaches to language and ethnicity*. Cambridge: Cambridge University Press.

Long, Jessica. 27 May 2016. The 15 nationalities of Norwich's Magdalen Street: a walk down the most diverse shopping area in Norfolk. *Eastern Daily Press*. https://www.edp24.co.uk/news/the-15-nationalities-of-norwich-s-magdalen-street-a-walk-down-the-most-diverse-shopping-area-in-norfolk-1-4552947 (accessed 28 April 2019).

Matras, Yaron. 2005. *Romani: a linguistic introduction*. Cambridge: Cambridge University Press.

Matras, Yaron. 2010. *Romani in Britain: the afterlife of a language*. Edinburgh: Edinburgh University Press.

Matras, Yaron & Alex Robinson. 2015. Multilingualism in a post-industrial city: policy and practice in Manchester. *Current Issues in Language Planning* 16(3). 296–314.

Meeres, Frank. 2012. *Strangers: a history of Norwich's incomers*. Norwich: Norwich HEART.

Moens, William. 1888. *The Walloons and their church at Norwich 1565–1832*. London: Huguenot Society.

Nevalainen, Terttu, Helena Raumolin-Brunberg & Peter Trudgill. 2001. Chapters in the social history of East Anglian English: the case of the third-person singular. In Jacek Fisiak & Peter Trudgill (eds.), *East Anglian English*, 187–204. Woodbridge: Boydell & Brewer.

Nielsen, Hans Frede. 1998. *The continental backgrounds of English and its insular development until 1154*. Amsterdam: John Benjamins.

Norwich City Council. 2017. New Lord Mayor and Sheriff take up honour. https://www.norwich.gov.uk/news/article/162/new_lord_mayor_and_sheriff_take_up_honour (accessed 15 June 2019).

Norwich Evening News. 9 July 2016. Shop owner describes arson attack at Eastern European store in Magdalen street, Norwich. *Norwich Evening News*.

ONS (Office for National Statistics). n.d. Nomis: official census and labour market statistics. https://www.nomisweb.co.uk (accessed 20 June 2019).

Papen, Uta. 2015. Signs in cities: the discursive production and commodification of urban spaces. *Sociolinguistic Studies* 9(1). 1–26.

Parsons, David N. 2001. How long did the Scandinavian language survive in England? Again. In James Graham-Campbell, Richard Hall, Judith Jesch & David N. Parsons (eds.), *Vikings and the Danelaw*, 299–312. Oxford: Oxbow.

Parsons, David N. 2006. Field-name statistics, Norfolk and the Danelaw. In Peder Gammeltoft & Bent Jørgensen (eds.), *Names through the looking-glass*, 165–188. Copenhagen: Reitzel.

Pestell, Tim. 2013. Imports or immigrants? Reassessing Scandinavian metalwork in late Anglo-Saxon East Anglia. In David Bates & Robert Liddiard (eds.), *East Anglia and its North Sea world in the Middle Ages*, 230–255. Woodbridge: Boydell.

Pigeon-Owen, Louise. 14 July 2016. Norwich shows solidarity with migrants, *Concrete*. http://www.concrete-online.co.uk/norwich-shows-solidarity-migrants (accessed 28 April 2019).

Pim, Keiron, Ellman Crasnow & Bente Elsworth. 2013. *Into the light: the medieval Hebrew poetry of Meir of Norwich*. Norwich: East Publishing.

Pound, John. 2004. Government to 1660. In Carol Rawcliffe & Richard Wilson (eds.), *Norwich since 1550*, 35–62. London: Hambledon & London.

Sampson, John. 1930. An East Anglian Romani vocabulary of 1798. *Journal of the Gypsy Lore Society* 9. 49–57.

Sandred, Karl Inge. 2001. East Anglian place-names: sources of lost dialect. In Jacek Fisiak & Peter Trudgill (eds.), *East Anglian English*, 39–62. Woodbridge: Boydell & Brewer.

Sandred, Karl Inge & Bengt Lindström. 1989. *The place-names of Norfolk I: the place-names of the City of Norwich*. Nottingham: English Place-Name Society.

Schulte, Michael & Henrik Williams. 2018. Den eldste tiden [The earliest time]. In Agnete Nesse (ed.), *Norsk språkhistorie IV: tidslinjer* [Norwegian language history IV: timelines], 51–117. Oslo: Novus.

Sebba, Mark. 2018. Awkward questions: language issues in the 2011 census in England. *Journal of Multilingual and Multicultural Development* 39(2). 181–193.
Shelley, Andy. 2015. South Conesford, Norwich: a Danish garrison port? *Medieval Archaeology* 59(1). 87–102.
Stoker, David. 1981. Anthony de Solempne: attributions to his press. *The Library: The Transactions of the Bibliographical Society* 6th ser. 17–32.
Sturge, Georgina. 2018. How has EU migration changed since the referendum? London: House of Commons Library. https://commonslibrary.parliament.uk/home-affairs/immigration/how-has-eu-migration-changed-since-the-referendum (accessed 21 June 2019).
Sturge, Georgina. 2019. Migration statistics: how many asylum seekers and refugees are there in the UK? London: House of Commons Library. https://commonslibrary.parliament.uk/insights/migration-statistics-how-many-asylum-seekers-and-refugees-are-there-in-the-uk (accessed 21 June 2019).
Töpf, Ana L. & A. Rus Hoelzel. 2005. A Romani mitochondrial haplotype in England 500 years before their recorded arrival in Britain. *Biology Letters* 1(3). 280–282.
Townend, Matthew. 2005. *Language and history in Viking Age England: linguistic relations between speakers of Old Norse and Old English*. Turnhout: Brepols.
Trudgill, Peter. 2002. *Sociolinguistic variation and change*. Edinburgh: Edinburgh University Press.
Trudgill, Peter. 2003. *The Norfolk dialect*. Cromer: Poppyland.
Trudgill, Peter. 2011. *Sociolinguistic typology: social determinants of linguistic complexity*. Oxford: Oxford University Press.
Trudgill, Peter. 2016. Contact-related processes of change in the early history of English. In Merja Kytö & Pahta Päivi (eds.), *The Cambridge handbook of English historical linguistics*, 318–334. Cambridge: Cambridge University Press.
Trudgill, Peter. 2021. *East Anglian English*. Berlin: Mouton de Gruyter.
van Riemsdijk, Henk 1978. *A case study in syntactic markedness: the binding nature of prepositional phrases*. Dordrecht: de Ridder.
Vertovec, Steven. 2007. Super-diversity and its implications. *Ethnic and Racial Studies* 30(6). 1024–1054.
Weaver, Matthew. 2 February 2020. 'Speak only English' posters racially aggravated, say police. *The Guardian*. https://www.theguardian.com/uk-news/2020/feb/02/norwich-anti-racism-protest-brexit-day-poster (accessed 2 February 2020).
Wright, Laura. 2001. Some morphological features of the Norfolk guild certificates of 1388/9: an exercise in variation. In Jacek Fisiak & Peter Trudgill (eds.), *East Anglian English*, 79–162. Woodbridge: Boydell & Brewer.

Bolormaa Shinjee and Sender Dovchin
10 The multilingual landscape of Ulaanbaatar, the capital city of Mongolia

1 Introduction

This chapter seeks to explore how multilingual practices are formed in Ulaanbaatar (UB), the capital city of Mongolia, by investigating the use of multiple linguistic resources displayed in the urban linguistic landscape. The research is timely, given the sociolinguistic significance of increasing linguistic diversity in post-socialist Mongolia. Before 1990, Mongolia was a satellite of the USSR (otherwise known as the Soviet Union), with Russian being the only significant foreign language. Cultural and linguistic elements from the West were perceived as "capitalist products" with negative ideological messages and were strictly banned by the ruling communist party. Alignment with the USSR was such that in 1941 the local communist authorities replaced the classical Mongolian Uyghur script with the Cyrillic alphabet, which remains the official orthographic system of Mongolia (Rossabi 2005). Soviet and post-Soviet cultural elements, including Russian films, music, literature, and cuisine, were (and some still are) widely popular in Mongolia, with a high number of Russian expatriates living and working in Mongolia.

By the late 1980s, with the impending conclusion of the Cold War, the Soviet Union started to collapse. This was the beginning of a new social, political, and economic order for Mongolia, marking the end of 70 years of Soviet dominance (Marsh 2010). After 1990, a newly democratic Mongolia quickly opened its internal and external market to the rest of the world, allowing economic liberalisation and the development of a free-market economy, complemented by the free flow of goods and capital in the country (Marzluf 2012). Mongolia also opened its internal and external borders, allowing the movement of individuals and groups, including both the arrival and free movement of tourists, volunteers, expatriates, missionaries, and professionals from overseas. The ability of local citizens to travel overseas has also risen dramatically since that time (Dovchin 2018).

Mongolia generally, but mainly its capital city, UB, has witnessed a significant shift in lifestyle since 1990. UB has experienced a dramatic increase in terms of its population, due to internal rural to urban migration, rising from just over half a million in 1990 to nearly 1.5 million people today, almost half of the country's entire population. By way of comparison, Mongolia's second-largest city, Erdenet, has less than one hundred thousand inhabitants. Nearly 60% of the UB population is under 35, now consisting of a mix of city and rural-bred young residents, making UB one of the most youthful cities in the world (Dovchin, 2018). The migration to the city is perpetuated not only by UB's rapid urbanisation, including the diverse job, business and education opportunities, but also by recurrent natural disasters such as *zud*, the snow blizzard which ruins the grassland for traditional livestock raising, playing a vital role in the acceleration of rural-to-city movement (Marzluf 2017). With this dramatic increase in urban population, urban Mongolians have also started enjoying various new media and technological resources, as the number of cable TV channels, urban radio stations, Internet cafés, CD and DVD shops has rapidly multiplied (Dovchin 2018). Western cultural and linguistic trends, which were previously considered to be the weapon of the capitalists' ideology, have become a part of the daily life of many urban Mongolians. In fact, globalisation today acts as a significant stimulus for urban Mongolians, as there is a stark contrast between the modern Westernised lifestyle centred around UB and the traditional life of nomadic herdsmen in rural areas (Campi 2006).

Overall, Mongolia has started to catch up rapidly with the rest of the world in terms of its economy, language, culture and technology. Urban Mongolians, primarily in UB, have begun to experiment with a range of language and cultural resources from the West since the political transformation (Marsh 2008). The new national government established in 1990 began to view linguistic diversity as both a powerful tool for creating new opportunities and a key to modernisation and success across all areas of society (Dovchin 2018). As a result, not only English but also other languages are, by extension, welcome in UB, with Russian, Chinese, Korean, Japanese, German, French and Turkish also found in both institutional and non-institutional settings. International tests such as TOEFL, and IELTS for English, the Japanese-Language Proficiency Test (JLPT) or the Korean-Language Proficiency Test (KLPT) are used locally for academic and professional purposes, and these languages are also taught across all levels of educational institutions as optional or core subjects. Foreign language high schools and private language and culture-specific educational institutions are in high demand, with numbers increasing each year (Dovchin 2018).

All these languages have also started blossoming in UB and elsewhere in Mongolia due to the influence of the Internet and new technology on cultural and economic expression. As Billé (2010: 245) acknowledges, English and the Latin script remain for instance highly visible in the contemporary musical landscape in UB, as the vast majority of urban Mongolian singers and bands write their names and titles in the Latin script, frequently translating titles into English. In addition, Dovchin (2018) notes that the linguistic practices of popular culture in Mongolia are diverse and vibrant since multiple other linguistic and cultural resources are integrated, notably in song lyrics, music videos, album covers, TV advertisements, and commercial websites. The languages present in these spheres include French, Russian, Spanish, Korean, Japanese and Chinese. Many TV channels broadcast bi/multilingual entertainment shows. In some of the most popular singing reality TV shows in Mongolia, "Universe Best Songs" and "The Voice of Mongolia", for example, contestants are expected to sing various popular foreign songs and are judged not only by local music experts but also by Japanese, American, Korean, Russian, and French representatives from the respective embassies. Other national singing competitions such as "Who can sing best in French?" or "Who can sing best in Japanese?" are widely popular among young people in Mongolia, not just in UB. The pop-opera band named "Nuance", based in UB, sings in French, Spanish, Italian, and Russian and has successfully performed outside Mongolia.

Meanwhile, the linguistic landscape of UB has been one of the most affected contexts in Mongolia with regard to multilingual diversity. It is common to see multilingual amalgamation and mixtures, loan translations and calques, and phonetic/grammatical change in the post-socialist context of UB, much more so than in its previous socialist incarnation, primarily due to rapid urbanisation and contact with the multiple languages. Nevertheless, there has been little sociolinguistic research to date about the urban linguistic landscape of UB. Most Asian studies in this field have so far been done in post-industrial urban contexts such as Beijing (Wang 2013; Lai 2013), Incheon, South Korea (Lee and Lou 2019), and Tokyo (Backhaus 2006; Wang 2013). Much less attention has been paid to the linguistic landscape of urban contexts in a peripheral Asian country such as Mongolia. This chapter, therefore, focuses on the sociocultural dynamics of the linguistic landscape in the post-socialist context of UB, a city very much under-represented in current sociolinguistic research. The chapter addresses two main questions:
(1) How are multilingual, cultural, and orthographic resources used in the post-socialist linguistic landscape of UB?
(2) What is the impact of these resources on the contemporary post-socialist Mongolian language?

2 Relocalisation of multilingual resources

The study presented here will approach the research questions from the perspective of "linguistic relocalisation" (Pennycook 2010: 4–5), in which language is examined in terms of its locality, space, and place. The focus is on how language creates the contexts where it is used, and how it becomes the product of socially mediated activities and a part of the action (Dovchin et al. 2015). Higgins (2009: 2) argues that English in the local context is a component of "urban vernaculars", or local ways of using language that are better understood as "amalgams rather than as codeswitches between languages". In this sense, English needs to be seen as part of local language practice. In order to understand how hybridised English is interpreted in the local context, Higgins (2009) reconceptualises English as an everyday social practice that is constantly being reconstructed in a specific locality (East Africa in her case). English can serve a local sphere through creatively mixing varied genres and resources, which means the localised English may involve more than just English itself.

Out of this mix, new locally relevant meanings and language practices may develop (Terkourafi 2010). Individuals mobilise different semiotic resources and adopt different negotiation strategies to make local meanings across linguistic boundaries rather than focusing on fixed grammar, forms, and discrete language systems (Canagarajah 2013). The concept of relocalisation – a form of language recontextualisation that creates new meaning – is thus important in understanding the multilingual resources used in local contexts (Pennycook 2010: 35–37). Multilingual relocalisation is not seen as a direct, borrowed or imported loan for describing the same concept as in the source language, but rather as an act of linguistic renewal, making new local linguistic meanings within this process (see also Dovchin 2017a, 2017b).

Drawing on this notion of relocalisation, this chapter analyses how the linguistic landscape of UB is formed through diverse linguistic, cultural, and orthographic resources to achieve its visual, communicative, and marketing purposes. The display of different languages will be understood as local language practices, which are useful for revealing how different local conditions influence a contemporary multilingual linguistic landscape in more complex yet localised ways (Li Wei 2018). Put simply, language relocalising processes are deeply historical and complex and depend on how different local societies and different contexts appropriate features from other languages. The relationship of any language with the local society is not random or meaninglessly contingent, but rather the relationship is context-dependent, producing meanings that manifest themselves in intensely local forms (Dovchin 2018, 2020).

3 Linguistic ethnography: Open ethnographic observation

The data used in this chapter derive from a larger ethnographic research project that explores the linguistic practices of urban culture in UB. Recent studies on bi/multilingual speakers, including our own, have found that the methodological framework of linguistic ethnography (LE) may be helpful to achieve a deeper understanding of the sociolinguistic realities of language users (Copland and Creese 2015). LE is characterised by the appropriation of both ethnographic and linguistic perspectives, where researchers are interested in understanding sociolinguistic experiences through ethnography. LE provides researchers with an improved explanatory power, enabling them to make statements about language and its actual connection with a socio-cultural reality. It focuses on people's daily lived experiences and on how language users' linguistic actions in particular local contexts are understood (Tusting and Maybin 2007).

One of the most common methods in LE – Open Ethnographic Observation (OEO) – gives the ethnographer the flexibility to record and note what they see, hear, smell, feel, and sense in the field (Dovchin 2019). In OEO, a researcher makes as many observations as possible about the people, social spaces, and practices in the site under investigation, documented through photographs, ethnographic notes, engagement with locals, and so on (Copland and Creese 2015). OEO has given the authors of this chapter the means to observe the language diversity in UB in a natural and unobtrusive manner. Based on photographs and ethnographic notes taken between 2014 and 2019, the analysis in this chapter examines how the linguistic landscape of UB is formed, and the ways in which it relates to local contexts. Both researchers are participant-observers, who consider themselves insiders, as one of them lives permanently in UB, while the other one is a Mongolian-background researcher based in Australia, who does fieldwork in UB.

In the next section, we analyse a series of examples taken from UB's linguistic landscape, representing the use of three different languages (English, Russian and Korean) not native to Mongolia and produced by the residents of UB. These three languages are selected because they are the most frequently occurring non-Mongolian resources in the linguistic landscape of UB observed during OEO. Data extracts have been selected to introduce a variety of ways in which such relocalised language resources are used in the socio-cultural, historical, ideological and political context of UB's linguistic landscape.

4 Relocalised linguistic resources in UB

4.1 Relocalised English linguistic resources in UB

Since the 1990s and at the expense of Russian (see section 4.2), English has clearly become the most common foreign language used across public places in UB, serving multiple visual, communicative, and marketing purposes for local urban Mongolians. Consider the example in Figure 1, where English orthographic and other linguistic resources are used to advertise the traditional Mongolian musical instrument *morin khuur*, 'horse-headed fiddle'. The shop *Морин хуурын дэлгүүр*, 'Morin khuur shop' is located in the city centre and specialises in making and selling the *morin khuur* – a two-string instrument, similar in sound to a violin or cello, identified by UNESCO as a Masterpiece of the Oral and Intangible Heritage of Humanity. The strings are made from horsetail hairs and run over a wooden bridge on the body of the instrument up a long neck, which is carved into the form of a horse head. The *morin khuur* is considered locally to reflect the spirit of the Mongolians and is an integral part of the nomadic culture because horses play a large role in the history and daily life of Mongolians (Marsh 2008). Each local household in Mongolia seeks to possess its own *morin khuur*.

Figure 1: Morin khuur shop in UB (Photo: Bolormaa Shinjee).

English is here aimed at the local audience as one needs to know the meaning and history of *morin khuur* in order to make complete sense of the content in English. The shop uses the standard Cyrillic writing system of the Mongolian language in its main header (Table 1, line 1), which is also ornamented by the figures of two *morin khuur*. The signage is further complemented by the English statement "Mongolian traditional musical instruments" (line 2). English orthographic

10 The multilingual landscape of Ulaanbaatar, the capital city of Mongolia — 255

Table 1: Morin khuur shopfront – visible text.

Transcript	Transliteration	Translation
(1) Морин хуурын дэлгүүр	Morin khuuriin delguur	The Shop of morin khuur (horse-headed fiddle)
(2) Mongolian traditional musical instruments	Mongolian traditional musical instruments	Mongolian traditional musical instruments
(3) Утас: 9909–4868 www.mori khuur.mn (Facebook page:) @PegasusBayaraa	Utas: 9909–4868: www.mori khuur.mn (Facebook *page*:) @PegasusBayaraa	Telephone: 9909–4868: www. morikhuur.mn (Facebook *page*:) @PegasusBayaraa
(4) *Morinkhuur* workshop Facebook page: @PEGASUSBAYARAA	Morinkhuur workshop Facebook page: @PEGASUSBAYARAA	Morinkhuur workshop Facebook page: @PEGASUSBAYARAA
(5) 9909–4868 English Japanese speaking available	9909–4868 English Japanese speaking available	9909–4868 English Japanese speaking available

resources are used to display its website "www.morinkhuur.mn" (line 3), while "telephone" is written in Mongolian Cyrillic (line 3). The name of the Facebook page, "PEGASUSBAYARAA" (lines 3 and 4), is the combination of Pegasus – a winged white divine horse in Greek mythology – and the shop owner's name, Bayaraa. Pegasus is related to the popular Mongolian myth of *morin khuur*, which describes how the horse rider who lost his white divine winged horse decided to create the musical instrument to commemorate his beloved horse. What seems interesting with this signage is that some of the meaning is local and not readily available to outsiders (e.g., tourists, business travellers etc.) who do not know about the traditions and connotations of Pegasus in this context, but the sign still addresses outsiders, including potential customers, through the use of English for its central message. What is even more interesting is the fact that the shop also offers service beyond English, seeking to attract Japanese speaking visitors to their shop, "English Japanese speaking available" (line 5). This line also illustrates the evidence that Japanese is a popular foreign language in UB due to the extreme popularity of Japanese TV dramas, sumo wrestling and Japanese food. Human mobility between Japan and Mongolia has also dramatically increased since 1990, largely due to scholarships provided by the Project for Human Resource Development Scholarship by Japanese Grant Aid (JDS), which have been awarded to 400 Mongolian students, allowing them to complete their postgraduate studies in Japan. The popularity of Japanese language and culture has also increased rapidly due to Japanese sumo wrestling in Mongolia. Many young Mongolian males started going to Japan to become sumo wrestlers, a momentum which made sumo very popular in Mongolia (Dovchin, 2017a). Since 2003, Mongolian-born Japanese sumo wrestlers have become the highest-ranking champions (Yokozuna) in Japan, including Hakuho (Munkhbat Davaajargal), a retired professional sumo wrestler, who became one of the most iconic sumo wrestlers in Japan.

Figure 2 shows the sign of a mobile phone trade and repair centre, which hundreds of mobile technology consumers visit on a daily basis.

Figure 2: Centre for mobile phone repair (Photo: Bolormaa Shinjee).

Table 2: Centre for mobile phone repair – visible text.

	Transcript	Transliteration	Translation
(1)	Super хальсан наалт	Super khalisan naalt	Super film screen protector
(2)	гар утас худалдааны төв	gar utas khudaldaanii tuv	mobile phone trade centre
(3)	гар утас засвар, дагалдах хэрэгсэл	gar utas zasvar, dagaldakh kheregsel	mobile phone repair and accessories

The actual signage is dominated by Mongolian Cyrillic (Table 2, lines 2 and 3), but English is also used for local purposes mainly targeted at locals, in line 1. Here, the English loan, "super" directly modifies the Cyrillic Mongolian, *хальсан наалт* 'film screen protector,' creating an anglicised Mongolian sign, referring to 'super film screen protector [for phone screens]'. In general, the English loan "super" is used widely by Mongolians to indicate something exquisite and exceptional and there are many local expressions such as *супер цавуу* [super tsavuu] 'super glue', or *Чи супершүү!* [Chi supershuu] 'You are super!'. "Super" has been relocalised into the

Mongolian vocabulary to the point that it is often viewed as "real Mongolian" and an authentic expression due to its deep absorption within the Mongolian language and culture. Note, however, that in these expressions, "super" is rendered in the Cyrillic alphabet and follows local morphosyntactic rules, different from the sign in Figure 2 where "super" appears in the Roman alphabet, making it foreign-looking.

Consider another example in Figure 3, where English has been relocalised.

Figure 3: Golden Point poster at a supermarket (Photo: Bolormaa Shinjee).

The poster in Figure 3 is located at the front door of a big supermarket in UB. It advertises the new "Golden Point" loyalty system that the supermarket is introducing and is marketed by Ca Lily Hair and Slimming Beauty Salon for its customers. The role of English here is local: even though phrases such as "Ca Lily Hair and Slimming Beauty Salon" and "golden point" (Table 3, lines 1 and 2) are presented in English, it is not very clear what they stand for. We need to be familiar with "golden point" and "Ca Lily" to make sense of the English part of the sign. Once we analyse these English linguistic resources in relation to the Mongolian language system, its

Table 3: Golden Point poster at a supermarket.

	Transcript	Transliteration	Translation
(1)	Golden Point Ca Lily Hair and Slimming Beauty Salon	Golden Point Ca Lily Hair and Slimming Beauty Salon	Golden Point Ca Lily Hair and Slimming Beauty Salon
(2)	Golden Point: хэмнэлт урамшуулал чанар	Golden Point: khemnelt uramshuulal chanar	Golden Point: save, reward and quality
(3)	Ca Lily Hair and Slimming Beauty Salon: Ca Lily гоо сайхны салон	Ca Lily Hair and Slimming Beauty Salon: Ca Lily goo saikhnii salon	Ca Lily Hair and Slimming Beauty Salon: Ca Lily beauty salon
(4)	Нэг стикерээр нэг хүн үйлчлүүлэх эрхтэй	Neg stickereer neg khun uilchluulekh erkhtei	Each sticker allows one customer
(5)	Уг стикер нь уутны хамт хүчинтэй	Ug sticker ni uutnii khamt khuchintei	The sticker is valid with the bag
(6)	5 ширхэг стикерээр 1 сугалаа аваарай	5 shirkheg stickereer 1 sugalaa avaarai	Buy one lottery [ticket] with five stickers
(7)	голден пойнтийн хөнгөлөлтийн хувьтай 1 ширхэг стикерээр 20% хөнгөлүүлээрэй	Golden pointiin khungulultiin khuvitai 1 shirkheg stickereer 20% khunguluuleerei	Get 20% discount through per sticker. Each sticker comes with the golden points.

meaning becomes easier to understand. From lines 4 to 7, English has been relocalised into the complex Mongolian syntax system. For example, the English stem word "sticker" has been Mongolianised in various ways based on Mongolian grammar and syntax, as seen in Нэг стикерээр нэг хүн үйлчлүүлэх эрхтэй 'With per sticker for per customer' (line 4). Here, "sticker" has been transliterated into Cyrillic Mongolian, mixed with the Mongolian suffix -ээр 'with', forming стикерээр 'with sticker'. In line 5, *Уг стикер нь уутны хамт хүчтэй* 'The sticker is valid with a bag', "sticker" is accompanied by the Mongolian verb нь 'is', creating стикер нь 'sticker is'. In the phrase *5 ширхэг стикерээр 1 сугалаа аваарай* 'Buy one lottery with five stickers' (line 6), it is again combined with the Mongolian prepositional suffix -ээр 'with', resulting in стикерээр 'with sticker'. Furthermore, the English phrase "Golden Point" has been integrated into the Mongolian syntax system in line 7. Here, "Golden Point" has been transliterated and then fully Mongolianised through the combination of the Mongolian suffix -ийн [possessive 's'], forming *голден пойнтийн* ['golden point's']. Overall, English is relocalised into the Mongolian syntax system to the point that it is difficult to recognise as English – certainly for an outsider – producing new local linguistic forms and novel terms. These types of relocalised multilingual signs in the urban linguistic landscape create not only new linguistic and cultural references but also new modes of meaning-making.

4.2 Relocalised Russian linguistic resources in UB

As noted previously, the Russian language was the most common foreign language in Mongolia before 1990. During the Soviet era, a majority of UB residents could speak fluent Russian as a second language. Since the collapse of the Soviet Union the presence of Russian has declined and been substantially replaced by English. Nevertheless, the impact of the Russian language and culture has not been fully erased. In fact, there are many deeply localised Russian examples in the linguistic landscape of UB which may make no sense to native Russian speakers but remain in common use in Mongolian. As Beery (2004: 106) highlights, "Mongolians seemed to have little need of Russian and concentrated on the learning of English [after the democratic revolution]". Yet, Russian is "so entrenched in Mongolia that it was never fully replaced". Such Russian examples are better understood through the sociolinguistic history and background of the Russian language and culture in Mongolia.

Due to geographic proximity and deep historical, cultural and linguistic ties with Russia, many Mongolians treat Russian cuisine as if it is their own. Not surprisingly, there are many Russian restaurants across UB, offering traditional Russian cuisine, apparent for example in the special Valentine's Day menu of a Russian restaurant called Россия ресторан 'Russia restaurant' (Table 4).

The menu of this restaurant displays some relocalised Russian phrases that are commonly used across Mongolia. Note, however, that all course sections are in English – "Soup" (line 3), "Salad" (line 4), "Main Course" (line 5) and "Dessert" (line 6), including the main heading "Valentine Dinner 14th February". In line 3, *борщ* ('Borscht', a sour soup common in Russia, which consists of beetroot as the main ingredient) and *солянка* ('Solyanka', a thick, spicy and sour soup), two very famous Russian soups that are loved by many Mongolians, are on offer. The original Russian words – *борщ* and *солянка* – are phonetically relocalised or, in other words, Mongolianised in this menu as they are phonetically transformed as *борш* and *салянка* with the Russian character *щ* replaced with the slightly different Mongolian character *ш*, and the Russian *о* in *солянка* replaced with the Mongolian *а*.

As one reads through the menu, it is clear that what many Mongolians think is Russian is often an appropriation from the west, especially French (and English), in which the use of Cyrillic and mediation via Russian are common. Many Mongolians

Table 4: Menu of a Russian restaurant in UB.

	Transcript	Transliteration	Translation
(1)	Россия ресторан	Rossia restauran	Russia restaurant
(2)	Valentine Dinner 14th February: 49000 ₮ хосын сэт	Valentine Dinner 14th February: 49000 ₮ khosiin set	Valentine Dinner 14th February: 49000 ₮ couple's set
(3)	Soup: Сонголтоор: Борщ Салянка	Soup: Songoltoor: Borsh Salyanka	Soup: By choice: Borscht Solyanka
(4)	Salad: Сонголтоор: Венегрет Цезарь Грек	Salad: Songoltoor: Venegret Tsezari Grek	Salad: By choice: Vinaigrette Caesar Greek
(5)	Main Course: Сонголтоор: Хонины нурууны стэйк – Жигнэсэн ногоо – Шарсан төмс – Тахианы горден блю – Хуурсан ногоо Гахайн нурууны стейк – Жигнэсэн ногоо – Будаа	Main Course: Songoltoor: Khoninii nuruunii steak – Jignesen nogoo – Sharsan tums – Takhianii gorden blu – Khuursan nogoo – Gakhain nuruunii steak – Jignesen nogoo – Budaa	Main Course: By choice: Lamb spine steak – Steamed vegetables – Fried chips – Chicken cordon bleu – Fried vegetables – Pork spine steak – Steamed vegetables – Rice
(6)	Dessert: Сонголтоор: Шоколадтай бялуу Мөхөөлдөс	Dessert: Songoltoor Shokoladtai byaluu Mukhuuldus	Dessert: By choice Chocolate cake Ice cream
(7)	Ирсэн бүх бүсгүйчүүддээ улаан сарнай дарсаар угтах ба Венус Спад хөнгөлөлтийн купон бэлэглэнэ. Амьд хөгжмийн тоглолт	Irsen bukh busguichuuddee ulaan sarnai darsaar ugtakh ba Benus Spad khungulultiin kupon beleglene. Amid khugjmiin toglolt	All women will be welcomed with the red rose and wine and will be rewarded with the Venus Spa's bonus coupon. Live music.
(8)	11-453475 99104402 БЗД Сансарын тунель Pizza Hut-ын чанх урд	11-453475 99104402 BZD Sansariin tunel Pizza Hutiin chankh urd	11-453475 99104402 Bayan Zurh district, Sansar tunnel, right opposite the Pizza Hut

do not necessarily know that these food terms are of western origin. For example, there is the Caesar salad, which is localised as *Цезарь*; Greek salad localised as *Грек*; vinaigrette as *Венегрет* (a Russian word of French origin, although the actual ingredients and style are very different from French vinaigrette) (line 4). Note further the transliteration of chicken cordon bleu as *Тахианы горден блю*, a dish of Swiss-French origin, mediated by Russian (line 5); and English steak mediated again by Russian as *стэйк* (line 5). In the dessert section (line 6), the combination of Russian and Mongolian linguistic resources has created *шоколадтай бялуу* 'chocolate cake'. Here, Russian *шоколад* 'chocolate' and the Mongolian preposition *-тай* 'with' and *бялуу* 'cake' are brought together. In line 7, *купон* ('coupon'), a word of French origin mediated through Russian, is localised into the Mongolian syntax by combining *хөнгөлөлтийн купон* 'discount coupon' and the Mongolian verb *бэлэглэнэ* 'will be rewarded'. The relocalised English term in the Mongolian Cyrillic orthography – *Венус Спад* 'Venus Spa's' – English Venus Spa attached to the Mongolian suffix *д* (possessive s') – is also used in line 7. Another western origin word – *тоннель* 'tunnel' – has been mediated through Russian and relocalised as *Сансарын тунель* 'Sansar's tunnel', referring to one of the central tunnels situated in UB (line 8), followed by Pizza Hut-*ын* 'Pizza Hut's', the combination of the name of the American pizza chain and the Mongolian suffix *ын* – a genitive ending in English. Overall, we see how this menu is formed by the relocalisation from western linguistic and cultural resources, especially French and English, in which the use of Mongolian Cyrillic orthography and the mediation via Russian are common.

4.3 Korean in the linguistic landscape of UB

Human mobility between Mongolia and South Korea has also rapidly expanded since 1990. South Korea has, in recent years, become one of the largest aid donors and important trading partners for Mongolia. Many Mongolians have started traveling to South Korea for different reasons, including to study, live, and work. As a result, Seoul hosts one of the largest Mongolian expatriate communities in the world, while South Korean merchants, businessmen, academics, tourists, and Christian missionaries have become long-term residents of UB. This mutual relationship has strongly reinforced the influence of South Korean linguistic and cultural resources in Mongolia. Korean TV dramas and movies, K-pop music, and Korean food have become tremendously popular in UB.

The linguistic landscape of UB is rich in Korean resources as seen in restaurants, karaoke bars, grocery shops, and beauty and hair salons. Mongolians today particularly enjoy Korean food such as kimchi, Korean BBQ, and noodles. Figure 4 shows the front of the Korean restaurant *Jang Su 2* in UB which interestingly makes no use of the Korean script. Instead it uses Romanised forms *Jang Su*, from the Korean 전라북도 [*Jangsu-gun*], a county in North Jeolla Province, South Korea, to convey the aura of the Korean language to those with reading ability in the Roman alphabet. Note that the romanised *Jang Su* has also been Mongolianised as Чансу embedded between two English terms leading to "Korean Чансу Restaurant" in order to make it more readable for locals.

Figure 4: Jang Su 2 Korean Restaurant in UB (Photo: Bolormaa Shinjee).

The use of Korean script has been avoided in this signage, mainly due to a new city regulation introduced in 2007 regarding city signage which requires all public signs to give priority to Mongolian over Asian languages such as Chinese and Korean. Restaurants bearing signs in Asian scripts were largely affected by this rule, and the owners were ordered to replace their existing Asian signs with Mongolian ones. In fact, according to Billé (2010: 241–242), the regulation did not only apply to Asian languages but to all foreign languages. However, it was enforced only regarding Asian languages/scripts. Billé (2010) suggests that Chinese signs were/are seen as representing cultural and political intrusion (and other Asian languages/scripts like Korean and Japanese were "collateral damage"), whereas signs with Cyrillic or Latin scripts (English in particular) are seen as representing modernity and cosmopolitanism (Billé 2010). In response to this regulation, many Korean restaurants have started replacing their signage with English or Mongolian, while still seeking to convey the aura and image of "Koreanness" through the relocalised Korean using Cyrillic Mongolian orthographic resources.

5 Conclusion

With reference to the data examples used in this study, we seek to address the two main research questions set out at the beginning of this chapter:
(1) How are multilingual, cultural, and orthographic resources used in the post-socialist linguistic landscape of UB?
(2) What is the impact of these resources on the contemporary post-socialist Mongolian language?

In addressing the first question, linguistic resources other than Mongolian are evident in the post-Socialist linguistic landscape of UB, Mongolia. It has become clear that the public urban linguistic landscape in UB has already extensively allowed for the inclusion of multilingual resources, while the users of these resources expand their linguistic creativity. However, the fact is that now, public signs in UB draw on different multilingual resources, and through the relocalising of such resources, relocalised meanings are created that are unique and not simply an echo of a source language. It is almost impossible to determine or comprehend the sole meaning of English, Russian, or Korean printed on these signs as they have become practically incomprehensible to English, Russian, or Korean speakers when in contact with Mongolian. We see how some examples in the linguistic landscape are formed by the relocalisation from western linguistic and cultural resources such as English (and French), either directly or mediated through the Russian language, while creating uniquely local Mongolian meanings. There are instances in the linguistic landscape where the meaning is local and not readily available to outsiders (such as tourists, and business travellers) who do not know about the local connotations, while the message still addresses outsiders, including potential customers, through the use of English for the central message. We also note the examples of Korean restaurants which display Roman or Mongolian signage, yet still convey the aura of Korean cuisine and Korean culture through relocalised Cyrillic Mongolian orthographic resources.

In addressing the second question, we found that these multilingual resources are deeply relocalised into Mongolian Cyrillic orthography, transliterated Roman Mongolian scripts, full Mongolian sentences, and the Mongolian grammatical, phonetic, lexical, and syntax systems. Rather than merely borrowing from these languages for the Mongolian context, the urban citizens in UB use English,

Russian, Korean and other languages alongside Mongolian to function in the space of relocalisation. The multilingualism in UB can no longer be considered as a separate linguistic system but rather as part of the local language. Multilingual resources are relocalised in creative ways in the local linguistic landscape of UB, which means that the Mongolian language is reformed and renewed in varied contexts, creating new locally relevant words, meanings, phrases, and terms. Overall, situated within the relocalisation of the increasing global spread of English and other languages (in this context Russian, Korean and to some extent French), the multilingual landscape in Mongolia is in a position of fluidity regarding what it means to be a modern Mongolian in a new post-socialist era. Because public signs and advertisements in languages other than Russian and Mongolian were not allowed in the public space prior to 1990, the current multilingual landscape presents an entirely new set of multiple and fluid linguistic relocalisations. The formation of these new post-socialist linguistic practices is a continuous process that reveals new sociolinguistic realities of belonging and identities in contemporary urban Mongolia (Barrett and Dovchin 2019). The multilingual landscape of UB is not a predetermined or prefixed entity, but rather a constant site for negotiation, shift, and reformation.

References

Backhaus, Peter. 2006. Multilingualism in Tokyo: a look into the linguistic landscape. *International Journal of Multilingualism* 3(1). 52–66.

Barrett, Tyler Andrew & Sender Dovchin (eds.). 2019. *Critical inquiries in the sociolinguistics of globalization*. Bristol: Multilingual Matters.

Beery, Kelli Erin. 2004. English in the linguistic landscape of Mongolia: indices of language spread and language competition. PhD thesis, Purdue University.

Billé, Franck. 2010. Sounds and scripts of modernity: language ideologies and practices in contemporary Mongolia. *Inner Asia* 12(2). 231–252.

Campi, Alicia. 2006. Globalization's impact on Mongolian identity issues and the image of Chinggis Khan. In Henry G. Schwarz (ed.), *Mongolian culture and society in the age of globalization*, 67–99. Bellingham: Center for East Asian Studies, Western Washington University.

Canagarajah, Suresh. 2013. *Translingual practice: global Englishes and cosmopolitan relations*. New York: Routledge.

Copland, Fiona & Angela Creese. 2015. *Linguistic ethnography: collecting, analysing and presenting data*: London: Sage.

Dovchin, Sender. 2017a. The ordinariness of youth linguascapes in Mongolia. *International Journal of Multilingualism* 14(2). 144–159.

Dovchin, Sender. 2017b. The role of English in the language practices of Mongolian Facebook users. *English Today* 33(2). 16–24.

Dovchin, Sender. 2018. *Language, media and globalization in the periphery: the linguascapes of popular music in Mongolia*. New York: Routledge.

Dovchin, Sender. 2019. Language crossing and linguistic racism: Mongolian immigrant women in Australia. *Journal of Multicultural Discourses* 14(4). 334–351.

Dovchin, Sender. 2020. *Language, social media and ideologies*. Cham: Springer.

Dovchin, Sender, Shaila Sultana & Alastair Pennycook. 2015. Relocalizing the translingual practices of young adults in Mongolia and Bangladesh. *Translation and Translanguaging in Multilingual Contexts* 1(1). 4–26.

Higgins, Christina. (2009). *English as a local language: post-colonial identities and multilingual practices*. Bristol: Multilingual Matters.

Lai, Mee Ling. 2013. The linguistic landscape of Hong Kong after the change of sovereignty. *International Journal of Multilingualism* 10(3). 251–272.

Lee, Jerry Won & Jackie Jia Lou. 2019. The ordinary semiotic landscape of an unordinary place: spatiotemporal disjunctures in Incheon's Chinatown. *International Journal of Multilingualism* 16(2). 187–203.

Li Wei 2018. Translanguaging as a practical theory of language. *Applied Linguistics* 39(1). 9–30.

Marsh, Peter K. 2008. *The horse-head fiddle and the cosmopolitan reimagination of tradition in Mongolia*. London: Routledge.

Marsh, Peter K. 2010. Our Generation is opening its eyes: Hip-Hop and youth identity in contemporary Mongolia. *Central Asian Survey* 29(3). 345–358.

Marzluf, Phillip P. 2012. Words, borders, herds: post-socialist English and nationalist language identities in Mongolia. *International Journal of the Sociology of Language* 218. 195–216.

Marzluf, Phillip P. 2017. *Language, literacy, and social change in Mongolia: traditionalist, socialist, and post-socialist identities*. Lanham: Lexington Books.

Pennycook, Alastair. 2010. *Language as a local practice*. London: Routledge.

Rossabi, Morris. 2005. *Modern Mongolia: from Khans to commissars to capitalists*. Oakland: University of California Press.

Terkourafi, Marina. 2010. Introduction: a fresh look at some old questions. In Marina Terkourafi (ed.), *The languages of global hip hop*, 1–19. London: Continuum.

Tusting, Karin & Janet Maybin. 2007. Linguistic ethnography and interdisciplinarity: opening the discussion. *Journal of Sociolinguistics* 11(5). 575–583.

Wang, Jingjing. 2013. Linguistic landscape of China: a case study of shop signs in Beijing. *Studies in Literature and Language* 6(1). 40–47.

Anu Bissoonauth and Jane Warren

11 Urban multilingualism in Mauritius: Exploring linguistic and ethnic diversity in Port-Louis

1 Introduction

The Republic of Mauritius is located in the southwestern Indian Ocean about 800 miles from Madagascar. The vast majority of the population of just over 1.2 million lives on the main island, also known as Mauritius, and there are a number of smaller islands and atolls.[1] Port-Louis, the capital city, is the economic, administrative and cultural centre of the country and also the main port and harbour, with a key outward-facing and international role. To date, there have been no published studies on multilingualism in Port-Louis, as far as we are aware, and this chapter aims to help fill this gap.

The language situation in Mauritius is complex, a legacy of its colonial past. Colonised in the early 18th century by the French who brought in slaves mainly from the east coast of Africa and Madagascar, it was ceded to the British in the early 19th century. Following the abolition of slavery, the British brought in indentured labourers from India, and Chinese traders also migrated there in the 19th century. Mauritius finally gained independence in 1968.

The country's history of colonisation and decolonisation has resulted in considerable linguistic diversity and various sociolinguistic paradoxes. Kreol is the Mauritian *lingua franca*, but does not have any official status. English is the *de jure* official language of government, administration and the education system (Corne 1999: 165), and French is the dominant language of the workplace, the media – daily newspapers are predominantly in French – and education. It was only in 2012 that Kreol began to be taught in schools, as an optional heritage or "ancestral" language[2] in primary school, alongside Hindi, Urdu, Tamil, Telugu, Marathi, Arabic and standard Mandarin.[3]

---

[1] According to the 2011 census, 97% of Mauritians live on the main island (1,196,383 of 1,237,091) (Statistics Mauritius 2012a). The majority of the rest of the population lives on Rodrigues, a smaller island to the north-east.
[2] The concept of 'ancestral language' has been viewed as a constructed political ideology (see e.g. Eisenlohr 2006, 2007; Rajah-Carrim 2005).
[3] Arabic is not strictly an ancestral language in that it is not directly linked to the ethnic origins of Mauritians but is the language of Muslim religious identity. Modern Arabic is seen as a

Scholars have shed light on the complex linguistic situation in Mauritius by linking language ideologies to ethnicity and the politics of nation building (Eisenlohr 2004; Eriksen 2004; Hookoomsing 2009; Miles 2000). The paradoxical attitudes of speakers towards their own multilingualism (Biltoo 2004; Rajah-Carrim 2007) have been described among the younger generations as multilingual pragmatism, enabling them to reconcile the various paradoxes related to language use. They share a consensus that "being Mauritian is equal to being born in Mauritius, speaking Kreol and living on a multicultural island" and accept "Kreol as their national language, whilst acknowledging at the same time that access to European languages is the key to social advancement" (Bissoonauth 2014: 263).

Port-Louis as the capital of Mauritius occupies a unique position, and it is also the only district in Mauritius that is officially classified as wholly urban. Neighbouring Plaines Wilhems, which is connected to Port-Louis via a new metro system, is the only other district that is predominantly urban.[4] The aim of this chapter is to explore whether and how multilingualism in Port-Louis differs from that in the rest of Mauritius. To do this, it will focus on the following research questions:

(1) How has linguistic and ethnic diversity evolved in Mauritius and Port-Louis?
(2) What are current patterns of language use in the capital, particularly among younger people, who are potentially at the forefront of linguistic change?

To answer these questions, the chapter will draw on a range of data sources, including Mauritian census and education statistics and a database of language use and attitudes among secondary school students collected by the first-named author in 2016 and 2018. Section 2 gives an overview of the evolution of multilingualism in Mauritius, to provide the context for the discussion of the past and current linguistic situation in the capital Port-Louis, set out in Section 3.

---

stepping-stone to understanding texts, prayers and sermons in Quranic Arabic. Standard Mandarin can be seen as an imported vehicular language, while other Chinese varieties such as Hakka, Cantonese and Hokkien are ancestral transmitted languages (Lefort 2019).

4 A minority of inhabitants of Black River and Moka districts live in urban areas, and the remaining five districts on the island of Mauritius are all officially classified as rural.

2 Multilingualism in Mauritius

2.1 Historical overview

To understand the complexity of present-day multilingualism in Mauritius and Port-Louis, it is useful to review how the country's language ecology evolved. Originally uninhabited, Mauritius was initially occupied in 1598 by the Dutch and subsequently abandoned. During French colonisation (1721–1810), slaves were brought from East Africa, Madagascar, Mozambique and to a lesser extent from West Africa and India (Baker, 1969: 73; Corne, 1999: 164) to work on sugar cane plantations. At the end of the 1730s Mauritius could be considered a multiethnic colony, with slaves from a number of different tribes and nationalities speaking mutually unintelligible languages (Baker 1982). Some fifty years later, a Pidgin language was born *in situ*, developing through the interactions between slaves and their French plantation owners, and gradually became a distinct Creole language, Kreol (Corne 1999: 164).

The 18th century multilingual situation in Mauritius involved three types of languages: (1) a French-based Creole, (2) dialectal varieties of French spoken by the French settlers in the 18th century (Corne, 1999: 165), and (3) varieties of Indian languages used by Indian artisans who came to Mauritius during the governorship of Mahé de Labourdonnais (Toussaint 2014: 38), most likely the Dravidian languages Tamil and/or Telugu.

In the early 19th century, during the Napoleonic wars, France lost Mauritius to Great Britain. During British jurisdiction (1810–1968), following the abolition of slavery in Mauritius, indentured labourers from India were brought in (Corne 1999: 164). About 70% were speakers of Indic languages from North East India and their mother tongue was Bhojpuri, while the remainder were speakers of Dravidian languages (Corne 1999: 164–165; Kriegel et al. 2019: 191).

Chinese migrants from Hong-Kong and mainland China, whose main mother tongue was Hakka, emigrated to Mauritius in the 19th century. The Chinese were traders and settled mainly in the eastern part of Port-Louis (Burrun 2009: 76). The arrival of Indians and Chinese in Mauritius created what has been called "Oriental" multiculturalism and multilingualism (Hookoomsing 2009), adding a number of Indian and Chinese languages to the already present European languages (French and English) and emerging Mauritian Creole.

2.2 Ethnicity and religion

Mauritius' unique history and evolution has given rise to a diverse population which can be grouped according to linguistic, ethnic and religious criteria. Religion and geographical origins have been two key elements in categorising ethnic identity. This is illustrated in the 1972 census, the last time Mauritians were explicitly asked about ethnicity. The population was asked to indicate to which of four "communities" they belonged to – Hindu, Muslim, Sino-Mauritian, and General Population (Central Statistics Office 1972). This latter category contrasts with the other three and is a catch-all grouping that included the Creole community, Franco-Mauritians, those of mixed-race descent, or those who did not identify with the other groups. "Creole" in Mauritius refers to "those Mauritians who are Catholic and have African, Malagasy, or mixed origins and/or who are seen by others and see themselves as Creoles" (Eriksen 2007: 173–174). Franco-Mauritians are descended from the original French settlers and plantation owners. In 1972, the four groups were ranked as follows: Hindu (50.3%), General Population (30.7%), Muslim (16.1%), and Sino-Mauritian (2.9%) (Statistics Mauritius n.d.: Table 4).

The removal of the question on ethnicity in subsequent censuses was designed to foster a sense of national unity (Christopher 2006: 347). However, these four communities continue to be recognised under the current Mauritian Constitution, in a section that deals with political representation (Mauritius National Assembly 2016: 68). The Constitution and the political system therefore continue to emphasise the importance of religion and Indian and Chinese heritage in the ethnic composition of the Mauritian nation. What is striking is that Creoles are not acknowledged officially as an ethnic or cultural group, in spite of being key in the formation of the country's *lingua franca* and making major contributions to Mauritian music and culture (Boswell 2006: 45).

Religion continues to be an important marker in Mauritius. It has been noted that "[a] leisurely walk through the capital, Port-Louis, may bring one past, within half an hour or so, a Buddhist pagoda, a Sunni mosque, an Anglican church and a Catholic one, and two Hindu temples – one North Indian, one Tamil" (Eriksen 1997: 175). Although the 2011 census has no explicit ethnicity question, it does ask respondents to report their religion, one of the key characteristics in defining Mauritian communities. There were 46 named religious groups in 2011, the majority of which can be classified into three groupings: Hindu (48.5%), Christian (32.7%) and Muslim (17.3%) (Statistics Mauritius 2012a: Table D5). Table 1 highlights the similarity between the 1972 figures on the size of the Hindu and Muslim communities and those from the 2011 census on the Hindu and Muslim religions.

It also shows the parallel between the size of the General Population community in 1972 (30.7%) and the proportion of Mauritians reporting a Christian faith in 2011 (32.7%).

Table 1: Mauritian ethnic identity according to religion, community and language of forefathers (Central Statistics Office 1972; Statistics Mauritius 2012a).

1972 Census: community	%	2011 Census: religion	%	2011 Census: language of forefathers	%
Hindu	50.3	Hindu	48.5	Indian languages	43.2
Muslim	16.1	Muslim	17.3	Kreol	51.7
General Population	30.7	Christian	32.7	French	3.2
Sino-Mauritian	2.9	Buddhist/Chinese	0.4	Chinese languages	1.2
		Other	1.1	English	0.2
				Other	0.5
Total	100		100		100

Table 1 also shows 2011 census figures on "language of forefathers", which can provide a partial picture of current ethnic affiliations in Mauritius. Given that Creoles and Franco-Mauritians are the key Christian groups,[5] we might expect under a third of the Mauritian population to report Kreol as the language of their forefathers. However, the proportion of Mauritians who claim Kreol as ancestral language – 51.7% – shows that for some, Kreol has supplanted their original ancestral language. Indian languages – and particularly Bhojpuri – remain an important means of asserting an ethnic identity even though they are not spoken very widely, with 43.2% claiming an Indian ancestral language. Only 0.2% of respondents reported English as their ancestral language, in spite of it being the *de jure* official language: of the few British people who settled in Mauritius, a number assimilated to the French-Mauritian group and culture (Rajah-Carrim 2005).

2.3 Current language situation

A key source of data on current language use in Mauritius comes from the census, conducted every ten years, which favours an analysis at national rather than district level. The 2011 census asked one question on language use, about languages usually

---

5 The majority of Sino-Mauritians are also Christian (Bissoonauth 2012: 87).

or most often spoken in the home.[6] These data do not provide a full picture of Mauritian multilingualism, as respondents were only able to give one or at the most two languages (Bissoonauth 2021: 68). However, the census can reveal the number of languages spoken and speakers. It lists 20 individual languages, with further unnamed languages subsumed under "Other". The top ten languages in 2011 were, in descending order: Kreol (86.7%), Bhojpuri (5.8%), French (4.7%), Hindi (0.8%), Bengali (0.6%), English (0.5%), Chinese languages (0.3%), Telugu (0.1%), Tamil (0.1%) and Malagasy (0.1%) (Statistics Mauritius 2012a: Table D8, single and two language responses combined). Bengali and Malagasy are both recent languages in Mauritius, brought in by migrant workers employed in the textile industry and services sector.

Behind these census figures lie a series of paradoxes. Although English is the *de jure* official language of state institutions and is an ethnically neutral language in the Mauritian context, it is more a written than a spoken language – only 0.5% of the population claim English as the language usually spoken at home. French, on the other hand, is a vehicular language frequently used in the workplace, media and education, and is the third most spoken language at home. Data on language attitudes and language choice of younger generations in education reveal that having a good command of English and French is associated with a high level of education, social mobility and good employment prospects (Bissoonauth 2011, 2019), which maintains the importance of these two languages. Kreol, which has no official status, is the *lingua franca* of the island and mother tongue of a large segment of the population spoken in informal situations and at home. Its use has increased in the media and government administration since the 1990s. However, there continues to be some stigma attached to Kreol, linked to the historical and social conditions in which it evolved (Bissoonauth 2012: 88).

The relationship between French and Kreol is one of classic diglossia between two related languages (Ferguson 1959), with Kreol having lower status and French higher status. Another classic diglossic relationship exists between standard Hindi, the higher status language which is taught in school alongside other standard Indian languages, and Bhojpuri (Hookoomsing 1986), the lower status language, which is mainly an oral variety and the second most spoken language at home. Bhojpuri has evolved in Mauritius through contact with local languages, and particularly Kreol, into a Mauritian variety (Bissoonauth 2012: 251). Originally spoken by Indians from Bihar and neighbouring regions, it became a *lingua franca* itself among Indo-Mauritians generally and "the predominant language of the Mauritian countryside" (Eisenlohr 2006: 207).

---

[6] Due to the Covid pandemic, the 2021 Census was postponed until 2022, and these most recent data were not available for this study.

Indian and Chinese ancestral languages (Bhojpuri, Gujrati, Hindi, Marathi, Tamil, Telugu, Urdu, Cantonese, Hakka, Hokkien and others) have shown a steady decline in a population in which around two-thirds are of Indian descent (Bissoonauth 2012: 248). Bhojpuri, for example, was spoken by 19.1% of Mauritians at home in 1990, 12.1% in 2000, and only 5.3% in 2011 (Central Statistics Office 2001; Statistics Mauritius 2012a; single language responses only). The low levels of usage suggest that the use of Indian languages is not important for Mauritians in asserting their ethnic and cultural identity (Bissoonauth 2011; Hookoomsing 1993).

In spite of the decline in Indian ancestral languages, a study of younger generations of Mauritians in secondary education has shown that the languages still maintain a societal role in interactions between young people and older generations of grandparents and in the rural areas (Bissoonauth 2011). They are also maintained through favourable education policies. However, the loss of this current generation of grandparents will mean that younger generations will have less motivation to use these languages outside the classroom. In addition, the growing shift from Bhojpuri to Kreol illustrates a non-classic diglossic relationship, that is, between two languages that are not related (Fishman 1967), in this case between higher status Kreol and lower status Bhojpuri. Kreol "has the prestige of a more useful language since it allows communication with members of other speech communities, and it represents the values of city living and white collar jobs" (Stein 1982: 136), whereas Bhojpuri is linked to rural and less prestigious ways of life.

3 Port-Louis: Urban multilingualism

3.1 The evolution of the capital

> Port-Louis is important for Mauritius because of its history, because it is not every day that you get the most important port in the Indian Ocean apart from South Africa, from 200 years and before. [. . .] Mauritius is the star and key of the Indian Ocean because of Port-Louis [male student, 20s, Port-Louis resident][7]

---

[7] The quotations that open sections 3.1 to 3.4 are from 15 short interviews recorded by the first-named author in July 2016 with a sample of members of the public living or working in Port-Louis, with the aim of eliciting their perceptions of the capital. The sample is not representative of the city's population, but it gives a flavour of how those in Port-Louis view the city. All interviewees claimed to be fluent in Kreol, French and English, and responded in the language of their choice.

Port-Louis, described as a "town where the past is also present" (Burrun 2009: 7), is situated in the north-west of the island between a natural sea harbour and a range of mountains in the shape of a crescent. The port was chosen as the capital of Mauritius island by both French and British administrations in the 18th and 19th centuries because it could welcome ships that could dock easily, unload and reload their goods (Charoux n.d: 5).

Port-Louis was the name given to Port-Nord-Ouest in honour of King Louis XV, by the French governor Denis Denyon, who arrived in Mauritius in 1722 (Burrun 2009: 5). Under the governorship of Mahé de Labourdonnais, stationed in Mauritius between 1735 and 1746 (Toussaint 2014: 55), Port-Louis developed into a thriving French military base and a capital city, in addition to being a trading port (Burrun 2009: 6). During French control, Port-Louis was a cosmopolitan city where the population was housed by the authorities according to their ethnic groups. Thus *Camp lascars et malabars* 'Camp for Indian sailors and people from the Malabar region' was reserved for sailors and workers from India, *Camp des noirs* 'Camp for Black people' for slaves and people of African descent, while the centre was reserved for the white population (Gautam 1998: 20; Burrun 2009: 9).

Nineteenth-century Port-Louis was marred by natural disasters such as fires, tropical storms and epidemics (Toussaint 1966: 103–118), and many survivors moved to the cooler central plateau in the bordering districts of Plaines Wilhems and Moka. Nonetheless, Port-Louis remained the administrative and financial centre with the only maritime port of the island.

The decade that followed independence from Great Britain in 1968 was a period of relative stagnation with high unemployment and low annual growth (Minogue 1992). Historically, the sugar industry has been important, but the textile industry based in the Export Processing Zone (EPZ) located outside central Port-Louis was responsible for the economy's take off in the 1980s (Hawkins & Holman 1994). This created employment in the country and the EPZ could thus draw upon a cheap yet literate multilingual work force to become one of the leading clothes exporters in the world (Holman 1992). Later on, the EPZ diversified its industry by adding electronics, manufacturing, and production of tea, tobacco and flowers. Economic recovery in the 1980s and 1990s meant that by the mid-1990s there was negligible unemployment (Hawkins & Holman 1994). Today, reclaimed land in the Port-Louis district has allowed for new developments with a free port, shipping industry, and a waterfront with commercial and business units.

3.2 Current size of population

> *Port-Louis, c'est un bouillon de cultures, c'est un carrefour [. . .] on trouve des gens des quatre coins de Maurice qui viennent travailler ici* [male journalist, early 30s, Port-Louis resident]
>
> Port-Louis is a melting pot, it's a crossroads [. . .] you find people from the four corners of Mauritius who come and work here

Port-Louis is one of two urban districts and the smallest of nine districts on the island of Mauritius, with an area of 43 square kilometres. In the 2011 census, the population of the island of Mauritius was just under 1.2 million, with 41.7% living in urban areas and 58.2% in rural areas. The district of Port-Louis had 10% of the national population with 118,431 inhabitants (Statistics Mauritius 2012a). The other mainly urban district is Plaines Wilhems, which borders Port-Louis and contained 29% of the population in 2011 (362,292 inhabitants) (see Figure 1 for a map of the districts).

Figure 1: Map of districts on the island of Mauritius.[8]

---

[8] https://commons.wikimedia.org/wiki/File:Mauritius_districts_named.png, reprinted under CC licence.

Census data give an indication of how Port-Louis has changed over the years. Although the data do not provide details about specific linguistic developments, they nonetheless provide useful information on demographic, social and linguistic trends (Bissoonauth and Offord 2001; Hookoomsing 1993; Stein 1986). The population of Mauritius grew by 14% between 1972 and 2011 (from 826,166 to 1,196,383 inhabitants), whereas the population of the district of Port-Louis decreased by 6% in the same period. In 1972, Port-Louis housed 16% of the nation's population with 133,996 inhabitants, while in 2011 that proportion had declined to 10% due to migration to neighbouring districts.

The decline in the resident population of Port-Louis has been the result of an expansion of urban commercial development at the expense of residential areas (Statistics Mauritius 2014). The last census data on five-year migration streams to and from each district (Statistics Mauritius 2014) show population movement from Port-Louis to the three bordering districts: Pamplemousses in the north, Black River in the southwest, and particularly Plaines Wilhems to the south, where housing is more affordable. Plaines Wilhems can be considered a suburban offshoot of Port-Louis, and the new Metro Express light rail, launched in October 2019, goes from central Port-Louis through the central length of the district. In 2011, Port-Louis was the district with the highest number of daily commuters (66,798) coming from all over the island of Mauritius (Statistics Mauritius 2014). The relatively small size of Mauritius means that Port-Louis is easily accessible (under an hour drive by car) from all parts of the island.

3.3 Linguistic and ethnic diversity

> *Port-Louis couma ou trouve ou gagne tou banne produits [. . .] li ene bon place pou vive, ou gagne tout accessib, pas bizin alle loin loin [. . .] ene culture* **assez diversifiée** [male lottery seller, 30s, Port-Louis resident]

> You find everything in Port-Louis [. . .] it's a good place to live, everything is accessible, there's no need to go very far [. . .] a fairly diverse culture

> Port-Louis is special because you still have a mix, a blend of the old and the new, of the poor and the rich and so it is a world in itself, not only the rich and the poor, the English and the French, this is all Mauritius [male academic, 50s, works in Port-Louis]

The opening quotations underline the diversity and history of Port-Louis, and illustrate the three key languages for Mauritians – Kreol, French and English. The first also shows code alternation between Kreol and French, with French signalled in bold. Kreol is the home language of the overwhelming majority of Port-Louisians (94.8%), according to the 2011 census data for language usually spoken at home. This is noticeably higher than the figure for the island of Mauritius as a whole (86.1%). A comparison between 1990 and 2000 census data for Port-Louis shows that Kreol is increasingly the main language spoken in the home (82.1% in 1990, 85.4% in 2000), with a similar trend evident for the island as a whole (60.5% and 69.2% respectively), although starting from a much lower base (see Figure 2).

An initial conclusion is that Port-Louis is leading the shift towards Kreol as the first language of the home, and a closer look at the linguistic profiles of other districts supports this. The outlying districts Savanne and Grand Port are the only other districts that show similar rates of Kreol use in the home in 2011 (93.5% and 91.6% respectively). However, unlike in Port-Louis, this is a fairly recent phenomenon in both districts: in the 1990 and 2000 census figures, the percentages of Kreol spoken in the home for Savanne were 63.3% and 78.6% respectively, and for Grand Port 54.2% and 73% (Figure 2).

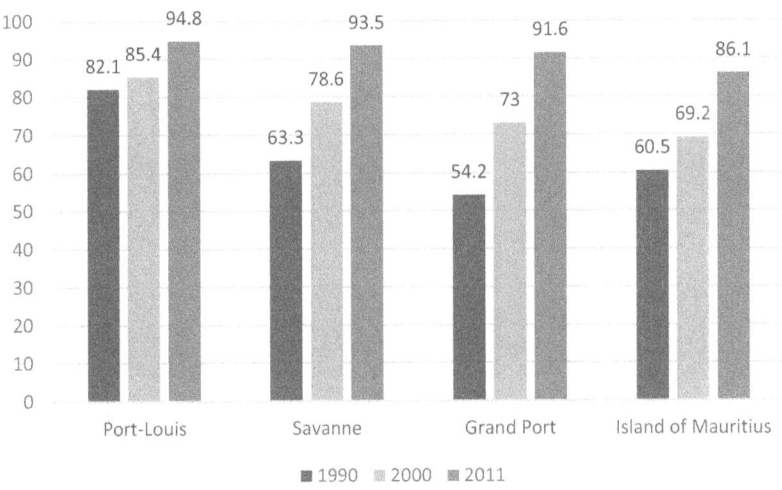

Figure 2: Use of Kreol at home from 1990 to 2011 (Central Statistics Office 1991 and Statistics Mauritius 2012a, single language responses as percentages).

We might expect that French and English, as the languages of government, administration, education and social advancement, would also be significant languages in Port-Louis, given its importance as an outward facing, international port, and its status as the capital. However, language use in the home does not reflect the instrumental value of the two languages. French is the second most common language spoken, albeit at only 1.6%, and English is hardly spoken at all in the home (0.2%). The proportion of French home speakers in Port-Louis has increased very slightly (by 0.6%) over the period from 1990 to 2011 (Figure 3).

The two districts in the 2011 census where French is spoken most in the home are Plaines Wilhems and Black River, at 7.8% and 10.4% respectively. These two districts started from a fairly high base of Kreol speakers in the home in 1990: 71% in Plaines Wilhems and 73.8% in Black River. In 2011 the use of Kreol at home rose to 86.1% and 82.1% respectively. These are also two of the three districts that have seen recent migration from Port-Louis. There has been little change in numbers in Plaines Wilhems from 1990 to 2011, but there has been a significant increase in French spoken at home in Black River (Figure 3). Anecdotal evidence suggests that the rise in French home speakers here is linked to a number of factors, including greater access to education and thus to French, a number of inhabitants for whom French signals social status and being educated in contrast to Kreol, and the increasing attraction of Black River's coast, amenities and new housing developments for wealthier Franco-Mauritians and expats from France. Overall, French has become a marker of Mauritian middle classes (Bissoonauth 2013: 142).

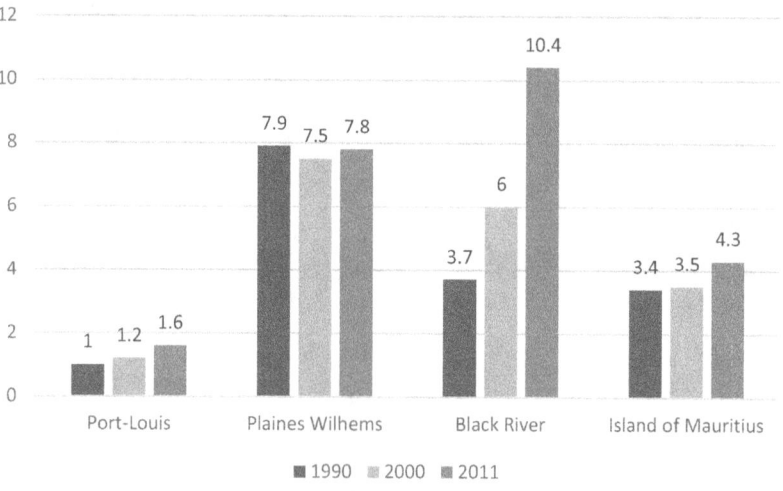

Figure 3: Use of French at home from 1990 to 2011 (Central Statistics Office 1991 and Statistics Mauritius 2012a, single language responses as percentages).

The main language affected by the shift to Kreol at home in Port-Louis has been Bhojpuri, Mauritius' other vernacular language, and its decline in the capital as a home language is nearing completion (0.9% spoke Bhojpuri at home in 2011 compared with 2.5% in 1990). The number of Bhojpuri home speakers in Plaines Wilhems and Black River is also very low (0.7% and 0.9% respectively), but these districts had slightly higher numbers of Bhojpuri home speakers than Port-Louis in 1990 and 2000 (Figure 4). In Grand Port, where, as we saw earlier, there has been a steep increase in Kreol spoken at home, this has also been at the expense of Bhojpuri, and in those rural districts where it has been a significant spoken language, such as Flacq, Bhojpuri is in sharp decline, which is echoed across the whole island (Figure 4). The reporting of other Indian languages in Port-Louis as languages usually spoken in the home is extremely low (0.3%).

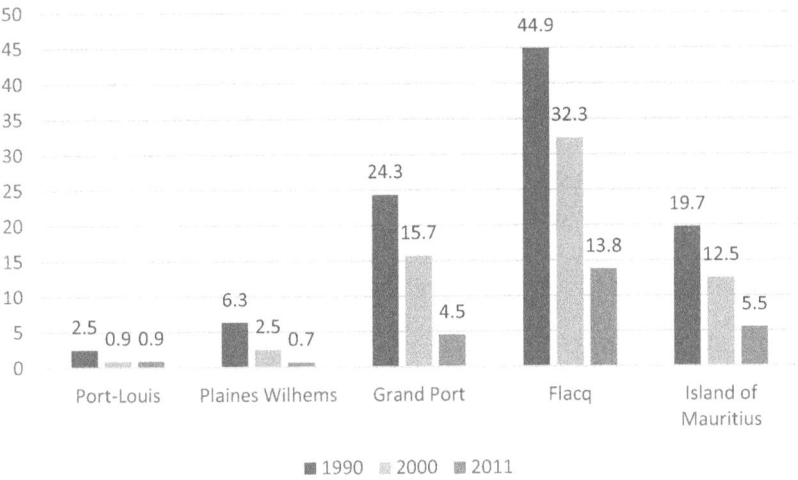

Figure 4: Use of Bhojpuri at home from 1990 to 2011 (Central Statistics Office 1991 and Statistics Mauritius 2012a, single language responses as percentages).

One possible explanation for the dominance of Kreol in Port-Louis homes could lie in the religious affiliations of the capital's inhabitants. In the 2011 census, Port-Louis was the only district in the whole of Mauritius where the majority of inhabitants were Muslim (40.2%), closely followed by those of Christian faith (38.4%), with Hindus in a clear minority (19.7%). The dominance of Muslims and Christians in the capital has been fairly constant in the recent past (in 1990 37.4% and 39.4% respectively), and both groups tend to speak Kreol as the language of daily interactions. The majority of Mauritian Muslims and Hindus are descendants of indentured labourers from north India who came to work on the sugar plantations in the 19th century and spoke Bhojpuri. As Muslims moved from the countryside to the towns where Kreol was the *lingua franca*, they tended to shift from Bhojpuri to Kreol as their home language. As Auleear Owadally (2011: 135–136) sums up: "[h]istorically, Islamic faith and culture and practices have been transmitted mainly through Urdu, the language of prayers has always been Arabic, and the language of everyday communication has shifted from Mauritian Bhojpuri to Creole" (Auleear Owodally 2011: 136). Bhojpuri has instead come to be linked to Hindu identity and Mauritians increasingly view Bhojpuri as a "Hindu language" (Eisenlohr 2004: 59–60), whereas Mauritian Muslims "are much less interested in laying a claim to Bhojpuri and are also less concerned about the language shift to Creole in their community" (Eisenlohr 2004: 61).

Another plausible explanation for the dominance of Kreol could be associated with a lower socioeconomic status. If we make the connection between the use of French and higher status occupations, for example, we might expect that Port-Louis would have a lower percentage of managerial, professional and technical workers than Plaines Wilhems and Black River, the two districts where French is spoken most in the home. It is certainly the case that numbers are lower in Port-Louis than in Plaines Wilhems. 2011 census figures show that in Port-Louis 21.3% (9,927/46,657) of workers are in higher status occupations, compared with 31.9% (50,812/159,205) in Plaines Wilhems. However, in Black River the percentage is only 18.9% (6,826/36,023), perhaps reflecting the more recent increase in French being the most spoken home language. Plaines Wilhems stands out as the only district with a large proportion of higher status workers, and Port-Louis sits at the higher end of the other districts, which range between 15.8% and 22% (Statistics Mauritius 2012b).

3.4 Multilingualism in everyday life: Younger generations

Pour être mauricien, c'est un peu c'est une fierté parce que on peut savoir sur la religion des autres comment on fête **how do we celebrate these things and we will also know how does the ancestors of us celebrate these, it's beautiful**' [Port-Louis student, female, 12 years old]

Being Mauritian it's a bit it's a matter of pride because you can learn about other people's religion, how we celebrate how we celebrate these things and we will also know how our ancestors celebrate them, it's beautiful

Pou moi etre morisien c'est pluto etre ene **citoyen multiculturel** *[. . .] moi pli banne langage mo konne, pli banne cultures mo konne, li ene* **plus** *pou moi. La cause sa meme mo bien content mo morisien, sa* **c'est un plus** *pou moi* [Port-Louis student, male, 14 years old]

For me being Mauritian it's more being a multicultural citizen [. . .] for me the more languages I know, the more cultures I know, it's a plus for me. That's why I am very happy that I am a Mauritian, that's a plus for me

The two quotations that open this section are from Port-Louis secondary school students. They are part of a set of student interviews undertaken by the first-named author in 2018 across Mauritius. The bold type indicates code alternation – between French and English in the first quotation and between Kreol and French in the second. This "back and forth movement between languages" (Auckle & Barnes 2011: 109) is the norm in multilingual and diglossic societies like Mauritius. Both utterances are typical of what Kriegel et al. (2019) call urban alternation in Mauritius, in which educated speakers alternate between Kreol, French and English.[9] They provide a sharp contrast with the predominantly monolingual portrait of Port-Louisians that has emerged from the census data analysis, at least as regards language usually spoken in the home. However, this is a rather reductive portrait of Port-Louisians' lived experience of language in their everyday lives, both within the intimate environment of the home and in more formal domains such as work, education and government.

The focus of this section is on education and the multilingualism of younger generations in Port-Louis, who are potentially at the forefront of change. School in Mauritius "plays an important role in social dynamics as it gives weight to the three "supracommunity" languages (Creole, French, English) to the detriment of Indian and Chinese languages" (Bissoonauth 2013: 149). Although English is officially the medium of instruction from the fourth year of primary school, there is a common tendency among teachers to revert to French and Kreol to aid and facilitate comprehension (Bissoonauth 2011; Ludwig et al. 2009; Sonck 2005).[10] At secondary level, informal conversation with teachers highlighted that they would use a mixture of English and French with Kreol to a lesser extent in their non-language classes. The use of Kreol, as a language of instruction, has also been found to be linked with pupils having a lower ability in English and French (Bissoonauth 1998: 272). For students, this learning context means that they "generally ask questions to the teacher in French but in Kreol to their classmates and answer examination questions in English" (Rajah-Carrim 2007: 54).

Alongside the predominantly trilingual nature of teaching and learning, English and French are also taught as school subjects throughout the primary and

---

9 In rural areas where the majority of the population is of Indian descent, Bhojpuri speakers alternate between Kreol and Bhojpuri, and with English and French to a lesser extent. Kriegel et al. (2019: 185) propose a continuum of "code hybridization", ranging from balanced alternation between languages to strict integration of an embedded element or copy in the dominant language.
10 The 1957 Education Ordinance recommended that in the first three years of primary education, any language deemed suitable by the minister may be used as a language of instruction (Stein 1982: 119).

secondary curricula, as the majority of children will have had little or no exposure to the two languages before starting primary school. Their linguistic repertoires are further expanded by the option of studying an Asian heritage language (Hindi, Marathi, Tamil, Mandarin, Urdu or Arabic), offered where there is demand from primary level.[11] As noted above, since 2012 Kreol has also been offered as a school subject in primary schools, albeit only where there is a minimum enrolment of five students and it is taught as another optional heritage language alongside Asian languages.[12] In 2018, Kreol as an optional subject was introduced in the first year of secondary education (year 7) with plans to continue its introduction to year 10 (Bissoonauth 2021).[13]

Figure 5 shows that Kreol is the only ancestral language with a marked increase in overall primary school enrolments from 2013 to 2019, both in Port-Louis and in the rest of Mauritius (MEHR n.d.). As we might expect, Port-Louis has a higher uptake of Kreol and Arabic, and it also has a small but steady demand for standard Mandarin. The capital has been a key area for the Chinese background community in Mauritius. In the 1972 census, 9.5% of the district's population identified as Sino-Mauritian – by far the highest percentage across the country, and it is where the country's Chinatown is located. The majority of the Sino-Mauritian population in Mauritius has shifted from a range of ancestral Chinese languages (Hokkien, Hakka, Cantonese) to Kreol, French and to some extent English as home language (Lefort 2019: 5). However, with the growing international influence of China, more young people have started to learn standard Mandarin (Lefort 2019).

At secondary school, although students have the option to study an ancestral language, it is generally recognised that fewer take up the opportunity, preferring the options of IT and English or French literature (Bissoonauth 2011). While there are no official figures publicly available on uptake of ancestral languages at secondary level, it is possible to explore how secondary students in Port-Louis use language generally in the public space of the school. The following analysis is based on data from a 2018 research project undertaken by the first-named author that investigates language use and attitudes among Mauritian secondary students.

---

[11] One important political decision from the 1980s was the official recognition and promotion of the multilingual character of Mauritian society in education by successive governments (Miles 2000; Tirvassen & Ramasawmy 2017). The master plan for education elaborated by the Ministry of Education in 1991 for 2000 highlighted the value of heritage languages as a means to preserve the ancestral languages, encourage links with one's cultural roots and appreciate other languages (MEAC 1991: 35).
[12] Bhojpuri was also introduced at primary school level in 2012, but only as an optional element in some Hindi language classes (MEHR 2014).
[13] The official standardised orthography for the Creole language (Grafi-larmoni) was devised by linguists at the University of Mauritius in collaboration with the Mauritius Institute of Education.

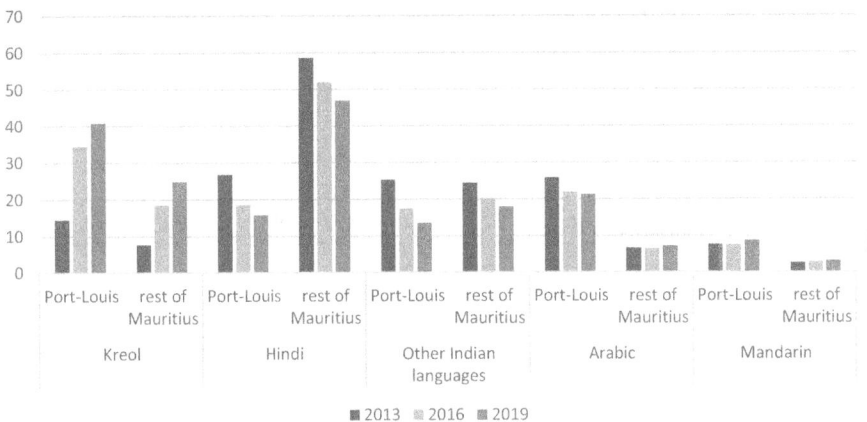

Figure 5: Ancestral languages studied at primary school as a percentage of all languages studied, Port-Louis and rest of Mauritius, 2013, 2016, 2019 (MEHR n.d.).

Initial reporting on this project, focusing on language use at home (Bissoonauth 2021), showed among other findings that Kreol was most often spoken with all family members (37%), followed by a trilingual combination of English, French and Kreol (32%), and then bilingual English and French (8%). Young multilingual Mauritians of various backgrounds increasingly accept Kreol "as the mother tongue of Mauritians as well as a symbol of Mauritian national identity" (Bissoonauth 2021: 75). They also show a positive attitude shift towards Kreol as a subject in school and as a medium of instruction compared with results from the previous two decades.

Twelve secondary schools were involved in the study, two of which were in Port-Louis – a boys' state secondary school and a private girls' Catholic confessional school. They provide a contrast, both as regards gender and also in terms of religious ethos. They both welcome students from different ethnic and religious backgrounds, but at the girls' school the majority are Catholic. Forty-five students completed a questionnaire on language use and attitudes, and 12 took part in an interview (see Bissoonauth 2021 for data collection methods).

By looking at the languages Port-Louis students report using with their friends at school and at home, it is possible to form a basic idea of their levels of multilingualism. When speaking with friends at school, there is a striking difference between the two schools/genders, with the girls more likely to report using three languages (43.5%, 10 of 23), and the boys more likely to use a single language (54.5%, 12 of 22). About a quarter of both groups report using two languages, and around one in ten students (9.1%, 5 of 55) use four or even five languages. Table 2 gives details on the languages used – the languages are presented in alphabetical order, not in order of preference or frequency of use. The boys show a marked preference for Kreol only, and the girls a modest preference for English, French and Kreol (39.1%, 9 of 23).

Table 2: Languages used when speaking with friends at school (N = 45).

	English	French	Kreol	FK	EFK	FKM	EFHK	EFHKU	BEFHK	Total
Girls	0	3	1	6	9	1	1	1	1	23
Boys	0	0	12	5	3	0	1	0	1	22
Total	0	3	13	11	12	1	2	1	2	45

B = Bhojpuri, E = English, F = French, H = Hindi, K = Kreol, M = Mandarin, U = Urdu.

This difference between the female and male students could be influenced by the school environment. It has been observed that "[i]n state schools, the language of the school-grounds is Kreol (especially in secondary schools) and/or French (especially in primary schools)" (Rajah-Carrim 2007: 54). The boys' more frequent reported use of Kreol with friends fits with this observation. It is also the case that the majority of boys in the sample from the Port-Louis state school came from outside the district, drawn by the prestige of the institution, which could be a factor in creating a school ethos in which Kreol dominates among peers. In the girls' reported usage, in contrast, French is much more present. This dominance of French in the Catholic school context can in part be explained by the status French has had as the language of the Roman Catholic church, reinforcing French-Kreol diglossia within the institution (see Auleear Owodally 2016).

However, if we look at language used with friends outside school in the home context, the contrast between boys and girls remains, although at a reduced level (Table 3). The girls continue to use more bilingual (38%, 8 of 21) and trilingual (38%, 8 of 21) combinations with European languages, whereas the boys tend to favour Kreol only (40%, 8 of 20).

Table 3: Languages used when speaking with friends at home (N = 41).

	English	French	Kreol	FK	EF	BK	EFK	FKM	EFHK	Total
Girls	0	1	4	7	1	0	7	1	0	21
Boys	0	0	8	5	0	1	4	0	2	20
Total	0	1	12	12	1	1	11	1	2	41

B = Bhojpuri, E = English, F = French, H = Hindi, K = Kreol, M = Mandarin.

The multilingual language combinations also include English and French, which is reflective of the Mauritian context. Overall, the data highlight the everyday multilingualism of young Mauritians when interacting with their peers.

4 Conclusion

The aim of this chapter was to explore whether and how multilingualism in Port-Louis differs from that in the rest of Mauritius. We have shown that in some respects language use in Port-Louis is distinct, whereas in other areas, similar patterns are evident across the country.

In response to the first research question regarding the ways in which linguistic and ethnic diversity has evolved in Mauritius and Port-Louis, census data have shown that Port-Louis differs from the rest of the island of Mauritius in two main, interconnected ways. It is the capital that is leading the shift towards Kreol as the first language of the home, with nearly 95% of the population choosing it as the language usually or most often spoken. This means that a language shift from Indian heritage languages seems irreversible in the capital, with other districts following close behind. We argue that the dominance of Kreol is in part linked to Port-Louis being the only district with a majority of inhabitants identifying as Muslim, for whom Kreol is the language of choice.

French and English are not significant home languages in the capital, in partial contrast to other districts such as Plaines Wilhems and Black River where French is more common. Overall, French and English in the capital remain very much languages of public spaces such as government, administration, education and international trade. French has been identified as the language of Mauritian middle classes, and a very small percentage of Port-Louisians predominantly speak French at home. We have seen that the proportion of Port-Louisians who work in higher status occupations is not significantly higher or lower than most of the other districts, apart from Plaines Wilhems. Could one explanation be that Port-Louis residents do not need to use French as a status marker because they have the status of living in the capital, in contrast to outlying areas? At this stage, such a hypothesis would require further research.

As seen earlier in the chapter, the language situation in Port-Louis and Mauritius is complex and constantly evolving. Language shift from Kreol to French occurs particularly in educated sections of the population. French is almost the "natural choice" for Mauritians because it is genetically linked to Kreol and it is easier to speak and understand than English. In addition, France is very present in the country and in the Indian Ocean for geopolitical reasons. It may well be that the next shift in Port-Louis would be from Kreol to French as the population becomes more educated. The 2022 Mauritian census would confirm, or contradict, the current trends in home language use in Port-Louis identified here.

To answer the second research question on current patterns of language use in the capital, our focus has been on the younger generations and language use in the educational domain. Kreol has been an optional language at primary school since 2012, and pupils in Port-Louis in particular, but also elsewhere, are increasingly taking up the opportunity to study the language, as seen from primary school language enrolments. Arabic and Mandarin are holding steady, with greater uptake in Port-Louis than in the rest of the island of Mauritius, due to the capital's particular demographics.

At secondary school, students operate in a primarily trilingual teaching and learning space – English, French and Kreol. In the two Port-Louis schools examined, French and Kreol dominate when students speak with friends, but there is a clear difference between male and female students. The boys in the study tend to favour Kreol and the girls tend to favour French, particularly in combination with Kreol and English. Further research is needed to determine to what extent gender and school culture play a role in the language choices of young people in Port-Louis. In addition, in a few years' time Kreol will have been fully introduced across the first nine years of compulsory schooling. This would be a key moment to undertake further studies of language choices and attitudes among young people in the capital and across the country.

References

Auckle, Tejshree & Lawrie Barnes. 2011. Code-switching, language mixing and fused lects: emerging trends in multilingual Mauritius. *Language Matters* 42(1). 104–125.

Auleear Owodally, Ambarin. M. 2011. Multilingual language and literacy practices and social identities in Sunni madrassahs in Mauritius: a case study. *Reading Research Quarterly* 46(2). 134–155.

Auleear, Owodally, Ambarin. M. 2016. Joseph . . . Yousouf. Changing names, navigating spaces, articulating identities. In Vally Lytra, Dinah Volk & Eve Gregory (eds.), *Navigating languages, literacies and identities: religion in young lives*, 161–175. New York: Routledge.

Baker, Philip. 1969. The language situation in Mauritius with special reference to Mauritian Creole. *African Language Review* 8. 73–97.

Baker, Philip. 1976. Towards a social history of Mauritian Creole. B.Phil thesis, University of York, UK.

Baker, Philip. 1982. The contribution of non-Francophone immigrants to the lexicon of Mauritian Creole. PhD thesis, SOAS University of London.

Biltoo, Anil K. 2004. Language maintenance and language shift in Mauritius: a sociolinguistic investigation into the language practices of Bhojpurias. PhD thesis, University of York, UK.

Bissoonauth, Anu. 1998. Language use, language choice and language attitudes among young Mauritian adolescents in secondary education. PhD thesis, University of Nottingham.

Bissoonauth, Anu. 2011. Language shift and maintenance in multilingual Mauritius: the case of Indian ancestral languages. *Journal of Multilingual and Multicultural Development* 32(5). 421–434.

Bissoonauth, Anu. 2012. Attitudes towards English in Mauritius: linguistic paradox or cultural pragmatism? In Cécile Coquet-Mokoko & Trevor Harris (eds.), *Crafting identities, remapping nationalities: the English-speaking world in the age of globalization*, 87–102. Newcastle upon Tyne: Cambridge Scholars Publishing.

Bissoonauth, Anu. 2013. Une analyse sociolinguistique du code switching chez les adolescents mauriciens de niveau secondaire. In Sibylle Kriegel & Daniel Véronique (eds.), *Contacts de langues, langues en contact*, 139–153. Aix-en-Provence: Presses de l'Université de Provence.

Bissoonauth, Anu. 2014. Language attitudes of Mauritian youth in secondary education: some preliminary results. In Arnaud Carpooran (ed.), *Langues créoles, mondialisation et éducation: Actes du XIIIe colloque du CIEC 2012*, 247–266. Réduit: University of Mauritius.

Bissoonauth, Anu. 2021. Language and attitude shift of young Mauritians in secondary education. *Journal of Multilingual and Multicultural Development* 42(1). 64–78.

Bissoonauth, Anu & Malcolm Offord. 2001. Language use of Mauritian adolescents in education. *Journal of Multilingual and Multicultural Development* 22(5). 381–400.

Boswell, Rosabelle. 2006. *Le malaise créole: ethnic identity in Mauritius*. Oxford/New York: Berghahn.

Burrun, Breejun. 2009. *Port-Louis-Ile Maurice*. Pereybère, Mauritius: Christian le Comte.

Central Statistics Office. 1972. *1972 Housing and population census of Mauritius: Volume V*. http://statsmauritius.govmu.org/English/CensusandSurveys/Documents/Archive%20Census/1972%20Census/Table%20Reports/1972-HPC-Volume%20V%20-%20Population%20General%20Tables%20-%20Island%20of%20Mauritius.pdf (accessed 10 November 2018).

Central Statistics Office. 1991. *1990 Housing and population census of Mauritius. Volume II: demographic and fertility characteristics*. http://statsmauritius.govmu.org/English/CensusandSurveys/Documents/Archive%20Census/1990%20Census/Table%20Reports/1990%20HPC%20Vol.%20II.pdf (accessed 11 November 2018).

Central Statistics Office. 2001. *2000 Housing and population census of Mauritius. Volume II: demographic characteristics*. http://statsmauritius.govmu.org/English/Documents/Demogra/index.htm (accessed 11 November 2018).

Charoux, Clément. n.d. *Le guide illustré de l'île Maurice*. Port-Louis: General Printing and Stationery Co.

Christopher, A. J. 2006. Questions of identity in the millennium round of Commonwealth censuses. *Population Studies* 60(3). 343–352.

Corne, Chris. 1999. *From French to Creole: the development of new vernaculars in the French colonial world*. London: University of Westminster Press.

Eisenlohr, Patrick. 2004. Register levels of ethno-national purity: the ethnicization of language and community in Mauritius. *Language and Society* 33(1). 59–80.

Eisenlohr, Patrick. 2006. *Little India: diaspora, time, and ethnolinguistic belonging in Hindu Mauritius*. Berkeley: University of California Press.

Eisenlohr, Patrick. 2007. Creole publics: language, cultural citizenship, and the spread of the nation in Mauritius. *Comparative Studies in Society and History* 49(4). 968–996.

Eriksen, Thomas. H. 1997. Multiculturalism, individualism and human rights: romanticism, enlightenment and lessons from Mauritius. In Richard Wilson (ed.), *Human rights, culture and context: anthropological perspectives*, 173–181. London: Polity Press.

Eriksen, Thomas. H. 2004. Ethnicity, class and the 1999 Mauritian riots. In Stephen May, Tariq Modood & Judith Squires (eds.), *Ethnicity, nationalism and minority rights*, 78–95. Cambridge: Cambridge University Press.

Eriksen, Thomas. H. 2007. Creolization in anthropological theory and in Mauritius. In Charles Stewart (ed.), *Creolization: history, ethnography, theory*, 153–177. Walnut Creek: Left Coast Press.

Eriksen, Thomas. H. 2018. Language and ethnic hierarchy in Mauritius. In Jacqueline Knörr & Wilson Trajano Filho (eds.), *Creolization and pidginization in contexts of postcolonial diversity*, 59–77. Leiden/Boston: Brill.

Ferguson, Charles. A. 1959. Diglossia. *Word* 15. 325–340.

Fishman, Joshua. A. 1967. Bilingualism with and without diglossia, diglossia with and without bilingualism. *Journal of Social Issues* 23. 29–38.

Gautam, Mohan. 1998. Immigration, settlement and identity formation: the Indians in Mauritius and La Réunion. Paper presented at *Globalization and the southwest Indian Ocean: Mauritius and neighbouring islands*, 21–23 September 1998, Réduit, Mauritius.

Hawkins, Tony & Michael Holman. 27 September 1994. Financial Times survey on Mauritius. *Financial Times*.

Holman, Michael. 14 September 1992. Financial Times survey on Mauritius. *Financial Times*.

Hookoomsing, Vinesh, Y. 1986. Langue et identité ethnique: les langues ancestrales. *Journal of Mauritian Studies*, 1(2). 117–137.

Hookoomsing, Vinesh, Y. 1993. L'île Maurice et ses langues. *Notre Librairie* 114. 26–32.

Hookoomsing, Vinesh, Y. 2009. Mauritius: Creole and/or multicultural? In Vinesh Y. Hookoomsing, Ralph Ludwig & Burkhard Schnepel (eds.), *Multiple identities in action: Mauritius and some Antillean parallelisms*, 19–29. Frankfurt am Main: Peter Lang.

Kriegel, Sibylle, Ralph Ludwig & Tabea Salzmann. 2019. Reflections on discourse ecology and language contact: the crucial role of some scalar terms. In Ralph Ludwig, Peter Mühlhäusler & Steve Pagel (eds.), *Linguistic ecology and language contact*, 179–213. Cambridge: Cambridge University Press.

Lefort, Julie. 2019. Chinese languages spoken in Mauritius: an overview. In Anu Bissoonauth-Bedford & Kumari Issur (eds.), *Lame dan lame? La main dans la main? Hand in Hand?*, 1–22. Réduit: University of Mauritius/Wollongong: University of Wollongong.

Ludwig, Ralph, Fabiola Henri & Florence Bruneau-Ludwig. 2009. Hybridation linguistique et fonctions sociales: aspects des contacts entre créole, français et anglais à Maurice. In Vinesh Hookoomsing, Ralph Ludwig & Burkhart Schnepel (eds.), *Multiple identities in action: Mauritius and some Antillean parallelisms*, 165–202. Frankfurt am Main: Peter Lang.

Mauritian National Assembly. 2016. *The Constitution of the Republic of Mauritius*. https://mauritiusassembly.govmu.org/English/constitution/Pages/constitution2016.pdf (accessed 18 May 2020).

MEAC (Ministry of Education, Arts and Culture). 1991. *Master plan for the year 2000*. Port-Louis: Ministry of Education, Arts and Culture.

MEHR (Ministry of Education and Human Resources). n.d. *Digest of Education Statistics 2013, 2016, 2019*. http://statsmauritius.govmu.org/English/StatsbySubj/Pages/Education.aspx (accessed 23 May 2020).

MEHR (Ministry of Education and Human Resources). 2014. *Education reforms in action 2008–2014*. http://ministry-education.govmu.org/English/downloads/Documents/Education%20Reforms%20in%20Action%202008-2014%20.pdf (accessed 23 May 2020).

Miles, William. F.S. 2000. The politics of language equilibrium in a multilingual society: Mauritius. *Comparative Politics* 32(2). 215–230.

Minogue, Martin. 1992. Mauritius: economic miracle or developmental illusion? *Journal of International Development*, 4(6). 643–647.

Rajah-Carrim, Aaliya. 2005. Language use and attitudes in Mauritius on the basis of the 2000 population census. *Journal of Multilingual and Multicultural Development* 26(4). 317–332.

Rajah-Carrim, Aaliya. 2007. Mauritian Creole and language attitudes in the education system of multiethnic and multilingual Mauritius. *Journal of Multilingual and Multicultural Development* 28(1). 51–71.

Sonck, Gerda. 2005. Language of instruction and instructed languages in Mauritius. *Journal of Multilingual and Multicultural Development* 26(1). 37–51.

Statistics Mauritius. n.d. *Historical series: population census*. http://statsmauritius.govmu.org/English/CensusandSurveys/Pages/census/Census---Series.aspx (accessed 10 November 2018).

Statistics Mauritius. 2012a. *2011 Housing and population census. Volume II: demography and fertility characteristics*. http://statsmauritius.govmu.org/English/CensusandSurveys/Documents/HPC/2011/HPC_TR_Vol2_Demography_Yr11.pdf (accessed 18 November 2018).

Statistics Mauritius. 2012b. *2011 Housing and population census. Volume V: economic characteristics*. http://statsmauritius.govmu.org/English/CensusandSurveys/Documents/HPC/2011/HPC_TR_Vol5_Economic_Yr11.pdf (accessed 18 November 2018).

Statistics Mauritius. 2014. *2011 Housing and population census: analysis report. Volume IV: migration*. https://statsmauritius.govmu.org/Documents/Census_and_Surveys/HPC/2011/HPC_AR_Vol4_Migration_Yr11.pdf (accessed 18 November 2018).

Stein, Peter. 1982. *Connaissance et emploi des langues à l'île Maurice*. Hamburg: Buske.

Stein, Peter. 1986. The value and problems of census data on languages: an evaluation of the language tables from 1983 population census of Mauritius. In Joshua Fishman (ed.), *The Fergusonian impact: in honor of Charles, A. Ferguson. Volume 2: Sociolinguistics and the Sociology of Language*, 265–277. The Hague: Mouton de Gruyter.

Tirvassen, Rada & Shalini Ramasawmy. 2017. Deconstructing and reinventing the concept of multilingualism: a case study of the Mauritian sociolinguistic landscape. *Stellenbosch Papers in Linguistics Plus*, 51(1). 41–59.

Toussaint, Auguste. 1966. *Une cité tropicale: Port-Louis de l'île Maurice*. Paris: Presses universitaires de France.

Toussaint, Auguste. 2014. *Port-Louis: deux siècles d'histoire 1735–1935*. Port-Louis: Vizavi editions.

María Irene Moyna
12 Pluricentricity in Río de la Plata address: Montevideo is alike and a little different

> El sabor de lo oriental
> con estas palabras pinto;
> es el sabor de lo que es
> igual y un poco distinto.[1]
> – J. L. Borges (*Milonga para los orientales*, 1965)

1 Introduction

Río de la Plata Spanish has long been recognised as a dialect area of Latin America, with several phonetic, morphological, and lexical peculiarities resulting from a common history of colonisation and later immigration (Henríquez Ureña 1976, Lipski 1996). Buenos Aires, a massive metropolitan area with over 15 million inhabitants, constitutes its centre, but several cities in the Province of Buenos Aires (La Plata, Mar del Plata, Bahía Blanca) and the Argentine interior along the Paraná and Uruguay rivers (Santa Fe, Rosario) share its main linguistic features (Fontanella de Weinberg 2000; Prevedello 1989; Prevedello et al. 1999; Siracusa 1977; Vidal de Battini 1964). My main focus is on Montevideo, the capital of Uruguay, and as such the only city in the dialectal area not located in Argentina. With a population of 1.3 million inhabitants, it feels the centripetal force of its neighbour across the estu-

---

1 The taste of what is Oriental (~Eastern, i.e., Uruguayan)/I paint with these words:/it is the taste of what is/alike and a little different.

Note: I would like to thank Magdalena Coll, Lindsey Cordery, María Alicia Correa, A. Cruz Cabral (Cruzca), Jorge Hipogrosso, Soraya Ochoviet, and Juan Sader for their assistance in the process of identifying study participants. My most heartfelt thanks go to all those who took time out of their busy lives to share their linguistic intuitions with me. This work was presented in some form at the first meeting of the International Network on Address Research, held at Freie Universität Berlin in June 2013, at the annual conference of the Linguistic Association of the Southwest held in San Diego in September 2014, and at ABRALIN ao Vivo in July 2020. I would like to thank the organisers, and the following colleagues in particular for their valuable comments and suggestions: Víctor Fernández Mallat, John Hajek, Leo Kretzenbacher, Bettina Kluge, Catrin Norrby, María Elena Placencia, Israel Sanz-Sánchez, Horst Simon, Sarah Sinnott, and one anonymous reviewer. The usual disclaimers apply.

https://doi.org/10.1515/9781501511974-013

ary. On the other hand, as the political capital of an independent state, it also exhibits a centrifugal pull fuelled by a distinct national identity.

Montevideo Spanish is virtually undistinguishable from that of Buenos Aires to the lay listener and even to the trained specialist (Lipski 1996: 369), as a result of several geographical and historical factors. Firstly, the two cities are only 200 kilometres apart across the Río de la Plata estuary, making them the closest national capitals in continental Latin America. Moreover, their histories have been intertwined since colonial times. Buenos Aires was founded on the southwestern shore in 1580, as the head of a Captaincy (and later, a Viceroyalty). By contrast, Montevideo was founded on a natural harbour on the north-eastern bank to serve as a military outpost and port, in a deliberate effort to strengthen Spain's claim to the territory and impede the advances of the Portuguese. The original population of the fortified city, which started to arrive in 1724, was made up in part of soldiers and settlers from Buenos Aires, some immigrants from the Canary Islands, Guaraní Indians, and African slaves. The city proved attractive to immigrants both during colonial times (Caetano and Rilla 2005: 27–28) and after independence in 1830 (Goebel 2010).

Today, Montevideo is home to over one third of Uruguay's population of 3.5 million, and is ten times larger than Salto, the country's second largest city (Instituto Nacional de Estadística 2011). This demographic imbalance is the result of several factors. Historically, Uruguay has been a supplier of raw materials for the global economy, so all major roads and railroads converge on Montevideo, out of which commodities are exported (Veiga 2010: 13). Moreover, the centralised political and administrative structure of Uruguay has led to the concentration of resources and population in the capital, which continues to be the undisputed centre of the country. It is the main economic engine and the seat of all three branches of government, most higher education institutions, hospitals, and other service providers.

Just as Montevideo has an outsized social and linguistic influence over other cities in Uruguay, so does Buenos Aires' demographic, economic, and cultural weight dominate the wider Plata region. It looms over its much smaller and younger sister, following a well described pattern of large cities influencing mid-size cities all over Latin America (Lipski 2002). This pull has long been recognised by linguists (Bertolotti 2011) and decried by non-linguists (Kühl de Mones 1981: 48). Even today, almost 200 years after independence from Spain and politically divergent paths, the two cities are in close contact. It is hard to overstate their longstanding and increasing interconnectedness, through cultural products (printed press, movies, television shows, popular music) and travel by air, land, and sea. Especially in the summer months, waves of Argentine tourists arrive in Uruguay, making up over 60% of the total number of visitors, and constituting the mainstay of an economic activity that generates 8.6% of Uruguay's GDP (Ministerio de Turismo 2018). For its part, Buenos Aires is as frequent an attraction to Uruguayans as Montevideo is to Argentines, for short term travel and long-term migration.

2 Background: Address in Río de la Plata Spanish

Linguists have found little to distinguish Buenos Aires from Montevideo Spanish phonetically (but cf. Michnowicz and Planchón 2020), and only recently have they started to focus systematically on other differences, such as lexicon (Coll and Resnik 2018). However, there is one morphological trait that does in fact offer a subtle contrast between the two varieties, namely, their informal address paradigm (Lipski 1996: 194: Fontanella de Weinberg 1999; Carricaburo 2010).

Like all Spanish dialects, Río de la Plata Spanish presents a formal address pronoun, *usted* (U), derived from *Vuestra Merced* 'your mercy', and accompanied by a third person paradigm. In informal address, these dialects diverge quite markedly from the generalised pattern of *tuteo*, i.e., the pronoun *tú* and second person singular verb forms. Instead, Río de la Plata varieties have preserved the pronoun *vos*, linked to the historical and previously formal second person plural, but used today as informal address towards a single interlocutor (Páez Urdaneta 1981), and combined with a verbal paradigm that mixes etymologically singular and plural forms (Fontanella de Weinberg 1976; 1977). Table 1 presents a dialect with informal *tú* (Mexico City), side by side with the Montevideo and Buenos Aires paradigms.

As seen in Table 1, in many respects Montevideo's second person informal forms are comparable to the Buenos Aires norm. However, a slew of studies has shown that the two dialects are not identical (Behares 1981; Bertolotti 2011; Bertolotti and Coll 2003; Elizaincín and Díaz 1979; Elizaincín and Díaz 1981; Lipski 1996; Mendoza 2005; Ricci and Malán de Ricci 1962–1963; 1977; Steffen 2010; Weyers 2009; 2012; 2013a; 2013b). The most important contrasts are found in the pronoun, since Montevideo still exhibits variation between *tú* and *vos* forms in the subject and prepositional object.[2] While this alternation has not been analysed quantitatively until now, the use of *tú* pronouns is typically considered prestigious in Mon-

---

[2] The classic universal nomenclature used in address studies since Brown and Gilman (1960) (T for informal, and V for formal) does not work well with a tripartite system like that of Montevideo. I have kept the initials used in the coding for the study, which were based on the most straightforward abbreviations, i.e., the first letter of each form. Both T and V stand for informal forms (T1 and T2), and U stands for a formal form (V), which was tangential to the study. This

Table 1: Informal second person paradigms in Buenos Aires and Montevideo, contrasted against standard *tú* (Mexico City).

Tense/mood	Mexico City	Montevideo	Buenos Aires
Pronouns			
Subject	tú	vos/tú	vos
Possessive pronoun	tu, tuyo	tu, tuyo	tu, tuyo
Object (accusative/dative)	te	te	te
Object of preposition	(a) ti	(a) vos/ti	(a) vos
Object of *con* 'with'	contigo	contigo/con vos	con vos
Verbs			
Imperative	toma	tomá	tomá
Present indicative	tomas	tomás	tomás
Pres. Subjunctive (subordinate)	tomes	tomes	tomes
Pres. Subjunctive (negative command)	tomes	tomes (tomés)	tomes (tomés)
Preterite	tomaste	tomaste(s)	tomaste(s)

tevideo (Bertolotti 2011). This may be connected to sociohistorical factors, which are hard to trace, given the dearth of informal address in historical documents. However, a quantitative historical study based on plays (Moyna and Ceballos 2008) showed that the early 20th century upper classes were represented as *tú* users, in particular the older women, while their younger counterparts showed increased preference for the formerly rural *vos*.

When it comes to the verbal manifestations of the informal paradigm, Buenos Aires and Montevideo are virtually indistinguishable. For example, both varieties employ stress-final verb forms in the imperative and present indicative, a feature of the *vos* paradigm (*hablás* vs. *hablas* 'you talk$_{V/T}$') that is virtually categorical in the two capital cities, and thus, represents the prestige norm of the region. Both dialects also exhibit vernacular *vos* features in the present subjunctive and preterite, but those require some clarification.

In Spanish, subjunctive forms have various pragmatic forces. In subordinate clauses, the subjunctive present expresses modalities such as uncertainty (e.g., *No creo que puedas* 'I don't think you'll be able to'). In negative commands, the subjunctive covers a range of prohibitions. For example, it can be a cessative, i.e., intended to stop an ongoing activity *(¡No cantes!* 'Stop singing!'). Alter-

---

language-specific nomenclature combines the advantages of being standard in Spanish studies, and providing the most straightforward way to retrieve full forms from initials. Since this study focuses entirely on informal forms, T/V should only be interpreted as the alternation between these two.

natively, it can be a preventive, when the negative command is intended to stop an activity that has not started (*¡No cantes!* 'Don't start singing!'). In some Río de la Plata varieties, these distinctions can be made explicit through the use of *tú* or *vos* forms. *Tú* subjunctive forms are almost categorical in subordinate clauses, while negative commands exhibit variation between *tú* and *vos* verbal forms. In cessative commands, *vos* frequency is higher, while in preventive commands it is lower (Fontanella de Weinberg 1979; Johnson and Grinstead 2011; Johnson 2016). Even then, there are some differences between Buenos Aires and Montevideo varieties, since *vos* subjunctives are more marked in the latter, and have been described as highly impolite and circumscribed to the lowest social groups (Behares 1981: 37).

The preterite exhibits a different kind of alternation, where the distinction between *vos* and *tú* forms lies not in the stress pattern, but in the presence or absence of a final *–s* (*tomaste* 'you drank$_T$' vs. *tomastes* 'id.$_V$') The direct link between this final segment and *vos* conjugation is controvertible, however, since it appears in many non-standard popular varieties of Spanish that do not employ *vos* (cf. Lapesa 1981: 470). In Montevideo Spanish previous studies have also shown the final *-s* is more acceptable among lower middle-class males (Elizaincín and Díaz 1979). In fact, the presence of the final *–s* may be attributable to hypercorrection in any dialect with syllable-final /s/ aspiration and/or to analogic pressure from the rest of the second person verbal paradigm, which is *-s* final (cf. *hablas, hablabas, hablarías* 'you talk-PRES, -IMPERF, -COND.').

A final difference between both dialects is that Montevideo speakers can match pronoun and verb forms in combinations that are not possible in Buenos Aires address, namely, a *tú-vos* hybrid (*tú tenés* 'you$_T$ have$_V$') (Lipski 1996: 373–374). The prestige variety of Montevideo Spanish exhibits frequent TV hybridisation (Bertolotti 2011), a qualitative observation that has been corroborated through matched guise tests (Moyna and Loureiro-Rodríguez 2017).

This study aims to provide fresh quantitative data on *vos/tú* paradigm variation in Montevideo. In particular, it aims to answer the following research questions:
(1) Is there variation in the use of informal address in Montevideo?
(2) If so, what are the social factors that influence this variation?
(3) To what extent are Buenos Aires models being favoured or disfavoured in Montevideo?

We now turn to the methodology employed in data collection and analysis.

3 Methodology

3.1 Questionnaire

The data comes from a large-scale survey carried out between July and August of 2012, partial results of which have been presented before (Moyna 2017; 2019; 2020). A paper version was distributed in several educational institutions and a digital version was disseminated online through *Survey Monkey*. The survey included a sociolinguistic section followed by questions on second person usage. In all, the questionnaire was answered by 579 respondents, 367 of whom were from Montevideo, and are thus the focus of the study.

3.2 Demographic questions

The purpose of the first section of the questionnaire was to ascertain the socio-educational variables of participants (age, gender, provenance, socioeconomic class, and education). Age was divided into five categories (18–30; 31–40; 41–50; 51–60; 61 or more), later consolidated into three (Age 1: 18–30; Age 2: 31–50; Age 3: 51 or older). Only two genders (Male and Female) were presented to the subjects; this binary choice was considered less confusing than alternatives. As it turns out, nobody left this question unanswered.

If a respondent chose Montevideo as their place of birth and longest residence, then they were included in the study. Also included were participants who had moved to Montevideo before the age of 18. Highly mobile respondents, who were not numerous, were only included if their place of longest residence was Montevideo. Respondents who had spent part of their lives in foreign countries were included if they had not been in long-term contact with other Spanish varieties abroad.

Finally, speaker social status was ascertained through four separate measures, two educational (schooling, educational attainment), and two occupational (employment, income). The first educational variable measured the type of schooling attended before college. Three categories were defined: Elite/Mostly Elite for participants who had attended prestigious schools and high schools; Private/Mostly Private, for those who had attended local parochial private schools; and Public/Mostly Public for those who had attended mostly state-run primary and secondary institutions. Final educational attainment was divided into three levels, namely, Secondary, for those who had attended secondary school or less; Technical, for those who had completed a post-secondary degree in a specialised trade; and University, for those who had completed a college degree.

The occupational measure of employment was divided into a Level 1, for service industry jobs, such as store clerk, cook, police officer, and domestic or industrial worker, and Level 2, which included teachers, doctors, and other professionals. The main criterion for the distinction was the centrality of writing to the job. Finally, income levels were grouped into three, including Low Income (monthly income under $20,000 Uruguayan pesos ~ $740 US dollars), Middle Income (between $U20,000 and $U50,000 ~ US$740 – US$1,850), and High Income (higher than $U50,000 ~ US$1,850). The middle group contained the mean national household income as measured in the last Census ($40,000 Uruguayan pesos) (Instituto Nacional de Estadística 2014), and the sample was spread approximately evenly among the three levels. The sample was better educated than the Montevideo average, and had more representation from the middle and upper middle classes, a consequence of the data collection instrument used.

A summary of all the factor groups considered in this study appears in Table 2.

Table 2: Summary of factors and factor groups considered in the study.

Factor group	Factors
Age	Age 1: 18–30
	Age 2: 31–50
	Age 3: 51+
Gender	Male
	Female
Income	Low: under $ U 20,000 a month
	Mid: $ U 20,000 – $ U 50,000 a month
	High: over $ U 50,000 a month
Occupation	Type 1: Professional
	Type 2: Non-Professional
Schooling	Public
	Private
	Elite
Educational Attainment	Secondary School (or less)
	Technical School
	University

3.3 Address usage questions

The main part of the questionnaire was made up of 34 questions worded as hypothetical situations, where participants were given options to choose what they would say. Twenty items represented the intimate and familiar relations where informal usage was expected, and are the only ones relevant for this study. The questions were paired, so that each situation was presented with a hypothetical male and a female addressee.

Six items focused on pronouns, including all the forms on Table 1: two were nominative, two prepositional (following *para* 'for'), and two comitative (following *con* 'with'). The latter form was singled out because it has retained a synthetic construction in the *tú* paradigm (*contigo*) which makes it quite distinct. For the verbs, two questions focused on the present indicative, two on the imperative, two on the preterite, and six on the present subjunctive. The latter were divided according to semantics: in two the verb appeared in subordinate contexts, in four it was a prohibition. These prohibitions were further subdivided following the distinction found in previous studies: two were preventive prohibitions (i.e., before the fact: *¡No comas!* 'Don't start to eat!') and two were cessative prohibitions (i.e. after the fact: *¡No comas!* 'Stop eating!').

Possible answers included a *vos* form, a *tú* form, and an *usted* variant. The last option in the questionnaire was always open, so that participants who felt that none of the responses reflected what they would say could fill in their own. Participants were given the option of choosing up to two forms they might use. To calculate the frequency of each form, all answers were added up. In the tabulation, *tú* forms were coded as T, *vos* forms as V, and *usted* forms as U. If a participant chose two possible categories, those answers were coded as mixed, and identified with the specific combination selected (i.e., T, V; T, U; V, U), as the most faithful representation of the degree to which respondents were aware of individual variability in address usage.

Filled-in answers were considered equivalent to the response that employed the same address category. Thus, for example, if the answer provided was *Andá al médico* 'Go$_V$ to the doctor,' it was coded as V, like the original choice *Yo que vos hablaría con el médico* 'If I were you$_V$, I'd talk to the doctor.' Naturally, a subset of the filled-in categories could not be used, either because they did not contain a second person form (e.g., *Yo hablaría con el médico* 'I'd talk to the doctor') or because they employed a form homomorphous between *vos* and *tú* (e.g., *Papá, ¿cuándo vas a ir al médico?* 'Dad, when are$_{V/T}$ you going to go to the doctor?'). An additional problem with the interpretation of filled-in verbal responses might have been the failure of some respondents to use written stress marks, especially when typing on the online questionnaire. For example, in *¿Por qué no consultas* *con el médico?* 'Why don't you consult with the doctor?' the verb *consultas* might have been a correctly spelled T form, or a V form missing its stress mark (*consultás*). These issues, coupled with the fact that some participants skipped questions, led to varying numbers of total usable responses per question.

3.4 Statistical analysis

The primary statistical analysis was multiple logistic regression in Rbrul (Johnson 2009). This program was chosen because it provides a bridge between standard statistical packages and outputs familiar to sociolinguistics (Tagliamonte 2012: 138), in addition to being open access and relatively easy to use. Rbrul provides several types of information to ascertain variation in address preference: the statistical significance of factor groups (independent variables), the ratio of the variant of interest to the total number of tokens (percent rate), the relative strength of a factor (factor weight, or FW), and which of the factors in the group favour or disfavour a particular form (logodds). In Rbrul, a factor weight over 0.5 favours the application value, while one under 0.5 disfavours it; factor weights around 0.5 are considered neutral. Statistical significance was set at $p \leq 0.01$; p-values between 0.01 and 0.05 were considered to be weakly significant, and are discussed where appropriate.[3]

3.5 Limitations of the study

The use of a questionnaire on reported usage poses some interpretive issues, especially with stigmatised vernacular forms that participants may be unwilling to acknowledge using. Other studies of address in Latin America have employed a variety of techniques in order to capture more spontaneous usage, such as oral elicitation based on hypothetical situations (Newall 2007, Baumel-Schreffler 1995), recordings of authentic speech (Moser 2003, 2008), a combination of authentic spoken and literary sources (Behares 1981), responses to linguistic atlas interviews (Mendoza 2005), and various kinds of semi-structured activities (Fontanella

---

[3] In choosing p values ≤ 0.01 to establish significance, I am taking an unusually stringent approach for the social sciences. However, it is demonstrably superior as a way to increase certainty in the findings and to avoid the replication crisis currently affecting many statistically-based fields. The only downside of choosing $p \leq 0.01$ is the increased chance of a Type II error (i.e., missing a significant correlation). However, so many solid correlations were found in this study that it is a risk much preferrable to its opposite, i.e., obtaining technically significant but shaky results (Patrick Bolger, personal communication).

de Weinberg 1979). However, the questionnaire format also offers many advantages and has been used in *voseo* studies profitably before (Rona 1967; Johnson 2016, to name just a few). First, it is a fast and economical way to reach a large number of respondents in a short time. Second, once responses are collected, they can be compared across respondents. Third, the survey allows for a controlled presentation of linguistic and pragmatic contexts. This is important when attempting to systematically compare forms such as the present subjunctive, which are infrequent and/or polysemic.

That said, it must be borne in mind that for some speakers of the older generation, it still holds true that spoken and written media call for different informal address choices. That may have resulted in higher reporting of *tú* forms in the questionnaire than would have obtained from an oral elicitation task. Additionally, written questionnaires are not an effective way to obtain data from working class respondents, for whom the experience of metalinguistic reflection and writing more generally may be alien. For that reason, no concerted effort was made to reach those populations specifically, and the sample essentially represents middle class usage. With that in mind, let us now turn to the main quantitative results of the study, including the overall address forms selected, and the independent variables that operated in the selection process.

4 Findings

4.1 Overall use of address forms by verb tense/mood

A simple cross-tabulation was performed to ascertain the address choices for each form (Table 3). The first observation is that in the informal relationships represented in the hypothetical situations, the use of *usted*, either exclusively or as an alternative, is vanishingly small, confirming our original assumption. To compare *vos/tú* usage, each form was considered separately to ascertain patterns of preference. In the pronouns, the nominative and prepositional cases exhibited a marked preference for *vos* forms (84% and 68%, respectively), while in the comitative, Montevideo speakers favoured *tú* (83.5%). In the verbs, the imperative and the present indicative exhibited a preference for *vos* forms (at 93% and 93.2%, respectively). On the other hand, the preterite favoured *tú* by a similar margin (92.7%), as did the subjunctive (90.2% overall). Finally, the semantics of the present subjunctive affected address choice, as predicted, with higher *vos* form frequency in prohibitions (cessative 13.5%, preventive 9.4%) and lower frequency in subordinate clauses (2.9%).

Table 3: Overall totals and percentages of address usage by morphological form.

	Vos Form (%)	Tú Form (%)	Informal (V+T) (%)	Usted Form (%)	Formal/ Informal (U+V/T) (%)	Total (%)
Pronouns						
Nominative	587 (84)	89 (12.7)	22 (3.1)	0 (0)	1 (0.1)	699 (100)
Prepositional	485 (68)	175 (24.6)	49 (6.9)	3 (0.4)	1 (0.1)	713 (100)
Comitative	66 (9.2)	598 (83.5)	66 (9.2)	0 (0)	0 (0)	716 (100)
Verbs						
Imperative	613 (93)	36 (5.5)	5 (0.8)	3 (0.5)	2 (0.3)	659 (100)
Pres. Indicative	599 (93.2)	37 (5.8)	4 (0.6)	2 (0.3)	1 (0.2)	643 (100)
Preterite	36 (5.7)	587 (92.7)	6 (0.9)	2 (0.3)	2 (0.3)	633 (100)
Pres. Subjunctive (Subordinate)	19 (2.9)	629 (95.9)	5 (0.8)	2 (0.3)	1 (0.2)	656 (100)
Pres. Subjunctive (Preventive)	62 (9.4)	589 (89.1)	9 (1.4)	1 (0.2)	0 (0)	661 (100)
Pres. Subjunctive (Cessative)	78 (13.5)	491 (85)	8 (1.5)	0 (0)	0 (0)	577 (100)

4.2 Rbrul analysis of address variation

Rbrul determined the independent variables with a statistically significant effect on each factor considered in binary opposition to all other responses (i.e., *vos* forms vs others; *tú* forms vs. others). Due to its small overall frequency, *usted* was not considered separately; responses that selected it and another form (either *tú* or *vos*) were counted under the latter. Responses that included both informal options (*tú* and *vos*) were counted in both tallies. Consecutive one-level logistic regression Rbrul runs were performed on the nominative, prepositional, and comitative pronominal cases, and on the imperative, present indicative, preterite, and present subjunctive verbal conjugations. The semantic values of the present subjunctive (subordinate vs. preventive vs. cessative) were included as an additional independent variable. The statistically significant factors in address selection are presented separately, starting with the pronouns and followed by the verbs.

4.2.1 Nominative pronoun

For the nominative, the informal expression *yo que vos* 'if I were you' offered the perfect context to guarantee the presence of the pronoun, with no accompanying verb to skew responses. Rbrul selected age as the only relevant predictor (Table 4). *Vos* was favoured markedly by the youngest age group (Age 1), and more moderately by the middle-aged respondents (Age 2), while it was disfavoured by the oldest participants (Age 3). That is, although *vos* forms were the most frequent across all ages, in the younger groups (50 and under) this preference exceeded 90% (Age 1 = 97.7%; Age 2 = 91.2%), while for the older participants it went down to 68.2%. The use of *tú* in the same position practically mirrored *vos*. Here, it was the oldest speakers who favoured *tú*, while the two younger groups disfavoured it. In fact, the frequency of *tú* for Age 3 speakers was ten and three times higher than for Age 1 and Age 2, respectively.

Table 4: Summary of multivariate analysis for the factor Age for nominative pronouns (N.B.: Age 1: 18–30; Age 2: 31–50; Age 3: 51 and over).

Speaker Age *Vos*	FW[4]	%	N	Speaker Age *Tú*	FW	%	N
Age 1	0.825	97.7	216	Age 3	0.811	35.8	148
Age 2	0.521	91.2	274	Age 2	0.491	12.4	274
Age 3	0.164	68.2	148	Age 1	0.194	3.7	216
$p = 1.2\,e\text{-}16$ (***)[5]				$p = 1.27e\text{-}16$ (***)			

4.2.2 Prepositional pronoun

Like for the nominative pronoun, age was the most statistically significant factor in determining address use in the prepositional case (represented in the question item by the sequence *para* 'for' + pronoun) (Table 5). The pattern of preference was also similar. Again, while all speakers were more likely to select *vos* forms, this choice was favoured in the two younger age groups (50 or younger), who selected *vos* at rates higher than 80%. By contrast, it was disfavoured by those older than 50, who selected *vos* only 55.8% of the time. *Tú* forms ([para] *ti*) reversed this

---

[4] In all tables, FW = Factor Weight.
[5] Following standard practice in statistics, significance is indicated through asterisks: (*) $p < 0.05$; (**) $p < 0.01$; (***) $p < 0.001$.

pattern, with the two younger groups disfavouring their selection, and thus contrasting with the older speakers.

Table 5: Summary of multivariate analysis for the factor Age for prepositional pronouns (N.B.: Age 1: 18–30; Age 2: 31–50; Age 3: 51 and over).

Speaker Age *Vos*	FW	%	N	Speaker Age *Tú*	FW	%	N
Age 1	0.659	85.2	216	Age 3	0.712	50.6	154
Age 2	0.596	81.9	281	Age 2	0.465	28.1	281
Age 3	0.26	55.8	154	Age 1	0.317	18.1	216
p = 4.47e-12 (***)				p = 3.78e-11 (***)			

One of the social variables, income level, also reached strong significance as a factor in the selection of *vos* forms, and one was weakly significant (0.01 < p < 0.05) in *tú* form selection for the pronominal case (Table 6). Although all income groups selected *vos* over *tú* forms more than half the time, *vos* forms were relatively favoured in the two lower income levels, and disfavoured among speakers of the highest income group. Inversely, *tú* form selection was disfavoured by the low- and mid-income levels, and favoured by the high-income group.

Table 6: Summary of multivariate analysis for the factor Income for prepositional pronouns.

Income *Vos*	FW	%	N	Income *Tú*	FW	%	N
Mid	0.659	85.2	413	High	0.627	44.2	95
Low	0.596	81.9	143	Mid	0.468	29.8	413
High	0.26	55.8	95	Low	0.404	21.7	143
p = 0.00575 (**)				p = 0.0128 (*)			

4.2.3 Comitative pronoun

The comitative items differ significantly from the nominal and prepositional cases in that across all factors the *tú* form (*contigo*) was preferred, rather than the *vos* form (*con vos*). However, the rates and likelihood of this preference were not uniform: Rbrul selected age and gender as the two individual factors determining choice. Starting with age, the oldest participants favoured *tú* forms and disfavoured *vos* forms, a pattern that was reversed in participants 50 and under, who chose *vos* forms at three times the rate of the oldest speakers (Table 7).

Table 7: Summary of multivariate analysis for the factor Age for comitative pronouns (N.B.: Age 1: 18–30; Age 2: 31–50; Age 3: 51 and over).

Speaker Age Vos	FW	%	N	Speaker Age Tú	FW	%	N
Age 1	0.603	21.2	217	Age 3	0.693	96.2	157
Age 2	0.585	18.9	280	Age 2	0.435	90	280
Age 3	0.318	7.6	157	Age 1	0.365	87.1	217
p = 0.000677 (***)				p = 0.00646 (**)			

Gender was also significant in the choice of comitative forms, with male respondents favouring *vos* forms, and females disfavouring them. In fact, men selected *con vos* at almost twice the rate as women, or one fourth of the time. The reverse was true for the *tú* form (*contigo*): women favoured this choice, and males disfavoured it (Table 8).

Table 8: Summary of multivariate analysis for the factor Gender for comitative pronouns.

Speaker Gender Vos	FW	%	N	Speaker Gender Tú	FW	%	N
Male	0.58	25.1	167	Female	0.597	92.6	487
Female	0.42	14.2	487	Male	0.403	84.4	167
p = 0.00575 (**)				p = 0.00831 (**)			

One socio-educational factor, i.e., schooling, influenced the choice of comitative forms (Table 9). This factor, which was the most significant for *tú* selection, was not statistically significant for *vos*. The likelihood of preference for the *tú* form (*contigo*) was highest among participants who attended private schools, while it was dispreferred by those who attended public institutions; those educated in elite schools were neutral. A summary of all the significant factors in address variation in the pronouns can be found on Table 10.

Table 9: Summary of multivariate analysis for the factor Schooling for comitative pronouns.

Schooling Tú	FW	%	N
Private	0.64	95.1	203
Elite	0.494	91.1	123
Public	0.365	87.5	328
p = 0.0061 (**)			

Table 10: Significant factors in *vos/tú* pronominal variation in Montevideo Spanish.

	Nominative	Prepositional	Comitative
Age	√	√	√
Income		√	
Speaker Gender			√
Schooling			√

4.2.4 Imperative

Rbrul selected age as a significant factor in both *vos* and *tú* imperative responses (Table 11). Although all speakers in the sample preferred *vos* forms over alternatives, this preference decreased with age. The biggest difference was between speakers 50 and younger, who favoured *vos* imperatives, and those older than 50, who disfavoured them. The reverse pattern was true for *tú* forms: the older speakers were three times as likely to select them as those in the two younger age groups.

Table 11: Summary of multivariate analysis for the factor Age for verbs in the imperative (N.B.: Age 1: 18–30; Age 2: 31–50; Age 3: 51 and over).

Speaker Age *Vos*	FW	%	N	Speaker Age *Tú*	FW	%	N
Age 1	0.614	96.3	217	Age 3	0.699	12.7	158
Age 2	0.601	95.8	284	Age 2	0.438	4.9	284
Age 3	0.294	88	158	Age 1	0.355	3.2	217
p = 0.00175 (**)				p = 0.00189 (**)			

Again, *vos* forms were preferred across all incomes, but they were favoured at significantly higher rates among those from the highest income group, for whom their use was almost categorical. Meanwhile, the low-income level speakers reported a preference for *tú* imperatives, with the middle-income respondents hovering in between (Table 12).

The final factor to influence address form choice in imperative verbs was schooling, in a pattern similar to income (Table 13). Speakers who had attended elite schools expressed a categorical preference for *vos* imperatives, which went down slightly among those who had attended other types of private school, and dipped further among those who had gone to public schools. The preference for *tú* imperative forms mirrored that of *vos*.

Table 12: Summary of multivariate analysis for the factor Income for verbs in the imperative.

Income Vos	FW	%	N	Income Tú	FW	%	N
High	0.732	98.5	203	Low	0.704	12.9	140
Middle	0.525	94.9	316	Middle	0.452	5.7	316
Low	0.249	85.7	140	High	0.337	2.5	203
p = 0.000449 (***)				p = 0.00483 (**)			

Table 13: Summary of multivariate analysis for the factor Schooling for verbs in the imperative.

Schooling Vos	FW	%	N	Schooling Tú	FW	%	N
Elite	> 0.999	100	124	Public	0.997	9.3	332
Private	0.007	96.6	203	Private	0.995	4.9	203
Public	0.003	90.4	332	Elite	< 0.001	0.0	124
p = 0.00286 (**)				p = 0.0019 (**)			

4.2.5 Present indicative

In the present indicative, Rbrul selected age as a relevant predictor, in a pattern parallel to the imperative (Table 14). Respondents expressed very high levels of preference for *vos* forms across all age groups. Among those 50 and younger, this preference was virtually categorical, while in the older group (51+) it was not. In fact, the oldest speakers were over twice as likely to select *tú* forms as their younger counterparts (13.9% vs. 5.5%).

Table 14: Summary of multivariate analysis for the factor Age for verbs in the present (N.B.: Age 1: 18–30; Age 2: 31–50; Age 3: 51 and over).

Speaker Age Vos	FW	%	N	Speaker Age Tú	FW	%	N
Age 1	0.699	97.2	217	Age 3	0.741	13.9	151
Age 2	0.545	95.3	275	Age 2	0.488	5.5	275
Age 3	0.265	86.8	151	Age 1	0.269	2.3	217
p = 0.000151 (***)				p = 5.61e-05 (***)			

4.2.6 Preterite

In preterite verbs, *tú* forms were preferred across all factor groups. Moreover, they exhibited patterns of variation that differed quite markedly from those identified for the imperative and present verbs. The only variable with a statistically significant effect on second singular variation in the preterite was educational attainment (Table 15). *Vos* (i.e., final -*s*) preterite forms were highly disfavoured by university graduates, and most favoured by those who had attended technical school. Speakers with the lowest levels of education (i.e., secondary school or less) did not strongly favour or disfavour this form. By contrast, *tú* forms were favoured by university graduates almost categorically, while secondary or technical school attendance decreased the likelihood of choosing *tú* preterite forms.

Table 15: Summary of multivariate analysis for the factor Educational Attainment for verbs in the preterite.

Educational Attainment *Vos*	FW	%	N	Educational Attainment *Tú*	FW	%	N
Technical	0.733	29.8	47	University	0.817	97.1	549
Secondary	0.555	16.2	44	Secondary	0.394	78.4	37
University	0.226	4	626	Technical	0.256	70.2	47
p = 2.54e-06 (***)				p = 1.21e-07 (***)			

4.2.7 Present subjunctive

Variation in the present subjunctive was the most complex in the entire paradigm. While *tú* forms were generally preferred across the board, selection was influenced by the most factors, including semantic value, schooling, gender and income of the speaker, and finally, gender of the addressee.

The most statistically significant factor identified by Rbrul was semantic value (Table 16); there was a clear difference between the two prohibitions (cessative, *¡No cantes!* 'Stop singing!' and preventive *¡No cantes!* 'Don't start singing!') and the subordinate clause uses of the subjunctive (*No creo que cantes* 'I don't think you sing'). The subordinate use disfavoured selection of *vos* forms, while prohibitions favoured it, with the cessative doing so at higher rates, as expected from the previous literature on Río de la Plata Spanish (Johnson 2016). Frequencies of *tú* form choice in the subjunctive were an exact mirror image of those trends, with the subordinate subjunctive favouring them and the two prohibitions disfavouring them.

Table 16: Summary of multivariate analysis for the factor Semantic Value for verbs in the present subjunctive.

Semantic Value Vos	FW	%	N	Semantic Value Tú	FW	%	N
Cessative	0.657	14.9	657	Subordinate	0.715	96.6	656
Preventive	0.564	10.7	763	Preventive	0.438	90.5	661
Subordinate	0.287	3.8	753	Cessative	0.338	86.5	577
p = 6.46e-12 (***)				p = 4.02e-11 (***)			

The next factor group in significance was speaker gender (Table 17), with males favouring *vos* forms in the present subjunctive, and females disfavouring them; in fact, men reported using *vos* subjunctive forms twice as frequently as women. The situation was reversed with *tú* forms, which were chosen by both genders over *vos* forms, but at lower rates by men than by women. Although the difference was small (93.1% for women, 86.5% for men), it was highly statistically significant.

Table 17: Summary of multivariate analysis for the factor Speaker Gender for verbs in the present subjunctive.

Speaker Gender Vos	FW	%	N	Speaker Gender Tú	FW	%	N
Male	0.618	15.8	495	Female	0.614	93.1	1399
Female	0.382	7.4	1399	Male	0.386	86.5	495
p = 4.03e-08 (***)				p = 8.09e-07 (***)			

Schooling was also a strong predictor of *vos/tú* variation in the subjunctive (Table 18). Although all speakers chose *tú* forms over 85% of the time, *vos* forms were favoured by public school attendance, and disfavoured by attendance at private and elite schools. In fact, speakers who had attended public education were over twice as likely to employ that form as those who had attended private/elite educational institutions. By contrast, attending private and elite schools increased the likelihood of *tú* forms, while attending public schools disfavoured it.

The next factor group in significance was addressee gender, a factor that was not relevant in the choice of any other second person form (Table 19). Although *tú* forms were selected more frequently overall regardless of addressee (>85%), female addressees received them at higher rates than males. Female addressee gender favoured *tú* forms while male addressee gender disfavoured them. The difference was clearer for *vos* form choice, which was almost twice as likely in speech addressed to men.

Table 18: Summary of multivariate analysis for the factor Schooling for verbs in the present subjunctive.

Schooling Vos	FW	%	N	Schooling Tú	FW	%	N
Public	0.664	13.8	943	Private	0.627	95.9	590
Private	0.422	5.6	590	Elite	0.536	94.7	361
Elite	0.41	5.3	361	Public	0.34	87.3	943
p = 1.14e-07 (***)				p = 1.47e-07 (***)			

Table 19: Summary of multivariate analysis for the factor Addressee Gender for verbs in the present subjunctive.

Addressee Gender Vos	FW	%	N	Addressee Gender Tú	FW	%	N
Male	0.589	12.4	954	Female	0.601	94.3	940
Female	0.411	6.8	940	Male	0.399	88.6	954
p = 1.4e-05 (***)				p = 3.23e-06 (***)			

Income level was the last significant factor (Table 20), in a pattern similar to schooling. Although frequencies of *vos* forms were always very low, the selection was favoured by low-income participants, and disfavoured by those in high- and middle-income brackets. In fact, *vos* subjunctives were twice as frequent in that group as in others. *Tú* forms were the mirror image, favoured by high- and middle-income participants, and disfavoured by low-income respondents. For a summary of all significant factors in address variation in verbs, see Table 21.

Table 20: Summary of multivariate analysis for the factor Income for verbs in the present subjunctive.

Income Vos	FW	%	N	Income Tú	FW	%	N
Low	0.601	15.3	405	High	0.618	95.4	582
Middle	0.486	9.4	907	Middle	0.508	91.7	907
High	0.413	6.0	582	Low	0.375	84.9	405
p = 0.00753 (**)				p = 0.000817 (***)			

Table 21: Significant factors in verbal *vos/tú* form variation in Montevideo Spanish.

	Imperative	Present	Preterite	Subjunctive
Age	√	√		
Schooling	√			√
Income	√			√
Speaker Gender				√
Ed. Attainment			√	
Addressee Gender				√
Semantic Value				√

5 Discussion

The first important generalisation is that the preferences of Montevideo speakers are well aligned with those of Buenos Aires, as expected. For example, the subjunctive exhibits the same split, with an almost categorical preference for *tú* forms in subordinate clauses (Fontanella de Weinberg 1979), and a pattern in negative imperatives (prohibitions) that distinguishes cessatives from preventives (Johnson and Grinstead 2011; Johnson 2016). The situation seems fairly stable, since frequency is not tied to age.

Second, as in Buenos Aires, in Montevideo *vos* forms were chosen almost categorically in the imperative and present second person, and they were also preferred in the nominative and prepositional pronouns. That said, even in these forms, which exhibit the highest *vos* frequencies, participants chose *tú* forms at non-negligible rates. While part of the preference for *tú* forms may have been an artifice of the data collection (written discourse), *tú* percentages in the present indicative and imperative were higher than those obtained for Buenos Aires even half a century ago (Siracusa 1977), and cannot be attributed entirely to self-monitoring when responding to the survey. For example, the use of *tú* forms was not linked to the final educational attainment, but rather to the type of school attended in the early years, which is a proxy for social class, rather than literacy level.

In spite of the differences between the two cities, the trend is unmistakable: variation by age group in Montevideo shows a consistent shift towards *vos*, and is thus further evidence of Buenos Aires' influence. Indeed, age was the most significant factor in five of the seven address forms analysed (Figure 1). In the nominative and present indicative, it was the only factor to reach significance, while in the imperative, prepositional, and comitative forms, it was the most statistically significant. In all cases, the two youngest age groups (50 or under) favoured *vos* forms and disfav-

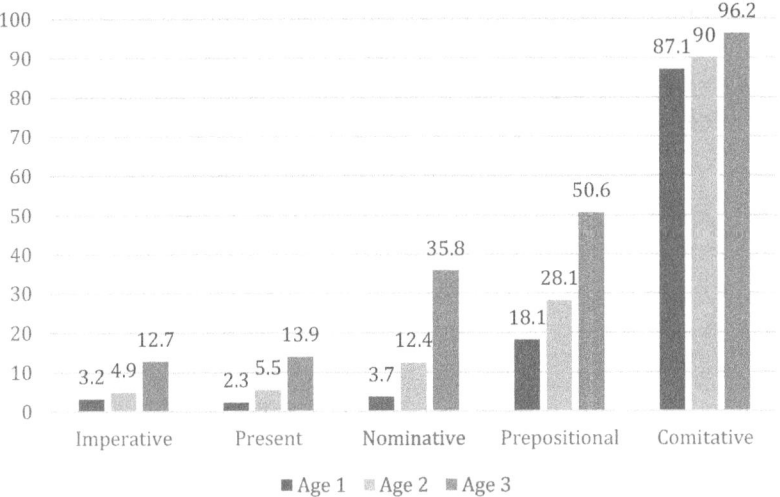

Figure 1: Percentage of *tú* form selection in Montevideo by age group in the imperative, present, nominative, prepositional, and comitative paradigms (N.B.: Age 1: 18–30; Age 2: 31–50; Age 3: 51+).

oured *tú* forms, with the oldest age group exhibiting the opposite pattern. The frequency presented a neat gradient, with each age group showing lower *tú* than the older one. In other words, younger Montevideo speakers are following trends already well-established in Buenos Aires, even in forms (such as the comitative) where the local norm continues to favour *tú* usage overall (for a similar trend in song lyrics, see Moyna 2015: 15). Conversely, there was no form in which the older age group exhibited higher levels of *vos* usage than its younger counterparts.

That said, not all *vos/tú* form variation in Montevideo was attributable to the influence of the sister city across the estuary. In fact, most of the socio-economic, educational, and interpersonal factors considered had some significance, with the lone exception of occupation. This suggests that Montevideo speakers continue to avail themselves of *vos/tú* variation to express subtle social and pragmatic meanings that would be impossible if the latter address form disappeared, as it has in Buenos Aires.

Let us begin by considering educational variables. The schooling attended in childhood proved to be significant for three forms (comitative, present subjunctive, imperative; see Figure 2). Private school attendees were most influenced by the normative standard forms promoted by the educational system; although their frequency of *tú* form choice wasn't always the highest, this social group was more likely to select *tú* verbs. For their part, public school attendees were the least likely to choose *tú* variants in the present subjunctive and the comitative, but they did favour *tú* imperatives and exhibited the highest *tú* rates for these forms. Finally, elite school graduates patterned with those from private schools when it came to the present subjunctive, but they categorically rejected *tú* imperatives, and in the comitative they stood halfway between the two other groups both in frequency and likelihood of *tú* form choice.

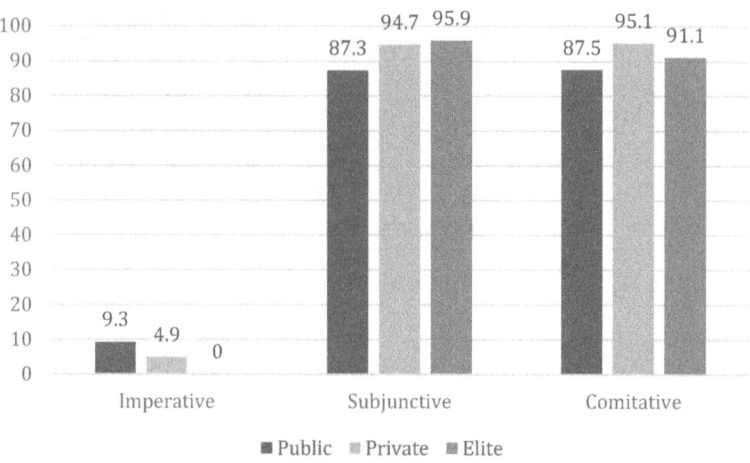

Figure 2: Percentage of *tú* form selection in Montevideo by schooling in the imperative, subjunctive, and comitative paradigms.

Final educational attainment had a limited effect on address variation, but it did matter for the choice of *vos* preterite forms (*tomastes* 'you drank$_V$' instead of *tomaste* 'you drank$_T$'). University educated participants rejected these forms soundly, but the two other groups favoured them, which suggests that the non-standard (analogical) form is only eliminated through instruction and normative pressure. These results are partially in line with those of earlier studies (Elizaincín and Díaz 1979), which found that young men from the lower middle class were most likely to accept -*s* final preterites. It seems that in the intervening years, the acceptability of these forms has extended to women of the same class, since this study found no statistically significant effect of gender. It is unclear whether Buenos Aires shares the same variation, since no quantitative studies of this variation are available for the Argentine capital.

Income also had some influence on address choice, particularly in the prepositional, imperative, and present subjunctive forms (Figure 3). The respondents in the highest income groups were most likely to choose *tú* forms in the present subjunctive verbs and prepositional pronouns, while the lowest income group was the least likely to do so; the middle-income respondents were neutral with respect to these forms. By contrast, in the imperative, it was the lowest two groups that favoured *tú* forms, in a pattern that parallels the situation of schooling. This suggests that different social groups use *tú* forms to convey different information: the lower classes mitigate direct commands through *tú* forms, while those with the most education do not feel compelled to do so, a strategy shown to operate more generally in Montevideo Spanish (Moyna 2019).

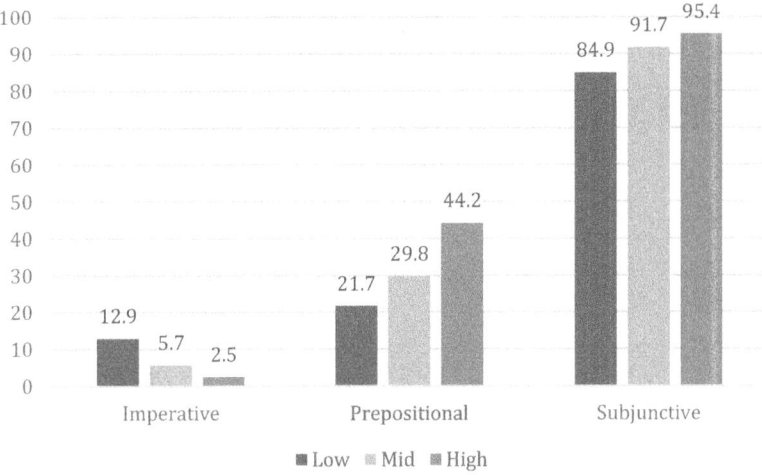

Figure 3: Percentage of *tú* form selection in Montevideo by income in the imperative, prepositional, and present subjunctive paradigms.

Finally, speaker gender had some influence on address choice (Figure 4). This factor was significant for the comitative and the present subjunctive, and in both cases, female speakers were more likely to employ *tú* forms by similar margins (over 5%).

Addressee gender was only significant in the present subjunctive, and again, it was more likely to address women than men, regardless of speaker gender. In fact, a cross-tabulation of speaker and addressee gender (Figure 5) revealed that male-to-male and female-to-female address exhibited the lowest and highest frequencies of *tú* form usage, respectively. Meanwhile, percentages of *tú* address between genders were identical (90%).

This result constitutes a change from earlier periods, when *tú* forms were more likely than *vos* forms in mixed-gender dyads (Moyna and Ceballos 2008: 79–81). The decreased scope of addressee gender as a significant variable – now restricted to the present subjunctive – suggests a historical erosion in the negative politeness value of *tú*, at least as far as its verbal manifestations are concerned (for pronouns, see Moyna 2020). For its part, the fact that *tú* form frequency is now

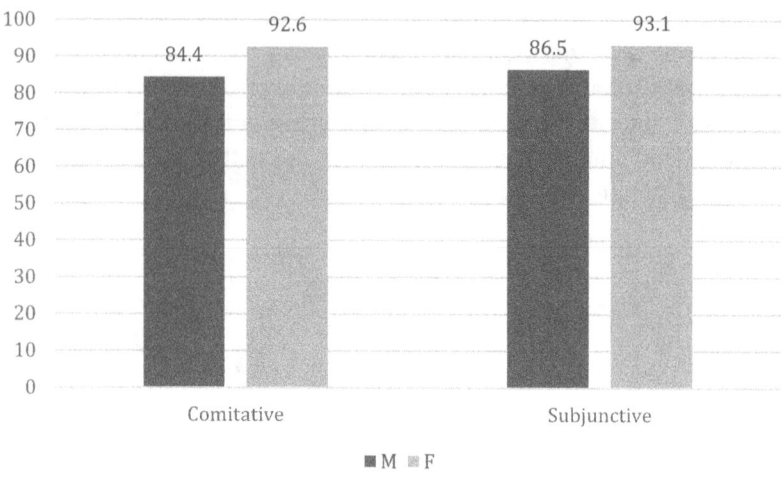

Figure 4: Percentage of *tú* form selection in Montevideo by speaker gender in comitative and subjunctive paradigms.

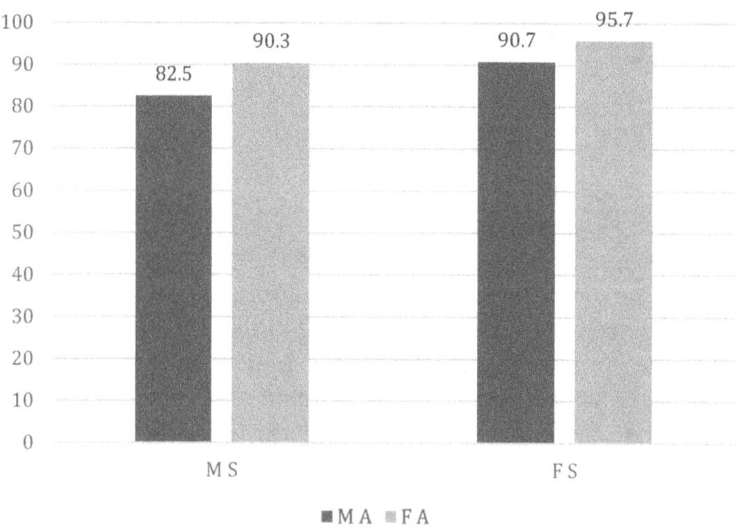

Figure 5: Percentage of *tú* form selection in Montevideo by speaker (S) and addressee (A) gender in the subjunctive.

higher among females than in mixed-gender discourse seems to index changes in gender relations, where distance between men and women is no longer prescribed as necessary and appropriate.

6 Conclusions

The first conclusion of this study is that second person address embodies well the convergent and divergent pulls of pluricentric languages. Address forms in Uruguay are not uniform or static, even in Montevideo, which represents the national standard norm. Thus, we can answer our first research question in the affirmative: there is still considerable variation in Montevideo informal address, even in forms that exhibit no variation in Buenos Aires. Moreover, we can also point to specific social factors behind this variation. The fact that age is a very important factor is evidence of the increasing convergence of Montevideo Spanish towards the paradigm of Buenos Aires, the larger dominant centre in the Río de la Plata region. This is clear, for example, from the virtually categorical preference for *vos* imperatives, present indicative, and nominative forms in the youngest group considered, i.e., those 30 or under. In those forms, *tú* is confined to older and lower income participants, and could very well be a reflection of prescriptive pressure or mitigation. In the present subjunctive, Montevideo is also close to the patterns presented by Fontanella de Weinberg (1979) and Johnson (2016) for Argentina. Thus, while it is still true that *vos* present subjunctives are infrequent in Montevideo (Behares 1981: 37), they are by no means absent, and their deployment matches the pragmatic and semantic contexts of Buenos Aires. This convergence should not come as a surprise, given the constant contact and trend-setting influence of Buenos Aires youth in the entire dialect area.

That said, Montevideo speakers continue to deploy non-negligible percentages of *tú* forms, the most obvious of which is the comitative pronoun (*contigo*), favoured at rates higher than 85% by all respondents. In the prepositional form, *tuteo* also ranges in frequency from 20 to 50%, and its presence is therefore quite high. Pronominal *tú* forms in Montevideo convey a range of sociolinguistic information, including schooling, income, educational attainment, and gender, and stands for overtly prestigious speech. All of these nuances are impossible to convey through the address system in Buenos Aires. While Buenos Aires speakers can easily identify Montevideo residents through their use of *tú* pronouns, neither of the two populations is explicitly aware of the social intricacies unveiled in this study. In particular, it is highly unlikely that the differences between social groups in Montevideo is the result of different degrees of influence from Buenos Aires. Rather, the variation that remains in Montevideo seems to have been resignified in dialect-specific ways, to mark gender and social class (i.e., type of schooling in childhood).

Many questions remain unanswered, in particular with respect to the influence of social class. This is partly due to the fact that the written instrument had a limited effectiveness in eliciting data from working class respondents, so different techniques are needed to tap into these speakers' intuitions. In addition, while Montevideo represents the prestige variety of Uruguay, one should be careful not to extend these conclusions to the rest of the country. For example, in the eastern seaboard pronominal and verbal *tú* forms are preferred (Rona 1967; Weyers 2014), while in the western border with Argentina, cities such as Paysandú deserve more attention as potentially influenced by the Buenos Aires system. This study should have made it clear that even areas typically considered representative of a single address pattern can exhibit dynamic strategies to encode complex social meaning.

References

Baumel Schreffler, Sandra L. 1995. The *voseo*: Second person singular pronouns in Guatemalan speech. *Language Quarterly* 33(1–2). 33–44.

Behares, Luis E. 1981. Estudio sociodialectológico de las formas verbales de segunda persona en el español de Montevideo. In Adolfo Elizaincín (ed.), *Estudios sobre el español del Uruguay*, 29–49. Montevideo: Universidad de la República, Facultad de Humanidades y Ciencias.

Bertolotti, Virginia. 2011. La peculiaridad del sistema alocutivo singular en Uruguay. In Angela di Tullio & Rolf Kailuweit (eds.), *El español rioplatense: lengua, literatura, expresiones culturales*, 23–47. Madrid: Iberoamericana/Frankfurt am Main: Vervuert.

Bertolotti, Virginia & Magdalena Coll. 2003. A synchronical and historical view of the *tú/vos* option in the Spanish of Montevideo. In Silvina Montrul & Francisco Ordóñez (eds.), *Linguistic theory and language development in Hispanic languages: Papers from the 5th Hispanic Linguistics Symposium and the 4th Conference on the Acquisition of Spanish and Portuguese*, 1–12. Somerville: Cascadilla.

Brown, Roger & Albert Gilman. 1960. The pronouns of power and solidarity. In Thomas A. Sebeok (ed.), *Style in language*, 253–276. Cambridge: Technology Press of Massachusetts Institute of Technology.

Bueno, Sergio. 5 December 2011. Impulsan plan de integración portuaria entre Montevideo, Buenos Aires y Río Grande. *Cronista.com*. http://www.cronista.com/especiales/Impulsan-plan-de-integracion-portuaria-entre-Buenos-Aires-Montevideo-y-Rio-Grande-20110512-0037.html (accessed 17 November 2012)

Caetano, Gerardo & José Rilla. 2005. *Historia contemporánea del Uruguay*. Montevideo: Fin de Siglo.

Carricaburo, Norma. 2010. Estudios fundantes del voseo en la Argentina: contextualización sociohistórica y pragmalingüística. In Martin Hummel, Bettina Kluge & María Eugenia Vázquez Laslop (eds.), *Formas y fórmulas de tratamiento en el mundo hispánico*, 465–481. Mexico City: El Colegio de México/Graz: Karl-Franzens-Universität.

Coll, Magdalena & Gabriela Resnik. 2018. Lexicografía y cambio lingüístico en el español del Río de la Plata. *Filología* 50. 33–52.

Elizaincín, Adolfo & Olga Díaz. 1979. Aceptación social y conciencia de hablantes montevideanos ante -s en la segunda persona singular del pretérito. *Revista de la Facultad de Humanidades y Ciencias. Serie Lingüística* 1(2). 20–36.

Elizaincín, Adolfo & Olga Díaz. 1981. Sobre tuteo-voseo en el español montevideano. In Adolfo Elizaincín (ed.), *Estudios sobre el español del Uruguay*, 83–86. Montevideo: Universidad de la República, Facultad de Humanidades y Ciencias.

Fontanella de Weinberg, María Beatriz. 1976. Analogía y confluencia paradigmática en formas verbales de voseo. *Thesaurus* 31. 249–272.

Fontanella de Weinberg, María Beatriz. 1977. La constitución del paradigma pronominal del voseo. *Thesaurus* 32. 227–241.

Fontanella de Weinberg, María Beatriz. 1979. La oposición "cantes/cantés" en el español de Buenos Aires. *Thesaurus* 34. 72–83.

Fontanella de Weinberg, María Beatriz. 1999. Sistemas pronominales de tratamiento usados en el mundo hispánico. In Ignacio Bosque & Violeta Demonte (eds.), *Gramática descriptiva de la lengua española. Volumen 1: sintaxis básica de las clases de palabras*, 1401–1425. Madrid: Espasa Calpe.

Fontanella de Weinberg, María Beatriz. 2000. El español bonaerense. In María Beatriz Fontanella de Weinberg (ed.), *El español de la Argentina y sus variedades regionales*, 37–61. Buenos Aires: Edicial.

Goebel, Michael. 2010. Gauchos, gringos, and gallegos: the assimilation of Italian and Spanish immigrants in the making of modern Uruguay. *Past and Present* 208. 191–229.

Henríquez Ureña, Pedro. 1976. *Observaciones sobre el español en América y otros estudios filológicos*. Buenos Aires: Academia Argentina de Letras.

Instituto Nacional de Estadística. 2011. *Censo, series históricas. Total País: población. Características Generales. Población por departamento de residencia habitual, según área y sexo*. https://www.ine.gub.uy/web/guest/censos-2011 (accessed 10 November 2022)

Instituto Nacional de Estadística. 2014. *Uruguay en cifras 2014*. Montevideo: Departamento de Difusión y Divulgación. https://www.ine.gub.uy/documents/10181/39317/Uruguay_en_cifras_2014.pdf/aac28208-4670-4e96-b8c1-b2abb93b5b13 (accessed 10 November 2022)

Johnson, Daniel E. 2009. Getting off the GoldVarb standard: introducing Rbrul for mixed-effects variable rule analysis. *Language and Linguistic Compass* 3(1). 359–383.

Johnson, Mary. 2016. Pragmatic variation in voseo and tuteo negative commands in Argentinian Spanish. In María Irene Moyna & Susana Rivera-Mills (eds.), *Forms of Address in the Spanish of the Americas*, 127–148. Amsterdam/Philadelphia: John Benjamins.

Johnson, Mary & John Grinstead. 2011. Variation in the *voseo* and *tuteo* negative imperatives in Argentine Spanish. *University of Pennsylvania Working Papers in Linguistics* 17(2). 99–104.

Kühl de Mones, Ursula. 1981. Actitudes lingüísticas frente al español de Montevideo (Uruguay). *Revista de la Facultad de Humanidades y Ciencias. Serie Lingüística* 1(3). 37–60.

Lapesa, Rafael. 1981. *Historia de la lengua española*. Madrid: Gredos.

Lipski, John. 1996. *El español de América*. Madrid: Cátedra.

Lipski, John. 2002. The role of the city in the formation of Spanish American dialect zones. *Arachne@Rutgers* 2(1).

Mendoza, Reinhild. 2005. *Der voseo im Spanischen Uruguays: eine pluridimensionale Makro- und Mikroanalyse*. Kiel: Westensee.

Michnowicz, Jim & Lucía Planchón. 2020. Sheísmo in Montevideo Spanish: not (yet) identical to Buenos Aires. In Sandro Sessarego, Juan José Colomina-Almiñana & Adrián Rodríguez Ricelli (eds.), *Language variation and evolution: aspects of language contact and contrast across the Spanish-speaking world*, 163–188. Amsterdam/Philadelphia: John Benjamins.

Ministerio de Turismo. 2018. *Anuario: estadísticas de turismo.* Montevideo: Área de Investigación y Estadística. http://gub.uy/ministerio-turismo/sites/ministerio-turismo/files/2019-09/ANUARIO_2018.pdf (accessed 8 November 2019)

Moser, Karolin. 2003. En torno a las formas de tratamiento para la segunda persona en el español de Costa Rica. *Káñina: Revista de Artes y Letras de la Universidad de Costa Rica.* 27(2). 153–161.

Moser, Karolin. 2008. Tres hipótesis sobre la (des)cortesía en el tratamiento diádico informal-familiar de San José, Costa Rica. *Revista Internacional de Lingüística Iberoamericana* 6/11. 129–145.

Moyna, María Irene. 2015. *Voseo/tuteo* variation in Uruguayan songs (1960–2010). *Romanische Forschungen* 127(1). 3–28.

Moyna, María Irene. 2017. *Voseo* vocatives and interjections in Montevideo Spanish. In Juan José Colomina Almiñana (ed.), *Contemporary advances in theoretical and applied Spanish linguistic variation*, 124–147. Columbus: The Ohio State University Press.

Moyna, María Irene. 2019. Variation in polite address in contemporary Uruguayan Spanish. In Bettina Kluge & María Irene Moyna (eds.), *It's not all about you: new perspectives on address research.* 191–219. Amsterdam/Philadelphia: John Benjamins.

Moyna, María Irene. 2020. Formas de tratamiento y mitigación en el español de Montevideo. In Tatiana Maranhão de Castedo & Ana Berenice Peres Martorelli (eds.), *El voseo en América: origen, usos y aplicación*, 165–197. Curitiba: Editora Appris.

Moyna, María Irene & Beatriz Ceballos. 2008. Representaciones dramáticas de una variable lingüística: tuteo y voseo en obras de teatro del Río de la Plata (1886–1911). *Spanish in Context* 5(1). 64–88.

Moyna, María Irene & Verónica Loureiro Rodríguez. 2017. La técnica de máscaras emparejadas para evaluar actitudes hacia formas de tratamiento en el español de Montevideo. *Revista Internacional de Lingüística Iberoamericana* 15/30. 47–82.

Newall, Gregory. 2007. The loss of the *voseo* in Chilean Spanish: evidence from literature. *University of Pennsylvania Working Papers in Linguistics* 13(2). 165–178.

Páez Urdaneta, Iraset. 1981. *Historia y geografía hispanoamericana del voseo.* Caracas: La Casa de Bello.

Prevedello, Nora Lilí. 1989. El voseo en el habla de Córdoba: dos fuerzas en pugna. In *Actas del II Congreso Argentino de Hispanistas*, 287–300. Mendoza: Universidad Nacional de Cuyo.

Prevedello, Nora Lilí, Susana Martorell de Laconi & Alicia Malanca de Rodríguez Rojas. 1999. Estudio del español hablado en la Argentina mediterránea: el voseo. In Elena M. Rojas Mayer (ed.), *Actas del VIII Congreso Internacional de la Asociación de Lingüística y Filología de América Latina (ALFAL), San Miguel de Tucumán, septiembre de 1987*, 2298–2304. San Miguel de Tucumán: ALFAL/Universidad Nacional de Tucumán.

Ricci, Julio & Iris Malán de Ricci. 1962–1963. Anotaciones sobre el uso de los pronombres *tú* y *vos* en el español del Uruguay. *Anales del Instituto de Profesores "Artigas"* 7–8. 163–166.

Ricci, Julio & Iris Malán de Ricci. 1977. La rotura del equilibrio vos(tú) - usted en el español del Río de la Plata. *Foro Literario (Montevideo)* 1. 51–54.

Rona, José Pedro. 1967. *Geografía y morfología del "voseo".* Porto Alegre: Pontifícia Universidade Católica.

Siracusa, María Isabel. 1977. Morfología verbal del voseo en el habla culta de Buenos Aires. *Filología* 16. 201–213.

Steffen, Joachim. 2010. El tratamiento en el Uruguay. In Martin Hummel, Bettina Kluge & María Eugenia Vázquez Laslop (eds.), *Formas y fórmulas de tratamiento en el mundo hispánico*, 451–464. Mexico City: El Colegio de México/Graz: Karl-Franzens-Universität.

Tagliamonte, Sali. 2012. *Variationist sociolinguistics: change, observation, interpretation*. Malden/Oxford: Wiley-Blackwell.
Veiga, Danilo. 2010. *Estructura social y ciudades en el Uruguay: tendencias recientes*. Montevideo: Universidad de la República, Facultad de Ciencias Sociales.
Vidal de Battini, Berta Elena. 1964. *El español de la Argentina*. Buenos Aires: Consejo Nacional de Educación.
Weyers, Joseph. 2009. The impending demise of *tú* in Montevideo, Uruguay. *Hispania* 92(4). 829–839.
Weyers, Joseph. 2012. *Voseo* in Montevideo's advertising: reflecting linguistic norms. *Studies in Hispanic and Lusophone Linguistics* 5(2) 369–385.
Weyers, Joseph R. 2013a. Linguistic attitudes toward the *tuteo* and *voseo* in Montevideo, Uruguay. *Spanish in Context* 10(2). 175–198.
Weyers, Joseph R. 2013b. Do consumers distinguish between verb forms in written advertising? Verbal *voseo* and *tuteo* in Montevideo. *International Journal of the Sociology of Language* 224. 25–41.
Weyers, Joseph R. 2014. The *tuteo* of Rocha, Uruguay: A study of pride and language maintenance. *Hispania* 97(3). 382–395.

Heinz L. Kretzenbacher, Doris Schüpbach, John Hajek and Catrin Norrby

Conclusion: Looking back and looking forward

The chapters in this volume, grouped into three thematic parts, present a broad picture of the diversity of multilingual cities across the world in the 21st century. They explore cities of vastly different size, ranging from megacities such as Jakarta down to small cities such as Fribourg/Freiburg, and cities situated in the Global North as well as in the Global South. The dynamics of and interaction between different languages in those cities also demonstrate great variation, from the presence of two or more languages in multilingual countries or regions to the status of immigrant languages in cities traditionally dominated by one majority language, and to post-colonial contexts where colonial languages often co-exist as official languages alongside indigenous languages. While national varieties of English, as well as English as a lingua franca, play an important role in the language make-up of many of the cities analysed in this volume, in others the focus is on other (originally) European and non-European languages. As a result, the specific circumstances of each of the cities sometimes demand different methodological approaches to do them justice, while other chapters share a common methodological approach to document multilingualism in the cityscape. This is the case with five chapters (identified in turn further below) across all three sections which use linguistic landscaping as their approach, carefully fine-tuning the methodology so as to fit the particular conditions of each site.

This concluding chapter has the task of taking stock of the research presented in the twelve chapters as well as opening up avenues for further research. It opens with a discussion on how two types of linguistic diversity – multilingualism and pluricentricity – are interrelated in general, and more specifically, how some of the chapters make use of both to account for the linguistic diversity and interaction encountered in a particular urban site. In section 2, we direct our attention to linguistic landscape studies, more recently also known as semiotic landscape studies (Jaworski and Thurlow 2010). We discuss how the field has developed over time, and show how fruitful such an approach can be when applied in different contexts. In the third section, we give a concluding survey of each of the three parts – *Multilingual policies in practice*, *Attitudes and identities*, and *Language across time and space* – to demonstrate ways in which research in these fields can go forward in the future.

https://doi.org/10.1515/9781501511974-014

1 Multilingualism and pluricentricity

In the introductory chapter we endeavoured to explain how the overarching topic of urban multilingualism, often together with a recurring theme of pluricentricity, is moving both fields of research forward. We argue that it does so by diversifying the exploration of urban settings of multilingualism, in terms of size, nature and geographical distribution and by highlighting the aspect of pluricentricity in some of the studies contained in the volume. While concepts such as superdiversity, metrolingualism, polylanguaging, and translanguaging are now frequently discussed in the literature on multilingualism, other concepts pertinent to linguistic diversity, such as pluricentricity, are still to be brought to the fore in this area of research.

The situations traditionally researched in studies on multilingualism are characterized by the coexistence of two or more different languages in a particular space (a nation, region or municipality) or in an individual speaker. For the most part, the chapters in the present volume treat named languages and named varieties of languages as 'real' to their speakers, and unproblematic in the sense that members of any community orient towards named languages and their varieties, and can talk and express opinions about them.

More recently, however, there has been a surge in research which challenges the existence of sharp boundaries between named languages. Such scholarship emphasises linguistic hybridity where, for instance, linguistic practices of individual speakers are open to the inclusion of different languages, or varieties of the same language, such as dialects or sociolects. Farr (2011) uses the term 'plurilingualism' for such practices. The concepts of polylanguaging (Jørgensen et al. 2016), translanguaging (García and Li Wei 2014; Li Wei 2018) and metrolingualism (Pennycook and Otsuji 2014) do not have the co-existence of different languages as a condition, but depart from a view where speakers draw on all their linguistic resources for meaning-making, no matter whether they represent named languages, varieties of such languages or hybrid representations. Speakers do not necessarily conceptualise their linguistic practices as expressions of separate languages or language varieties, rather they are thought to move along a linguistic continuum or space where there are no hard boundaries between them. In particular, the concept of heteroglossia (above all in linguistic anthropology) has been applied to intra-language varieties of the same language co-existing in the hybrid linguistic competence of individuals and "encompasses both mono- and multilingual forms" (Bailey 2007: 258). A recent example of a study applying the heteroglossia concept to varieties of the same language spoken in different countries is Radke (2021), who reflects on the role of Namibia German multilingual slang in contrast to Standard German from Germany or Standard Namibia German (cf. Kellermeier-Rehbein 2016) – as part of ingroup construction by heteroglossic means. Given the varied regional origins of Italians in Munich discussed in Chapter 8 by Riehl and Ingrosso, the coexistence of different regional varieties and the standard variety of Italian in this group is also part of their constitution as a cultural community. However, we also recognise that not all scholars, including contributors to this volume, are sympathetic to the use of new terms such as polylanguaging and metrolingualism to reconsider and/or account for any patterns observed in Munich or elsewhere. Goebel in Chapter 3 on Jakarta is clear on what he considers to be their limitations, including difficulties they have in accounting for the language labels they use, as well as insufficient consideration of the multimodal nature of communication.

Turning our attention to pluricentricity – or pluriareality for that matter – most studies have involved some discussion or focus on features of phonological, morpho-syntactic, lexical or, to a lesser extent, pragmatic features of a particular variety of a pluricentric language, which have been explicitly or implicitly compared to one or more varieties of the same language. This is also the case in two contributions to this volume. Moyna (Chapter 12) compares two local urban manifestations of the Rioplatense variety of Latin American Spanish (Montevideo and Buenos Aires), and Diskin-Holdaway (Chapter 7) investigates immigrant perceptions of Irish English, particularly Dublin English. However, the latter analysis also demonstrates that the Chinese and Polish participants in the study display rather mixed, or sometimes even opposite attitudes, to the English(es) that surround them. In turn, this highlights the importance of also taking the linguistic diversity and multilingual nature of a community into account when dealing with pluricentric languages. Most prior research into pluricentric languages has tended to treat a national or regional variety of a certain language as uniform, thereby playing down the diversity in attitudes and in use among its speakers. How migrants with other language backgrounds orient towards the local, national or even supranational varieties of a pluricentric language has been studied to a much lesser degree and deserves more attention in future investigations (but see Oakes and Warren 2007 for a study on how migrants to Quebec navigate the available varieties of pluricentric French).

Diatopic (geographical) varieties – national ones in the case of pluricentric languages and/or regional ones in the case of cities with their own urban linguistic standards determined by their geographic situation within a country – are relevant factors in the dynamic interaction of languages in multilingual cities. As demonstrated by a number of studies referred to above, both the discussion of pluricentricity/pluriareality and of multilingualism benefit if both perspectives are merged, seen as two sides of the same coin to a degree. This is likely to be the view taken by those who contribute to the linguistic diversity of multilingual cities, above all for those whose L1 is not the respective national standard variety of the country that their city is situated in.

2 Linguistic landscaping – different contexts for a common approach

Nearly half of the contributions across all three sections of the volume share the approach of linguistic landscaping – in its understanding as semiotic landscaping, with verbal messages often accompanied by visual elements such as photos – applying it in different ways in order to do justice to the particular situation in each city, as well as to target their specific research focus. Two of the chapters in the first section, *Multilingual policies in practice,* apply linguistic landscaping approaches to European cities. In Chapter 2 on Mariehamn and Kotka, Nelson and Henricson focus on the visibility of what are in effect minority languages in each city rather than on the respective majority languages, Swedish in Mariehamn and Finnish in Kotka (which are both national languages of Finland). While in Mariehamn Finnish is much less visible than the international language English, in Kotka Swedish, together with Russian, the language of Finland's eastern neighbour, is prominent in second rank after the majority language. By charting language diversity in these two Finnish cities through urban signs, the authors thus show that the linguistic complexities are far greater than the official language policy of bilingual Finland would indicate.

In Chapter 4, Goglia focusses on one particular multicultural neighbourhood in his study on Padua and adds a qualitative discussion of the function of some non-Italian shop signs to the quantitative overview of languages visible in the neighbourhood, showing how different immigrant groups and different commercial contexts shape the linguistic landscape (LL) of the area and specific streets within it.

Chapter 5 by Hajek, Hasnain and Hanson in Part 2, *Attitudes and identities,* explores Lygon Street in the Melbourne suburb of Carlton, traditionally characterised by strong post-WWII Italian immigration. The contribution shows that Italian language, often subject to modification, alongside other indicators of Italian identity and way of life persist in the LL long after most Italians have left the area – as part of a shift to a food-oriented transclave, i.e. a "commercialized ethnic space that exists exclusively for consumption, leisure, and entertainment" (Kim 2018: 277).

Two chapters in Part 3, *Language across time and space,* focus on the impact that history had on LL in two very different cities: in Chapter 9 on Norwich,

Trudgill and Warren demonstrate how developments such as the UK's membership in the EU and Brexit as well as recent refugees, alongside the established post-WWII immigration, form and change the LL of the city. But they also trace the presence of other languages than English much further back into history as they document, for example, how the Viking presence in medieval Norwich still is reflected in street names of Old Norse origin. In this sense, their chapter illustrates how the LL approach can be successfully utilised to expose the layers of history that are still present in the contemporary city.

Shinjee and Dovchin (Chapter 10) explore the LL of Ulaanbaatar, where the development of a post-socialist Mongolia opening up to international influences is clearly visible in the streetscape, both in terms of the languages used and the types of cultural artefacts that are depicted in the signs across the city. Mongolian appears alongside English (and other languages), or is fused into hybrid representations, and through renditions of cultural objects traditional ways of life are meshed with expressions of transnational global culture.

Drawing on Shohamy's (2019) overview of LL research to date, the five contributions in this volume fall – at least in part – under the theme of "LL as a *representation* of languages in public spaces" (p. 27, original emphasis). While they all collected linguistic items in the public space of the respective cities, some are exhaustive for a certain area (Mariehamn/Kotka, Padua), others contain a selection of representative items (Ulaanbaatar, Norwich) or focus on a particular language (Italian in Melbourne). These data are often analysed quantitatively and subsequently interpreted against the backdrop of relevant concepts and frameworks such as the local and national language policy and practice (Mariehamn/Kotka, Padua) or language demography and migration, i.e. with a focus on immigrant languages (Padua, Melbourne). Others apply a more qualitative or discursive approach by discussing a selection of items to illustrate historic and present language contact (Norwich, Ulaanbaatar).

If LL is understood in a broader sense than the traditional one applied in the chapters mentioned above, the mediated contexts which both Schüpbach and Brohy (Chapter 1) and Goebel (Chapter 3) explore – official written online discourse and oral discourse in mass media respectively – can be viewed as extensions of linguistic landscaping, thus expanding the notion of what we understand the 'landscape' to be beyond the actual visible and physical urban streetscape. Thus, linguistic landscaping can be taken as a common approach or "metaphor that guides particular ways of collecting and organizing research data" and "seeing the world in a spatially and historically organized way" (Hovens 2021: 648), which has been fruitfully applied in a variety of contexts and settings in the contributions to this volume, although there remains scope for further development. Among such further pathways, which could be investigated in more detail in future research, is, for example, the use of more ethnographic methods. Through the use of interviews and observations, these explore people's interaction with specific semiotic signs, thus highlighting the discursive aspects of LL (Blommaert 2013: 32–33). Another perspective which deserves more attention is the issue of authorship in the LL, leading to questions about ownership and "the right to write in the public space" (Shohamy 2019: 31).

3 Thematic sections and avenues for future research

In the following, we outline possible avenues of further research emerging from contributions in this volume. The contributions in Part 1, *Multilingual policies in practice*, explore connections between official and unofficial language policies and ideologies to apparent language use. While they all deal with approaches and responses to official discourses on multilingualism, they do so in widely differing contexts and media.

The contribution by Schüpbach and Brohy (Chapter 1) leads to questions of how (more or less officially) bi- or multilingual cities present themselves linguistically – in communication with their residents and in their official presentation in different media – and how their multilingual status is reflected in their semiotic landscapes. These issues have been brought to the fore also in other studies, mostly with regard to Western cities, for example the recent study on the bilingual linguistic landscape of Montreal by Leimgruber and Fernández-Mallat (2021), but also with regard to cities in other world regions, such as Yaoundé, the capital city of Cameroon (Pütz 2020), or Tang's (2020) study on Singapore. All show a developing trend of work comprehensively addressing how official or semi-official multilingualism is inscribed in the physical and/or virtual context of cities.

Goebel's contribution on Jakarta (Chapter 3) addresses inter-ethnic language commodification in the mass media of metropolitan centres, as seen through the lens of a popular TV series where the characters seamlessly move between several languages, thereby presenting a rather different and linguistically diverse reality than official policy of promoting a common Indonesian language would suggest. This perspective deserves further exploration, in particular for Africa (for a recent example, cf. Ibrahim 2021 on Nollywood films and TV productions in Lagos, Nigeria) as well as for Latin America and Asia.

In the context of bi/multilingual cities, an interesting field of research considers tourist-oriented language use, with studies such as Schedel (2018), investigating how local authorities in the German/French bilingual city of Murten/Morat in

Switzerland capitalize on local bilingualism to attract visitors, or Kallen (2009) and Moriarty (2014), both focusing on Irish/English linguistic landscapes in tourist-oriented cities in Ireland. Such studies on the role of tourism in multilingual semiotic cityscapes tap into studies on multilingualism from a specific, previously under-researched point of view, namely the fact that tourists are consumers of cultural and linguistic diversity to which they then might add their own linguacultural experiences. This points to the need for increased interdisciplinary studies into such questions; in this instance collaboration between researchers in areas such as linguistics, tourism studies, communication studies, and marketing would be highly desirable.

The aspect of tourist-orientation also adds an additional facet to questions of the commodification of language(s) – as explored in Chapter 5 with respect to Italian in the LL of Lygon Street, at the heart of Melbourne's Little Italy. More specifically, pluricentric language commodification towards dominant national varieties in the tourism industry of urban centres where non-dominant varieties are spoken is an important field to explore further, for instance in the context of global Englishes. In a world where people travel frequently to consume tourist sites, globally transmitted languages like English take centre stage. This has an impact on the multilingual life of cities and nations. How strongly is the official tourist marketing of cities, or the individual marketing of tourist businesses in those cities, linguistically targeted towards tourists from countries speaking dominant varieties of English, e.g., tourist destinations in Anglophone Caribbean countries towards US English? However, tourist-targeted language commodification cuts both ways: how much does the consumable 'quaintness' of national varieties of English in tourist countries – as opposed to the dominant national varieties in the countries from which tourists are attracted – contribute to the touristic attractiveness of cities, and how is it reflected in the semiotic landscape of such cities? An example here would be the use of traditional Gaelic-style typeface noted in some of the examples shown by Moriarty (2014). Examples for other dominant/non-dominant varieties constellations in tourist-oriented semiotic landscapes are the choice between the non-dominant national standard of Austrian German and the tourist-targeted dominant variant of German German on menus in Austrian tourist restaurants (cf. Dannerer and Franz 2018: 177–179), and the use of Low German alongside (German) Standard German in the municipality of Krummhörn (cf. Reershemius 2011). Studies such as these highlight the value of investigating the use of different national and regional varieties of pluricentric languages for commercial identity purposes. While 'commodification' is defined differently in different studies (see, e.g. Kim 2018), research on the commodification of languages in tourism such as Heller et al. (2014), who compare sites of cultural and heritage tourism in Switzerland, Catalonia and francophone Canada, have proven useful. Yan

(2019) combines an analysis of linguistic commodification in tourism with that of tourist-targeted linguistic landscapes in multilingual cities in his study on Macau, where languages on signs relevant for tourists often include the former colonial language Portuguese as well as Japanese as the language of a large number of tourists alongside Chinese. However, the Chinese texts are usually not written in simplified Chinese characters (as used in Mainland China and Singapore), but in traditional Chinese characters as used in Hong Kong and Taiwan, two important source areas for Macau tourism.

A special case compared to – usually short-term – tourism on the one hand and – usually longer-term or permanent – labour migration is 'lifestyle migration', a relatively privileged type of (part-time or full-time) migration primarily motivated by lifestyle choices (O'Reilly and Benson 2009) rather than economic or political factors. Such migration, often in the form of retirement migration, shares its travel direction with tourism, but its timeframe with labour migration. There is some sociolinguistic research on career-based expatriates, such as the inclusion of this group in Alenezi's (2022) PhD thesis on English in Kuwait or the studies by Luef (2020) on the linguistic enclaves of North-American academics in East Asia and by Castle (2021) on English-speaking expatriates in Prague (both focussing on L1/L2 interaction and L2 uptake by the expatriates). Gustafson and Laksfoss Cardozo (2022) study the sociolinguistic effects of Scandinavian retirement migration to Alicante in southern Spain. A very recent phenomenon involves post-COVID pandemic remote workers who are able to move easily from city to city, country to country. Their impact on multilingualism and language patterns also deserves attention. Given the increasing extent and geographical distribution of lifestyle migration (often southwards within Europe and the Americas or increasingly from the Global North to the Global South, e.g. in the case of Europeans or Australians moving to South-East Asia), its sociolinguistic consequences merit more analysis.

Part 2, *Attitudes and identities,* presents contributions exploring different aspects of the status of minority (immigrant) languages, including their relationships (and that of their speakers) with more dominant languages, in particular the local majority language or language variety. This is seen in Chapter 5 in the LL of Lygon Street where Italian coexists and shows the influence of contact with English. In terms of future research directions, the issues of 'embedded linguistic minorities' (such as the Mixtecs in New York, Chapter 6) and of attitudes towards non-dominant national varieties of a pluricentric language (as noted in Chapter 7 on Dublin) seem particularly promising pathways for further research.

Kaufman's chapter on the plight of the Mixtec speaking minority in New York places the searchlight on a much under-researched topic – the attitudes and identities among and towards linguistic minorities *within* linguistic minorities. The

Mixtec speakers in New York are just one group of Latin American Indigenous language-speakers within the Hispanic minority in the US, and many other indigenous language groups also deserve our attention. In Europe, examples would include Kurdish speakers within the Turkish immigrant minorities in Berlin or Berber speakers within Arabic-speaking immigrants from the Maghreb in Brussels, in South-East Asia, speakers of different Chinese languages and dialects other than Mandarin within the Chinese ethnic group in Singapore. This also has a pluricentric aspect; there are (locally) non-dominant varieties of Latin American Spanish in US cities where specific varieties (such as Puerto Rican or Mexican) are dominant minority language varieties. Similarly non-dominant in their new urban settings are the Italian varieties in Munich mentioned in the contribution by Riehl and Ingrosso (Chapter 8) or the Nigerian and Bangladeshi varieties of English in Padua mentioned in Goglia's Chapter 4.

Diskin-Holdaway's contribution (Chapter 7) explores the attitudes of immigrants and their communities towards a non-dominant national variety of a pluricentric language spoken in their new home. In the case of English as in her chapter, one of the questions is whether previous schooling and media contact with a dominant variety of English is relevant for the attitude. In future research it would be interesting to follow up on how immigrants respond to the locally dominant English variety they hear around them, such as Arabic-speaking Syrian immigrants in Sydney or Mozambican immigrants in Cape Town, for example.

Finally, the contributions in Part 3, *Language across time and space*, add diachronic and territorial perspectives to the discussion of urban language contact. A diachronic approach is generally rare in the research on multilingual cities (but see Pavlenko 2010, who employed historic and contemporary photographs as well as inscriptions to reconstruct aspects of the LL of Kyiv over time). The contribution by Trudgill and Warren (Chapter 9) explores the historical layers of multilingualism in the city of Norwich through the remaining linguistic traces of Danish, Norman and Dutch migration of past centuries before looking into the multilingualism of contemporary Norwich, a city rarely described as ethnically or linguistically diverse. The argument for integrating a temporal dimension, particularly into LL research, is made by Pavlenko and Mullen (2015), who also highlight difficulties potentially arising from "partial and often decontextualized evidence" (p. 129). Depending on the archival situation, linguistic change and multilingual influence can be seen in the correspondence of urban merchants, as Conde-Silvestre (2021) shows with English wool merchants in late-Medieval Calais, or in the changing LL of cities from colonial to post-colonial times. The history of a city such as the Namibian capital Windhoek from German colonial times over the decades of the South African mandate to post-1990 independence could be a great example to explore (Schulte 2021 is one study following that path). One recent study focussing (amongst other things) on the changing language of street names in post-colonial cities is Tan and Purschke (2021) who consider Kuala Lumpur in Malaysia as well as Windhoek. Further studies on the impact of changing geopolitical circumstances on multilingual cityscapes would also be invaluable in other contexts. A case in point would be Indonesian cities, where Chinese characters completely disappeared from public view under the total assimilation policy of President Suharto's New Order regime (cf. Ling 2016), and slowly reappeared after the regime collapsed.

Another avenue for further research – emphasising the territorial perspective in the discussion of urban language contact and change – is foreshadowed in Chapter 11 by Bissoonauth and Warren. The authors note a demographic decline in the city of Port-Louis in favour of surrounding districts and different rates of language shift across and between urban and rural districts of Mauritius. This shows that not only urbanisation, but also suburbanisation and counterurbanisation (where urban residents move into the surrounding rural areas) are promising areas for further exploration (cf. e.g. Britain and Grossenbacher 2021 on counterurbanisation and dialect contact) and a focus on urban-rural contact zones could be added to the research agenda.

In final conclusion of this volume, we note that much remains to be explored about the rich linguistic complexity of cities large and small (and beyond). The diversity of urban settings around the world is matched not only by the questions to investigate and respond to, but also increasingly by the rise of new concepts and approaches, tools and ways of understanding, only some of which we have highlighted in this chapter.

References

Alenezi, Mohammad. 2022. *English in Kuwait: a pattern-driven perspective*. PhD thesis, University College Dublin.
Bailey, Benjamin. 2007. Heteroglossia and boundaries. In Monica Heller (ed.), *Bilingualism: a social approach*, 257–274. London: Palgrave Macmillan.
Blommaert, Jan. 2013. *Ethnography, superdiversity and linguistic landscapes: chronicles of complexity*. Bristol: Multilingual Matters.
Britain, David & Sarah Grossenbacher. 2021. Counterurbanisation, dialect contact and the levelling of non-salient traditional dialect variants: the case of the front short vowels in Eastern England. In Arne Ziegler, Stefanie Edler & Georg Oberdorfer (eds.), *Urban matters: current approaches of international sociolinguistic research*, 89–118. Amsterdam: John Benjamins.
Castle, Chloe Michelle. 2021. L1 English speakers in Prague: motivators in language use and language borrowing. *Linguistica Pragensia* 31(2). 161–187.

Conde-Silvestre, J. Camilo. 2021. Multilingualism and language contact in the Cely letters. *Anglia* 139(2). 327–364.

Dannerer, Monika & Marianne Franz. 2018. Language and tourism in Austria with a focus on Tyrol. *Sociolinguistica* 32(1). 169–184.

Farr, Marcia. 2011. Urban plurilingualism: language practices, policies, and ideologies in Chicago. *Journal of Pragmatics* 43(5). 1161–1172.

García, Ofelia & Li Wei. 2014. *Translanguaging: language, bilingualism and education*. London: Palgrave Macmillan.

Gustafson, Per & Ann Elisabeth Laksfoss Cardozo. 2022. Language use in international retirement migration: the case of Scandinavian retirees in Alicante, Spain. In François Grin, László Marácz & Nike K. Pokorn (eds.), *Advances in interdisciplinary language policy*, 488–507. Amsterdam: John Benjamins.

Heller, Monica, Joan Pujolar & Alexandre Duchêne. 2014. Linguistic commodification in tourism. *Journal of Sociolinguistics* 18(4). 539–566.

Hovens, Daan. 2021. Language policy and linguistic landscaping in a contemporary blue-collar workplace in the Dutch–German borderland. *Language Policy* 20(4). 645–666.

Ibrahim, Muhsin. 2021. *Kannywood and the cultural and linguistic contestations on Hausa films*. PhD thesis, University of Cologne.

Jaworski, Adam & Crispin Thurlow (eds.). 2010. *Semiotic landscapes: language, image, space*. London: Continuum.

Jørgensen, Jens Normann, Martha Sif Karrebæk, Lian Malai Madsen & Janus Spindler Møller. 2016. Polylanguaging in superdiversity. In Karel Arnaut, Jan Blommaert, Ben Rampton, & Massimiliano Spotti (eds.), *Language and superdiversity*, 137–154. New York: Routledge.

Kallen, Jeffrey. 2009. Tourism and representation in the Irish linguistic landscape. In Elana Shohamy & Durk Gorter (eds.), *Linguistic landscape: expanding the scenery*, 270–283. New York: Routledge.

Kellermeier-Rehbein, Birte. 2016. Sprache in postkolonialen Kontexten II: Varietäten der deutschen Sprache in Namibia. In Thomas Stolz, Ingo H. Warnke & Daniel Schmidt-Brücken (eds.), *Sprache und Kolonialismus*, 213–234. Berlin: de Gruyter.

Kim, Jinwon. 2018. Manhattan's Koreatown as a transclave: the emergence of a new ethnic enclave in a global city. *City & Community*, 17(1). 276–295.

Leimgruber, Jakob R. E. & Víctor Fernández-Mallat. 2021. Language attitudes and identity building in the linguistic landscape of Montreal. *Open Linguistics* 7(1). 406–422.

Li Wei. 2018. Translanguaging as a practical theory of language. *Applied Linguistics* 39(1). 9–30.

Ling, Chong Wu. 2016. Rethinking the position of ethnic Chinese Indonesians. *SEJARAH: Journal of the Department of History* 25(2). 96–108.

Luef, Eva Maria. 2020. North American academics in East Asia: life in the English-speaking enclave. *Journal of Intercultural Communication* 20(2). 56–71.

Moriarty, Máiréad. 2014. Contesting language ideologies in the linguistic landscape of an Irish tourist town. *International Journal of Bilingualism* 18(5). 464–477.

Oakes, Leigh & Jane Warren. 2007. *Language, citizenship and identity in Quebec*. Basingstoke: Palgrave Macmillan.

O'Reilly, Karen & Michaela Benson. 2009. Lifestyle migration: escaping to the good life? In Michaela Benson & Karen O'Reilly (eds.), *Lifestyle migration: expectations, aspirations and experiences*, 1–13. Farnham: Ashgate.

Pavlenko, Aneta. 2010. Linguistic landscape of Kyiv, Ukraine: a diachronic study. In Elana Shohamy, Eliezer Ben Rafael & Monica Barni (eds.), *Linguistic landscape in the city*, 133–150. Bristol: Multilingual Matters.

Pavlenko, Aneta & Alex Mullen. 2015. Why diachronicity matters in the study of linguistic landscapes. *Linguistic Landscape* 1(1-2). 114–132.

Pennycook, Alastair & Emi Otsuji. 2014. Metrolingual multitasking and spatial repertoires: "Pizza mo two minutes coming". *Journal of Sociolinguistics* 18(2). 161–184.

Pütz, Martin. 2020. Exploring the linguistic landscape of Cameroon: reflections on language policy and ideology. *Russian Journal of Linguistics* 24(2). 294–324.

Radke, Henning. 2021. Language contact and mixed-mode communication: on ingroup construction through multilingualism among the German-Namibian diaspora. In Christian Zimmer (ed.), *German(ic) in language contact: grammatical and sociolinguistic dynamics*, 127–158. Berlin: Language Science Press.

Reershemius, Gertrud. 2011. Reconstructing the past? Low German and the creating of regional identity in public language display. *Journal of Multilingual and Multicultural Development* 32(1). 33–54.

Schedel, Larissa Semiramis. 2018. Turning local bilingualism into a touristic experience. *Language Policy* 17(2). 137–155.

Shohamy, Elana. 2019. Linguistic landscape after a decade: an overview of themes, debates and future directions. In Pütz, Martin & Nele Mundt (eds.), *Expanding the linguistic landscape: linguistic diversity, multimodality and the use of space as a semiotic resource*, 25–37. Bristol: Multilingual Matters.

Schulte, Marion. 2021. The linguistic landscape and soundscape of Windhoek. In Anne Schröder (ed.), *The dynamics of English in Namibia: perspectives on an emerging variety*, 83–107. Amsterdam: John Benjamins.

Tan, Peter K.W. & Christoph Purschke. 2021. Street name changes as language and identity inscription in the cityscape. *Linguistics Vanguard* 7(s5). 20200138.

Tang, Hoa K. 2020. Linguistic landscaping in Singapore: multilingualism or the dominance of English and its dual identity in the local linguistic ecology? *International Journal of Multilingualism* 17(2). 152–173.

Yan, Xi. 2019. A study of language choices in the linguistic landscape of Macao's heritage and gaming tourism. *Journal of Multilingual and Multicultural Development* 40(3). 198–217.

Biographical notes

Anu **Bissoonauth** is a graduate of the University of Nottingham. She taught at the University of Lincoln, University of the West Indies (Trinidad and Tobago) and the University of Bath and is now Senior Lecturer in French at the University of Wollongong, Australia, where she teaches across all subjects of the French major and supervises research projects in sociolinguistics. Her research is concerned with factors that impact the sustainability of minority languages in the French-speaking Indian and Pacific oceans, where French comes in contact with Creoles, other regional/indigenous languages and global English.

Claudine **Brohy** grew up bilingually at the French-German language border in Fribourg/Freiburg, Switzerland. She holds a PhD in Sociolinguistics and has taught Linguistics and German and French as second/foreign languages mainly at the University of Fribourg/Freiburg. Her research interests and publications focus on language contact, bilingual education and immersion, language policies and minorities, and the interface between individual plurilingualism and institutional multilingualism. She is also active in teacher training and in the development of teaching/learning materials.

Chloé **Diskin-Holdaway** is Senior Lecturer in Applied Linguistics at the University of Melbourne. Her research focuses on the sociolinguistics of migration, with expertise in language and identity, sociophonetics, language attitudes and ideologies, and discourse-pragmatic variation. She is the author of '*You know* and *like* among migrants in Ireland and Australia' (*World Englishes*) and 'New speakers in the Irish context: Heritage language maintenance among multilingual migrants in Dublin, Ireland' (*Frontiers in Education*). She is the current chair of the Discourse-Pragmatic Variation and Change research network.

Sender **Dovchin** is Associate Professor, Director of Research and Principal Research Fellow and at the School of Education, Curtin University, Australia. She is also a Discovery Early Career Research Fellow of the Australian Research Council. Previously, she was Associate Professor at the University of Aizu, Japan and was awarded Young Scientist (Kakenhi) by the Japan Society for the Promotion of Science. She is editor-in-chief of the *Australian Review of Applied Linguistics* and was identified as "Top Researcher in the field of Language & Linguistics" by The Australian's 2021 Research Magazine and as among the Top 250 Researchers in Australia in 2021. She has authored numerous articles in international peer-reviewed journals and authored six books with international publishers.

Zane **Goebel** is Associate Professor at the University of Queensland, Brisbane, where he teaches Indonesian and Applied Linguistics. He works on language and social relations in Indonesia and has extensive publications in this area, including *Language, Migration, and Identity: Neighbourhood Talk in Indonesia* (Cambridge University Press, 2010); *Language and Superdiversity: Indonesians Knowledging at Home and Abroad* (Oxford University Press, 2015), *Global Leadership Talk* (Oxford University Press, 2020); *Reimagining Rapport* (Oxford University Press, 2021); *Rapport and the discursive co-construction of social relations in fieldwork settings* (Mouton De Gruyter, 2019); and *Contact Talk* (with Deborah Cole and Howard Manns, Routledge, 2020).

Francesco **Goglia** is Associate Professor of Migration and Multilingualism in the Department of Languages, Cultures and Visual Studies at the University of Exeter. His research interests are multilingualism, language maintenance and shift, and language contact in immigrant communities in particular in Italy, the United Kingdom, East Timor and Australia. His current research, supported by the Leverhulme Trust, focuses on the process of onward migration from Italy to the UK and its sociolinguistic implications.

John **Hajek** is Professor of Italian Studies and Director of the Research Unit for Multilingualism and Cross-Cultural Communication (RUMACCC) at the University of Melbourne. He completed his university education in Australia, Italy and the United Kingdom. He has a broad range of research interests including in all aspects of multilingualism and pluricentricity in cities and countries around the world.

Carlie **Hanson** received a BA in Linguistics from the University of Wisconsin-Madison, and an MA in Linguistics from the University of Manchester, specialising in Kurdish Language Documentation. She has since worked on research projects including the Dialects of Kurdish archival project at the University of Manchester and the LinguaSnapp project at the University of Melbourne, and is currently living in Montreal, Canada.

Ambrin **Hasnain** is a research assistant at the Research Unit for Multiculturalism and Cross-Cultural Communication (RUMACCC) at the University of Melbourne. She has a background in Arts and Cultural Management, and now conducts independent as well as collaborative research in the fields of education, sociolinguistics, media communication, and in interdisciplinary fields.

Sofie **Henricson** is Associate Professor in Scandinavian languages at the University of Helsinki. She received her PhD from the University of Helsinki in 2013 and her title as Docent from the University of Turku in 2020. She is interested in a broad range of variational and sociolinguistic perspectives on language use, interaction research, linguistic landscape studies, and language learning and teaching.

Sara **Ingrosso** studied German at the University of Bari, Italy, and obtained her PhD in Italian philology from the Ludwig-Maximilians-Universität in Munich. She is a Lecturer at the Institute for German as a Foreign Language at the Ludwig-Maximilians-Universität and a member of the Committee of Italians Abroad (Com.It.Es.) for the Consular District of Munich. Her research interests are language biographies, language and migration, and conversation analysis.

Daniel **Kaufman** is Associate Professor of Linguistics at Queens College and the Graduate Center, City University of New York. He is also a founding Co-Director of the Endangered Language Alliance (www.elalliance.org), a non-profit organisation based in New York City that collaborates with Indigenous and immigrant New Yorkers on various aspects of language documentation and conservation. He received his PhD from Cornell University in 2010 and specialises in the Austronesian languages of Island Southeast Asia.

Heinz L. **Kretzenbacher** is a Senior Fellow in the School of Languages and Linguistics at the University of Melbourne. His main research areas include sociolinguistics, academic communication and German studies.

María Irene **Moyna** (Ph.D. University of Florida) is Professor in the Department of Global Languages and Cultures at Texas A&M University. Her work focuses on variation and change in Spanish morphology, especially compounding and address forms. She is the author of *Compound Words in Spanish: Theory and history* (John Benjamins, 2011), and co-editor of *Recovering the U.S. Hispanic Linguistic Heritage* (Arte Público Press, 2008), *Forms of Address in the Spanish of the Americas* (John Benjamins, 2016), and *It's Not All About You: New Perspectives on Address Research* (John Benjamins, 2019). Her articles have appeared in 30 journals and collections.

Marie **Nelson** is Senior Lecturer and a former Director of Studies for Swedish as a Second Language at the Department of Swedish Language and Multilingualism at Stockholm University. She previously worked as a visiting lecturer in Estonia and China. She received her PhD in Scandinavian languages from Uppsala University in 2010. Her broader research interests cover sociolinguistics, variational pragmatics, Swedish as a second language, and communication in the workplace.

Catrin **Norrby** is Professor of Scandinavian Languages at Stockholm University, Sweden, and an Honorary Fellow at the University of Melbourne. Her main research interests are in sociolinguistics and interaction analysis. She takes a special interest in issues concerning multilingualism and cross-cultural communication. Most recently, she led a binational research programme on interaction and variation in pluricentric languages, in particular communicative patterns in Swedish in Sweden and Finland.

Claudia Maria **Riehl** is Professor of German Linguistics and German as a Foreign Language. She is Chair of the Institute of German as a Foreign Language and Director of the International Research Unit of Multilingualism (IFM), all at the Ludwig-Maximilians-Universität in Munich. Her research interests are sociolinguistic and cognitive aspects of multilingualism, language contact, minority languages and language policy, multiliteracy, and second language teaching.

Doris **Schüpbach** grew up near Biel/Bienne, Switzerland, and now lives in Melbourne, Australia, where she is a Research Fellow at the Research Unit for Multilingualism and Cross-Cultural Communication (RUMACCC) at the University of Melbourne. Her main research interests are in sociolinguistics and concern issues around multilingualism and migration as well as societal and individual multilingualism and their interaction.

Bolormaa **Shinjee** is currently a PhD candidate at the School of Education, Curtin University, Australia. Previously, she worked as Senior Lecturer at the National University of Mongolia. She obtained her Master's degree in TESOL from Flinders University, Adelaide, Australia. Her main research interests include the sociolinguistics of globalization, language policy and translanguaging.

Peter **Trudgill**, FBA, is a sociolinguist, academic and author, and was born in Norwich. He is Professor Emeritus of English Linguistics at the University of Fribourg and Honorary Professor of Sociolinguistics at the University of East Anglia. He is honorary president of the Friends of Norfolk Dialect and contributes a regular column to the *New European* newspaper. He is a well-known authority on dialects, as well as being one of the first to apply Labovian sociolinguistic methodology in the UK, and to provide a framework for studying dialect contact phenomena. His latest book is *East Anglian English* (2021).

Jane **Warren** is an Honorary Fellow in the School of Languages and Linguistics, University of Melbourne. She was born in Norwich where she now lives. She has published in the areas of French and francophone sociolinguistics and cultural studies. She is co-author of *Language, citizenship and identity in Quebec* (2007, with Leigh Oakes) and of *Language and human relations: Address in contemporary language* (2009, with Michael Clyne and Catrin Norrby).

Index

address in Rio de la Plata Spanish 291–319
address variation 293, 295, 301–305, 311, 315
addressee gender 308–310, 313, 314
adequation 173, 174, 186–189, 194
age 296, 302–306, 310, 311
Åland islands 55, 59, 67
ancestral languages 267, 271, 273, 282
Arabic 36, 45, 100, 104, 106, 114, 118, 131, 239–242, 267, 279, 282, 283, 286, 329
Australia 123, 124, 126

Bahasa Indonesia See Indonesian
Bengali 116, 118
Betawi 81, 89–92
Bhojpuri 269, 271–273, 278–280
Biel/Bienne 11–14, 27–53
bilingual education 155, 209
bilingual signs *See* multilingual signs
bilingualism 14, 27–30, 39–44, 48–50, 78, 231–234 *See also* de facto bilingualism; official bilingualism
bottom-up signs 64–66, 71, 72, 75, 76, 102
branding 31, 33, 43, 129, 140, 141
Breton 234
Brexit 227, 239, 243, 244, 325
Buenos Aires 291, 292, 310, 315

Carlton *See* Melbourne
census data 125, 126, 177, 178, 228, 238, 239, 241, 268, 270, 271, 276–286
Chinatown 103, 104, 108, 110, 118, 178, 282 *See also* Little Italy; linguistic enclaves; transclaves
Chinese 70, 100, 104, 106, 108–111, 117, 118, 132, 143, 144, 163, 239, 240, 283, 328, 329
Christianity 270, 271, 279
codeswitching 13, 107, 214, 219, 276, 281 *See also* signswitching
codification 232
colonisation 5, 150, 152, 156, 165, 267, 269
commodification of ethnic identity 129, 140–143
commodification of languages *See* language commodification
communicative function of signs 129, 242

contact register 82, 87, 91–96
counterurbanisation 276, 278, 330
Cyrillic script 249, 254, 256, 259

de facto bilingualism 38, 44, 49, 50, 100
demography 100, 124, 177, 178, 201–206, 271, 275 *See also* census data
dialects
– Italian 99, 200, 201, 207–209, 219, 220
– Swiss-German 27, 47, 48
diglossia 13, 27, 47–49, 220, 272, 273, 284
discourse analysis 175, 176
discrimination 162, 167
distinction 173, 174, 182–186, 194
domains 154, 157–161, 214, 215, 281–283, 286
Dublin 16, 173–197, 323
Dublin English 11, 16, 174, 175, 179, 180, 182–189, 191–194
Dutch 235, 236

East Anglia 227, 229–232
educational attainment 296, 307, 310, 312
embedded linguistic minorities 33, 49, 328, 329
emblematic function of signs *See* symbolic function of signs
Endangered Language Alliance (ELA) 147, 148
English 11, 44, 45, 56, 60, 63–78, 87, 95, 153, 154, 160, 161, 163, 168, 227–248, 253–258, 267, 269, 271, 272, 276, 277, 281–286
– as a lingua franca 9, 11, 15, 44, 45, 78, 100, 103, 111–114, 116, 118, 209, 217, 218, 264, 321, 323
– as a pluricentric language 9, 11, 173–197, 321, 327
– as a second language 173–197, 218–220
ephemeral signs 67, 77, 245
ethnic enclaves 15, 123, 128, 141, 143 *See also* Chinatown; Little Italy; transclaves
ethnic languages in Indonesia 81, 85–88
ethnicity 238, 270, 271, 276, 285
ethnolinguistic identities 7, 83, 87, 102, 129, 140–143, 270
European Union (EU) 227, 239, 243, 244

family domain *See* home domain
Finland 55–80
Finnish 55–78
Flemish 234, 235
folklinguistic notions 28, 48, 49, 82
food-related businesses 67, 70, 110, 114, 118, 123, 125, 131, 132, 134, 137, 139, 143, 203
French 27–53, 114, 234–236, 244, 245, 267, 269–272, 274, 276–278, 280–286
Fribourg/Freiburg 27–53

"*Gastarbeiter*" *See* migrant workers
gender 84, 296, 303, 304, 308–310, 313
gentrification 125, 128, 180
German 27–53, 208, 209, 213, 214
– as a pluricentric language 8, 9, 322
– as a second language 211, 217–220
Germanisation 44, 49
Global North 321, 328
Global South 4, 321, 328
globalisation 3, 83, 202, 218, 243, 250
"guest-workers" *See* migrant workers

healthcare domain 157, 158
heritage languages *See* ancestral languages; migrant languages
heteroglossia 175, 220, 322, 323
Hindi 272
Hinduism 270, 279, 280
historical sociolinguistics 228–238, 325, 329
home domain 158–161, 214, 215
Huguenots 235
Hungarian 239, 240, 242

ideologies of standardness *See* language ideologies
imperative 305, 306
income level 296, 303, 306, 309, 310, 312, 313
indentured labour 267, 269
Indigenous languages 148, 154, 321, 329
Indonesia 5, 6, 86–88
Indonesian 6, 81, 87, 89, 90, 91, 93, 95
informal address 17, 293, 315
institutional bilingualism *See* official bilingualism
interethnic communication 14, 87–96

intergenerational communication 156, 158–161, 165
intergenerational language transmission *See* language transmission
international students 125, 202, 239, 240
Internet 3, 251
interpreting services 154, 157, 240
interviews 148, 175, 210, 273, 281
Ireland (Republic of Ireland) 176–178
Irish English 175, 177, 179, 180, 183, 185–189, 191, 193, 194
Islam 114, 116, 270, 279
Italian 32–34, 37, 99, 103, 106, 107, 109, 112, 114, 115, 117, 118, 123, 124, 126, 130, 131, 133–143, 199–224, 324
Italian dialects 99, 200, 201, 207–209, 219, 220
Italianità 123, 124, 126, 134, 136, 137, 140–143, 208
Italianness *See Italianità*
Italiano popolare 212–214, 220
Italy 99, 103, 104, 202, 205
Italy (migrants from) 34, 124, 126, 200–203, 205, 206, 208–210, 213–219

Jakarta 5, 14, 81–98, 326
Japanese 255
Javanese 81, 87, 89, 91, 95
Jews 234

Korean 261–263
Korean script 262
Kotka 7, 55–80, 324
Kreol 17, 267–269, 271–273, 276–286

L2 identities *See* second language identities
Ladino 234
language attitudes 15, 16, 167, 175, 182, 191, 194, 282, 283
language by-laws 99, 103, 104, 115, 117, 262 *See also* language legislation
language change 17, 231, 236, 245
language commodification 14, 15, 43, 45, 83, 87, 92, 94, 95, 250, 326–328
language contact 13, 14, 16, 18, 28, 124, 173, 177, 186, 188, 195, 215, 220, 228, 231, 237, 245, 250, 263, 323, 329

language demography 30, 32, 34–36, 55–57, 59–62, 78, 100, 125, 126, 228, 229, 239–241, 271, 276–280, 325
language hierarchies 6, 15, 55, 76, 82, 85, 87, 88, 102
language ideologies 10, 13, 48, 81–84, 87, 91–93, 95, 96, 164, 167, 168, 174, 179, 185, 186, 188, 189, 191, 192, 194, 195, 268, 326
language legislation 28, 30, 37, 38, 58, 262
language loss 208, 216, 235
language maintenance 154, 167, 168, 208, 221 *See also* language transmission
language mixing 13, 90, 91, 96, 136, 141, 143, 213, 252, 322 *See also* codeswitching
language policies 13, 14, 17, 28, 30, 37, 38, 56–58, 78, 87, 103, 107, 118, 324–326
language prestige 201, 208
language promotional discourses 29, 31, 42–44, 50
language repertoires 14, 15, 29, 102, 173, 200, 207–211, 213, 218–221, 282, 322
language rights 58, 158
language shift 18, 154, 166, 208, 216, 277, 279, 285
language shock 183–185
language standardisation 151
language transmission 16, 147, 148, 158–161, 164–167, 220 *See also* language maintenance
language visibility 55–57, 59, 72, 76–78, 102–104, 114, 117, 127, 140, 153, 169, 245, 324
lexical transference 211, 212, 214, 217, 218
lifestyle migration 328
lingua franca 102, 118, 208, 267, 272 *See also* English as a lingua franca
LinguaSnapp Melbourne 130
linguistic ethnography 13, 252, 253
linguistic justice 9
linguistic landscape
– Kotka 64–66, 70–77
– Mariehamn 64–70, 76, 77
– Melbourne 123, 130–144
– Norwich 241–243
– Padua 99, 105–119

– Ulaanbaatar 249, 251, 253–264
linguistic landscape approach 7, 14, 15, 17, 62–64, 102, 104, 105, 127–130, 229, 321, 324–326
linguistic relocalisation *See* relocalisation
linguistic repertoires *See* language repertoires
literacy 161, 210, 220
Lithuanian 239–242
Little Italy 15, 123–125, 128–130, 140–143 *See also* Chinatown; ethnic enclaves; transclaves
localisation *See* relocalisation

Mandarin *See* Chinese
Mariehamn 55–80, 324
mass media *See* mediated contexts
Mauritian Kreol *See* Kreol
Mauritius 5, 267–289
mediated contexts 14, 218, 325, 326
Melbourne 123–146, 324
Mestizo gaze 149, 161, 162
metalinguistic discourse 174, 191
metasemiotic commentaries 84, 93
metrolingualism 82, 322, 323
migrant languages 28, 45, 99, 321, 325, 328
migrant workers 199, 201, 207, 211, 212
migration 3, 6, 17, 57, 62, 99, 123, 124, 126, 149, 150, 173, 200, 202, 227, 228, 239, 249
Mixtec 147–171
mobility *See* migration
Mongolia 249–251, 254, 255, 259, 261, 264
Mongolian 249, 251, 254–264
Montevideo 4, 291–319, 323
multiethnic area 99, 100, 117, 245
multilingual signs 63, 65–69, 71–75, 77, 78, 103, 106–109, 111, 114, 116, 118, 134
Munich 199–224
mutual intelligibility 229, 231

nation building 86, 268
New York 147–171
Nigeria (migrants from) 100, 111–113
Norfolk 227
Norman conquest 234
Norwich 5, 227–248, 324, 325

official bilingualism 13, 33, 37, 38, 49, 50
official discourses on languages and multilingualism 13, 28, 30, 39, 46, 49, 326
Old Danish 229, 231, 233
Old English 229–233
Old Norse 229–232
orthography 249–251, 254–256, 258, 259, 261–263

Padua 99–120, 324
pluriareality 9, 323
pluricentric languages
- English 9, 11, 173–197, 321, 327
- German 8, 9, 322
- Swedish 10
- Spanish 10, 291–319, 323
pluricentricity 8–10, 322, 323, 327, 329
Polish 66, 70, 186–188, 193, 239–242
polylanguaging 82, 322, 323
port cities 59, 61, 267, 274
Port-Louis 267–289
Portuguese 33, 36, 37, 45, 241, 242
power relations between languages 8, 9, 15, 55, 102, 127 *See also* language hierachies
pragmatic bilingualism *See* de facto bilingualism
pronominal address 293, 294, 298, 300–305, 315

questionnaires 296–300

Rbrul 299, 301
refugees 235, 240, 244
religion 157, 270, 271, 279
relocalisation 17, 85, 94–96, 251, 252, 256–264
restaurants *See* food-related businesses
Rio de la Plata Spanish 291–319
Roman script 250, 254, 255, 262
Romani 238
Romanian 100, 101, 106, 114, 115, 117, 118, 242, 243
Russian 58, 62, 66, 69, 70, 73, 75–77, 259–261

school domain 215, 281–283, 286
schooling 296, 304, 306, 308–312
scripts
- Cyrillic 249, 254, 256, 259
- Korean 262
- Roman 250, 254, 255, 262
second language identities 173–197
self-perception *See* urban identity
semantic restructuring 215
semantic transference 215, 218
semantic value 307, 308
semiotic landscape 7, 102, 128, 321, 324–327
semiotic register 84, 85, 87, 89, 95
signswitching 82, 87, 92, 95, 96
slavery 267–269
soap operas 82, 88, 89
social media 3, 161, 210, 218
social status 296, 313, 314
Spanish 147, 148, 153–161, 163, 164, 166, 167, 169, 291–319
- as a pluricentric language 10, 291–319, 323
speaker gender 308, 310, 313, 314
street names 232, 233, 237, 241, 325, 330
suburbanisation 330
superdiversity 3, 4, 173, 227, 322
Swedish 55–73, 75–78
- as a pluricentric language 10
Swiss-German dialects 27, 47, 48
Switzerland 27, 28, 31–33, 48
symbolic function of signs 127, 129, 141–143, 242, 243

television 81, 85, 86, 88, 95, 213, 251
temporary migration 126, 200
territoriality principle 27, 28, 32, 58
top-down signs 64–66, 71, 72, 76, 102
tourism 57, 59, 70, 71, 73–78, 141–143, 326–328
transclaves 140–143, 324 *See also* Chinatown; ethnic enclaves; Little Italy
transference 211, 212, 214–218, 221
translanguaging 82, 322
translation services 154, 157, 240
transliteration 258, 261
transnational migration *See* migration

Ulaanbaatar 7, 249–265, 325
United Kingdom 227, 239, 240, 243, 244, 325
University of East Anglia 239
urban gaze 1, 12
urban identities 14, 29, 30, 33, 39, 42–44, 50, 242

urban redevelopment *See* gentrification
urbanisation 249–251
urban-rural contact 191, 192, 276, 279, 330
Uruguay 4, 292
Uruguayan Spanish 291–319

Valentine's Day 66, 78, 259, 260
vehicular language *See* lingua franca

verbal address 305–310
Vikings 229, 230, 232
visibility *See* language visibility

websites 13, 30, 39, 43–46
WhatsApp 210, 218

www.ingramcontent.com/pod-product-compliance
Lightning Source LLC
Chambersburg PA
CBHW061931220426
43662CB00012B/1872